CAPITOL WOMEN

Texas Female Legislators, 1923–1999

NANCY BAKER JONES AND RUTHE WINEGARTEN

CAPITOL

☆

WOMEN

University of Texas Press, Austin

First edition, 2000

Requests for permission to reproduce material from this work should be sent to
Permissions, University of Texas Press, Box 7819, Austin, TX 78713-7819.

(∞) The paper used in this book meets the minimum requirements of ANSI/NISO
Z39.48–1992 (R1997) (Permanence of Paper).

LIBRARY OF CONGRESS CATALOGING-IN-PUBLICATION DATA
Jones, Nancy Baker.
    Capitol Women : Texas female legislators, 1923–1999 / Nancy Baker Jones and
Ruthe Winegarten.— 1st ed.
    p.   cm.
    Includes bibliographical references (p.   ) and index.
    ISBN 0-292-74062-x (cloth : alk. paper) — ISBN 0-292-74063-8 (pbk. : alk. paper)
    1. Women legislators—Biography. 2. Texas. Legislature—Biography. 3. Texas—
Biography. 4. Texas—Politics and government—1951–　5. Texas—Politics and govern-
ment—1865–1950.　I. Title. II. Winegarten, Ruthe.

F391.3.J66 2000
328.764'0082 21—dc21　　　　　　　　　　　　　　　　　　　　99-044225

Above: Texas women won the right to vote in general elections with the passage of the 19th Amendment
to the U.S. Constitution. Mrs. L. W. Evans of San Antonio is shown voting here in 1924. Courtesy
University of Texas Institute of Texan Cultures, *San Antonio Light* Collection.

CONTENTS

★

SNAPSHOTS

★

APPENDICES

PREFACE

This book is the first compilation in one volume of information about the eighty-six women who have served as Texas legislators from January 1923 to January 1999 (38th–75th Legislatures). We decided to produce it after spending countless and often frustrating hours—as have others—searching for information about women elected to serve in the Capitol. We hope this book benefits scholars and students of women's history; Texas and U.S. history and government; political junkies; officeholders and potential candidates; and writers and journalists. Over three years of research included conducting video interviews of past and current legislators and former governor Ann Richards as well as combing archives, libraries, newspaper and magazine articles, private collections, books, theses, and dissertations. We hope this volume is a user-friendly compendium of what we found. Our goal was also to inform and empower people—women in particular—to consider candidacy as a way of enriching our democracy.

Writing this book has presented us with several challenges. As historians, our first goal was to provide information about these eighty-six women, many of whose names have been forgotten. We wanted to present not just the "what" about them, but also the "so what"—not only *when* women first appeared as legislators but *why,* not only how many served, but what it was like for them; not only how much legislation women passed, but what kinds of issues they pursued; and, certainly, whether being a woman in the legislature made a difference.

Our desire to present context as well as factual information led us to design a format that is a hybrid of historical synthesis and biographical reference work. This book consists of four essays, fifty-eight biographies, twenty-eight brief "snapshots," and appendices containing various analyses of the information we gathered. The essays are "Women in Red," Ruthe Winegarten's personal response to the project; "Entering the 'Men's Room': Women inside the Texas Legislature," which presents the conclusions we have drawn from our research; "Texas Women as Politicians: A Historical Overview," a look at the context within which Texas women became involved in party politics as candidates; and "How the Texas Legislature Works," a brief civics lesson.

We have arranged biographies in chronological rather than alphabetical order to provide a sense of the passage of time, of relationships among and between women, and of the issues of their eras. This structure will allow readers to approach the book either as a narrative (reading it from front to back) or as a reference (picking and choosing from among entries). Because some women's names have changed over time due to marriage or divorce, we have listed women under the names used when they served and have added subsequent name changes in parentheses. Thus, the entry for Kay Bailey Hutchison, who married after she left the House, appears as Kathryn A. "Kay" Bailey (Hutchison).

Within the entries, we have included factual information common to all women in almanac-like headings at the beginning, along with an image of each woman from the period when she served in the legislature. We have written biographies for fifty-eight of the eighty-six legislators. The remaining twenty-eight women are included in a section called "Snapshots."

Deciding which legislators would get biographies was difficult. We knew that assessing the career of the first women to serve in the legislature was appropriate because we could examine their performance within the context of their times and with the perspective of intervening decades. But this became increasingly difficult as we moved closer to the present; assessing the "histories" of women who are relative newcomers to the legislature would mean coming to conclusions before the story is over—risky business for historians.

We could have solved this puzzle at one extreme by limiting the book to deceased women, but that would have prevented us from including the many living women who served and moved on. Including them not only allowed us to study their legislative years as closed chapters within their lives, but also added essential information to the contextual pool. We decided that the most objective criterion to use would be to write biogra-

MIRIAM A. FERGUSON
Candidate for Governor
SECOND TERM
SUBJECT TO THE ACTION OF THE DEMOCRATIC PRIMARY, JULY 24, 1926

1. Read what Ferguson-ism has done for Texas.

2. A man who will not read both sides of a question is dishonest.—Abraham Lincoln.

3. Do not send a boy to mill.

4. The State is now on a cash basis, and there is money in the Treasury.

5. The penitentiary is paying its way.

6. Taxes have been reduced.

7. No strikes or lynchings.

8. The schools are being run economically and efficiently.

9. The insane have been taken out of jails.

10. Mercy and forgiveness is extended to the friendless and unfortunate.

11. All these a woman Governor has brought to Texas.

12. Why change?

PLATFORM

To the People of Texas:

Some weeks ago in a formal statement I announced for re-election to the office of Governor subject to the Democratic primaries. As I have never scratched the Democratic ticket or violated the party pledge, I felt that I was justified in making this announcement.

In that statement I gave my personal reasons for asking the same second term that has been given to men, and I promised later to give to the people such an account of my administration as would justify my re-election. I now give to the people of Texas that information.

This discussion necessarily involves the statement of past performances and future promises. What has been done and what will be done. Tried by this rule I am willing to be weighed in the balance of public opinion and abide the consequences.

Tax Reduction.

In the first place I promised the people if they would elect me that there would be a reduction in State taxes, and that appropriations would not be allowed to exceed the constitutional limit. To insure the full performance of this promise, I asked the co-operation of the Legislature and stated that I would not approve any special appropriation until the actual needs of the State government were first taken care of and within the constitutional limit. The preceding Thirty-eighth

Legislature appropriated for all purposes $46,855,772.85 and the Thirty-ninth Legislature appropriated for all purposes $36,095,803.95, or a reduction of $10,759,968.90—yes more than ten and three-quarters millions of dollars reduction for the first two years of my administration. To bring about this result it became necessary for me to veto more than two million dollars in appropriations to keep the total within the constitutional limit.

On account of my administration having inherited a two million dollar deficiency (including about $800,000 to pay the debts of the prison system) from the preceding administration, it was not possible to reduce the State rate for 1925, but the constitutional limit was respected and the State rate for 1926 will be reduced from 35 cents to 25 cents—a fraction over 30 per cent reduction.

As a result of these economies there has been brought about a very prosperous condition of the State Treasury. On April 1, 1925, seventy days after I came into office, there was to the credit of the general fund $1,664,372.06, while on April 1, 1926, there was to the credit of the general fund $7,147,904.99, or a gain of nearly five and one-half million dollars.

It is needless to say that the State can be kept on a cash basis, and there will be no necessity for the discount of warrants drawn against the regular appropriation.

I submit that the promise of tax reduction has been fully redeemed.

Miriam A. (Ma) Ferguson was the first woman elected governor of Texas. She served two terms—from 1925 to 1927 and from 1933 to 1935. Courtesy Texas State Library and Archives Commission.

phies only about those women elected before 1990 *unless* those elected in or after 1990 had left office (as of the 75th Legislature), thereby presenting us with a completed legislative career. We invite those who follow us to fill in the picture of women legislators serving in the last decade of the twentieth century. Finally, we stopped our research with the 75th Legislature (January 1997–January 1999). We have not included snapshots of women elected in November 1998 to the 76th Legislature (January 1999–January 2001), although we have mentioned the effects of this election in the essay "Entering the 'Men's Room'" and, where appropriate, we have noted whether women in the 75th were affected by the 1998 election results. Appendix E lists the women of the 76th Legislature.

Our research included conducting videotaped interviews with twenty-eight current and former male and female members of the legislature, searching libraries and archives, and sending a two-page questionnaire, requesting basic information, to all living current and former members. Readers will notice differences in length and depth of the biographies. This is a consequence of the reality that historians can go no further than existing sources allow. In most cases, we found the opportunity to interview subjects to be beneficial because we were able to pursue answers to questions left silent in family and archival materials. We offer these biographies as a beginning.

A further word about the interviews: in 1995 Dr. Linda Schott, director of the Center for the Study of Women and Gender at the University of Texas at San Antonio, and Representative Sylvia Romo of San Antonio invited us to participate in producing a video history of women in the Texas Legislature to celebrate the centennial anniversary of the first woman to have been elected to a state legislature (Colorado, 1895). As a member of the House, Romo secured permission for us and the three videographers of MultiMedia Associates, Molly Dinkins, Dick DeJong, and Jim Cullers, to set up shop in Speaker Pete Laney's private conference room. In the last days of May 1995, during the hectic finale of the 74th legislative session, Romo invited her colleagues to tell us the stories of their lives ("the good, the bad, the ugly," Romo advised them) as numerical minorities in what had been an exclusively male world from 1846 to 1923. Even by 1995, women constituted less than 20 percent of the legislature's population.

We also invited two of the "oldest living graduates" to talk with us, Virginia Duff and Myra Banfield Dippel. In later months, we interviewed many others, including Frances (Sissy) Farenthold, who ran for governor after two terms as the only woman in the House; Sarah Weddington, a state representative when she argued *Roe vs. Wade* before the U.S. Supreme Court; U.S. senator Kay Bailey Hutchison, the first Republican woman elected to the Texas House; Senfronia Thompson and Eddie Bernice Johnson, the first two African American women elected to the House; Irma Rangel, the first Latina elected to the legislature; Judith Zaffirini, the first Latina elected to the Senate, and Barbara Jordan, in one of her last video interviews. We also interviewed Speaker Laney and former governor Ann Richards, who had once been a legislative aide to Sarah Weddington. These and our other interviews are now part of UTSA's Archives for Research on Women and Gender. They formed the core of the 36-minute video history, *Getting Where We've Got to Be: The Story of Women in the Texas Legislature*, completed in 1996.

As independent scholars, we could have neither undertaken nor finished this book without help from many individuals. We received a small advance from the University of Texas Press to help defray costs of photograph and document reproduction. We are also deeply thankful to the many legislators (and their staffs) who spent their own time, energy, and money by filling out the questionnaire we sent them, sending us copies of photographs and documents from their own collections, and even cheering us on with their support for the project. Our families could not have been more supportive or encouraging emotionally, or more practically productive, for they volunteered their own time to assist with the myriad of small and large tasks required to turn this book into a reality. To Nancy's husband, Al King, and to Ruthe's children, Debbie Winegarten, Marc Sanders, and Martha Wilson, our boundless gratitude and appreciation for your help and your patience with us during those inevitable hours that we would rather have spent with you than on the manuscript. Nancy also especially values the encouragement expressed by her mother, Marjorie Allmond Jones, and her sister, Judith Allmond Moore; she remembers fondly the advice of her father, David Willard Jones, during what turned out to be the last year of his life in 1998: "Stay brave!" Friends and colleagues David Mauzy, Mary Beth Rogers, Frieda Werden, David C. Humphrey, and Sharon Kahn generously shared their own work with us, read drafts, and encouraged us along the way.

In addition, we could not have completed this project without the essential assistance of librarians, archivists, and others throughout the state. We are especially thankful to Marvin Stone, Dallas Public Library; Steve Green and Tom Shelton, University of Texas Institute of Texan

Cultures; Caroline Geer and Courtney Gardner, Legislative Reference Library, Texas Capitol; Patrick Johnson, legislative aide to Representative Senfronia Thompson of Houston; Carol Johnson, Houston Public Library; Dianna Evans, Bryan Public Library; Marvin Thurman, Office of the Secretary of State; John Anderson, Texas State Library and Archives; Jill Jackson, Archives for Research on Women and Gender, UTSA; Dawn Letson and the reference staff of Special Collections, Texas Woman's University Library; Jimi Davis, Palestine Public Library; Patricia Rodriguez and Catherine Brush, *Fort Worth Star-Telegram*; Sherry Adams, *Houston Chronicle*; and Judy Zipp, *San Antonio Express-News*. We are also grateful for assistance from Colonel Ray Burley, San Antonio; Myrna Cantrell, Groesbeck; and Katie Jones, San Antonio. The staffs of the following institutions have provided invaluable assistance as well: Perry-Castañeda Library, University of Texas at Austin; Barker Texas History Center of the Center for American History, University of Texas at Austin; State Bar of Texas; Texas Collection, Baylor University; Austin Public Library; El Paso Public Library; Waco Public Library; Moore Memorial Library, Texas City; Groesbeck Memorial Library; Texas Southern University Library; Lyndon Baines Johnson Library and Museum; *San Marcos Daily Record*; *Waco Tribune-Herald*; and Austin Prints for Publication.

Finally, this book is not intended to be a comprehensive history of the Texas Legislature or of women in Texas politics. We recognize that one danger inherent in focusing our lens of inquiry on individual women is that we have surely missed capturing some of the larger picture, including the roles that men have played in this history and also some of the relationships that women built with each other and through organizations like the League of Women Voters, Texas Women's Political Caucus, Women's Legislative Days, Business and Professional Women, and Democratic and Republican women's clubs. However, no other text currently provides this basic information. As an offering to the history of women in Texas politics, we see this book's purpose as similar to that of the archaeologist who unearths the bones and shards of past lives: here they are for your consideration and contemplation. Please join us in the reconstruction of the story that goes with them.

Nancy Baker Jones
Ruthe Winegarten

CAPITOL WOMEN

THE POLITICAL CONTEXT

WOMEN IN RED

☆

She came to the interview wearing a red chiffon jumpsuit, sequined belt, red patent leather pumps and purse, a red bow in her silver ponytail, and lots of rhinestone jewelry. If Myra Banfield Dippel were serving in today's Texas Legislature, she would be a media star, a reporter's dream—quick with a quip and a quotable quote. She kept our video crew in stitches—a very funny woman with a mind and memory like a steel trap. In her first race for the legislature, her husband had provided matchbooks with her platform printed on them. She had to raise her own money for ads: "I sold my kids' piano; I sold everything in the house I could get by with that he wouldn't miss," she said, to finance her campaign and win. "New male legislators could expect lobbyists to provide them with a case of liquor, a carton of cigarettes, and gorgeous call girls," she told us. She refused a bribe to support a certain candidate for House speaker, and when he won, she lost a chance for choice committee assignments. She refused to support legalized horse racing despite threats from one of its proponents. When asked what advice she would give young people considering a political career, she said firmly, "They need to get 'em a job somewhere, waiting tables, working in a filling station. Learn what it's like to work and make a living." Then, looking at me with raised eyebrows and a throaty chuckle, she asked, "You follow me?" I did, indeed.

Virginia Duff, a tiny woman under five feet and weighing in at ninety pounds, entered wearing a red tailored suit, sensible shoes, and carefully coifed hair. Duff had served throughout the 1950s and into the early 1960s, when she met Myra Banfield Dippel. Duff was a model of propriety, an

3

Had These Women Stayed Strictly At HOME
The World Would Have Been Much POORER

Clare Boothe Luce
Former Ambassador to Italy, Playright and Actress

Madame Pandit
India's Representative To The United Nations

Ivy Baker Priest
United States Treasurer

Georgia Neese
Former U. S. Treasurer

Madame Eve Curie
Great Scientist, Discoverer of radium for cancer treatment

Judge Sarah T. Hughes
Texas Own First Lady of the Bench

Joan of Arc
Saviour of France, Now a canonized Saint

Perle Mesta
Former Minister to Luxembourg, "The hostess with the mostest on the ball!"

Eleanor (Cissy) Patterson
Who published the Washington (D.C.) Times Herald until her death

Frances Perkins
"Madame Secretary" FDR's Secretary of Labor

Mrs. Myra D. Banfield
Candidate for State Rep.
30th District Election June 4
(Paid Pol. Ad. By Friends)

Eleanor Roosevelt
Only her name is necessary

Margaret Chase Smith
U. S. Senator from Maine

Evelyn Walsh McLean
Once owned the Washington (D.C.) Post

Susan Anthony
Whom women can thank for the privilege of voting

Jane Addams
Philanthropist, founder of Hull House, Chicago

Amelia Earhart
First Woman to fly the Atlantic, writer of note

Elisabet Ney
Famous Texas Sculptor

Oveta Culp Hobby
First WAC Commander, First Secretary of Health, Education and Welfare, also "works" for the Houston P

Lady Nancy Astor
First Woman Member of Parliament, American girl made good in England

Ruth Bryan Rhode
Once Minister to Denmark, daughter of Wm. Jenn Bryan

Campaign ad for Myra Banfield. Courtesy of Myra Banfield Dippel.

attorney who had worked almost her whole life as a laboratory assistant
for an oil company. During her seven races Duff took no donations, using her own funds and vacation time to campaign. She remembered the
hazards of seeking votes door to door—water moccasins, a dog that almost tore her dress off, and one voter (male, we presume) who offered
her a dip of snuff. Duff recalled that, after her election, she always wore a
hat to the House floor. She and state representative Dorothy Gurley were
treated "like ladies," she said, and were showered with flowers by lobbyists and male representatives.

Banfield and Duff, both now in their late seventies, were among my
favorites of the women legislators we interviewed. Turn to their entries
and see if you don't agree with me that these are two interesting women.

Even though I had been working in the field of Texas women's history
for twenty years, beginning with the Texas Women's History Project, sponsored by the Foundation for Women's Resources under the leadership of
Ann Richards (later governor) and Mary Beth Rogers, I had never heard
of Banfield or Duff. Where were all the biographies, the theses, the dissertations? Inquiring minds wanted to know.

When I wrote *Texas Women, A Pictorial History: From Indians to Astronauts* in 1986 and included what I thought was a comprehensive list of all the female legislators, I omitted Laura Burleson Negley of Bexar County, the third woman elected, who had served from 1929 to 1931. She had not been on any lists I could find at that time. Who was she and where could I find information about her? In desperation I turned to the San Antonio phone book, intending to call any Negley listed. Luckily my first call reached Negley's son who said, yes, his daughter, Laura Negley Gill, named for her legislator-grandmother, had a collection of papers in an old trunk. Laura Gill and her husband kindly opened their home (where Laura Burleson Negley had lived) and the trunk. Accompanying me on this fact-finding adventure was Jill Jackson, director of the Archives for Research on Women and Gender, the University of Texas at San Antonio. We could barely conceal our excitement as we opened the trunk and began pulling out yellowed and crumbling seventy-five-year-old clippings and flyers of Laura Negley's work as a suffragist in Washington, D.C., where her father had been a U.S. representative and later postmaster general under Woodrow Wilson. We knew we had hit pay dirt. There were not only clippings about Negley's suffrage activities and legislative career but also other valuable materials about her great-grandfather, Edward Burleson, a fighter in the Texas Revolution and a vice president of the Republic of Texas. With these new materials, we were able to produce an informed biographical piece about Laura Negley.

Moving closer to the present, even though most Texas historians are familiar with the careers of Barbara Jordan, Sissy Farenthold, Sarah Weddington, and Kay Bailey Hutchison, we didn't know many of the "behind the scenes" stories of these nationally prominent women. We were determined to interview each of them.

Barbara Jordan agreed to give us just thirty minutes. Because it usually takes that long or longer for a video crew to set up equipment for a "shoot," we were challenged for time. To speed the process, one of us posed as Jordan so that we would not use precious interview time adjusting cameras, lights, and props. When Jordan was wheeled in, we all felt somewhat intimidated. We had boiled down our questions to the absolute minimum as we knew time was limited. But when Jordan opened her mouth and that sonorous voice emerged, we were mesmerized. Her face lit up as she talked about how exciting it was when hundreds of residents of Houston's Fifth Ward "closed the town down to come to Austin to see me take the oath of office." There was one poignant moment when one of her earrings fell to the floor and her assistant picked it up and put it back on. Jordan bristled when asked about her identity as a female politician. She retorted, "I'm not a black politician. I'm not a female politician. I'm a politician. And a good one." The interview stretched to almost an hour, and we left with memorable footage. As it turned out, this would be one of her last interviews. It was September 1995, and Jordan died four months later. I admire Jordan most for her work in extending the Voting Rights Act of 1965 to cover Mexican Americans in the Southwest, despite opposition by the Texas congressional delegation, the Texas governor, and the secretary of state.

Sissy Farenthold spent almost all day with us answering questions. We met on the University of Texas campus in the Tarlton Law Library, named for her grandfather, Benjamin Dudley Tarlton. Farenthold came from a family of leaders; an aunt, Lida Dougherty, was the first female school superintendent in Texas (Beeville). Farenthold and Jordan had each been the only woman in their respective chambers from 1969 to 1973. Whereas Jordan consciously decided to be an insider and make friends with her fellow senators to facilitate the passage of legislation she thought was important, Farenthold embarked on a course of reform. She said she came to the legislature knowing that blacks and Mexican Americans weren't represented, but that within two weeks she had concluded "that Texans weren't even represented." Her colleagues tried to trivialize her. On February 14, 1969, they declared her their "valentine." That infuriated her. She didn't want to be a "pet." Although she initially opposed a state Equal Legal Rights Amendment (ELRA), she changed her mind and co-sponsored ELRA legislation with Jordan. Farenthold led a successful revolt of other reform-minded legislators known as the Dirty Thirty to uncover the roles played by legislative and statewide leaders who accepted bribes in order to pass favorable legislation for a Houston banker. Those efforts eventually ended the political careers of the speaker of the House, governor, and lieutenant governor.

U.S. senator Kay Bailey Hutchison, who was a member of the largest class of female legislators (six) ever elected when she won in 1972, had such a busy schedule that it took weeks for us to pin her down. But the wait was worth it. We were fascinated with her account of how she, Weddington, and the other new women legislators drove through significant legislation because they were united. Other women serving in the House were two African American women, the first there—Eddie Bernice Johnson of Dallas and Senfronia Thompson of Houston—and Chris

Miller of Fort Worth. "The Democratic women could work the Demo-cratic side of the aisle, and I could work the Republican side of the aisle," she said with pride, "and because of that, we overwhelmingly passed a landmark piece of legislation for the victims of rape." Although Hutchison has contributed to the improvement of the legal status of women, she shies away from the feminist label. "My gender does not determine my ideology." But, she said, "as a woman in the Texas Legislature, I thought of and pursued issues that men often would not think of pursuing."

Sarah Weddington is best known for having successfully argued *Roe vs. Wade* (which legalized abortion) before the U.S. Supreme Court. She got news of the decision the same month she was sworn into the legisla-ture in 1973. The women's movement was "in the air," and certain issues affected Weddington directly. She was outraged when, after graduating from law school and supporting her husband, who was still a law student, she was denied credit. She explained that she was a licensed attorney, she was putting her husband through law school, the couple were living on her salary, "and I didn't think I ought to have to have his signature." She refused to accept credit on that basis and "passed the Equal Credit Bill and went back and got my credit card." Weddington was named one of the top ten freshmen during her first term and one of the ten best legisla-tors in the state her second. She recalled, "They were wonderful years, and part of what made it so wonderful was that the injustices involving women were so clear and that some of the women were Republicans and some of the women were Democrats, but anytime all of the women in the Texas Legislature could agree on a piece of legislation, it passed."

I was delighted with these examples of women working together across party lines. Did their gender interests override other philosophical differ-ences, and how did they negotiate these spaces? Why does it seem so surprising today, and even heart-warming, that Sarah Weddington and Kay Bailey Hutchison, one a Democrat, the other a Republican, could work together so effectively? It all seems so long ago. Yet why has it been so difficult for female legislators to organize a formal women's caucus, as Hispanic and African American legislators have? Would such a caucus be valuable? Will it ever be organized?

I was particularly interested in fund-raising, an area where women have had not only less experience but also fewer "old boy" business and professional networks to solicit for funds; what's more, they have felt that asking for money might not be "ladylike." So we interviewed an expert, former governor Ann Richards, whom I had known for almost forty years—since the 1960 Kennedy-Johnson presidential campaign. Richards had worked for Democrats for decades at the grassroots level, then had run the winning campaigns of former state representatives Sarah Weddington and Wilhelmina Delco before winning her own races for Travis County commissioner, state treasurer, and governor. Richards is one of the most popular speakers in the country today and one of the most successful fund-raisers. "There's no secret to fund-raising," Richards told us. "It's all asking. And the worst thing that could happen is that they say no, and then you go on and ask someone else. . . . If you can't sell yourself to a person who might give you $10 or $10,000, you're not going to be able to sell yourself to the public." Richards' two campaigns for statewide office in the 1980s and 1990 paved the way for the successful candidacies for statewide office of Republican women like Kay Bailey Hutchison and Susan Combs. In 1990 Hutchison succeeded Richards as treasurer, and in 1993 she became the first female U.S. senator from Texas. In 1998 Combs was elected Texas' first female state commissioner of agriculture.

For the first forty years of female presence in the legislature—from 1922 when the first woman was elected until 1966 when Barbara Jordan won—the twenty women were all white Democrats. As the face of the legislature, male and female, has changed, so has the ethnic and political composition of its members. Today the legislature is much more diverse. How have redistricting, urbanization, the women's and civil rights movements, and the rise of the Republican Party contributed to a changing legislature, both in terms of increased numbers of women, more blacks and Hispanics, and an emphasis on different issues?

Can women ever achieve 50 percent parity instead of the almost 20 percent they now have? Will reclaiming the history of women legislators stimulate careers in public service? We don't have all the answers, but we still have lots of questions. We encourage future researchers and writers to pay more attention to women who have served in the legislature, not only as elected officials but also as staff members, aides, administrative assistants, speech writers, fund-raisers, lobbyists, and more. We hope that comparisons will be made between the backgrounds and achievements (or failures) of women legislators with their male counterparts. There are biographies to be written and plays to be produced, plus lots of materials for graduate theses and dissertations. We look forward to those works.

Ruthe Winegarten

ENTERING THE "MEN'S ROOM"

WOMEN INSIDE THE TEXAS LEGISLATURE

☆

Along with barrooms and bordellos, there has not been a more male-focused institution in Texas history than the Texas Legislature. These three worlds have a lot in common, such as liquor, tobacco, money, fistfights, and, of course, politics. They are also arenas of male social bonding—in other words, "men's rooms"—where women have traditionally had quite specific, limited roles. Before 1923, when Dallas attorney Edith Wilmans entered the capitol as Texas' first female lawmaker, women had participated in legislative culture as wives, support staff, social companions, and call girls, but not as lawmakers.

Before the 1970s, when some reforms were introduced, the Texas Legislature was distinguished by what has been called a "low degree of professionalism" in which brief, biennial sessions, low pay, unregulated lobbying, manipulation of the legislative process, freewheeling socializing after hours in bars and hotels, and accommodation to large economic and legal interest groups defined the culture as the quintessential "old boys' network." In the 1930s and 1940s, for example, the culture took its toll on Frances Goff, a politically astute legislative aide and staff member for four governors. Although Goff had grown up in a small-town hotel where drinking, gambling, and partying were common and she was comfortable socializing with the legislators and governors she worked for, she also knew that the primary responsibility for maintaining her good reputation was on her shoulders. Goff left Governor W. Lee (Pappy) O'Daniel's administration in part because of offensive advances from one of the governor's aides. Even since the 1970s, much of this culture has survived. As a lobbyist from the 1980s said about men's responses to their female colleagues, "It's as if they are another legislator's wife or a daughter of a legislator that they knew. It's just that Old South mentality of 'Now sweet thing, I'll tell you how to handle this.'" And, as Barbara Jordan said to us in 1995, "This is Texas. We are a macho state. We just are."[1]

The female legislators with whom we spoke told us they continue to experience such attitudes: "They're not used to having women around," said San Antonio representative Christine Hernández. "[There is] a lot of concentration on looks, and what good girls we are. We tease them a lot about being 'law bubbas.'"[2] Particularly in the House, social relationships have constituted the most significant factor for gaining and maintaining power. Telling off-color jokes, joining golfing, fishing, and hunting trips, and engaging in late-night smoking and drinking in the speaker's quarters have marked the road to influence. "The way the speaker picks his buddies [is, they're] the ones who go out drinking with him," observed a male legislator in 1988. Becoming one of the speaker's "buddies" has been an important part of legislative life because it usually results in appointment to committee chairmanships and, consequently, the potential for making or breaking legislation. But a double standard has existed where female legislators are concerned. "Men get drunk and we just put up with it," said another male legislator of the 1980s. "A woman would be less effective if she got drunk, slept around."[3]

The women who have stepped through the capitol's doors as lawmakers, then, have continued to enter a highly defined, culturally male space, a *men's room*, where a gendered dynamic exists and where expectations of women have been slow to change. As numerical minorities, women in the legislature have a difficult task to accomplish. Regardless of ideology, age, race, profession, or time period, the women who enter the Texas Legislature must face their status *as women*, and all must decide how they will behave as a result of that consciousness.

We have reached several conclusions about the gendered dynamic that exists within the Texas Legislature. First, there is a "no-win conundrum" imposed upon women who enter the legislature. Second, in the face of this situation, women must choose a strategy for operating effectively in spite of it. Third, the strategy women choose affects their chances for advancement. Fourth, gendered dynamics have an effect on the issues that women choose to support once they get to the legislature and on their relationship to "women's issues." And, fifth, we have concluded that, despite the fact that since 1846 only eighty-six women have ever served (compared with about 6,000 men), women *have* made a difference, and their presence has signaled the beginning of the end of the Texas Legislature as the largest and most influential men's room in the state.

THE "NO-WIN CONUNDRUM"

The "no-win conundrum" that female legislators have faced since 1923 consists of this: whether women conform to societal mores of female propriety or fail to do so, they are not likely to be taken seriously—in the first case because they will not be regarded as capable, and in the second case because they will not be regarded as worthy of respect.[4] Women are continually required to strike a behavioral bargain with the legislature's cultural expectations about female behavior. If you behave like a lady, the bargain goes, you will be tolerated. This value has been held by women as well as men. House parliamentarian Oveta Culp (later Hobby) called Carthage senator Margie E. Neal (who served from 1927 to 1935) "unique" because "she was so unlike those driving, militant, admirable women—but not always enchanting women—that we were left to expect after the suffragettes had made their march in the United States. Miss Margie felt as free to be feminine as a senator as she had as a private citizen of Carthage."[5] Women understand quickly that they will be most valued by colleagues as long as they do not challenge the cultural status quo.

The implication of the bargain, however, is that those women who do not "behave" will suffer. This bargain is usually struck when women are asked, almost invariably, whether they have come to the legislature to support women's causes. The implication of this question is usually negative—that the woman is a "feminist," a hot-headed lobbyist for a narrow special-interest group. As Waco representative Margaret Gordon (later Amsler) said when she entered the House in 1939, "The opinion seemed to be that any woman who would get out and run for public office would have to be a sort of fish-wife type with a sharp tongue. They were so relieved to find that neither Mrs. [Neveille] Colson or I was that type, that we came to the legislature to be working members without any chips on our shoulder or any special interests to serve." Then one can hear the inference of threat in Gordon's conclusion that their male colleagues were "so relieved, that we were treated beautifully."[6]

Even when they do "behave," however, women are likely to be dismissed. In the 1950s, Del Rio representative Dorothy Gillis Gurley assured the press that she was "no feminist" and that she was not there to "champion women's rights." As one paper reported, Gurley "Asks No Favor." She was described as the "Legislature's Glamour Gal," and her colleagues were reported to "gallantly swarm about her chair, whistle and applaud when she gets up to speak." Even so, El Paso representative Anita Blair, who served with Gurley, recalled that Gurley was "deliberately bedeviled by some legislators" over a water bill affecting her ranch. "She had to break down and cry before they would pass that bill," Blair said.[7]

The no-win conundrum and its companion, the behavioral bargain, have not evaporated over time. "In the beginning, I could have been a pet," Corpus Christi representative Frances (Sissy) Farenthold said of her first year in the House in 1969. "There was a sort of pethood ordained for you, if you accepted it. . . . If I had quietly gone about what was expected of me, I probably would have had a few perks." But Farenthold did not regard herself as a guest in the House. As a result, she responded angrily when her male colleagues declared her their valentine, and she rejected the title.[8] "We are still in token positions where they have us placed," San Antonio representative Karyne Jones Conley told us in 1995. "You can go hunting with them, and you can go golfing with them, but there's still a role for women."[9]

WOMEN'S STRATEGIES

Women's responses to the no-win conundrum generally parallel the strategies they use to survive and to try to flourish in the legislature. Faced with the reality of being a minority identified primarily by gender and secondarily by ideology or ability, women must find solutions for getting over the hurdle of gender to the reality of doing what they were elected to do. Women have tended to use one of three strategies for doing so. First, like Houston senator Barbara Jordan and Austin representative Lena Guerrero, they have tried to adapt to the system, to become "one of the boys" by studying how the system works, finding mentors, and adopting its behavior, such as telling off-color jokes, cursing, or joining social expeditions with influential colleagues. Jordan was quite conscious of being the only black female among thirty men, but she still wanted to become an insider. "I knew that the best way for me to operate as a player in the Senate was to become friends with my colleagues and not have them uncomfortable because there was a woman in their presence," Jordan said to us. "I wanted to be *inside* the Senate." On Jordan's first day as a senator in 1967, when a colleague apologized to her for saying "sonofabitch," she replied, "Listen, Senator, if you say he's a sonofabitch, he's a sonofabitch. Period." That comment, she said, "took care of them deferring their language to me."[10] Jordan's choice of strategy worked for her; she became a successful state senator.

Lena Guerrero had an early reputation, in 1985, as an undisciplined radical—a "bomb thrower." But she also knew that "perception was an important thing. Did they think you were young and stupid? . . . Did they think you were vulnerable?" She chose to improve her image by seeking guidance from Hale Center representative Pete Laney, who later became speaker of the House (which reveals Guerrero's astute judgment in a mentor). In addition, she said, "I noticed that much got done in the legislature by hunting, fishing, and golfing . . . the kinds of things guys like to do," so she joined in these outings with her male colleagues. Over time, she learned how to trade favors with them and how to write a bill that would pass. Eventually, she became an effective lawmaker who had an influence on the passage or defeat of legislation and who passed much of her own, including several pieces that supported women and Mexican Americans.[11]

The second strategy women have adopted is rare: to reform the system, as Sissy Farenthold did in 1971. Having vocally rejected "pethood" during her first term, in her second term Farenthold led efforts to reveal which House members were involved in the Sharpstown bank fraud scandal and subsequently to lead a statewide movement for political reform. Although she gained widespread public support for her efforts, Farenthold was the object of political retribution from the men in power she sought to unseat. Little to none of her legislation passed during her second session, and Speaker Gus Mutscher had a man follow and photograph her antiwar activist son. After two unsuccessful bids for the governorship, Farenthold left politics.[12]

The third strategy women tend to take is a combination of the two: to learn how the system works from someone who has experience (whether male or female), to refrain from socializing, to decide consciously not to seek power if it requires compromising their principles, and to influence the operation of the chamber and to pass legislation through persistence and hard work, which they often refer to as "doing my homework." In 1991 Austin representative Wilhelmina Delco became speaker pro tempore, the second-highest position in the House. She did not, however, attempt to ingratiate herself with Speaker Gib Lewis and his inner circle.

Instead, she spent her off hours with her family or brought her husband to social functions. "In Texas, power politics often is played out away from the public eye—in backroom, after-hours meetings," she said. "I wasn't one to sit around and sip coffee and drink a beer." Her relationship with Lewis remained somewhat tentative, and when he threatened to "unappoint" her because—in violation of the speaker's team ethic—she had supported legislation he opposed, she told him, "You've gotta do what you've gotta do. And I've gotta do what I've gotta do." Lewis left her alone. "He clearly understood that I wasn't giving up my sex or my ethnicity or my principles for the honor of being speaker pro tem."[13]

Similarly, Houston representative Senfronia Thompson, one of the first two African American women in the House, responded to a colleague's joking reference to her as his mistress by delivering a scathing personal privilege speech on the House floor "to put everyone on notice that I was a duly elected official, just like they were."[14] Laredo senator Judith Zaffirini, one of the hardest-working and most productive senators in the history of that chamber, has developed her own practical approach. In 1993, when Lieutenant Governor Bob Bullock told her that if she "cut her skirt off about six inches and put on some high heels, she could pass anything she wants," Zaffirini laughed it off and praised Bullock's record for hiring, promoting, and paying women. When a fellow senator congratulated her for passing a bill by a 28-2 margin by saying, "You have to understand what this means coming from me, because . . . for me, the only purpose for women is to entertain men between wars," Zaffirini simply said to herself, "Twenty-eight to two—who cares what he thinks?"[15]

ADVANCING WITHIN THE MEN'S ROOM

The strategy that women choose, affected as it is by the no-win conundrum, has an effect on women's ability to advance within the culture of the men's room. Austin representative Sarah Weddington recalled of her time in the House in the 1970s that "there were situations when there were individual members, especially after late evenings when there was drinking, who had a hard time telling women who were the members from women who were not. So I just decided I wouldn't go to those late-night activities."[16] In a culture where socializing affects advancement, to withdraw from the fray has career consequences. No woman has ever been speaker of the House, yet even the woman widely regarded as the one with the best chance, Manchaca representative Libby Linebarger, said in 1989 that she looked forward to the time when she could walk down the floor of the House and not be called "little lady, sugar, or darlin'."[17] Not surprisingly, women have felt justifiably disadvantaged by a process requiring that they either behave in ways they do not value or give up ambitions for leadership. And, of course, even when they do play by the rules, they may not necessarily advance. "They say they [make committee appointments] by seniority," Karyne Jones Conley told us in 1995, "but they really don't. It's who the speaker decides he wants, and I guess that none of us as women have met his criteria."[18] As El Paso representative Nancy McDonald told us, "We're very similar to women in other fields. We get so high up on the executive ladder, but we don't get quite [high enough] and break that glass ceiling."[19]

We have found, too, that the strategies women use are mediated by their concerns for their families. Karyne Jones Conley decided that she would commute to Austin daily so that she could be at home for her children, thereby making attendance at after-hours meetings impossible. "I made the decision that it doesn't make any sense to go out and save the rest of the world and have four nuts growing up at home," she explained.[20] Even Wilhelmina Delco, who reached the highest point of any woman yet in the House, believed that her devotion to her family cost her politically. And Libby Linebarger, regarded as the first woman with a serious chance to become speaker, left the legislature to raise her two daughters.[21] Although we are increasingly seeing males decide to leave politics for family reasons, many more women than men continue to make family the determining factor in their political careers.

WOMEN AND "WOMEN'S ISSUES"

The culture of the men's room affects the issues that women support once they become lawmakers. In particular, it affects women's relationship to what is commonly referred to as "women's issues." Since 1920, male legislators, the press, and the public have assumed that women legislators are interested *primarily* in "women's issues," which we define as those concerns that involve women's equality under the law and that have evolved from women's traditional roles as caregivers in family and society: health care, education, and the welfare of children and family.[22] Because of the negative implications of entering the culture of the men's room with a "feminist agenda," however, many women have, as we have already seen, denied their interests in women's issues. Neveille Colson, who served in the House and the Senate for almost thirty years, refused to carry bills for women, fearing they would be ridiculed as "petticoat legislation."[23]

With the exception of the 1920s, when all four of the women in the legislature were former suffragists, and the 63rd Legislature in 1973, in which all five women in the House publicly supported feminist issues, most legislative sessions have seated women who were reluctant to identify themselves with women's issues. As a result, there has never been a formal women's caucus in either the House or the Senate, although African American and Mexican American caucuses do exist. Women have met *informally* for years to discuss issues, cross party lines to support mutual interests, and to share "am I crazy, or did this just happen?" stories with their female colleagues. The closest women have come to forming a caucus was the lunch group that Alice representative Ernestine Glossbrenner described to us, the "Ladies' Marching, Chowder, Terrorist, and Quasi-Judicial Society," which existed in the 1980s and printed its own letterhead. Other research has already recorded that women in the Texas Legislature are reluctant to commit to creating a formal caucus because their male colleagues can perceive such action as "plotting." Such a reaction would imply negative consequences for the women and imperil the bargain struck under the terms of the no-win conundrum.[24]

Certainly some women who deny an interest in women's issues are telling the truth. But we also know that for centuries women have been under pressure to avoid the "sex antagonism" that advocacy of female-related issues can produce.[25] So it is also likely that the negative implication attached to supporting women's issues causes women to become defensive. One modern indicator of this dynamic in Texas is that the term "women's issues," so popular in the 1970s, became "people's issues" in the 1980s as the backlash against the women's movement progressed. In addition, as more women join the legislature and as issues related to women, children, and the family become more commonly addressed over time (because of women's presence), more men have felt comfortable joining in support of them. As Houston representative Debra Danburg said, "Where people considered me to be somewhat strident or radical on sexual assault legislation fifteen years ago, now every guy and his dog is ready to sign on as a joint author. Some even try to be the primary author."[26]

Further, as more women enter the legislature, they invariably represent more diverse ideological viewpoints, and they have also become less inclined to identify with each other as women. In the 63rd Legislature in

1973, for example, as Sarah Weddington said, "Anytime all of the women in the Texas Legislature could agree on a piece of legislation, it passed." By the 1980s, however, Danburg noted a new, "strange dynamic. . . . [I]f something is pegged as a feminist issue, it will lose more votes [if a feminist carries it] than if a woman who is seen as more traditional is seen carrying the identical issue."[27]

Simply put, there is no typical female legislator. While the dynamic has changed, however, the reality remains that women, whether progressive, moderate, or conservative, continue to be the legislators most likely to support women's issues. Researchers have concluded that women will continue to carry the responsibility for these matters until they become between 25 and 40 percent of the population of legislatures. Lena Guerrero believes when that time comes, "when there are so many women on the floor of the Texas House and Senate that we're not counting anymore, . . . [we'll be] looking at substance and character and personalities" of legislators instead of their gender. It will take that, she thinks, before advocating women's issues will no longer be unpopular.[28]

As long as women's issues continue to remain important to the public, however, both the public and legislators need to consider who will take responsibility for them, for research indicates that male-dominated legislatures usually do not act with the interests of their female constituents in mind. The irritation of Progressive Era Texas suffragists Minnie Fisher Cunningham and Jane Y. McCallum with the legislature's inability to represent women adequately was one of the driving forces behind their support of woman suffrage.[29] The same concern drove women like Sarah Weddington and Houston representative Kay Bailey (later U.S. senator Kay Bailey Hutchison) to run for the legislature in 1972. As Hutchison recalled, "We did bring some new issues to the table that, because we were women, we were uniquely able to address and able to bring to focus. A man wouldn't have been experienced in the trauma of rape or the discrimination in getting credit."[30] Recent research indicates that a distinct gender gap indeed exists in the issues that state legislators regard as important and are willing to make legislative priorities and that gender differences in attitudes remain in place regardless of similarities in age, seniority, or party, generation, ideology, or race.[31]

WOMEN MAKE A DIFFERENCE

If men are not representing women adequately, and women appear to represent women's concerns better than men do, then we can only conclude that women, per se, do make a difference where women's issues are concerned. Women in the Texas Legislature have made a difference; they have represented issues of concern to women that were not addressed adequately before they became lawmakers. Some of their efforts were quickly successful, while others took decades and the repeated efforts of many legislators to win. During the 1920s the four women who served in the legislature—Edith Wilmans, Margie E. Neal, Laura Burleson Negley, and Helen Moore—supported most of the lobbying efforts of the women's Joint Legislative Council to pass much social reform legislation, including small, successful steps toward equalizing married women's property rights (this was not fully achieved until 1967). In the 1930s Moore and Dallas representative Sarah T. Hughes proposed to legalize jury service for women, but Hughes would become a judge before she could be a juror.[32] And the presence of a woman, Miriam Ferguson, as governor from 1933 to 1935 was of little assistance to activists. During the 1940s Waxahachie representative Rae Files Still continued Hughes' efforts to secure child support payments from noncustodial parents, but she was no more successful than Hughes had been.

In the late 1950s Texas women began to support passage of a state Equal Legal Rights Amendment, and in the early 1960s El Paso representative Maud Isaacks openly, but unsuccessfully, supported it. With the resurgence of the women's movement in Texas in the 1970s, women's issues became as central to the legislative process as they had been in the 1920s, and women helped to pass an equal credit act, reform sexual assault laws, obtain job protection for pregnant teachers, create a fair housing commission, and provide access to kindergarten for five-year-olds. Since then, women have been instrumental in or responsible for passing legislation, among other things, to obtain financial support for displaced homemakers, create a bill of rights for the ill elderly, reform the educational finance system, and provide alimony for spouses with no other means of support.

During the 72nd and 73rd Legislatures (1991–1995), Texas experienced a situation unique in its history: the existence of a reform-minded female governor—Ann Richards—and the highest numbers of women serving in the legislature to that time. "Naturally, when I became governor, a lot of people thought of me as a safekeeper for issues related to children, old people, the sick and the needy," Richards said. Knowing that access to power was a form of power within the legislature, Richards worked to "elevate women so that the impression would be left that they had access to me. I wanted their influence to be enhanced by the fact that I was there." Citing cooperative efforts with Lena Guerrero, Ernestine Glossbrenner, Debra Danburg, Wilhelmina Delco, Judith Zaffirini, Nancy McDonald, Dianne Delisi, Christine Hernández, and Patricia Gray, Richards reported successful legislation to fund health and mental retardation facilities, expand the rights of crime victims, create the offense of "stalking," eliminate spousal immunity in sexual assault cases, enhance punishment for acts of family violence, pass a public school finance bill, provide for widespread child immunization, and create the Texas Commission on Children and Youth.[33]

Despite the fact that by the time the 75th Legislature ended in January 1999, only eighty-six women had served in the Texas Legislature, and despite the strength of the men's-room culture they found there, women's presence has made a difference. Since 1923, there has been only a slight edge in the number of female lawmakers who have defined themselves or behaved as overt supporters of women's issues compared with the numbers of those who have not. Even so, it appears that in Texas, as in legislatures throughout the country, women in general tend to be more supportive of issues affecting women and children and of "feminist and liberal" positions, even though they may not describe themselves as feminists. The result is that the state policy agenda is being reshaped to reflect their concerns. In other words, electing women to office matters.[34]

The three women senators of the 76th Legislature, which opened in January 1999, agree. Jane Nelson (R), Florence Shapiro (R), and Judith Zaffirini (D) have all expressed the desire for more women. Shapiro said, "Many of the issues in today's legislative agenda are about women, family and children." Zaffirini joined Nelson in supporting a bill by Shapiro to notify parents when their daughters plan to have an abortion. Zaffirini and Shapiro have supported Nelson's efforts to punish domestic abusers more strictly, and Shapiro and Nelson have backed Zaffirini's welfare-reform bills. Zaffirini said, "We need more women to run and more women to win." Nelson agreed: "For a long time, politics was a field for men. I think that will change significantly over the next few years. I look forward to the day you don't have to interview me because I'm a female legislator." Shapiro's advice to women is "Jump in. The water's fine."[35]

THE END OF THE MEN'S ROOM

The men's-room culture was still alive and well in the legislature in 1999. "[Men] oftentimes view us as little sisters, which I don't think any of us appreciates," Senator Florence Shapiro observed. "Several members find

The three women of the Texas Senate, 76th Legislature, May 12, 1999. *Left to right:* Senators Florence Shapiro (R), Judith Zaffirini (D), and Jane Nelson (R). All three are businesswomen. All three say family is their highest priority. And all three wish there were more than three of them. Courtesy Associated Press; photo by Harry Carbluck.

themselves frequently apologizing for vulgar language," noted Senator Judith Zaffirini. And Senator Jane Nelson added, "A female senator will be interrupted on the Senate floor, which you wouldn't see happen to a male senator."[36]

Even so, the presence of women in the capitol has signaled the beginning of the end of the Texas Legislature as one of the largest and most powerful men's rooms in the state. When Edith Wilmans walked into the Texas House in 1923 as the state's first female lawmaker, gender boundaries in the political landscape became more fluid. Once women began to vote, in Texas as in the nation, definitions and images of "citizen" widened to include women. And once women became lawmakers, women began to wield the direct power of officeholding as well as the indirect influence of the organizing and lobbying at which they had become so experienced during the seventy-year fight for suffrage. Men could no longer necessarily assume, or claim, without contradiction, that they represented all women. Further, despite resistance and even open hostility to the presence of women in the legislature, women did not, and have not, stopped running for office.[37]

Since 1923, only two of thirty-eight legislative sessions in Texas have had no women members, and the numbers of women have grown steadily since the 1970s. They doubled between 1972 and 1978, then doubled again between 1978 and 1990. More than one woman served in the Texas Sen-

% FEMALE	STATE
0–5	AL
6–10	KY, OK
11–15	AK, LA, MS, PA, SC, TN, VA, WV
16–20	AR, GA, HI, IN, NJ, NY, NC, ND, SD, **TX**, UT, WY
21–25	CA, DE, FL, ID, IL, IA, ME, MA, MI, MO, MT, OH, WI
26–30	CT, KS, MD, NE, NH, NM, OR, RI
31–35	MN, NV, VT
36–40	AZ, CO, WA

SOURCE *"Women in State Legislatures 1998," fact sheet, Center for the American Woman in Politics (CAWP), National Information Bank on Women in Public Office, Eagleton Institute of Politics, Rutgers University, 1998.*

ate for the first time in 1987, when three appeared, including Judith Zaffirini, the first Latina senator. In the 75th legislative session (January 1997–January 1999), thirty-three women served in both chambers, the highest number yet. While these numbers have risen, the *percentage* of women members of the legislature has yet to reach 20 percent in Texas, far below their percentage within the general population. Texas is not among the ten state legislatures with the lowest percentage of female members, but it does fall within the group of twenty-three states with 20 percent or fewer. Twenty-seven states had 21 percent or more women members in the terms ending in 1998. The chart above shows how states compared in their percentages of female state legislators in 1998.

Because nothing indicates that women will cease running for office, we predict that the Texas Legislature will never have only men in it again. We cannot predict precisely when the culture of the men's room in the Texas Legislature will disappear, although we do think it will no longer exist when females constitute half of the membership of both houses and thereby more nearly represent their percentage of the general population. In order to become half of the legislature's population, however, women's numbers in the capitol must triple. If the proportion of women continues to expand at the current rate—an average of only two per biennium since 1973—it will take sixty years, until 2058, to reach that goal. (This does not allow for net losses such as those that occurred in the November

1998 election in which only twenty-nine women were elected to the Texas House—a loss of one. The Senate retained its three female members.) Texas is not unusual in this regard. After the 1998 elections, the population of women members of state legislatures hovers around 20 percent, with a high of almost 41 percent in Washington and a low of almost 8 percent in Alabama. Given these statistics, the entire country will have to wait until half of the next century is over before all legislatures reach 50 percent female membership.[38]

Figuring out how to speed up the process may be in question, but the goal itself is not. Because the presence of women in the state legislature does make a difference and because women are steadily making more incremental gains in statehouses than in the U.S. Congress (just over 22 percent compared with 12 percent, respectively), we urge politically active women to run for the legislature, particularly for open seats (those for which no incumbent is running). As illustrated in the biographies presented here, women have developed a variety of successful campaign strategies since 1923, from soliciting small donations at the grassroots level to networking with large-scale fund-raising groups, from using donated coffin lids for car-top advertisements to marshaling wide-ranging print and television media, from enlisting family members to hiring professional consultants. As a result of winning seats in the legislature, several women have found the service to be valuable experience for moving to higher office or into larger spheres of influence. Sarah T. Hughes became a federal judge; Barbara Jordan and Eddie Bernice Johnson were elected to the U.S. House of Representatives; Kay Bailey Hutchison became Texas' first female elected to the U.S. Senate; Frances Farenthold was nominated for vice president and later became chair of the National Women's Political Caucus; Susan Combs became Texas' first female state commissioner of agriculture.

In addition, as the ethnic and racial composition of the legislature has broadened through reapportionment, more women of color are emerging as public officials. For those women who are already in the legislature, we hope you will run for reelection—the power of incumbency is a real advantage. We also hope you will create a formal women's caucus. Given the number and kinds of caucuses that exist, the diversity among women in party, position, age, and ethnicity, and particularly the fact that female legislators do make a difference in shaping legislative agendas, creating a women's caucus is legitimate as well as long overdue.[39]

In the words of Senator Judith Zaffirini, "Cumulatively, women comprise half the population, and, cumulatively, we are the mothers of the other half. . . . We need a population in the legislature that reflects the population of the state."[40] Contemplating the fate of the culture of the men's room when we reach that goal may engender fear in some lawmakers about what women will do once their numbers equal men's. On the other hand, consideration of the value of reaching gender parity should keep us working toward it. In an echo of John Stewart Mills' conclusion about the benefits of freeing women from inequality, U.S. representative Eddie Bernice Johnson (who represented Dallas in both the Texas House and Senate) has said, "Look at all the gray matter we have missed. Can you imagine what this nation would be if we had had all of this brain power at work . . . all these years that women were left out?"[41]

NOTES

1. See Jeanie R. Stanley and Diane D. Blair, "Gender Differences in Legislative Effectiveness: The Impact of the Legislative Environment," in *Gender and Policy Making: Studies of Women in Office,* ed. Debra L. Dodson, pp. 115, 122; Nancy Beck Young and Lewis L. Gould, *Texas, Her Texas: The Life and Times of Frances Goff;* Barbara Jordan, videotape interview by Nancy Baker Jones, September 12, 1995, Archives for Research on Women and Gender, University of Texas at San Antonio (hereafter ARWG).

2. Christine Hernández, videotape interview by Nancy Baker Jones, May 26, 1995, ARWG.

3. Stanley and Blair, "Gender Differences," pp. 120, 122.

4. Stanley and Blair found this conundrum operating in the 1980s in both the Arkansas and Texas legislatures; see "Gender Differences," pp. 122–123. See also Camilla Stivers, *Gender Images in Public Administration: Legitimacy and the Administrative State.*

5. Walter L. Harris, "Margie E. Neal: First Woman Senator in Texas," *East Texas Historical Journal* 9, no. 1 (Spring 1973): 41.

6. "Oral Memoirs of Margaret [Gordon] Amsler," transcript, 1972, Baylor University Project, Baylor University Program for Oral History, Waco, p. 70.

7. *Austin American-Statesman,* January 10, 1951; *San Antonio Evening News,* January 22, 1953; Anita Blair, telephone interview by Ruthe Winegarten, July 14, 1995.

8. Frances Farenthold, videotape interview by Ruthe Winegarten, June 12, 1995, ARWG.

9. Karyne Jones Conley, videotape interview by Molly Dinkins, May 28, 1995, ARWG.

10. Jordan, interview, ARWG.

11. Lena Guerrero, videotape interview by Nancy Baker Jones, August 11, 1995, ARWG.

12. Farenthold, interview, ARWG.

13. Wilhelmina Delco, videotape interview by Ruthe Winegarten, July 20, 1995, ARWG.

14. Senfronia Thompson, videotape interview by Nancy Baker Jones, May 26, 1995, ARWG.

15. *El Paso Times*, January 22, 1993; *Houston Post*, January 22, 1993; Judith Zaffirini, videotape interview by Molly Dinkins, October 1995, ARWG.

16. Sarah Weddington, videotape interview by Nancy Baker Jones, June 18, 1995, ARWG. This concern is also discussed in Stanley and Blair, "Gender Differences," pp. 120–121.

17. *Austin American-Statesman*, April 17, 1989.

18. Conley, interview, ARWG.

19. Nancy McDonald, videotape interview by Ruthe Winegarten, May 29, 1995, ARWG.

20. Conley, interview, ARWG.

21. Delco, interview, ARWG; *Austin American-Statesman*, September 11, 1993; Libby Linebarger, "The Miracle Worker: Libby Linebarger on the Art of Compromise," talk to Leadership Texas, Austin, February 24, 1994; Pete Laney, videotape interview by Nancy Baker Jones, May 29, 1995, ARWG; see also Kristi Anderson, *After Suffrage: Women in Partisan and Electoral Politics before the New Deal*, p. 169.

22. Anderson discusses political women and women's issues in *After Suffrage*, pp. 17, 131–132. We define "women's issues" as do Debra L. Dodson and Susan J. Carroll in *Reshaping the Agenda: Women in State Legislatures*, pp. 92, 93. We also subscribe to Susan J. Carroll's additional assertion that women's issues are those whose policy consequences are likely to have a more immediate and direct impact on significantly larger numbers of women than of men; see *Women as Candidates in American Politics*, p. 15.

23. David Mauzy, draft of history of Texas women legislators, typescript, [1996], Senate Research Office, State of Texas, p. 63, Edith Wilmans Collection, Archives Division, Texas State Library, Austin.

24. Ernestine Glossbrenner, videotape interview by Ruthe Winegarten, July 20, 1995, ARWG; Stanley and Blair, "Gender Differences," p. 124.

25. Nancy F. Cott discusses this in *The Grounding of Modern Feminism*, esp. pp. 113, 266–267. The situation Cott describes for women in the 1920s sounds similar to the situation today: "There were also defensive reasons why women in partisan politics did not pursue or speak of their goals in terms of mobilizing a woman bloc. The notion of a woman bloc was harshly condemned by mainstream male politicians as well as by right-wing ideologues, described as against the American grain, portrayed as the deployment of destructive 'sex antagonism'" (p. 113).

26. Debra Danburg, videotape interview by Ruthe Winegarten, May 26, 1995, ARWG. Danburg's analysis is not unique to Texas. See R. Darcy, Susan Welch, and Janet Clark, *Women, Elections, and Representation*, pp. 181–184.

27. Weddington, interview, ARWG; Danburg, interview, ARWG.

28. Jane Sherron De Hart, "Rights and Representation: Women, Politics, and Power in the Contemporary United States," in *U.S. History as Women's History: New Feminist Essays*, ed. Linda K. Kerber, Alice Kessler-Harris, and Kathryn Kish Sklar, p. 237; Guerrero, interview, ARWG.

29. See Judith Nichols McArthur, "Motherhood and Reform in the New South: Texas Women's Political Culture in the Progressive Era" (Ph.D. diss., University of Texas at Austin, 1992), for a comprehensive discussion of the motivations and strategies of Texas suffragists. Our next chapter, "Texas Women as Politicians: A Historical Overview," provides a summary.

30. Kay Bailey Hutchison, videotape interview by Nancy Baker Jones, August 18, 1995, ARWG.

31. Carroll, *Women as Candidates*, p. 17; Dodson and Carroll, *Reshaping the Agenda*, pp. 11–35, 73, 91–92, 95–96; Janet K. Boles, "Advancing the Women's Agenda within Local Legislatures: The Role of Female Elected Officials," in *Gender and Policymaking*, ed. Dodson, p. 41; Sue Thomas, "Women in State Legislatures: One Step at a Time," in *The Year of the Woman: Myths and Realities*, ed. Elizabeth Adell Cook, Sue Thomas, and Clyde Wilcox, pp. 148–155; Darcy, Welch, and Clark, *Women, Elections, and Representation*, pp. 182–184.

32. Women won the right to jury service in Texas in 1954. Hughes became a judge in 1935.

33. Ann W. Richards, telephone interview by Ruthe Winegarten, November 19, 1998; "Report to the 74th Legislature by Ann W. Richards" (Austin: State of Texas, 1995).

34. Dodson and Carroll, *Reshaping the Agenda*, p. 94; Susan Welch and Sue Thomas, "Do Women in Public Office Make a Difference?" in *Gender and Policymaking*, ed. Dodson, p. 94; Lyn Kathlene, Susan E. Clarke, and Barbara A. Fox, "Ways Women Politicians Are Making a Difference," in *Gender and Policymaking*, Dodson, pp. 31–38; Susan Gluck Mezey, "Increasing the Number of Women in Office: Does It Matter?" in *Year of the Woman*, ed. Cook, Thomas, and Wilcox, pp. 255–270.

35. *Austin American-Statesman*, May 17, 1999.

36. *Austin American-Statesman*, May 17, 1999.

37. For an extended discussion of the shifting boundaries of gender and politics, see Anderson, *After Suffrage*, esp. pp. 163–170.

38. In 1998 Washington's became the first statehouse to cross the 40 percent female line. Whether this will affect its gendered dynamic remains to be seen. Election results for 1998 are from "Women in State Legislatures: Modest Gains Set New Record in 1998 Elections, Exciting Opportunities Lie Ahead," press release, Center for the American Woman and Politics (hereafter CAWP), National Information Bank on Women in Public Office, Eagleton Institute of Politics, Rutgers University, November 24, 1998.

39. Ibid.; "Women Who Will Serve in the 106th Congress," fact sheet, CAWP, November 4, 1998; "Women's Electoral Success: A Familiar Formula," press release, CAWP, November 25, 1998; see also Darcy, Welch, and Clark, *Women, Elections, and Representation*, for a discussion of the benefits to women of their becoming state legislators and the power of incumbency, esp. pp. 122–126, 176–178.

40. Zaffirini, interview, ARWG.

41. Eddie Bernice Johnson, videotape interview by Mike Greene, October 19, 1995, ARWG.

TEXAS WOMEN AS POLITICIANS

A HISTORICAL OVERVIEW

☆

Even before Texas women could vote or hold elective office, they were politicians, because they had influence on their communities and their governments. In some Native American tribes, women were leaders with significant authority. Among the matrilineal Caddos of East Texas, for example, the Kadohadachos had a woman chief. In another Caddo tribe, Santa Adiva was renowned as a "principal lady" with many men and women in her service.[1]

Spanish women settlers also exercised power as landowners of huge estates. Doña María Hinojosa de Ballí owned one-third of the lower Rio Grande Valley around 1800. María Cassiano married the Spanish governor of Texas in 1814 and ran the affairs of state in his absence. The officers called her "Mrs. Brigadier General," and she reviewed the troops while mounted on her spirited horse. The widowed Patricia de la Garza de León, co-founder of the city of Victoria, was the richest woman in Texas around 1835 and became one of the backers of the Texas Revolution.[2]

Despite slavery, black women exercised power that can be considered political, from fighting against slave owners and suing them in court to petitioning the Texas Legislature on behalf of their rights. Mary Madison, for example, a Galveston nurse and a free woman of color, petitioned the Texas Legislature around 1849 for the right to remain free in Texas after a law was passed outlawing free people of color from remaining in the state. Her petition, signed by eighty white friends and patients, was granted around 1850.[3]

Among early white settlers, women pursued distinctive political agendas, with mixed success. In Jane Long's inn the Texas Revolution was hatched. Jane Cazneau championed Texas annexation to the United States through fiery articles, and she played an important, although unofficial, part in a secret peace mission to Mexico City during the Mexican War.[4]

Elise Waerenskjold, a Norwegian immigrant, was a strong opponent of slavery and a strong supporter of public education. Melinda Rankin, a Presbyterian missionary, was fired from her job as director of the Rio Grande Female Seminary for abolitionist sympathies. And, according to writer Amelia Barr, there were several women in the balcony of the legislature when Texas signed the Articles of Secession to join the Confederacy. Barr writes that a passionately Unionist sixteen-year-old named Lucille leaned over the balcony to spit on the articles as the lieutenant governor stepped up to take the oath of office: "There was a little soft laughter from the women sympathizers who saw the action."[5]

WOMEN BECOME CANDIDATES

The transformation of women into political candidates, in Texas as in the nation, occurred within the context of women's participation in cultural and public roles and their increasing insistence on achieving legal and social equality. From the earliest days of the United States, women voiced their opinions in public spaces, but in doing so they often incurred the wrath of authority and became the subjects of public policy debates. Societal expectations that middle-class women remain primarily in the private rather than public domain were powerful. Citizenship was equated with manliness; women's images were equated with abstractions such as goddesses of liberty or the republic itself and with civic virtues like sobriety and domesticity. As for flesh-and-blood women, their early roles were expected to be indirect. "Republican mothers," for example, served the country best by training their sons for public life. And even Progressive Era women's involvement with voluntary associations, while bringing women into public, were couched, through their mostly decorous, if insistent approaches to reforming society, in terms of social housekeeping and often based on a belief in the moral superiority of women and motherhood. The U.S. suffrage movement, the largest effort among women to agitate publicly for a political goal, eventually won because it focused on a single objective and used a strategy that placed a premium on propriety, eschewing feminist demands for "emancipation whole and . . . immediate." Suffragists, particularly those in the National American Woman Suffrage Association (NAWSA), honed the skills they had used in the reform-minded work of voluntary associations, focused on the single goal of the vote, adapted publicity and propaganda tactics to confront the male political power structure, and created what we now recognize as a single-interest pressure group. Women, then, have long inhabited a separate political culture. Only in the last seventy-five years, since women have increasingly won the legal right to vote and become candidates, have they chosen to enter the male-dominated realm of party politics and to add the more direct power of officeholding to their long-standing talent for indirect influence through lobbying and persuasion.[6]

THE LINK TO SUFFRAGE

Women's presence in the Texas Legislature *as legislators* was a direct result of their having won the right to vote. While women first began calling for the vote nationally around 1848, it was not until after the Civil War that there is recorded evidence of Texas women organizing to seek the vote. A small group of Texas women submitted a petition to the Texas Reconstruction Convention of 1868–69 asking that the new constitution grant suffrage to both sexes. A resolution to this effect failed, but it is noteworthy that six of the ten black delegates to that convention supported it. Anecdotal evidence suggests that many black women were enthusiastic about the men in their lives exercising the long-withheld franchise and would have liked to have it for themselves.[7]

In 1868 the newly ratified 14th Amendment introduced the word "male" into the U.S. Constitution, equated the word with "citizen," and opened to question, particularly by suffragists, whether women were still citizens. The 14th Amendment was followed quickly by the 15th in 1870, which guaranteed that the right to vote could not be abridged on account of race or previous condition of servitude, but not on account of sex. Article VI of the Texas Constitution of 1875 defined voting eligibility, but women were excluded once again. By implication, they felt classified with idiots, lunatics, paupers, and felons, other Texans whom the Constitution prohibited from voting. It took Texas women fifty years, from 1868 to 1918, and three waves of organizing, to win this right.[8]

Among the incentives for winning suffrage was the desire to use the vote to achieve a number of political objectives held by more women than men. The Woman's Christian Temperance Union, the first widespread, organized political movement of Texas women, endorsed suffrage in 1888. Its *primary* goal, however, was to pass prohibition of alcohol amendments to the state and federal constitutions.[9] Other women's organizations—

Texas women won the right to vote in general elections with the passage of the 19th Amendment to the U.S. Constitution. Mrs. L. W. Evans of San Antonio is shown voting here in 1924. Courtesy University of Texas Institute of Texan Cultures, *San Antonio Light* Collection.

such as the Texas Federation of Women's Clubs, the National Council of Jewish Women, La Liga Femenil Mexicanista, and the Texas Association of Colored Women's Clubs—were addressing social problems and attempting to improve the health, education, and everyday lives of women and children.

Around 1900, as the economy changed and urbanization increased, more white women entered the workforce, joining the black women and Latinas who had always been there. Women who worked as sales clerks, teachers, secretaries, home demonstration agents, and nurses began looking toward politics as a means of acting on their concerns. Perhaps the most influential group of professional women to join the suffrage struggle were women journalists, who organized to flood newspapers with pro-woman suffrage pieces that they hoped would turn public sentiment in favor of their efforts. The second female member of the Texas Legislature,

Margie Neal, was a suffragist newspaper publisher and editor. Although suffrage marked women's entrance into the state's political life as voters, however, Texas suffragists, like their cohorts nationally, were not political novices. Texas women were busy throughout the Progressive Era forming women's voluntary associations and pushing for wide-ranging social reform. Between 1902 and 1918, for example, the Texas Federation of Women's Clubs and the Texas Congress of Mothers formed coalitions with other women's organizations to secure child labor legislation. In 1913 the federation and the Texas Congress of Mothers organized women to press for a married women's property law, a direct result of the clubwomen's having read and circulated among themselves the 1905 digest "The Legal Status of Women in Texas."[10] Winning the vote had required that they learn essential political skills such as organization building, persuasive communication, educating the public, and lobbying. Alice Paul's Congressional Union (later the National Woman's Party) established a Texas branch in 1916, but most Texas suffragists did not consider themselves feminists. The leadership of the Texas Equal Suffrage Association (TESA) avoided publicly denouncing the Woman's Party but privately rejected Paul's radical, public tactics in favor of the noncombative approach of Carrie Chapman Catt's NAWSA. While Minnie Fisher Cunningham, TESA president, and Jane Y. McCallum, president of the Austin Woman Suffrage Association, knew that male politicians were not representing women's interests, they believed they could change men's minds by convincing them that middle- and upper-class white women armed with the vote would improve society because they were wives and mothers. As occurred nationally, white Texas suffragists excluded African American and Mexican American women (who were working within their own organizations, such as the Texas Association of Colored Women's Clubs and La Liga Femenil Mexicanista) and demonstrated that their efforts could be as "fractious and ego-driven" as male party politics.[11]

In 1918 Texas women won the right to vote in primaries, an enormous victory in a one-party state where primary winners were virtually assured of winning general elections. The primary suffrage achievement was therefore as close to full suffrage as women had ever moved, and it was largely the result of a practical political deal offered by Minnie Fisher Cunningham to Governor William P. Hobby. If he would sign the bill granting women the right to vote in primaries, which until that point he had neither supported nor opposed, she would marshal the support of newly enfranchised women to help him defeat former governor James Ferguson's bid to regain the governorship in the upcoming election. Cunningham and other Texas suffragists despised Ferguson for his opposition to both suffrage and Prohibition, and they feared that if Ferguson were reelected, he would oppose or try to rescind female primary suffrage. Cunningham's strategy worked. Hobby signed the bill, Cunningham delivered the votes, and Hobby beat Ferguson in a landslide. In addition, the female vote that suffragists produced helped elect Annie Webb Blanton state superintendent of schools, thereby making her the first woman elected to a statewide office in Texas history. Early in 1919 Hobby recommended that state election laws be amended to enfranchise women and citizens, which would have *dis*franchised aliens such as Germans and Mexicans. The amendment was soundly defeated in May, in part due to opposition from aliens. In June Hobby called a special session of the Texas Legislature to consider the federal woman suffrage amendment to the U.S. Constitution. At the end of the month, Texas became the first state in the South to ratify the Nineteenth Amendment, causing Cunningham later to describe herself and her cohorts as "the smartest group of politicians in the state."[12] Cunningham's astute definition of Texas suffragists as "politicians," despite their being barred from holding most elected offices, reveals her understanding that "politics" existed outside of the party system and that women, although excluded from that male world, could nevertheless get what they wanted from it. She was, in essence, asserting that women had created a political world of their own in which getting elected was irrelevant. The reality of ensuing years, however, would prove her to be too optimistic.[13]

With the ballot won, many Texas suffragists assumed that women voters would transform society by voting for *the right man*, as Representative Charles Metcalfe reminded Cunningham in 1918, rather than by becoming candidates themselves. And, in fact, Cunningham was not inclined to urge women to vote for a woman unless, as had happened with Annie Webb Blanton, the woman supported the "right" issues. In 1922 Cunningham and other activists again supported Blanton in her unsuccessful run for the U.S. House of Representatives. But in 1924, when Jim Ferguson ran his wife, Miriam Amanda "Ma" Ferguson, for governor with the slogan "Two Governors for the Price of One," Cunningham and thousands of other women left the Democratic Party to support Republican George C. Butte. The ironic result was that the first woman elected governor of Texas won with the support of antisuffragists and the opposition of a substantial bloc of new women voters. In 1926, when Attorney General Dan Moody opposed Miriam Ferguson, women voters, galvanized by Jane Y. McCallum's vigorous campaigning for him, came out in force for Moody. This time they won, and Moody made McCallum his secretary of state. (The record is as yet silent about women voters' knowledge of or support for Edith Wilmans' candidacy for governor in both 1926 and 1928.)[14]

A significant indication of the importance of the suffrage victory in turning women into legislators is the fact that all of the women who served in the Texas Legislature during the 1920s—Edith Wilmans, elected in 1922; Margie Neal, elected in 1926; Laura Negley and Helen Moore, both elected in 1928—were suffragists. Furthermore, each was elected in her own right, not to serve out the term of a male relative. The first woman to run for the legislature may have been Houston's Mrs. R. L. Yocome, an African American who ran in 1920 on the Black and Tan ticket of the Republican Party and lost. Seven women besides Wilmans ran unsuccessfully for the legislature in 1922 alone, indicating that the level of victory among women candidates is not an accurate method for assessing women's interest in becoming elected officials.[15] Even if women did not become state legislators in large numbers, they fairly quickly started becoming county treasurers, school superintendents, clerks, tax assessors, and commissioners.[16]

Because some women showed interest in running for office did not mean they would be welcome contenders. Women who wanted to enter party politics had many barriers to overcome: at least four states ruled in 1920 that women were not eligible to hold office at all, and women were not legally allowed to hold high state office in Oklahoma until 1942. In addition, social mores had long resisted women's participation in public life on an equal footing with men. The whole zeitgeist of political campaigns had evolved into a male social ritual during the nineteenth century: voting often occurred in saloons, barbershops, or poolhalls, and men were used to taking an entire day to participate in parades, rallies, and other gatherings, where smoking and drinking were common.[17] Women's nonpartisan approach to winning the vote had not prepared them for the realities of party politics, and neither the federal government nor the two major parties tried to educate the new voters in the specifics of voting, party operations, or running for office. The *Woman Citizen* lamented in 1922 that barriers obstructing women from being elected were "almost insurmountable," and that the parties "do not nominate women for political office if there is a real chance for winning."[18]

WOMEN IN OFFICE UPHOLD SUFFRAGE

Miss Margie Neal
First senator

Mrs. Edith Wilmans
First legislator

First all-woman supreme court: Miss Ruth Brazzil, member; Mrs. Hortense Ward, chief | Justice; Miss Hattie L. Henenberg, member, now assistant attorney general.

Mrs. Espa Stanford
First governor's secretary

Mrs. Miriam A. Ferguson
First governor

Mrs. Clara Driscoll Sevier
National committeewoman

Miss Ethel Hilton
First legal official (Now Mrs. Cone Johnson)

Miss Annie Webb Blanton
First elected official

Mrs. Laura Burleson Negley
Legislator

Mrs. Helen Moore
Legislator

Mrs. Jane Y. McCallum
Secretary of State

Mrs. S. W. Meharg
First secretary of state

Miss Oveta Culp
First parliamentarian

By RAYMOND BROOKS
(Copyright, 1929, The Austin
American-Statesman)

STRANGE as it may seem in Texas, where women have held offices in every branch of the public service, it was less than eight and one-half years ago when the state officially proclaimed them the equals and partners of men in things political, and just a decade ago they were admitted to party primaries.

If one any longer questions women's ability to take care of themselves in politics and public affairs, compare the record of that eight and one-half years of feminine endeavor, with the achievements of men in any similar period of the world's history. His question will answer itself.

A woman has been governor of Texas. Four women have served as lawmakers, including one in the office of state senator. An all-woman supreme court has handed down decrees from the loftiest judicial bench of Texas. Women's share in things political is so much an accepted fact now, that it seems like going back into the dim and dusty past to read the proclamation of the governor of Texas, published in the fall of 1920, when women were first welcomed to full equality in the responsibilities and duties of citizenship.

An official proclamation on file in the state department—presided over by a woman—recounts that the day "marks an epoch and a turning point in the history of this nation * * * The tremendous significance of this achievement, affecting as it does the "political" status of half the people of this nation, and promoting the political well-being of all the people of the nation, at once taxes our imagination with its magnitude, and makes

our hearts rejoice with its roseate promise for the future."

Five years after that, a woman occupied the governor's chair.

This proclamation was written by Gov. W. P. Hobby in September of 1920, when Tennessee had been the 36th state to ratify the 19th amendment to the national constitution, conferring full suffrage upon women. Gov. Hobby caused the law to be changed to admit women to vote in the 1918 primary election.

"It is appropriate and proper," the Texas proclamation set forth, "that we pause and give expression to our deep gratitude, for it is impossible to conceive a more far-reaching achievement or to estimate its outstanding influence upon the future progress of the human race." Sept. 4, 1920, was set aside as a holiday to celebrate the political freedom of women.

At that, woman suffrage has never been written into the constitution of Texas; but was rejected by the he-men voters who passed on it last, in May, 1919, less than a decade ago.

Feminine Leaders

Already the roster of women who have held high public office is getting to be a lengthy one. This list speaks for itself of the success of the experiment in government that is no longer an experiment. Here are some of the women who have taken part in the official affairs of the state.

Mrs. Miriam A. Ferguson, first of her sex to be inaugurated governor of an American state.

Miss Annie Webb Blanton, first woman elected to state office, first superintendent of public instruction.

Mrs. Edith E. Wilmans, first

legislator.

Miss Margie Neal, first state senator.

Mrs. Emma Griggsby Meharg, first secretary og state.

Mrs. Espa Stanford, first private secretary to a governor; member of state industrial accident board.

Mrs. Hortense Ward, first chief justice of supreme court.

Mrs. H. J. O'Hair of Coleman, first university regent.

Miss Oveta Culp, first parliamentarian of the house.

Mrs. Cone Johnson, assistant attorney general.

Mrs. Clara Driscoll Sevier, president national democratic committee from Texas.

Mrs. J. D. Claybrook, first messenger of presidential electoral college.

Mrs. Jane Y. McCallum, secretary of state.

Mrs. Laura Burleson Negley, member of the legislature.

Mrs. Helen Moore, member of the legislature.

Miss Hattie L. Henenberg, assistant attorney general and member of Texas' only all-woman special supreme court.

Miss Ruth Brazzill, member of first all-woman supreme court.

Mrs. Elizabeth M. Speer, secretary of Texas prison commission.

Miss Elizabeth M. West, first state librarian.

Women officeholders support suffrage. Courtesy family of Laura Negley.

THE 1920S: REFORMERS AND REACTIONARIES

During the entire 1920s, only eleven women served in the U.S. Congress (in the House); of these, ten were elected because they were relatives of male politicians, usually filling their unexpired terms. The eleventh was an antisuffragist who was defeated after one term and denounced politics as "too unclean" for women. This small number of women who won at the national level did not nearly reflect the far larger numbers of women who ran and lost, however. Women were more successful at the local and state level; the number of women in state legislatures rose from 33 to 149 between 1921 and 1929. Almost 10,000 men served. In Texas, the 1920s were more socially reactionary than they were liberating. Social reform was not a major concern among politicians. Rather, three issues dominated: prohibition, "Fergusonism" (the abuse of ethics exemplified by Governors Jim and Miriam Ferguson), and the Ku Klux Klan. Texas women were a significant percentage of Klan membership, and in Houston enough members of the League of Women Voters joined the Klan to cause a serious split within the league. The Klan's efforts to terrorize and intimidate blacks, along with the appearance of the White Primary Law, meant that the federal suffrage amendment held no benefits for black women in Texas, and many of them, like those of the Texas Association of Colored Women's Clubs, turned their attention to securing antilynching legislation. Given these kinds of obstacles, that four women reached the Texas Legislature in the 1920s is more an accomplishment than a failure.[19]

Politically active women in Texas, like women nationally, tended to follow three paths during the 1920s. Most continued as they had in the past, lobbying for social and workplace reform and for peace. Others tackled the political system itself by becoming active in party politics and running for office—Minnie Fisher Cunningham staged an unsuccessful campaign for the U.S. Senate in 1928 to defeat the incumbent, Klansman Earle Mayfield. The smallest number followed the new National Woman's Party (NWP) and supported passage of the newly written Equal Rights Amendment. Mainstream activists closed the TESA and opened a state chapter of the League of Women Voters to educate women about their new voting rights and to provide all voters with nonpartisan information about candidates. In a move similar to the 1920 formation of the Women's Joint Congressional Committee, a nationwide collaboration among women's organizations to lobby Congress, five women's groups in Texas joined to form the Joint Legislative Council (JLC) in 1922 to lobby the Texas Legislature.[20]

Called the "Petticoat Lobby" by legislators weary of it, the JLC persuaded the Democratic Party to include two of its measures in the 1922 platform, a prison survey and a state match of federal funds for mother-infant health care available through the Sheppard-Towner Act. These and the four other JLC recommendations making up its entire agenda—an education survey, emergency appropriation for the public schools, and two prohibition enforcement measures—passed the 38th Legislature in 1923, despite the opposition of one representative who described the lobby's program as "the most audacious piece of Bolshevism ever permitted to clutter up this chamber." The JLC succeeded with Edith Wilmans' support, but because the lone female representative could not pass the plan by herself, the JLC clearly had to marshal most of its support from male legislators. Perhaps male legislators' fear of the new women's block vote—exhibited with such success in 1918—influenced them to give the women what they wanted in 1923. As the decade progressed, however, the JLC's programs met with rising resistance. Three of its ten proposals (including strengthened child labor laws and funding for rural schools and a girls' correctional facility) failed to pass the 39th Legislature in 1925, in which no women served. In 1927 the JLC recorded fewer successes. It won its fight to establish a state board of education, for example, but, despite support from state senator Margie E. Neal, failed to pass its bill requiring political parties to make women half of their state executive committees. The coalition fractured after the 40th Legislature ended in 1929 when most of its member organizations decided to pursue increasingly divergent agendas, and in the 41st Legislature neither Representative Helen Moore nor Representative Laura Burleson Negley supported the bills advanced by the Woman's Christian Temperance Union, a JLC member. A severely diminished JLC secured state oversight of day nurseries, children's homes, and adoption agencies during that session, but for all intents and purposes, it no longer existed. "Even new, enthusiastic citizens sometimes weary in well doing," sighed the JLC's first head, Jane Y. McCallum.[21]

Organized support for passage of an Equal Rights Amendment (ERA) to the U.S. Constitution, the reform measure that Alice Paul and her National Woman's Party introduced in 1921 to eliminate all discrimination based on sex, remained virtually nonexistent in Texas, despite the fact that the Texas Supreme Court ruled in 1924 that a married woman's identity was submerged in her husband's. (One result of the court's deci-

Women were front-page news. Courtesy family of Laura Negley.

sion was that in 1926, before Governor Miriam Ferguson could sign state property over to the U.S. War Veterans' Bureau as the legislature had directed her to do, the attorney general had to research whether this action by a married woman would be legal.) Activists in Texas had become used to lobbying the legislature issue by issue, and they continued the strategy. In 1913 Houston attorney Hortense Ward had led the successful effort to pass the Married Woman's Property Law, which gave married women partial control over both separate and community property. In 1927 the League of Women Voters and other women's groups won from the legislature a statute giving wives the authority to dispose of community property; in 1929 the JLC supported, and Representative Laura Burleson Negley sponsored, a married persons' property rights bill that defined the rent and revenues from the separate properties of a married couple as community property. The bill passed, with Negley calling it "a piece of remedial legislation which will be of benefit to a number of women."[22]

NWP members believed that such an issues-based strategy was too slow. Like the federal suffrage amendment, they held, a federal ERA would strike down all gender-based legislation at one time. This was necessary, the NWP believed, because such laws insulted women by assuming their inferiority. The ERA's opponents, who included the Women's Bureau of the Department of Labor, the American Association of University Women (AAUW), the League of Women Voters, and similarly influential groups, believed that women's physical limitations and their domestic roles often necessitated different treatment from men. Most of all, they feared the amendment would leave women workers without protective labor legislation for which they had fought. These separate visions among activists accelerated the unraveling of the solid coalition that women of diverse views had forged in order to win their focused campaign for the vote. "Suffrage was a symbol, and now you have lost your symbol," said suffragist Anna Howard Shaw. With suffrage won, women followed interests they had put aside for years. Minnie Fisher Cunningham believed that the "next 'big job' in Texas" was prison reform, and this was the effort to which many Texas women devoted their energies throughout the 1920s.[23]

THE 1930S: ACTIVISM RECEDES

By 1930, then, activists in Texas, as elsewhere, did not see in the ERA or any other single issue the galvanizing force that suffrage had offered. Although the legislative victories achieved by Progressive Era women resulted in more women running for office and working for newly formed local, state, and federal departments, bureaus, boards, and commissions, the Depression forced most women to turn their attention away from activism toward economic survival. Nationally the sense of emergency engendered by the Depression and the presence of Franklin and Eleanor Roosevelt in the White House resulted in more women serving in high-level federal positions than at any time in the past. Among these were Texas senator Margie E. Neal, who worked for the National Recovery Administration and the Social Security Administration in the 1930s, and

Minnie Fisher Cunningham, who left her job of nine years as an editor for the Texas A&M University Extension Service in 1939 to work in Washington for the Women's Division of the Agricultural Adjustment Administration. More women served in Congress during the 1930s than had served in the 1920s, but only incrementally so. One woman reached the Senate, and no more than four or five women served in the House in any one session. In Texas only six women served in the House throughout the 1930s—Helen Moore, Frances Rountree, Cora Strong, Sarah T. Hughes, Margaret Gordon (Amsler), and Neveille Colson. Of these, Rountree and Strong were widows elected to serve out their deceased husbands' terms. No women served in the Senate, and no women at all served in the 45th Legislature (1937–1939). Houston's Oveta Culp ran for the legislature in 1930, but she was defeated by an opponent who criticized here as "a parliamentarian and a Unitarian." She never ran for office again. Jane Y. McCallum served Governors Daniel J. Moody and Ross Sterling as their secretary of state from 1927 until Miriam Ferguson won her second race for governor in 1932. By then, the "women's bloc" of voters no longer existed.[24]

Many of the Progressive Era voluntary associations foundered during the 1930s, and several feminist pioneers died, including Jane Addams, the founder of Hull House; Florence Kelly, the founder of the National Consumers' League; Grace Abbott, director of the federal Children's Bureau; and intellectual Charlotte Perkins Gilman. The Women's Joint Congressional Committee began to lose its members, as had the Joint Legislative Council in Texas during the late 1920s. In addition to these setbacks, women's groups after the Russian Revolution and World War I came under increasing accusation and outright attack from red-baiters who branded feminists and other reformers Bolsheviks and radicals. Elizabeth Dilling's *The Red Network* claimed to have evidence of radical infiltration in 460 organizations. Near the end of the decade, a national coalition of women's groups tried to revive the "woman movement" by issuing the Woman's Charter, a declaration of objectives for women's increased participation in public life. But its assertion that remediation of poor working conditions be undertaken through legislation angered supporters of the ERA and widened the split among feminists over the best strategy for winning equality. In the end, Woman's Charter organizer Mary Anderson declared the effort "a complete flop."[25]

In Texas, support for protective labor legislation was pervasive, making the state's atmosphere hostile to ERA supporters. (Although the National Federation of Business and Professional Women decided to support the campaign for the ERA in 1937, the Texas chapter would not do so for another twenty years.) Texas women who worked in laundries were "restricted" to working an eleven-hour day, but no limits existed for stenographers, waitresses, sales clerks, domestics, or farm workers. Representative Helen Moore tried to end such inconsistencies and to enact an eight-hour day while she was in the legislature, but her bills failed. Texas working women engaged in a number of strikes in the 1930s but with limited success: unionized garment workers in Dallas and San Antonio struck several times from 1935 to 1938, and Emma Tenayuca led a strike by San Antonio pecan shellers (primarily Mexican American women) in 1938 to protest earning three dollars for a sixty-hour week. As the state's unemployment rate rose, working women, particularly married women, came under increased pressure to relinquish their jobs to men. The Dallas city manager even considered a proposal to fire all married women whose husbands were employed.[26]

Married women in Texas were more restricted by legislation than unmarried women. For example, the law "protected" a married woman from controlling her own wages, signing contracts, or disposing of her own property without her husband's approval. Concerned that marriage rendered them legally incompetent, women worked for change. In 1935 Representatives Helen Moore and Sarah T. Hughes proposed a bill to legalize jury service for women, thereby eliminating legal "protection" for women from hearing sordid courtroom testimony. Their effort failed, and Hughes would become a judge (in 1935) before she could serve on a jury. Texas women did not win this right until 1954.[27]

Nationally, organizations that remained relatively healthy during the 1930s included the Women's International League for Peace and Freedom, the League of Women Voters, Ladies LULAC (League of United Latin American Citizens), and Mary McLeod Bethune's National Council of Negro Women. In 1930, Texas suffragist Jessie Daniel Ames founded the Association of Southern Women for the Prevention of Lynching, and its Texas chapter secured the pledges of seven gubernatorial candidates in 1934 to use the power of the governorship to stop lynching. Socially, birth control gained wide acceptance during the Depression. In Texas, Kate Ripley opened the first birth control clinic in Dallas with financial support from her husband's shirt manufacturing company. To circumvent the federal law against mailing contraceptives, she had Margaret Sanger send diaphragms to her in shirt boxes.[28]

Overall, however, the decade appeared to be one of transition for the women's movement. The economic concerns of the Depression overshadowed, and were often regarded as unrelated to, women's issues. "Is Feminism Dead?" asked a 1935 article in *Harper's*. Women's attention focused increasingly on the war in Europe, and in Texas Jewish and non-Jewish women turned their energies to founding the Texas State Cause and Cure of War Committee in 1938. In 1940 Minnie Fisher Cunningham looked back ruefully and wrote Jane Y. McCallum with this question: "It was maddening to think that we somehow didn't carry on as vigorously as we could have done. . . . Did the League of Women Voters turn us away from fighting to studying? Something happened. What?"[29]

THE 1940S AND 1950S: THE DOLDRUMS

During the 1940s and 1950s, the women's movement did not die, but it did enter what has been called the "doldrums." World War II offered expanded employment opportunities for women inside and outside of the military, increasing public awareness about gender inequities in the workplace, but the postwar years saw many women relinquish their jobs to returning male veterans. In 1945 a Gallup Poll revealed that only 18 percent of those surveyed approved of a married woman working if her husband could support her. The Baby Boom increased women's domestic responsibilities, while antifeminism and McCarthyism further marginalized even moderately activist, political women as antifamily radicals. Academic and popular publications overwhelmed progressive viewpoints with outright attacks on feminism. Ferdinand Lundberg and Marynia Farnham's *Modern Woman: The Lost Sex*, published in 1947, invoked Freudian psychology to declare that feminists were neurotics responsible for the country's problems and advocated federal subsidization of psychoanalysis for feminists. Throughout the 1950s, popular women's magazines like *Colliers* and *Ladies' Home Journal* waved the flag of antifeminism as well, calling activism dangerous and urging women to devote themselves to home and family. In such an atmosphere, women's organizations were reluctant to tackle issues larger than those affecting their own members. In addition, race and class divisions continued to prevent women from collaborating productively.[30]

For many women, of course, winning suffrage had made little difference in their lives. People born in China and Japan were ineligible to become U.S. citizens at all, and Japanese Americans suffered internment in U.S. concentration camps during World War II. Native Americans,

Mexican Americans, and African Americans remained virtually disfranchised by state laws and customs: in 1940 fewer than 2 percent of southern blacks voted. With the U.S. Supreme Court's 1944 decision in *Smith vs. Allwright*, a Texas case, the white-only primary was declared unconstitutional, and black voter registration in Texas more than tripled by 1947. Even so, by 1952, 87 percent of southern black women (and 65 percent of men) had never voted.[31]

Not surprisingly, the energies of most African American activists during this period focused on ending segregation and lynching, fighting racial discrimination, and winning basic civil rights. Some white women's organizations that had previously committed themselves to women's interests stopped. The League of Women Voters increasingly disassociated itself from women's issues, defined itself as nonpartisan, and in 1953 debated whether to rename itself the League of Active Voters. In Texas the league studied local school systems, water problems, and the United Nations. Groups like the AAUW and B&PW encouraged and prepared women to run for public office, but the numbers of women in elected office did not rise appreciably. The women who did focus on women's equality were overwhelmingly white, well-educated professionals, members of a variety of organizations who shared a commitment to "women's rights" but not to a single issue. They found some measure of agreement around equal pay, and both houses of Congress reported an equal pay bill favorably in the 1940s and 1950s, but did not pass one. Congress similarly considered and then delayed action for federal legislation allowing women to serve on juries, but by 1950 most state legislatures still barred women from jury service. The loosely defined "women's movement" of the postwar period was less interested in these specifics and more interested in three larger goals: moving women into policymaking positions, supporting the development of women's history as a field, and passing the Equal Rights Amendment.[32]

As the ERA's creator and sponsor, the National Woman's Party was the only thread of feminist activism that tied the postwar period to the heady days of the suffrage victory. But it was not a healthy organization. Its membership had plummeted from 60,000 in the 1920s to only 200 in 1952. It remained a group of elite, white, generally conservative women unwilling to diversify its membership, and it suffered from internal disagreements, not the least of which was founder Alice Paul's support of Senator Joseph McCarthy. While some ERA opponents denounced the measure as Communistic, the Communist Party itself opposed the ERA, a position Paul used to try to gain support for it. Organized opposition, however, especially from labor unions and the Women's Bureau, meant the NWP won only piecemeal support for the ERA during the 1940s and 1950s. The National Education Association, General Federation of Women's Clubs, and the National Association of Colored Women endorsed the ERA, the American Association of University Women stopped opposing it, and both the Republican and Democratic parties included platform planks supporting the concept of constitutional equality. President Harry S. Truman affirmed his support in 1945; in the following year, the Senate debated the ERA seriously for the first time, but the resulting vote failed to generate the majority required to send the amendment to the states for ratification. And in the 1950s Eleanor Roosevelt, who had opposed the ERA because she supported protective labor legislation, began to see its benefits. Despite such trends, however, state legislatures continued to prohibit women from holding certain jobs.[33]

Despite the regressive atmosphere of the postwar years for women, they continued to be active politically. Although no more than eleven women served in any one session of Congress in the 1940s (and they generally declined to call themselves feminists), several—like Representative Mary T. Norton of New Jersey and Representative Helen Gahagan Douglas of California—nevertheless noted that they received different, and sometimes discriminatory, treatment from their colleagues. They also felt comfortable sponsoring antidiscrimination legislation, such as Maine senator Margaret Chase Smith's efforts to equalize the status of women in the peacetime military. They remained divided over the ERA, however, with Republicans tending to favor it and Democrats tending to oppose it. They united around support for day care centers, but their numbers were too small to make a difference. In 1952 both the Republicans and the Democrats nominated (but did not run) women for vice president, and President Dwight D. Eisenhower added twenty-six women to his administration. (Not all were interested in women's rights: Texan Oveta Culp Hobby, secretary of health, education, and welfare, tried to reverse some New Deal social reforms.) During the 1950s, however, seeds of reaction against conservatism were sown: in 1950 the U.S. Supreme Court declared, in *Sweatt vs. Painter*, that the separate law school established by the University of Texas for its one black student, Heman Sweatt, was not equal to the school white students attended and ordered the law school to integrate. In 1954 the U.S. Senate censured Senator Joseph McCarthy, and the U.S. Supreme Court rejected the doctrine that separate public schools for blacks were equal in *Brown vs. the Board of Education of Topeka, Kansas*. More silently, young women began to sense their own mothers' discontent with women's lives, and a female generation gap developed. Times were beginning to change.[34]

The 1940s and 1950s in Texas have been described as "primitive years" politically, a time of conservative, corporate hegemony characterized by "harsh antilabor laws, the suppression of academic freedom, a segregationist philosophy, elections marred by demagoguery and corruption, the devolution of the daily press, and a state government that offered its citizens, especially the minorities, very few services."[35] Although much is left to learn about Texas women's political action in the 1940s and 1950s, we do know that in this atmosphere Texas women made few public forays for women's rights. Christia Adair, one of the state's few African American suffragists, turned her attention to civil rights when she was denied the right to vote because of her race, and spent these decades working through the Houston chapter of the National Association for the Advancement of Colored People (NAACP) to desegregate the city. White women activists invested their energies in helping keep liberalism alive within the Democratic Party, believing that such a victory would ensure a hearing for women's issues. Only six women served in the legislature during the 1940s—Neveille Colson (in both the House and Senate), Rae Files Still, Florence Fenley, Elizabeth Suiter, Maribelle Stewart, and Persis Henderson. Of these, Stewart and Henderson were elected to fill the terms of their deceased husbands and served only briefly. With the support of former Representative Sarah T. Hughes, Rae Files Still introduced legislation mandating child support payments from noncustodial parents, but her efforts failed.[36]

In 1944 the liberal Minnie Fisher Cunningham, by then in her sixties, ran for governor to force incumbent Coke Stevenson to take a position in the party fight between liberals and conservatives over support for Franklin D. Roosevelt. She came in second in a field of nine primary candidates, but Stevenson won in a landslide. In 1945 Cunningham and Jane Y. McCallum launched their last substantial effort at activism when they formed the seventy-five-member Women's Committee for Educational Freedom (WCEF). Its purpose was not to foster gender equality, but to demand reinstatement for University of Texas president Homer P. Rainey, who had been charged by the university's conservative board of regents with allowing subversives to infiltrate the faculty and then had been fired.

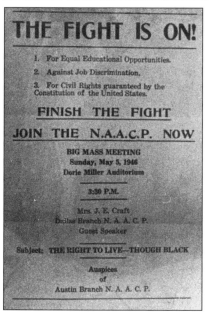

THE FIGHT IS ON!

1. For Equal Educational Opportunities.
2. Against Job Discrimination.
3. For Civil Rights guaranteed by the Constitution of the United States.

FINISH THE FIGHT

JOIN THE N.A.A.C.P. NOW

BIG MASS MEETING
Sunday, May 5, 1946
Dorie Miller Auditorium

3:30 P.M.

Mrs. J. E. Craft
Dallas Branch N. A. A. C. P.
Guest Speaker

Subject: THE RIGHT TO LIVE—THOUGH BLACK

Auspices
of
Austin Branch N. A. A. C. P.

Juanita Craft of Dallas, a state leader of the National Association for the Advancement of Colored People, organized dozens of NAACP chapters throughout the state. Courtesy Center for American History, University of Texas at Austin, Juanita Craft Collection.

The WCEF faltered not only because of a lack of funding but in larger measure because, as it became more political and less civic in identity, its members began to fear repercussions from conservatives. Democratic Party activist Margaret Carter said one woman dropped out fearing her husband would lose his job. Cunningham and McCallum also supported Rainey's unsuccessful run for governor in 1946 but met similar resistance to the participation of women in such political action. In the same election that Rainey lost, New Deal state district court judge and former state representative Sarah T. Hughes also lost her race for the U.S. Congress to a conservative Dallas businessman whose antilabor campaign characterized his opposition as "left-wing political terrorists."[37]

Such defeats helped answer the question that India Edwards, national Democratic Party women's division director, had asked of Texas party activist Margaret Carter in 1947: "When is Texas going to send us a Congresswoman or a woman Senator?"[38] The political climate prevented women from succeeding as candidates at the national level. In 1952 Sarah T. Hughes was nominated for the vice presidency at the Democratic National Convention, but the move was a gesture, sanctioned by Democratic Party chair and Speaker of the House Sam Rayburn (a fellow Texan) only on the condition that Hughes immediately withdraw her name from consideration. She did. Only five women served in the Texas Legislature during the 1950s—Neveille Colson in the Senate and Dorothy Gillis Gurley, Virginia Duff, Anita Blair, and Maud Isaacks in the House. Of these, only Isaacks openly agitated for women's equality. The others claimed little or no interest in such a role, although Blair supported women's right to serve on juries. Duff, the most conservative of the group, supported school segregation bills throughout her tenure. The ascendance of conservative governors like Allan Shivers, the reality of political corruption, and the lack of interest in women's issues shown by powerful but pragmatic congressional Democrats like Senator Lyndon Johnson, Representative Wright Patman, and Speaker Rayburn, combined to make the Texas political climate an unhealthy one for overt support of women's equality. In 1952 Margaret Carter, Minnie Fisher Cunningham, and other former WCEF members formed a statewide women's group to preserve Democratic Party liberalism. Rayburn discouraged them, however, and Johnson declined to support their efforts to defeat a bill in the Texas Legislature permitting cross-filing between parties. The women helped defeat the bill anyway. Cunningham and other liberals supported Adlai E. Stevenson's presidential bid in a year when conservative Texas Democrats bolted to Dwight D. Eisenhower. In 1954 Cunningham offered to mortgage her farm to ensure that the *Texas Observer* would remain a liberal newspaper. In 1954 Texas women finally won the right to serve on juries, but the victory was an isolated one. In 1957 Cunningham turned seventy-five, and Jane Y. McCallum died, two events that signaled the demise of the state's suffrage generation.[39]

The same year, however, a new figure emerged to lead another generation of politically astute women's rights activists: Hermine Tobolowsky, Dallas attorney, legal counsel to the National Federation of Business and Professional Women, and later president of the Texas B&PW. Tobolowsky and the B&PW had long supported improving the legal status of married women and jury service for women, but in contrast to the national office, they had advocated a piecemeal approach to winning equal legal rights law by law and had opposed the single-law approach embodied in the Equal Rights Amendment. In 1957, however, Tobolowsky represented the state B&PW at legislative hearings in Austin for bills granting married women control of their own property. She became so irritated by the paternalistic treatment of her by Senator Wardlow Lane and others that she left convinced the piecemeal approach was futile. She then persuaded the Texas B&PW to reverse its stand and support a *state* Equal Legal

Rights Amendment and poured her energy into leading the campaign for an amendment to the Texas Constitution that would take the next fifteen years—until 1972—to win.[40]

The fight for the national ERA, begun when it was first introduced in Congress in 1923, had served as the continuous, if sometimes tenuous, thread that linked the activism of the suffrage years to the reemergence of public feminism in the 1960s by keeping interest in women's rights alive throughout the doldrums of the 1940s and 1950s. If nothing else, ERA supporters kept issues related to women's equality in front of legislators, bureaucrats, journalists, and other public officials, but they also contributed both tangible and intangible resources (such as membership newsletters, office space, time, and commitment) to the effort to keep the women's movement alive through hard times. In addition, they provoked thought and conversation about the state of women's rights among their opponents, who consisted of women's rights advocates as well as reactionaries. By 1961 the pendulum of the country's mood, awakened by the civil rights movement, had swung back slightly from conformity toward support for social change. While women were not particularly visible as professional politicians, they held substantial positions in government and took note of politicians' opinions about sex equality. In this atmosphere three actions at the federal level occurred in quick succession that helped contribute to the reappearance of an energized women's movement shortly thereafter.[41]

THE 1960S: ACTIVISM REEMERGES

In 1961 opponents of the ERA, like Women's Bureau head Esther Peterson, encouraged President John F. Kennedy to create the first of these federal actions, the President's Commission on the Status of Women, because they believed it would disprove the need for the amendment. Although the commission's final report neither supported nor opposed the ERA, it supported equal legal rights for women. One of its recommendations resulted in the second federal action, the Equal Pay Act of 1963, the underlying concept of which the National Federation of Business and Professional Women had supported since 1919. While the Equal Pay Act had several problems (it did not cover some jobs held by both poor and professional workers and did not require equality in hiring practices), it came to be regarded as an early step toward ending gender-based job discrimination. The third of these actions was the passage of Title VII of the 1964 Civil Rights Act, which prohibited discrimination on the basis of sex as

well as race in employment. Ironically, the bill's southern opponents introduced the word "sex" into Title VII as a joke, because they believed it
would doom the bill to defeat. But NWP and B&PW members lobbied
hard for passage, invoking as persuasion their influence with women voters. While these groups could not take full credit for passing Title VII,
they considered it a great victory.[42]

As a result of these actions at the federal level, state commissions and
national conferences on the status of women emerged, providing a locus
for conversation and study across the country. In 1963 Betty Friedan's *The
Feminine Mystique* appeared and served as a lightning rod for revealing a
widespread mood of personal dissatisfaction among white, middle-class
women. When Friedan and others realized that the Equal Employment
Opportunity Commission, created to enforce Title VII, was likely to ignore the amendment's sex discrimination provision, they tapped the diverse but electric energy of "a seething underground" of women to form
the National Organization for Women (NOW) in 1966. Modeled on the
NAACP, NOW brought together a wide range of women into the service
of achieving equal rights for women. Although NWP founder Alice Paul
joined NOW, the two organizations remained distant from each other,
and as the decade progressed, NOW became the more successful of the
two, committed to winning a wide range of advances that included, but
were not limited to, the ERA. By decade's end, the women's movement
was fully revived. The word "sexism" had entered the language as a companion to "racism," and a new body of sex discrimination law existed, a
result of the many cases brought under Title VII. But the new women's
movement was not a cohesive one. Although NOW was often perceived
as radical by the general public, its goals and tactics were actually more
reflective of mainstream liberal activism. In contrast to NOW, many
younger women defined themselves as socialist ("politicos") or radical
feminists who supported "women's liberation." The former put a priority
on left-wing or New Left politics as a way of ensuring socialist revolution
to overturn capitalism, thereby advancing women as a class. Radical feminists saw the problem as patriarchy rather than class and placed a priority
on women's issues; some advocated gender separatism, became "women-
identified women," and supported lesbianism as a political act. Fundamental differences erupted over definitions, strategies for dealing with
"the system," the inclusion of poor and minority women, and men. Far
from focusing on a single issue, the new women's movement turned into
a multifaceted critique of the entire culture and a heated debate about

how to change it. By 1970 the movement had its first serious volume of feminist criticism, Kate Millett's *Sexual Politics*.[43]

In Texas the resurgence of women's rights activism was slower to appear than it did in other areas of the country. The larger political landscape shifted significantly in the state during the decade: the 1964 Civil Rights Act passed because of the efforts of the new president, Lyndon Johnson; the same year the poll tax was abolished in federal elections by the 24th Amendment, and in 1966 the poll tax was outlawed by the Supreme Court in state and local elections as well. This, coupled with legislative reapportionment the same year, resulted in increasing numbers of African Americans being elected to office. Barbara Jordan entered the Texas Senate that year. With regard to women's rights, the decade was marked by Hermine Tobolowsky's and the B&PW's relentless efforts to win passage of the state ELRA, but it would take a significant change in both the culture and in the legislature before they would succeed during the 1970s. The ELRA was first introduced in the Texas Legislature in 1959, but attitudes such as those of Lieutenant Governor Ben Ramsey, who argued that women did not want to lose the protection of law, and probably could not manage their own lives anyway, prevented its passage. In 1961 Tobolowsky's efforts won her national attention from columnists Sylvia Porter and Clair Boothe Luce as well as an article in the *Saturday Evening Post*, "The Revolt of Texas Women." Women in the legislature during the 1960s included Neveille Colson and Barbara Jordan in the Senate and Maud Isaacks, Myra Banfield, Sue Hairgrove, and Sissy Farenthold in the House. Of these, the ELRA had only three supporters, Isaacks, Jordan, and Farenthold. In 1961 Isaacks became the first female Texas legislator to actively support the amendment. During the same session, Myra Banfield, who had won B&PW support by saying she would vote for the ELRA, continued to vote against it, telling Tobolowsky that she did not want her husband to stop behaving like a gentleman should the amendment pass.[44]

Tobolowsky and B&PW members increasingly understood not only the importance of educating their own membership to lobby for the ELRA, but also the need to prevent its opponents from entering or returning to the legislature. In 1960 their electioneering contributed to the defeat of one of Lieutenant Governor Ramsey's allies, Senator William Fly; in 1962 they helped defeat Senator Wardlow Lane and prevent Senator Crawford Martin from becoming lieutenant governor; in 1964 they rallied to defeat Representative James Cotten; and in 1966 they helped defeat Senator

Neveille Colson, a twenty-eight-year veteran, because she would not commit herself to the ELRA. Although the ELRA still did not have enough support to pass the legislature, by the mid-1960s Tobolowsky and the B&PW had established a track record for targeting opponents successfully and had built a statewide network that enabled them to keep their members well informed and able to lobby quickly and accurately when critical votes occurred. Perhaps most important, they had awakened candidates to the realization that their stand on the ELRA could be an important element of their campaigns.[45]

In 1965 the B&PW met its most significant opponent, the State Bar Association, which had previously opposed jury duty for women. To counter arguments about the need for the ELRA, the association's Louise Raggio, a Dallas attorney, began drafting a new section of the Family Code to equalize married women's legal rights. Raggio's Marital Property Act passed the 1967 session, during which Raggio and Tobolowsky found themselves opposing each other, for Tobolowsky thought Raggio's act would undercut hopes for passing the ELRA. The act may have passed because ELRA opponents wanted to hand Tobolowsky a defeat, but in the end the new legislation finally achieved what Tobolowsky had originally set out to accomplish—end discrimination against married women. Debate over the ELRA became more sophisticated during the 1967 session, with Senators Dorsey Hardeman, Franklin Spears, Martin Dies, Jr., and Representative Rayford Price voicing concern over the legal chaos the amendment would cause by clogging the courts with cases to remove special legal protections for women. The amendment failed to pass the 1969 session as well, with help from House Speaker Gus Mutscher, who kept it bottled up in committee.[46]

THE 1970S: REFORMERS AND REACTIONARIES—AGAIN

During the 1970s, differences among feminists became less distinct, and women of varying approaches used the terms "women's movement" and "women's liberation" interchangeably. Issues raised by more radical women in the late 1960s and early 1970s—abortion, wife abuse, rape, and sexual preference—became part of mainstream debate and resulted in the creation of women's centers, rape crisis centers, battered women's shelters, women's bookstores, and the growth of women's history as a discipline. But the issue on which most organized women's groups focused during the 1970s was passage and ratification of the national Equal Rights Amendment. By the late 1960s, the ERA had earned bipartisan support at high levels in the federal government. In 1969 President Richard M. Nixon's Presidential Task Force on Women's Rights and Responsibilities urged the president to persuade the U.S. Congress to pass the ERA. Republican women like Representative Martha Griffith and presidential aides Anne Armstrong (a Texan) and Jill Ruckelshaus actively worked for its passage. In 1970 members of NOW disrupted Senate hearings to insist on a vote on the ERA; as a result, the first hearings since 1956 were held that year. In addition, Elizabeth Koontz, the new director of the Women's Bureau, invited hundreds of women of differing opinions to a conference to celebrate the bureau's fiftieth anniversary and produce a set of resolutions. As a result, the Labor Department, at Koontz' urging, reversed its decades-long opposition to the ERA and openly supported it. By this time, public opinion about the ERA had shifted from opposition to support; both parties had included endorsement in their platforms for years, six presidents had endorsed it, and nearly every major woman's group supported it. The ERA passed both houses of Congress, with wide margins of support, by March 1972. Less than one month later, in an April special session, the 62nd Texas Legislature ratified the national amendment, becoming one of the first southern states to do so.[47]

With such support, failure to ratify the ERA seemed impossible. In 1973 NOW had over 600 local and international chapters and was growing, but internal disagreements over organization, philosophy, and personality sapped NOW's energies for much of the decade. In the meantime, conservative and right-wing opposition to the ERA grew, contributing to popular confusion about the amendment's intent and possible consequences. By 1979, when time ran out for ratification, politically active women were fighting uphill for an extension of the ratification period and against a backlash against the women's movement. Despite the enormous disappointment the impending failure of the ERA caused during the 1970s, the decade witnessed unprecedented growth in the participation of women in electoral politics. In 1971 Texan Liz Carpenter helped found the National Women's Political Caucus (NWPC) to develop a feminist political strategy. The bipartisan NWPC's purpose, to support candidates who supported women's rights issues, made an immediate difference when it pressured the Democratic National Committee to adopt demographic quotas to open the party to increased participation by women, minorities, and young people. As a result, women were 40 percent of delegates to the 1972 Democratic convention, compared with only 13 percent in 1968. The Republican Party convention changed similarly,

Liz Carpenter was chair of ERAmerica in the 1970s. Courtesy Liz Carpenter.

from 17 to 30 percent. But both the NWPC and NOW remained unde-cided about whether their political strategy should involve backing a woman or backing a winner. By the time of the 1972 Democratic presi-dential convention, feminists felt betrayed by their leading presidential candidate, Senator George McGovern, on several key issues. When Rep-resentative Shirley Chisholm dropped her own run for the nomination, the NWPC backed a surprising bid for the vice presidential nomination by Frances (Sissy) Farenthold, the former Texas legislator and defeated gubernatorial candidate. Unlike Sarah T. Hughes' nomination twenty years before, Farenthold's was not a gesture, and she came in second to Senator Thomas Eagleton. Although the successful nomination of a woman to run on a major political party ticket as vice president would have to wait until 1984, the numbers of women elected to state legislatures continued to rise throughout the 1970s, nearly doubling during the decade. By mid-decade, the women's movement had become so widespread that the United Nations declared 1975 the "International Year of the Woman," and Presi-dent Gerald R. Ford established a national commission to observe the year and promote equality.[48]

By 1971 the women's movement had caught hold in Texas. Although no chapters of NOW existed, women met informally in consciousness-raising groups, women's centers were springing up in communities, col-leges and universities were teaching women's literature and history, Liz Carpenter helped found the Texas Women's Political Caucus (TWPC), and Governors John Connally and Preston Smith had each authorized a Committee on the Status of Women. The 62nd Texas Legislature that convened in 1971 proved to be a turning point for women in elective politics. No more than four women had served in the legislature at one time throughout the 1960s, and in 1971 only two women served, Barbara Jordan in the Senate and Sissy Farenthold in the House. But Farenthold, who had opposed the state ELRA during the 61st session, changed her mind during the 62nd and, with Jordan, she co-sponsored the amendment. Hermine Tobolowsky and the B&PW hired former Speaker of the House Waggoner Carr to lobby Gus Mutscher to support the ELRA. With support from Lieutenant Governor Ben Barnes, the state amendment passed the Senate in late March, then passed the House without objection from Mutscher. In November 1972 Texas voters overwhelmingly ratified the ELRA, by 4-1.[49]

Mutscher may have lost interest in opposing the ELRA because he had a bigger problem. In March 1971 Farenthold introduced a resolution calling for an investigation of bills that had benefited Houston banker Frank Sharp and to determine the roles that Mutscher and others had played in the stock fraud scandal that came to be known simply as "Sharpstown." Farenthold's efforts, along with those of a bipartisan group called the "Dirty Thirty" by an angry lobbyist, ultimately ended Mutscher's political career, along with those of Governor Preston Smith and Lieutenant Governor Ben Barnes. The scandal and its aftermath spread the desire for political reform throughout the state: Farenthold ran for governor as a Democrat and Alma Canales ran for lieutenant governor as a member of the newly created Raza Unida Party in 1972. The spirit of reform, combined with the growth of the women's movement, the increasing successes of civil rights movements among both blacks and Mexican Americans, the rise of the Republican Party, and reapportionment, caused the face of the Texas Legislature to change as it had not before. Although Farenthold and Canales lost, six women were elected to the legislature that year, more than had ever been seated at one time in the state's history. They were Representatives Kay Bailey (later Hutchison), Sarah Weddington, Chris Miller, Eddie Bernice Johnson, and Senfronia Thompson and Senator Betty Andujar. Bailey and Andujar were the first Republican women elected, and Johnson and Thompson were the first African American women elected to the House. In addition, Barbara Jordan was elected to the U.S. House, becoming the first female Texan to serve there in her own right. "This was the first time in Texas that we'd

Eddie Bernice Johnson, a former member of the Texas House of Representatives and Senate, was elected to the U.S. Congress in 1992. Courtesy Office of Eddie Bernice Johnson.

had that kind of diversity in the House," Eddie Bernice Johnson recalled. "There was a great deal of questioning and suspicion and challenge we could see on the faces of those who had been there longer, because this was a new crop of people for a new era. And we ushered in that era, and we made a lot of changes."[50]

The suddenly successful involvement of women in electoral politics galvanized the state's women's movement. Martha Dickey helped found a state chapter of NOW in 1973, and chapters spread across the state. The TWPC grew as well, and its lobbyist, Cathy Bonner, worked with the newly elected women to pass a series of reform measures unlike anything since the efforts of the Joint Legislative Council of the 1920s. "Women's issues" that had surfaced through the women's movement now entered the legislative arena as bills supporting child care funding, family planning services, maternity leave, equal access to credit, and homestead law reform. Representatives Sarah Weddington and Kay Bailey successfully co-sponsored the Equal Credit Act, which prohibited discrimination against women, allowing them to have credit cards in their own names. Representative Chris Miller sponsored a successful amendment allowing single unmarried adults a homestead exemption and preventing husbands from selling a homestead without the wife's consent. Representative Eddie Bernice Johnson sponsored successful legislation allowing pregnant teachers to use maternity benefits and not lose their jobs. And Weddington and Bailey, both attorneys, sponsored successful legislation reforming the state's rape statutes. The presence of women in the legislature did not always assure the success of reform legislation, however. Senator Betty Andujar blocked attempts to pass state-funded day care centers for women on welfare. In 1973 the U.S. Supreme Court ruled in *Roe vs. Wade*, a case argued by Sarah Weddington, that state laws prohibiting abortion were unconstitutional. In 1975 Lila Cockrell became the first female mayor of a major Texas city, San Antonio. In 1976, encouraged by the previous formation of the Raza Unida Party and Mujeres por la Raza groups, and supported by the TWPC, Irma Rangel became the first Latina elected to the legislature.[51]

In 1977 the National Women's Conference met in Houston, probably marking the high point of the modern women's movement in both the state and the country. The first meeting of its kind since the Women's Rights Convention at Seneca Falls in 1848, the conference was supported with federal funds and charged with writing a national plan of action and submitting it to the president and Congress. Although the conference attracted thousands of delegates and observers described as a "rainbow of women" from across the country, its participants were primarily liberal activists. Delegates produced resolutions on spousal abuse, rape, abortion rights, and sexual preference, but perhaps their most immediate success was the U.S. Senate's granting a three-year extension for ratification of the national ERA, which the conference had also endorsed. Conservative and right-wing participants like attorney and John Birch Society member Phyllis Schlafly, who opposed the ERA, abortion rights, and sexual preference, found little audience for their views at the conference, and many held alternative meetings or walked out.[52]

INTO THE PRESENT

As the 1970s progressed, feminists finally took such opposition seriously. Schlafly had formed Stop ERA in 1972, and by 1975 Texas antifeminists had succeeded in getting a resolution to rescind the ERA introduced in the legislature. Rather than progress with reform legislation, political activists inside and outside the capitol found themselves spending energy trying to save the ERA and other legislation they had already achieved. Liz Carpenter chaired ERAmerica, a coalition of groups intent on saving the amendment. Hermine Tobolowsky and the B&PW formed a coalition with the AAUW, Common Cause, Women in Communication, and the League of Women Voters to stop the rescission attempt, which they succeeded in doing. Nationally, however, Schlafly and like-minded activists succeeded in defeating the ERA in 1982, when its extension finally ran out.[53]

Antifeminism has existed as long as feminism has. The suffragists of NAWSA counteracted it by refusing to call themselves feminists and defining the suffrage movement as the woman movement. Their concern with propriety and their insistence on working toward a single goal rather than a wider agenda for women was calculated to ensure winning their one goal, the vote. NAWSA leaders knew that agitating for more than that—for something as fundamental as change in gender roles—would open the suffrage movement to opposition powerful enough to defeat it. In assuming this strategy, NAWSA ultimately won, but at a high price: the sacrifice of principles and alliances that might have left the women's movement healthier and more cohesive once suffrage was won.[54] Maintaining a women's movement through the decades after suffrage was difficult, and by the end of the 1970s, when its renaissance was waning, the new generation of feminists was experiencing what the leaders of NAWSA had feared. In aspiring for a sea change in society, and especially in advocating rights to abortion and sexual preference, the new feminists opened themselves to enormous and eventually well-organized opposition of the New Right. With the rise of groups like Schlafly's Eagle Forum, Right to Life, the Conservative Caucus, the Moral Majority, and the Christian Coalition, the women's movement encountered enough resistance to the issues it championed that the 1980s and 1990s became known as "postfeminist."[55]

WHERE DO WE GO FROM HERE?

Not enough time has passed for historians to declare the fate of feminism and the fight for gender equality under the law. Their effects on women's entry into public office seem to remain, however. Women's presence in the U.S. Congress continued to grow, if slowly, throughout the 1970s and 1980s. In 1992 more women than ever were elected, resulting in a total of six female senators and forty-seven representatives. It was a similarly good year for women seeking seats in state legislatures. Almost 2,400 ran, and enough won to push the national percentage of women in statehouses to 20 percent (up from 5 percent in the early 1970s). In Texas, women continued to enter elective politics in increasing numbers. Ann Richards became the first woman to win statewide office in fifty years when she became state treasurer in 1982, and she became the first woman elected

Ann Richards was the second female governor of Texas (1990–1994). Photo by Danna Byrom, ©1990.

governor in her own right in 1990. The same year, Kay Bailey Hutchison became the first Republican woman elected to a statewide office when she became state treasurer; in 1992 Eddie Bernice Johnson was elected to Congress, and Judge Rose Spector became the first woman elected to the Texas Supreme Court. In 1993 Hutchison became Texas' first female U.S. Senator. Unfortunately, the elections of 1994, 1996, and 1998 saw fewer women running for state legislatures than the 1992 all-time high figure. The 1998 elections in Texas resulted in a net loss of one woman (in the House); as a result, the 76th Legislature opened in January 1999 with thirty-two women, the first session in twenty years to seat fewer women than its predecessor. Nevertheless, 1998 election results nationwide resulted in enough modest gains to push the female population in statehouses to an average of 22.3 percent (up from 21.7). In contrast, women made up only 12 percent of the 106th Congress.[56]

The two surges of widespread social reform favoring gender equality, known in the early decades of the century as the suffrage crusade and fifty years later as the women's liberation movement, had a direct and positive impact on women's ability to think of themselves as candidates and officeholders as well as voters and politicians. The result has been a steady, if slow, increase in the numbers of women running for and being elected to public office. Yet impediments remain to women's running for office. One social scientist has classified these as internal and external.

Kay Bailey Hutchison, a former member of the Texas House of Representatives, was the first woman elected to the U.S. Senate from Texas in a special election in 1993; she was elected to a full term the following year. Courtesy Office of Kay Bailey Hutchison.

Internal impediments include women's own socialization and gender role conceptions; external impediments include limitations imposed by the political structure itself, such as male domination of party operations, voter prejudice against women candidates, one-party domination, party recruitment of women candidates in viable races, fund-raising, and the power of incumbency.[57]

Clearly, both kinds of impediments were solidly in place before 1920, when most women could not even vote, much less run for office. In addition, socialization of gender roles was formidable enough that mainstream suffragists rejected feminism in favor of propriety. Even with the vote won, the majority of women did not see themselves as candidates but looked toward "the right man." Some suffragists, like Ida Husted Harper, thought that women's having the vote would, by itself, transform society. Others, like the League of Women Voters and hundreds of Texas women who continued to work for other kinds of social reform, looked toward nonpartisan strategies that avoided involvement with the party structure. And still others, like Minnie Fisher Cunningham, attempted to work within the male-dominated party structure, only rarely, if ever, running for office themselves. One result was that the total number of women in the Texas Legislature during any one session did not surpass five for fifty years after suffrage was won. But before we hang the reason for this low number on the hook of women's internal limitations, we need basic information about the women who ran for office in Texas *and lost* between 1923 and 1973. If the data collected since 1974 are any indication, many more women ran than won, which would mean that external factors were also significant reasons for their losses. Such a study would also tell us much about the state of feminism and politics in Texas during those years.[58]

As with the suffrage victory, the women's movement of the 1970s had a direct and positive impact on the number of women elected to the legislature. In 1973 six women were victorious in one election, breaking the all-time record of five and also introducing the first Republican women to the legislature and the first African American women to the House. Again, we need more information about what women in Texas were doing politically if we are to reach any conclusions, but it seems apparent—from the numbers and from what we do know about those fifty years—that both internal and external factors had to be changing, slowly but incrementally, to allow this to occur.

We know, for example, that the efforts of NOW not only resulted in women's engaging in consciousness-raising about their own gender roles, but also helped reform Democratic and Republican party rules regarding the makeup of convention delegations, meaning that many more women were included in the party process, thereby increasing their knowledge of and experience within the political structure. In addition, the formation of such successful fund-raising groups as EMILY's List began to target women as sources of financial support for female candidates. We also know that while nine women were seated in the Texas Legislature in 1975, there were nineteen who ran, meaning that about half won. By 1994, the number of women candidates had more than doubled, to forty-three, and thirty-two won; thus the rate of victory had increased to almost 75 percent. In the 1998 elections the numbers of both candidates and victors slipped, but the percentage of victors rose to 78, with twenty-nine of thirty-seven candidates winning legislative seats. That women's presence as candidates and as victors has grown since 1973 seems to be evidence that reforms in both internal and external impediments have not only occurred but have spread.[59] Researchers Darcy, Welch, and Clark have concluded recently that times have changed for the better, at least where attitudes about women are concerned. Voters and party leaders are no longer likely to discriminate against female candidates, and there is little evidence that women's campaigns are being underfinanced. So women who are reluctant to run for the legislature because they fear gender discrimination should worry no more, these researchers assert.[60]

Although we predict the Texas Legislature will never consist only of men again, a significant problem remains—how to increase women's presence at a faster rate. Given that more and more women are running for office, but not enough are winning to reach parity, it appears that external factors are the cause. One political scientist has identified the problem as incumbency. Incumbents tend to win, but few women are incumbents. A corollary to this reality is that candidates who run against incumbents rarely win, and women are most often those candidates. Apparently women will continue to remain disadvantaged until incumbents retire or are in other ways disadvantaged, such as through redistricting.[61]

Others have named such likely barriers, in addition to incumbency, as women's comparatively lower educational and occupational status (particularly women's experience in business and law, most often the backgrounds of state legislators), women's age and family commitments, and stability of party representation around election cycles (in other words, dramatic shifts by voters from one party to another tend to benefit female candidates). These researchers suggest that women would benefit from the creation of multi-member districts, a shift from PAC- and candidate-centered fund-raising to party fund-raising, support for term limits (which weaken the power of the incumbent), and an increase in women's participation in leadership positions in state legislatures (which would encourage women to remain in office longer, thereby strengthening their status as incumbents).[62]

One novel approach to reaching the goal of 50 percent women (to more nearly reflect their percentage of the general population) in state legislatures and the U.S. Congress more rapidly is the suggestion that a percentage of all seats be set aside for female candidates, an idea adopted by parties in Norway, Sweden, Denmark, Germany, and France. Another idea is simply to double the number of representatives and mandate that a male and a female occupy each pair of seats. Still others look to campaign finance reform as the most practical way of leveling the playing field and ending the advantage of incumbency. Time will tell whether any of these ideas takes hold in Texas. Worth noting, however, is that research conducted since the 1970s shows that seeking a seat in the state legislature may be the most promising option for women interested in high-profile political offices. Although, with the exception of a few states, women are not making striking inroads into statehouses, they do continue to make incremental gains that result in net growth far beyond women's presence in the U.S. Congress.[63]

Until that time, when women are fully represented in the Texas Legislature in numbers equal to their population in Texas, and when our assessment of the capitol as the largest and most powerful men's room in the state is an anachronism, we recall the admonition of Barbara Jordan: "We cannot stand to have, in a democracy, any significant portion of the people who do not have a voice in what happens to them. All I know is that we as a people, black, white, Asian, Hispanic, must keep scratching the surface until we get where we've got to be, and that's all-inclusiveness for all people."[64]

NOTES

1. W. W. Newcombe, Jr., *The Indians of Texas* (Austin: University of Texas Press, 1978), pp. 291, 304; Fray Gaspar de Solís, "Diary of a Visit of Inspection of the Texas Missions in the Year 1767–1768," trans. Margaret Kenney Kress, *Southwestern Historical Quarterly* 35, no. 1 (July 1931): 61. Historian Paula Baker has defined politics as "any action . . . taken to affect the course of behavior of government or the community." See Baker, "The Domestication of Politics: Women and American Political Society, 1780–1920," *American Historical Review* 89 (June 1984): 622.

2. Minnie Gilbert, "Texas' First Cattle Queen," in *Roots by the River* (Mission, Tex.: Border Kingdom Press, 1978), pp. 15–25; Teresa Palomo Acosta, "María Gertrudis Perez Cassiano," *New Handbook of Texas*, 1:1016 (hereafter *NHOT*); Paula Stewart, "Patricia de la Garza de León," *NHOT*, 2:571–572; Cynthia E. Orozco, "Mexican-American Women," *NHOT*, 4:680.

3. Ruthe Winegarten, *Black Texas Women: 150 Years of Trial and Triumph*, pp. 1–13; Memorial No. 251, File 64, Letter "M," Archives Division, Texas State Library, Austin.

4. Ellen Garwood, "Early Texas Inns: A Study in Social Relationships," *Southwestern Historical Quarterly* 60, no. 2 (1956): 227; Robert E. May, "Jane Maria Eliza McManus Cazneau," *NHOT*, 1:1052.

5. Elise Waerenskjold, *Lady with the Pen*, ed. C. A. Clausen, (Clifton, Tex.: Bosque Memorial Museum, 1976); William Stuart Red, *A History of the Presbyterian Church in Texas* (Austin: Steck, 1936), pp. 329–331; Amelia Barr, *All the Days of My Life: An Autobiography* (New York: D. Appleton, 1913), p. 227.

6. For historical treatments of women's roles in public and in politics, see Aileen Kraditor, *The Ideas of the Woman Suffrage Movement, 1890–1920*; Linda K. Kerber, *Women of the Republic: Intellect and Ideology in Revolutionary America*; Baker, "The Domestication of Politics," pp. 620–647; Nancy F. Cott, *The Grounding of Modern Feminism*; Evelyn Brooks Higginbotham, "In Politics to Stay: Black Women Leaders and Party Politics in the 1920s," in *Women, Politics, and Change*, ed. Louise A. Tilly and Patricia Gurin, pp. 199–220; Mary P. Ryan, *Women in Public: Between Banners and Ballots, 1825–1880*; Sara

Hunter Graham, *Woman Suffrage and the New Democracy*; Kristi Anderson, *After Suffrage: Women in Partisan and Electoral Politics before the New Deal*; and Eleanor Flexner and Ellen Fitzpatrick, *Century of Struggle: The Woman's Rights Movement in the United States*. The extent to which gender was a nullity in public law between 1825 and 1880 can be seen in Mary Ryan's conclusion: "No equal rights statutes, no acts to enfranchise women, no legislative remedies for sex discrimination, no public provision of services expressly for women, were placed before municipal governments between 1825 and 1880. Rather, gender rarely appeared on the statute books; when it did, it was largely within those articles of the municipal code that defined punishable sexual acts" (*Women in Public*, p. 96). Quotation from Cott, *Grounding*, p. 80.

7. J. Mason Brewer, *Negro Legislators of Texas* (Dallas: n.p., 1935; rpt., Austin: Jenkins, 1970), p. 25; Winegarten, *Black Texas Women*, pp. 66–68; *Journal* of the Texas Reconstruction Convention, 1868–69.

8. See Flexner and Fitzpatrick's discussions of the impact of the 14th and 15th Amendments on suffragists and the suffrage movement in *Century of Struggle*, pp. 136–145; Ruthe Winegarten and Judith N. McArthur, eds., *Citizens at Last: The Woman Suffrage Movement in Texas*, pp. 70, 87–171.

9. A. Elizabeth Taylor, "The Woman Suffrage Movement in Texas," *Journal of Southern History* 27, no. 2 (May 1951): 194–215, reprinted in *Citizens at Last*, ed. Winegarten and McArthur, pp. 13–25; "The WCTU Endorses Votes for Women," in *Citizens at Last*, ed. Winegarten and McArthur, p. 79.

10. Judith N. McArthur, "Saving the Children: The Women's Crusade against Child Labor, 1902–1918," in *Women and Texas History: Selected Essays*, ed. Fane Downs and Nancy Baker Jones, pp. 57–71; Judith N. McArthur, *Creating the New Woman*, pp. 101–102. For additional studies of women in Progressive Era Texas, see Megan Seaholm, "Earnest Women: The White Woman's Club Movement in Progressive Era Texas 1880–1920" (Ph.D. diss., Rice University, 1988); Judith N. McArthur, "Women and Politics," *NHOT*, 6:1051–1055; Elizabeth Hayes Turner, *Women, Culture, and Community: Religion and Reform in Galveston, 1880–1920*; Jacquelyn McElhaney, *Pauline Periwinkle and Progressive Reform in Dallas*; and Elizabeth York Enstam, *Women and the Creation of Urban Life: Dallas, Texas, 1843–1920*.

11. Sherilyn Brandenstein, "National Woman's Party," *NHOT*, 4:947; Roberta S. Duncan, "Jane Legette Yelvington McCallum," *NHOT*, 4:369–370; Ann Fears Crawford and Crystal Sasse Ragsdale, "Texas's 'Petticoat Lobbyist': Jane Yelvington McCallum," *Women in Texas: Their Lives, Their Experiences, Their Accomplishments*, pp. 231–243; Winegarten, *Black Texas Women*, pp. 209–210; María Cristina García, "Liga Femenil Mexicanista," *NHOT*, 4:194. See Judith McArthur, "Motherhood and Reform in the New South: Texas Women's Political Culture during the Progressive Era" (Ph.D. diss., University of Texas at Austin, 1992), for a comprehensive discussion of Progressive Era political activities among white

Texas women, and Graham, *Woman Suffrage*, for a comprehensive discussion of tactics adopted by NAWSA. Quotation from McArthur, "Motherhood," p. 9.

12. Judie Karen Walton Gammage, "Quest for Equality: An Historical Overview of Women's Rights Activism in Texas, 1890–1975" (Ph.D. diss., North Texas State University, 1982), pp. 82–88. Winning the federal suffrage amendment vote, like winning primary suffrage, had the practical effect of enfranchising white women. African Americans and Mexican Americans were disfranchised by custom and by the state's white primary law, which was not rescinded until 1944. African American women in Austin, for example, were allowed to register but not to cast votes. The requirement that voters be literate reportedly prevented Mexican American women in Corpus Christi from even registering. Winegarten, *Black Texas Women*, pp. 209–210; McArthur, "Motherhood," pp. 506–509, 530–557, 562, 569. McArthur argues convincingly that Texas suffragists, led by Cunningham and Jane Y. McCallum, made the difference in the gubernatorial election of 1918, noting that Cunningham gave Representative Charles Metcalfe of San Angelo, one of the suffrage bill's co-sponsors, a letter assuring that TESA would support Hobby's candidacy if the governor would recommend passage of the bill: "[V]ote in hand, we will quite naturally concentrate on the man who enfranchised us.   .   .   . But without us, it is Ferguson with a plurality" (p. 509). With the bill signed, Cunningham and her forces undertook a massive voter registration campaign. Persuading Annie Webb Blanton to run for state superintendent of public instruction was one of her strategies to get women out to the polls by providing them a female candidate. Suffragists also formed Women's Hobby Clubs to educate women about their new right and to encourage them to exercise it by voting for Hobby. In addition, Cunningham knew that with 100,000 men away in World War I, a female turnout could make the difference she wanted. Almost 400,000 women registered in seventeen days, "enough to make Ferguson sick," Cunningham said (p. 537). In the end, Ferguson conceded that women had probably voted 10 to 1 for Hobby, and the *New York Times* described the election results with the headline "Woman Vote Sweeps Texas." McArthur estimates that 80 percent of women voters chose Hobby (p. 555). See also Taylor, "The Woman Suffrage Movement"; "Texans Vote on a State Constitutional Amendment," in *Citizens at Last*, ed. Winegarten and McArthur, pp. 188–189; Debbie Mauldin Cottrell, *Pioneer Woman Educator: The Progressive Spirit of Annie Webb Blanton*, pp. 42–76; and Janet G. Humphrey, "Texas Equal Suffrage Association," *NHOT*, 6:327–328. Cunningham quotation from Minnie Fisher Cunningham to Jane Y. McCallum, April 5 [1940?], Jane Y. McCallum Papers, Austin History Center, Austin Public Library. Both U.S. senators from Texas, Morris Sheppard and Charles A. Culberson, voted for the 19th Amendment.

13. Cunningham's definition of suffragists as politicians supports historian Sara Hunter Graham's assertion that the suffrage movement created a political culture for women as well as Paula Baker's definition of politics as "any action . . . taken to affect the course of

behavior of government or the community." Under such a large tent, suffragists would clearly find seats as politicians. See Graham, *Woman Suffrage*, esp. pp. 161–162, and Baker, "The Domestication of Politics," p. 622.

14. Cott, *Grounding*, p. 100; Anderson, *After Suffrage*, p. 111; McArthur, "Motherhood," pp. 563–565; McArthur, "Women and Politics," p. 1053; Cottrell, *Pioneer Woman Educator*, pp. 72–76; Emma Louise Moyer Jackson, "Petticoat Politics: Political Activism among Texas Women in the 1920's" (Ph.D. diss., University of Texas at Austin, 1980), pp. 61–62, 318–328. Some suffragists, like Jessie Daniel Ames, did support Miriam Ferguson's bid for governor because of her anti-Klan platform.

15. Winegarten, *Black Texas Women*, p. 211; Jackson, "Petticoat Politics," p. 60. According to Jackson, the seven women who ran unsuccessfully for the Texas Legislature were Lola Dale, Miller County (Senate); Katie Daffan, Houston (House); Mrs. Sidney H. Huston, Houston (House); Anna Kilpatrick Fain, Livingston (House); Mrs. J. A. McConnell, Crockett (House); Hattie de Walker, Alto (House), and Julia Sue Gott, Rosebud (House). A study of the relationship between the numbers of women who threw their hats into the ring and those who won will teach us much about the phenomenon of women transforming themselves into candidates.

16. Jane Y. McCallum compiled a list of over 250 women in county positions during the 1929–1930 biennium. See McCallum's "Activities of Women in Texas Politics," reprinted in *Citizens at Last*, ed. Winegarten and McArthur, pp. 226–230. Women in Texas had actually been winning elective office since 1908, when Adella Kelsey Turner and Ella Isabelle Tucker joined the Dallas school board, thereby becoming the first women public officials in a major city in Texas. See McArthur, "Women and Politics," p. 1052.

17. Anderson, *After Suffrage*, pp. 13, 28–33, 122–123, 142–144. The four states that prevented women from holding public office were Massachusetts, Oklahoma, Missouri, and Arkansas.

18. *Woman Citizen*, November 18, 1922; Graham, *Woman Suffrage*, pp. 153–154.

19. Graham, *Woman Suffrage*, p. 153; Dorothy M. Brown, *Setting a Course: American Women in the 1920s*, p. 68; Anderson, *After Suffrage*, pp. 113–114; Ryan, *Women in Public*, p. 168; Cott, *Grounding*, p. 110; Jackson, "Petticoat Politics," p. 266. For a definitive discussion of Texas politics in the 1920s, see Norman D. Brown, *Hood, Bonnet, and Little Brown Jug: Texas Politics, 1921–1928*, which defines and discusses the three issues of 1920s Texas. Georgetown suffragist Jessie Daniel Ames became director of the interracial Texas Council of the Commission on Interracial Cooperation during the 1920s and founded the Association of Southern Women for the Prevention of Lynching in 1930.

20. Dorothy M. Brown, *Setting a Course*, pp. 50–74; Ann Fears Crawford and Crystal Sasse Ragsdale, "Mrs. Democrat: Minnie Fisher Cunningham," *Women in Texas*, p. 220; Jackson, "Petticoat Politics," pp. 572–575; Brandenstein, "National Woman's Party," pp. 947–948. Whether the Texas NWP actually supported the ERA is unclear. It did analyze

state statutes for sex discrimination, and chair Mary Rowena Maverick Green prepared and submitted statutes to the legislature to secure equal rights in a number of areas in 1925. Whether the Texas NWP survived the 1920s is also unknown.

21. McCallum, "Activities of Women in Texas Politics," pp. 221–226. The five groups forming the JLC were the Texas Federation of Women's Clubs, Texas League of Women Voters, Texas Congress of Mothers and Parent-Teacher Associations, Federation of Business and Professional Women's Clubs, and the Woman's Christian Temperance Union (the Texas Graduate Nurses Association joined later). See also Gammage, "Quest for Equality," esp. pp. 88–95; McArthur, "Motherhood," pp. 565–569; Jackson, "Petticoat Politics," pp. 88–185, 364–366, 430–437, 459–462, 471. During the 39th Legislature (1925–1927), in which no women served, Miriam Ferguson was serving her first term as governor. Although the JLC was successful that term, Ferguson was likely not one of the reasons. Suffragists had opposed her election, and Ferguson had promised to abolish the Child Hygiene Bureau. See Brown, *Hood, Bonnet, Little Brown Jug*, pp. 269–270, 488.

22. Jackson, "Petticoat Politics," pp. 517–522; Kathleen Elizabeth Lazarou, *Concealed under Petticoats: Married Women's Property and the Law of Texas, 1840–1913*, pp. 92–98; Elizabeth York Enstam, "Women and the Law," *NHOT*, 6:1047.

23. Susan Ware, *Holding Their Own: American Women in the 1930s*, p. 87; Cott, *Grounding*, pp. 117–142, 263–264; Paul Lucko, "The Next 'Big Job': Women Prison Reformers in Texas, 1918–1930," in *Women and Texas History*, ed. Downs and Jones, pp. 72–87; McArthur, "Woman and Politics," p. 1053. For a detailed discussion of the transition of public thought about women's legal rights, see Jo Freeman, "From Protection to Equal Opportunity: The Revolution in Women's Legal Status," in *Women, Politics, and Change*, ed. Tilly and Gurin, pp. 457–481.

24. Ware, *Holding Their Own*, pp. 87–115, passim; Patricia Ellen Cunningham, "Minnie Fisher Cunningham," *NHOT*, 2:451; William P. Hobby, Jr., "Oveta Culp Hobby," *NHOT*, 3:638. Miriam Ferguson ran for governor for the last time in 1940 and lost.

25. Ware, *Holding Their Own*, pp. 87–115, quote from p. 107. Organizations involved in the Woman's Charter effort included the National Women's Trade Union League, National League of Women Voters, General Federation of Women's Clubs, National Consumer's League, American Association of University Women, Young Women's Christian Association, and American League Against War and Fascism.

26. Gammage, "Quest for Equality," pp. 129, 106, 109–111; Sherilyn Brandenstein, "International Ladies' Garment Workers' Union," *NHOT*, 3:862–863; Richard Croxdale, "Pecan-Shellers' Strike," *NHOT*, 5:117–118. Because the full history of the ERA in Texas is as yet unwritten, little is known about the extent to which the measure had support before the 1950s.

27. Gammage, "Quest for Equality," pp. 110–111, 114–116.

28. Ware, *Holding Their Own*, pp. 87–115; Jacquelyn Dowd Hall, *Revolt against Chiv-*

alry: Jessie Daniel Ames and the Women's Campaign against Lynching; Gammage, "Quest for Equality," pp. 113–114; Cynthia E. Orozco, "Ladies LULAC," *NHOT*, 4:1–2.

29. Ware, *Holding Their Own*, p. 87; Minnie Fisher Cunningham to Jane Y. McCallum, September 1940, Jane Y. McCallum Papers, Austin History Center, Austin Public Library; Ruthe Winegarten and Cathy Schechter, *Deep in the Heart: The Lives and Legends of Texas Jews, A Photographic History*, p. 153.

30. Among the military opportunities women seized during World War II were to join the Women's Airforce Service Pilots (WASPs), which trained at Avenger Field in Sweetwater, and the Women's Army Corps (WACs), which was headed by Texan Oveta Culp Hobby. Sherwood Inkley, "Women's Airforce Service Pilots," *NHOT*, 6:1055; William P. Hobby, "Oveta Culp Hobby," *NHOT*, 3:637–640; Leila J. Rupp and Verta Taylor, *Survival in the Doldrums: The American Women's Rights Movement, 1945 to the 1960s*, pp. 15, 18–44, 30; Susan M. Hartmann, *The Home Front and Beyond: American Women in the 1940s*, esp. pp. 123–161.

31. Hartmann, *Home Front*, pp. 123–141; Sanford M. Greenberg, "White Primary," *NHOT*, 6:940–941.

32. Hartmann, *Home Front*, pp. 123–141; Rupp and Taylor, *Survival*, pp. 45–84.

33. Rupp and Taylor, *Survival*, pp. 24–44, 141–147; Hartmann, *Home Front*, pp. 123–141; Eugenia Kaledin, *Mothers and More: American Women in the 1950s*, p. 99; Susan Ware, "American Women in the 1950s: Nonpartisan Politics and Women's Politicization," in *Women, Politics, and Change*, ed. Tilly and Gurin, pp. 281–299.

34. Hartmann, *Home Front*, pp. 123–141. Kaledin, *Mothers and More*, pp. 84–86; Ruth Rosen, "The Female Generation Gap: Daughters of the Fifties and the Origins of Contemporary American Feminism," in *U.S. History as Women's History*, ed. Kerber, Kessler-Harris, and Sklar, pp. 313–334. The Republican Party nominated Maine senator Margaret Chase Smith, and the Democrats nominated both India Edwards, head of the party's women's division, and Judge Sarah T. Hughes.

35. George Norris Green, *The Establishment in Texas Politics: The Primitive Years, 1938–1957*, p. xi.

36. Nancy Baker Jones, "Christia V. Daniels Adair," *NHOT*, 1:21.

37. Green, *Establishment*, pp. 88–89, 98; Nancy Beck Young, "Margaret Carter and Texas Politics: Women and the Battle for Control of the Democratic Party" (paper presented to the Fourth Southern Conference on Women's History, Southern Association for Women Historians, June 14, 1997), pp. 1, 5–6; Hartmann, *Home Front*, pp. 143–161; Patricia Ellen Cunningham, "Bonnet in the Ring: Minnie Fisher Cunningham's Campaign for Governor of Texas in 1944," in *Women and Texas History*, ed. Downs and Jones, pp. 102–115; Crawford and Ragsdale, "Mrs. Democrat," pp. 221–225. The WCEF also sought the resignation of regents who had approved Rainey's dismissal and revision of laws under which regents were selected. See also Janet G. Humphrey, *A Texas Suffragist:*

Diaries and Writings of Jane Y. McCallum, p. 155. For a look at roles open to African American women in Texas in the 1950s, see Sherilyn Brandenstein, "*Sepia Record* as a Forum for Negotiating Women's Roles," in *Women and Texas History*, ed. Downs and Jones, pp. 143–157; Winegarten, *Black Texas Women*, pp. 252–253, 261–262, 269, 271; and Winegarten, *Black Texas Women: A Sourcebook*, pp. 303–304.

38. Young, "Margaret Carter," p. 7.

39. Robert S. LaForte, "Sarah Tilghman Hughes," *NHOT*, 3:774–775; Sarah T. Hughes and Joe B. Frantz, "Oral History" [1968], Lyndon Baines Johnson Library, Austin, p. 15; Young, "Margaret Carter," pp. 9–11; Cunningham, "Minnie Fisher Cunningham," p. 451.

40. Gammage, "Quest for Equality," p. 131; Natalie Ornish, "Hermine Dalkowitz Tobolowsky," *NHOT*, 6:512.

41. Rupp and Taylor, *Survival*, pp. 188–193.

42. Ibid., pp. 166–179; Blanche Linden-Ward and Carol Hurd Green, *Changing the Future: American Women in the 1960s*, pp. 1–27; Freeman, "From Protection to Equal Opportunity," pp. 466–469; Paula Giddings, *When and Where I Enter: The Impact of Black Women on Race and Sex in America*, pp. 299–300.

43. Rupp and Taylor, *Survival*, pp. 179–183; Linden-Ward and Green, *Changing the Future*, pp. 1–27, 408–439; Winifred D. Wandersee, *On the Move: American Women in the 1970s*, pp. xiv, xv.

44. Gammage, "Quest for Equality," pp. 133–139. See also Sherilyn Brandenstein, "Texas Equal Rights Amendment," *NHOT*, 6:326.

45. Gammage, "Quest for Equality," pp. 139–144, 165.

46. Ibid., pp. 152–158, 165–166; Enstam, "Women and the Law," p. 1049.

47. Wandersee, *On the Move*, pp. 176–177. Via Senate Concurrent Resolution 1, Texas ratified the ERA on April 19, 1972, two weeks after Tennessee became the first southern state to ratify the amendment. Legislative Reference Library, Austin; *New York Times*, April 5, 1972.

48. Wandersee, *On the Move*, pp. 16–35, 36–54.

49. Gammage, "Quest for Equality," pp. 167–171; Debbie Mauldin Cottrell, "Texas Women's Political Caucus," *NHOT*, 6:448–449; the state ELRA passed the Senate on March 29, 1972, and the House passed it the following day. Legislative Reference Library, Austin.

50. Frances Farenthold, videotape interview by Ruthe Winegarten, June 12, 1995, ARWG; Suzanne Coleman, "The Politics of Participation: The Emergent Journey of Frances Farenthold" (M.A. thesis, University of Texas at Arlington, 1973), pp. 24–28; Eddie Bernice Johnson, videotape interview by Mike Greene, October 19, 1995, ARWG. The Raza Unida Party was formed in 1970. See Teresa Palomo Acosta, "Raza Unida Party," *NHOT*, 5:462–463.

51. Gammage, "Quest for Equality," pp. 173–176; McArthur, "Women and Politics," p. 1054.

52. Debbie Mauldin Cottrell, "National Women's Conference," *NHOT*, 4:948–949; Wandersee, *On the Move*, pp. 175–196.

53. Gammage, "Quest for Equality," pp. 180–184; Wandersee, *On the Move*, pp. 175–196. See also Toni Carabillo, Judith Meuli, and June Bundy Csida, *The Feminist Chronicles: 1953–1993* (Los Angeles: Women's Graphics, 1993).

54. Graham, *Woman Suffrage*, pp. 150–152, 162; Cott, *Grounding*, p. 243.

55. For an analysis of women involved in the New Right, see Rebecca Klatch, "The Two Worlds of Women of the New Right," in *Women, Politics, and Change*, ed. Tilly and Gurin, pp. 529–552.

56. For representative analyses of women in modern politics, see Jeane Kirkpatrick, *Political Woman* (New York: Basic Books, 1974); Janet K. Boles, "The Texas Woman in Politics: Role Model or Mirage?" *Social Science Journal* 21, no. 1 (January 1984): 79–89; Anne Phillips, *Engendering Democracy*; R. Darcy, Charles D. Hadley, and Jason F. Kirksey, "Election Systems and the Representation of Black Women in American State Legislatures," *Women and Politics* 13, no. 2 (1993): 73–89; Susan J. Carroll, *Women as Candidates in American Politics*; Sue Thomas, *How Women Legislate*; and Jane Sherron De Hart, "Rights and Representations: Women, Politics, and Power in the Contemporary United States," in *U.S. History as Women's History*, ed. Kerber, Kessler-Harris, and Sklar, pp. 214–242 (1992 statistics on women in state legislatures from p. 233); "Women in State Legislatures," press release, Center for the American Woman and Politics (hereafter CAWP), National Information Bank on Women in Public Office, Eagleton Institute of Politics, Rutgers University, November 24, 1998; "Women's Electoral Success: A Familiar Formula," press release, CAWP, November 25, 1998; "Women Who Will Serve in the 106th Congress," fact sheet, CAWP, November 4, 1998.

57. Carroll, *Women as Candidates*, pp. 4–5; Graham, *Woman Suffrage*, p. 163; see also Darcy, Welch, and Clark, *Women, Elections, and Representation*.

58. Carroll, *Women as Candidates*, pp. 4–5; Graham, *Woman Suffrage*, p. 163; Nancy Baker Jones, "A Forgotten Feminist: The Early Writings of Ida Husted Harper, 1878–1894," *Indiana Magazine of History* 73, no. 2 (June 1977): 79–101.

59. Statistics from "Women in State Legislative Elections, 1974–1994," fact sheet, CAWP, 1994, and "Women Candidates for State Legislatures 1998," fact sheet, CAWP, 1998.

60. Darcy, Welch, and Clark, *Women, Elections, and Representation*, pp. 51–73, 175–180.

61. Carroll, *Women as Candidates*, pp. 119–120, 162.

62. Darcy, Welch, and Clark, *Women, Elections, and Representation*, pp. 104–118, 122–127, 169–171, 186–190, 194–195.

63. Ibid., pp. 166, 169; Phillips, pp. 84, 152–153; Thomas, "Women in State Legislatures"; "Women's Electoral Success."

64. Barbara Jordan, videotape interview by Nancy Baker Jones, September 12, 1995, ARWG.

HOW THE TEXAS
LEGISLATURE WORKS

☆

The Texas Legislature convened for the first time in February 1846. It now meets once every two years—in odd-numbered years—for no more than 140 days (almost five months) in regular session. The governor may call 30-day special sessions to address specific issues after the regular session has ended.

All members of the legislature are elected from single-member districts configured so that each representative or senator represents an approximately equal number of citizens. Boundary lines for these districts are redrawn during the first regular session each ten years after the U.S. census is complete. Called "redistricting," this process usually generates intense competition among members to create districts that will benefit themselves or their party.

If a senator or representative dies or leaves during the course of the designated term, special elections are held to fill the seat for the remainder of the term. This results in some members' serving during years that do not neatly fit the two- or four-year cycles.

Because regular sessions are short and meet only every two years, legislators have a great deal of information to assimilate in a short time—far more than any one person can master. As a result, a system of committees has developed that allows members to become familiar with a subset of legislation. Permanent committees are called *standing* committees. These may also have *subcommittees*, and there may also be *ad hoc* (temporary) committees. *Interim* committees may be established for operation during special sessions. Standing committees generally range in size from seven to twenty-three members who can wield significant influence over the

Myra McDaniel was appointed Texas secretary of state in 1984. She is shown here opening the legislative session in 1985. Courtesy Texas Senate Media Services; photo by Bill Malone.

fate of bills assigned to them for review. (The most powerful committees are generally regarded to be State Affairs, Ways and Means, Finance, and Calendars.) Further, House and Senate members depend heavily on their paid staff to provide them with information and services. Lobbyists—individuals paid by special-interest groups to advocate for the passage or defeat of particular pieces of legislation—are also a significant part of the legislative process.

The House of Representatives has 150 members who are elected for two-year terms in even-numbered years. A candidate elected in November 1972, for example, would have served in the 63rd Legislature that met in regular session from January through May of 1973 and then in any special sessions called through December of 1974. Her term would officially end on January 1, 1975. The presiding officer of the House is the speaker, who is elected by a majority of House members. The speaker appoints chairs and members of all House committees, refers all bills to committees, and decides all questions of order in the House. In addition, the speaker may vote, as other House members do, but may also delay voting in order to cast a deciding vote. The Calendars Committee schedules bills for consideration on the House floor. The House is responsible for all revenue-raising legislation and also originates charges of impeachment.

The Senate has thirty-one members who are elected for four-year terms in even-numbered years. Terms are staggered; as a result, one-half of the Senate membership stands for election every two years. The lieutenant governor, elected by statewide popular vote, serves as president of the Senate but is not a member of the Senate and may not vote except in the event of a tie. The lieutenant governor appoints all chairs and members of Senate committees, refers all bills to committees, and schedules most bills for consideration on the Senate floor. The Senate has the power of advice and consent on gubernatorial appointments and tries individuals against whom the House has brought charges for impeachment.

The lawmaking process is straightforward, but there are several steps at which "politics" may affect the outcome. Members of either chamber introduce a bill; it is then referred to the appropriate standing committee by the speaker or the lieutenant governor; the committee may take action on the bill or do nothing, in which case the bill "dies in committee." If the committee refers the bill out, it is placed on the calendar for floor discussion, debate, and vote. In the event of a disagreement between House and Senate versions, a conference committee makes changes and returns the bill to the chamber of origin for a vote. If the bill passes, its final form is signed by the speaker and the lieutenant governor and is sent to the governor for approval or veto.

According to a study of the 74th Legislature (1995–1997), House bills passed at a rate of 18 percent, Senate bills at a rate of 28 percent. Bills entered by Anglos were more successful than those entered by others. House bills with male authors were more successful than those with female authors, but Senate bills with female authors were more successful than those with male authors (even though there were only four female senators during this session).[1]

The responsibilities of the speaker of the House and the lieutenant governor make them the two most powerful political figures in the state, because they control the memberships of the committees that can support or kill legislation. Although the governor is the state's chief executive, the position is relatively weak. Its two primary powers are to make appointments (which must be confirmed by the Senate) and to approve or veto all legislation passed by the legislature (which can override a veto with a two-thirds vote of each chamber).

Because of the expense of running for the legislature and the low salary paid to members ($7,200 annually, with a supplemental daily allowance of $30), members have tended to be financially secure. Historically, most members have been conservative, male, white, Protestant Democrats who are often involved in business or law. The 75th Legislature that opened in 1997, however, saw Republicans take a majority of Senate seats for the first time since Reconstruction.

NOTE

1. Harvey J. Tucker, "Bill Authors, Bill Sponsors, and Bill Passage in the Texas Legislature" (paper prepared for delivery at the annual meeting of the Midwest Political Science Association, April 10–12, 1997).

BIOGRAPHIES

THE 1920s–1930s

EDITH EUNICE THERREL WILMANS

HOUSE 38th Legislature (1923–1925)
Democrat, Dallas
DISTRICT 50
COMMITTEES Common Carriers; Public
Health; Counties; Education; Oil, Gas,
and Mining

DATES December 21, 1882–March 21, 1966
BIRTHPLACE Lake Providence, Louisiana
FAMILY Jacob Hall Wilmans (died); three
children; Henry A. Born (divorced)
EDUCATION Licensed to practice law, 1918
OCCUPATION Attorney; rancher

EDITH WILMANS was the first woman elected to the Texas Legislature and the first to preside as speaker of the House, although this was likely an honorary appointment. She was active in Dallas Democratic and women's causes, as well as PTA and church work, while she was raising her family. In 1914 she helped organize the Dallas Equal Suffrage Association, helped found the Dallas Housewives League and the Democratic Women of Dallas County, and was also active in the Woman's Christian Temperance Union, the League of Business and Professional Women, and later two anti-Communist groups, the Minute Women and the Paul Revere Club. She was also president of the Democratic Women's Association of Texas. She studied law to help improve the status of women and children and was admitted to the bar in 1918.[1]

In 1922 Wilmans was one of eight women to run for the legislature, and the only one to win. Her platform advocated four issues: to create a domestic court in Dallas County, mandate health certificates before marriage, fund state support for children whose fathers were in prison or asylums, and raise the age of compulsory school attendance to sixteen. Wilmans' position on the Ku Klux Klan, an important issue that year, remains unclear. The Dallas County Citizens' League, which opposed the Klan, refused to endorse either Wilmans or her opponent because neither had provided the league with sufficient assurance of their opposition to the KKK. Wilmans eventually defeated multiterm House member John E. Davis of Mesquite with 54 percent of the vote.[2]

When Wilmans was sworn in, the *Austin American*, in a section "printed for women only," described Wilmans as wearing a gold and gray turban, a gray sport coat, brown shoes and hose, and a brown satin dress. "She did not have the proverbial bouquet," the paper added. As the chamber's only "lady member," Wilmans was then allowed to choose which desk she wanted. On her second day, Wilmans rebuked legislators at an informal gathering at the Driskill Hotel for making the event ridiculous instead of professional. Although she was the only female member of the legislature at the time, Wilmans organized Women Legislators of the House and, as its sole member, served as president during her term.[3]

Only one of the five bills Edith Wilmans introduced became law, an education appropriations bill that the Senate reduced by 14 percent. Her bills to create a domestic relations court and to provide pensions to women whose husbands did not contribute to child care passed the House but failed in the Senate. Her bill to increase the number of days in the school year was endorsed by the Education Committee but not considered by the House. She was unsuccessful in her attempt to require women as well as men to submit to health tests to receive marriage licenses. In called sessions of the legislature, she was one of six sponsors of a successful bill to increase funding for rural schools, but again failed to secure a domestic relations court or to tax attorneys filing petitions for divorce. Wilmans also supported the efforts of the Joint Legislative Council (JLC), called "the Petticoat Lobby" by legislators and the press, to pass several pieces of social reform legislation. A coalition of Progressive Era women's groups that formed after suffrage was won, the JLC saw all six of its measures pass the 38th Legislature. These included a prison survey, a state match of federal funds for mother-infant health care available through the Sheppard-Towner Act, an education survey, emergency appropriations for the public schools, and two prohibition enforcement measures.[4]

Although Wilmans regarded being in the House as "difficult, thankless, and unprofitable," she ran again in 1924, also against John E. Davis. This time she and the three other women who ran for the legislature lost. As a result, no women served in the 39th Legislature that opened in 1925. In the 1924 elections, Wilmans supported Democrat Miriam A. "Ma" Ferguson's successful campaign for governor, despite the fact that the majority of Texas suffragists, led by Minnie Fisher Cunningham, Jane Y. McCallum, and thousands of newly enfranchised women voters, threw their support to Republican George C. Butte rather than elect a governor who they believed would be a puppet for her husband, the impeached former governor Jim Ferguson. Wilmans apparently supported Miriam

Ferguson primarily because she wanted to see a woman prove her compe-
tence to hold high office. In 1925, before his term ended, Governor Pat
M. Neff appointed Wilmans to the All-Woman Supreme Court (nearly
thirty years before women could serve on juries in Texas), but she could
not serve because she lacked the seven years of law practice required.[5]

In 1926 and 1928 Wilmans ran for governor. Two other women also
ran in 1926, the incumbent Governor Miriam Ferguson and Kate Miller
Johnston of San Antonio, a rancher and antiprohibitionist. Wilmans'
primary purpose in running was to prove that women were serious candidates. Disappointed by Governor Ferguson's lack of independence from
her husband, Wilmans pledged not to marry while she was in office. In
addition, she supported prison reform, tax equalization, stricter child labor laws, protection of freedom of the press, health protection for industrial workers, and more rigid enforcement of prohibition laws. She also
criticized the costs of campaigns, saying that they made it impossible for
a poor man—or woman—to compete in a fair election. "I do not think
that any candidate who has spent over $100,000 . . . to be elected is a
proper person to be governor of the state," she said, because "the whole
amount of the salary for the two year term is only $24,000."[6]

Her campaign also attacked the legislature for promoting the interests
of corporations while neglecting the common people. As governor, she
said, her foremost intent would be to "work to better conditions for every
citizen of this state. It seems that the financial interests and oil companies
. . . make their money from Texas people and Texas natural resources, but
spend it in the northern and eastern states." Further, she believed, Texas
officials cooperated with big oil companies to "take from the small land
owners their inherent right to their acreage and what is in, on, and under
it." In addition, she said that as governor she would submit a measure "to
remove all legal discrimination against women, and place woman—so far
as legal rights are concerned—the equal of man." Despite a vigorous campaign, she finished fifth in a field of six in the Democratic primary.
Ferguson finished second behind the victorious Dan Moody, and Johnston
finished sixth.[7]

In 1926 Wilmans resumed her law practice in Dallas, and in 1928 the
National Woman's Party endorsed her as a candidate for vice president of
the United States, although she declined to run. She ran for governor
again in 1928, coming in last in a field of four in the Democratic primary.
Her name was left off the primary ballot in Cameron County by Democratic Party officials in retribution for her refusal to support Al Smith's

Democratic presidential campaign. In 1935 she ran unsuccessfully for another term in the House. That year she moved to Vineyard, Jack County, where she raised goats and cattle and campaigned unsuccessfully for the 13th Congressional District seat in 1948 and 1951. In 1958 she broke her hip and returned to Dallas to stay with her oldest daughter, where she lived until her death in 1966.[8]

NOTES

1. Jack County Historical Survey Committee, "Edith Eunice Therrel Wilmans: First Woman Legislator in Texas," typescript, 1973, pp. 1–2, Edith Wilmans Collection, Archives Division, Texas State Library, Austin (hereafter EWC); Edith Eunice Therrel Wilmans, holographic ms., n.d., EWC; Edith Eunice Wilmans Malone, "Edith Eunice Wilmans," *New Handbook of Texas*, 6:1003–1004; Sue M. Hall, "The 1925 All-Woman Supreme Court of Texas," typescript, 1978, Woman's Collection, Texas Woman's University Library, pp. 23–24.

2. David Mauzy, draft of history of Texas women legislators, typescript, [1996], Senate Research Office, State of Texas, pp. 9–11, EWC; Emma Louise Moyer Jackson, "Petticoat Politics: Political Activism among Texas Women in the 1920s" (Ph.D. diss., University of Texas at Austin, 1980), pp. 60, 62. According to Jackson, the seven women who ran unsuccessfully for the legislature in 1922 were Lola Dale, Miller County (Senate); Katie Daffan, Houston (House); Mrs. Sidney H. Huston, Houston (House); Anna Kilpatrick Fain, Livingston (House); Mrs. J. A. McConnell, Crockett (House); Hattie de Walker, Alto (House); and Julia Sue Gott, Rosebud (House).

3. *Austin American*, January 10, 1923, quoted in Sarah Weddington, Jane Hickie, Deanna Fitzgerald, Elizabeth N. Fernea, and Marilyn P. Duncan, "Edith Eunice Therrel Wilmans," *Texas Women in Politics*, p. 8; Mauzy, draft, p. 12; Vivian Anderson Castleberry, *Daughters of Dallas: A History of Greater Dallas through the Voices and Deeds of Its Women* (Dallas: Odenwald Press, 1994), p. 255.

4. Hall, "The 1925 All-Woman Supreme Court of Texas," pp. 24–25; Jackson, "Petticoat Politics," pp. 18–189; Mauzy, draft, pp. 1–14; Judie Karen Walton Gammage, "Quest for Equality: An Historical Overview of Women's Rights Activism in Texas, 1890–1975" (Ph.D. diss., North Texas State University, 1982), pp. 88–95, 104; Jane Y. McCallum, "Activities of Women in Texas Politics," reprinted in *Citizens at Last: The Woman Suffrage Movement in Texas*, ed. Ruthe Winegarten and Judith N. McArthur, pp. 221–226. See also Judith Nichols McArthur, "Motherhood and Reform in the New South: Texas Women's Political Culture in the Progressive Era" (Ph.D. diss., University of Texas at Austin, 1992), pp. 565–569.

5. Malone, "Edith Eunice Wilmans," p. 1003; Jackson, "Petticoat Politics," pp. 273, 309; McArthur, "Motherhood," pp. 564–565. According to Jackson, the three other women

who ran for the legislature and lost in 1924 were Anna Kilpatrick Fain, Livingston (House); Mrs. G. Frank Coffey, Fort Worth (House); and Mrs. L. S. Holstead, McLennan County (House).

6. Norman D. Brown, *Hood, Bonnet, and Little Brown Jug: Texas Politics, 1921–1928*, p. 326; *Austin Statesman*, March 22, 1966; Jackson, "Petticoat Politics," pp. 315–317; Wilmans, holographic ms., EWC. According to Jackson, Wilmans' sister, Helen Viglini, ran unsuccessfully for the House to represent Dallas in 1928; see "Petticoat Politics," p. 571.

7. Wilmans, holographic ms., EWC; Brown, *Hood, Bonnet*, p. 372.

8. Brown, *Hood, Bonnet*, p. 404; Jack County Historical Survey Committee, "Edith Eunice Therrel Wilmans," p. 2; Malone, "Edith Eunice Wilmans," p. 1004.

☆

MARY ELIZABETH (MARGIE) NEAL

SENATE 40th–43rd Legislatures (1927–1935)
Democrat, Carthage
DISTRICT 2
COMMITTEES Educational Affairs (Vice Chair); Rules; Privileges and Elections (Chair)

DATES April 20, 1875–December 19, 1971
BIRTHPLACE Near Clayton
FAMILY Single; no children
EDUCATION Sam Houston State Teachers College (no degree)
OCCUPATION Teacher; newspaper publisher; federal administrator

MARGIE NEAL was the second woman elected to the Texas Legislature and the first woman to serve in the Texas Senate. She passed tests to get her teaching certificate and taught one year in Jacksonville, Florida, before returning to Texas where she taught in Carthage, Forney, Marlin, and Fort Worth. She returned to Carthage in 1903 to care for her mother and become editor and publisher of the *Texas Mule*, a newspaper her father bought for her. She renamed it the *East Texas Register* and operated it until she sold it in 1911, using it in part to advocate for woman suffrage. Support for World War I brought the community's women into more public view. Neal observed that before the war "not more than three" women had been willing to speak in public, but that several had emerged as effective public speakers by the war's end. She herself made her first speech selling Liberty Bonds from the back of a pickup truck in the town square. Active in the Democratic Party as a volunteer and a fund-raiser, Neal was the second woman to register to vote in Panola County (she regretted she was not the first) and the first female member of the Texas Democratic Executive Committee. She chaired the district organization for woman suffrage and in 1920 was a delegate to the Democratic National Convention. In 1923 Governor Pat M. Neff appointed her the first female member of the board of regents of state normal schools (teachers colleges), where she became so frustrated with the reluctance of the state legislature to raise academic standards that she decided to run for the Senate. After discussions with her father, who approved of her decision, Neal campaigned, at her own expense, on a platform supporting improved rural schools, better highways, and aid to farmers. She won, carrying four of five counties in her district.[1]

During Neal's first term, she was the only woman in the legislature. She remained the only female senator throughout her four terms. Early in 1927, in an attempt at reform, newly elected Senator Thomas B. Love of Dallas proposed an amendment to Senate rules to require lobbyists to register under oath their clients' names and which legislation they supported or opposed. Margie Neal was one of only six senators to support Love's measure, which was ultimately defeated by a margin of over three to one. As chair of the Committee on Privileges and Elections, she ensured that a bill supported by the Joint Legislative Council (JLC) giving women equal representation on all executive committees of the Democratic Party was reported out favorably. Although the Senate approved the bill, the House defeated it.[2]

As a senator, Neal focused on education issues. She submitted an amendment to teacher certification laws, an effort supported by the Texas State Teachers' Association (TSTA), but eventually voted against her own bill because of unacceptable amendments tacked on to it by fellow senators. Some of her colleagues apparently thought she was not aware that she had voted against her own legislation, but Neal assured them she knew what she was doing. She was successful in passing a Senate bill, supported by the Texas Congress of Mothers (TCM), to require that physical education classes be taught in all public schools and requiring normal schools to train teachers in health and physical education, but it failed in the House. Later Neal also supported the partially successful efforts of the TCM, JLC, and TSTA to reconstitute the state board of education.

In addition, Neal joined with Tom Love to persuade the Senate to increase salaries and the numbers of attendants (usually women) at state hospitals for the insane so that the women would not have to work twelve to fourteen hours a day for fifty dollars a month. That effort failed, in part because the chair of the Finance Committee did not think the attendants' work was "appreciably harder" than work in private homes.[3]

Neal also played an important role in securing the largest appropriation for rural education to that time in Texas and helped pass legislation to provide rehabilitation for disabled people. She also sponsored a joint resolution authorizing the statehood centennial celebration and secured the adoption of "Texas, Our Texas" as the state song.[4] She supported Governor Dan Moody's progressive legislative agenda and was particularly interested in prison reform; she was a member of the inspection team that visited South Texas prison farms in 1927. In 1931, with a three-hour filibuster near the end of the session, she briefly defeated a bill permitting oil drilling in river beds, but was ultimately outmaneuvered at the last minute by Governor Ross Sterling, with whom she had a somewhat chilly relationship. With Governor Miriam A. "Ma" Ferguson, who succeeded Sterling in 1933, Neal had little difficulty; she supported Ferguson's plan for "bread bonds" for the unemployed. Neal also served on the first board of directors of the Texas Society for Crippled Children, was a delegate to the 1932 Democratic National Convention, and was state co-director for Franklin D. Roosevelt and John Nance Garner's presidential campaign that year. Her friend Oveta Culp, who was parliamentarian of the Texas House while Neal was a senator, described Neal as "unique, because she was so unlike those driving, militant, admirable women—but not always enchanting women—that we were left to expect after the suffragettes had made their march in the United States. Miss Margie felt as free to be feminine as a Senator as she had as a private citizen of Carthage."[5]

After eight years as a senator, paid ten dollars a day and ten cents a mile, Neal said she could no longer afford to serve and left for Washington, D.C., to work with the National Recovery Administration (NRA). After her departure, the Texas Senate remained without a female member for twelve years. At the NRA Neal became chief of its women's division before transferring to the Social Security Administration. Later she transferred to the San Antonio office of that agency. During World War II she worked in the federal War Manpower Commission in San Antonio and Dallas until her resignation in 1945. She returned to Carthage where she was active in community affairs, particularly clubs such as the Carthage Book Club, which she had helped organize. She was also a member of Delta Kappa Gamma, the honorary society for women in education founded by Texan Annie Webb Blanton in 1929. In 1952, when Neal was seventy-seven years old, she was honored for her public service by U.S. senator Lyndon B. Johnson, Governor Allan Shivers, and Federal Security Agency chair Oveta Culp Hobby. Although she remained a Democrat, Neal was a conservative. She supported the Eisenhower-Nixon presidential ticket and introduced Richard Nixon to Longview audiences when he ran for president. She died in 1971.[6]

NOTES

1. "Margie E. Neal," *New Handbook of Texas*, 4:962–963 (hereafter *NHOT*); Judith N. McArthur, *Creating the New Woman: The Rise of Southern Women's Progressive Culture in Texas, 1893–1918*, p. 135; *Longview Journal*, November 20, 1977; *Dallas Morning News*, June 9, 1952; *Panola Watchman*, December 20, 1971; Emma Louise Moyer Jackson, "Petticoat Politics: Political Activism among Texas Women in the 1920's" (Ph.D. diss., University of Texas at Austin, 1980), pp. 368, 464. According to Jackson (p. 337), one other woman ran for the legislature in 1926, Mrs. R. Thompson of Amarillo (House). She lost.

2. Norman D. Brown, *Hood, Bonnet, and Little Brown Jug: Texas Politics, 1921–1928*, pp. 34–344; Jackson, "Petticoat Politics," p. 465. The Joint Legislative Council was a coalition of Progressive Era women's groups that formed in 1922 to lobby the legislature for reform legislation. It was also called the "Petticoat Lobby" by the press and legislators. See Sherilyn Brandenstein, "Joint Legislative Council," *NHOT*, 3:974–975.

3. Jackson, "Petticoat Politics," pp. 465, 476–478, 511–512. When Governor Dan Moody appointed the first members of the new state board of education in 1929, he named Progressive Era reformer and suffragist Minnie Fisher Cunningham as one of its two female members. Cunningham and Jane Y. McCallum had marshaled women voters to support Moody in his successful 1926 campaign against Miriam A. "Ma" Ferguson. McCallum was serving as Moody's secretary of state in 1929.

4. Senate Resolution 507, *Senate Journal of Texas*, 59th Legislature, Regular Session, 1965.

5. Walter L. Harris, "Margie E. Neal: First Woman Senator in Texas," *East Texas Historical Journal* 9, no. 1 (Spring 1973): 41, 45. Oveta Culp later married former governor William Pettus Hobby and became the first commanding officer of the Women's Army Corps, the first secretary of the Department of Health, Education, and Welfare, and chair of the board of the *Houston Post*. See William P. Hobby, Jr., "Oveta Culp Hobby," *NHOT*, 3:637–640.

6. "Margie E. Neal," p. 963; *Panola Watchman*, December 20, 1971; Nancy Baker Jones, "Delta Kappa Gamma," *NHOT*, 2:582–583.

LAURA BURLESON NEGLEY

HOUSE 41st Legislature (1929–1931)
Democrat, San Antonio
DISTRICT 78
COMMITTEES Criminal Jurisprudence;
Education; State Affairs

DATES November 7, 1890–January 23, 1973
BIRTHPLACE Austin
FAMILY Richard van Wyck Negley; three
children
EDUCATION University of Texas at Austin
(B.A., 1911)
OCCUPATION Rancher

LAURA BURLESON NEGLEY and Helen Moore were the first two women to serve in the Texas Legislature at the same time, and Negley was the first woman to be elected from San Antonio. Her parents were Adele Lubbock Steiner Burleson, a well-known author and playwright, and Albert Sidney Burleson, Texas congressman and postmaster general for President Woodrow Wilson. Her great-grandfather, Edward Burleson, fought in the Texas Revolution and was vice president of the Republic of Texas as well as a member of the republic's congress and legislature. As a young woman in Washington, D.C., Laura Burleson actively supported woman suffrage and appeared as a speaker at one of the city's largest pro-suffrage rallies with others such as attorney Belva Lockwood and Idaho senator William E. Borah. Laura and Richard Negley moved to San Antonio where she cared for their three sons and was active in the Red Cross, Daughters of the American Revolution, and the Equal Franchise Society. Her family remembers her as a principled but gentle mother who succeeded in getting English taught as a subject in her children's school. She also refused to brand the polled Hereford cattle on the family ranch near Kyle, preferring instead to name each one and attach collars with numbered tags on them. She hired the ranch staff and kept its logs. Richard Negley, an engineer, founded and operated Negley Paint Company. Two of their sons died in World War II.[1]

Believing that women should use part of their leisure time for public service, Laura Negley accepted an invitation from Bexar County judge Arthur Seeligson to run for the legislature in 1928. "I have no idea why they picked me," she said, "but now that I am in the race, I am going to fight until the last vote is counted." Her name's appearance on the ticket surprised others as well. According to newspaper accounts, district court judge Robert W. B. Terrell suggested the socially prominent Negley when the idea of running a woman was raised during a Democratic Party caucus. She ran as part of a slate of candidates called the "People's Progressive Ticket." As a result of the fractious 1928 presidential campaign, in which prohibitionist ("dry") Texas Democrats bolted the party, deserting the Catholic, "wet" Al Smith for the victorious Republican Herbert Hoover, Negley decried factionalism, saying, "I am just a plain, old-fashioned Democrat. . . . I have no prefixes for the word." She also claimed no association with "any women's organization which either have their purposes outlined for them by others or which outline them for themselves." The same year, Negley was an alternate Smith delegate (and the only woman in her congressional district's delegation) to the Democratic National Convention in Houston and served on the Democratic Party presidential campaign committee. After the convention, Negley criticized Democratic women thinking of bolting the party because of Smith's stand against prohibition. "Governor Smith is for temperance," Negley said. "The Prohibition laws as they now stand are responsible for much of the crime of the day because crime now, for the first time, is profitable. Prohibition has given criminals money and power."[2]

On Negley's first day in the House, Secretary of State Jane Y. McCallum presided over the election of a speaker by passing around a ten-gallon Stetson hat into which ballots were tossed. Negley seconded the nomination of Edinburg representative W. R. Montgomery, but he lost to Bryan representative W. S. Barron. Within her first month, Negley startled her colleagues with an "anti-bolter" amendment that would have abolished primary elections and made party executive committees the authority for choosing candidates. It was ruled out of order, but the subsequent bill sponsored by Negley and Seguin senator A. J. Wirtz (which gave party state executive committees the power to decide voter and candidate qualifications in primaries) passed the House (in "an uproar of cheers") and the Senate. It went to Governor Dan Moody's desk amid charges that it was a "dripping wet" measure that would bar 300,000 "Hoovercrats" from voting in the primary, drive "preachers and the drys" out, and wreck the Democratic Party. Moody vetoed it.[3]

The first debate on the floor in which Negley participated concerned the creation of junior college districts around the state, which she opposed as an unnecessary burden on taxpayers and because she thought children should go to college away from home. Another debate in which she participated concerned a bill prohibiting the teaching of evolution in schools and prohibiting teachers from declaring the story of Genesis to be false. "You will make illegal the teaching that the world is round," Negley said. In addition, she proposed a bill that exempted women working in state orphanages and eleemosynary institutions from a law limiting the number of hours in a work day and work week because she believed the women were "merely on call in 'motherly duty.'" This measure was denounced by the state labor commissioner as unfair to these women. Another effort, House Bill 59, was a successful attempt to equalize, if only partially, the property rights of husbands and wives. Co-sponsored by New Boston representative R. M. Hubbard and Georgetown representative H. N. Graves, and supported by the Joint Legislative Council and the League of Women Voters, the bill made the income from the husband's as well as the wife's separate property a part of the couple's community property. "Marriage is a contract to share lives," Negley said. "Why shouldn't that mean to share incomes?" Although the act still required a husband's signature before the wife could convey or encumber her property, stocks, or bonds, it was a step forward from the husband's having complete control over his wife's property. This bill, eventually signed into law by Governor Moody, was one of many passed before married women finally achieved fully equal property rights in 1967. As a member of the Committee on Criminal Jurisprudence, Negley helped kill a bill in that committee that would have permitted a wife testifying on behalf of her husband to be cross-examined by the state prosecutor. Negley said the bill ran counter to the natural law of a woman's loyalty to her husband. Both Negley and Texas City representative Helen Moore, the only other woman in the House, had the opportunity to sit briefly as speaker of the House. Negley presided over a discussion about prison reform. Neither Negley nor Moore supported bills advanced by the Woman's Christian Temperance Union, a signal that the influence of the Joint Legislative Council, the women's lobby to which the WCTU belonged, was waning.[4]

Although she had been active as a suffragist in her youth, Laura Negley was not inclined to identify with her gender. By 1928, she objected to the term "women voters" because she believed women had been in politics long enough that their vote did not need to be distinguished from men's. "We should all be classed as citizen voters," she said. After House Bill 59 passed, the *Houston Chronicle* assured its readers, "Woman legislator takes job seriously but she is not out to remake world" and added, "Don't get the idea that this handsome daughter of former Postmaster General A. S. Burleson is a feminist. She denies it." Negley also rejected any identity as a club woman and claimed not to seek reform through "trick legislation." At the end of her seventh week in the House, she said of her colleagues that they had "extended me every courtesy of Southern gentlemen." The standard of chivalry inferred by Negley's assessment was also understood as a criterion among her male colleagues. When Dallas representative George Purl was charged with "unchivalrous" procedural action toward Negley, he defended himself by saying, "I considered the greatest act of chivalry was to treat Mrs. Negley like any other member. . . . I think [the women members] realize we are not here to pass laws by courtesy."[5]

Although Negley was regarded as a "chip off the old block" of her father, and she was discussed as a potential candidate for lieutenant governor, her term in the House apparently caused strains in her marriage. She nevertheless encouraged her children to inform themselves on political issues and to support the best available candidates. In 1958 Negley and her sisters endowed the Albert Sidney Burleson professorship at the school of law at the University of Texas in honor of their father.[6]

NOTES

1. *San Antonio Express*, January 25, 1973; Seymour V. Connor, "Albert Sidney Burleson," *New Handbook of Texas*, 1:836 (hereafter *NHOT*); Helen Burleson Kelso, "Edward Burleson," *NHOT*, 1:837; *Houston Post-Dispatch*, February 1, 1929; William Negley, telephone interview by Ruthe Winegarten, December 12, 1997; *Washington Times*, March 31, 1912.

2. *San Antonio Evening News*, June [3?], 1928, authors' files; *San Antonio Express*, June 3, 1928; *San Antonio Express*, August 3, 1928; *Austin Statesman*, August 2, 1928; *San Antonio Light*, [August 2?], 1928, authors' files; Emma Louise Moyer Jackson, "Petticoat Politics: Political Activism among Texas Women in the 1920's" (Ph.D. dissertation, University of Texas at Austin, 1980), p. 464. According to Jackson (p. 571), four women ran for the legislature in 1928 in addition to Negley and Moore: Mrs. C. W. Satterfield, San Antonio (House); Mrs. E. J. Anderson, Waxahachie (House); Mrs. R. Thompson, Amarillo (House); and Helen Viglini (Representative Edith Wilmans' sister), Dallas (House). All four lost.

3. *San Antonio Express*, January 9, 1929; [*Austin American*], January 17, 1929, [March ?], 1929; *Houston Post-Dispatch*, February 1, 1929; *Dallas Morning News*, February [13?] and March 6, 1929; unidentified newspaper clipping, March 5, [1929], March 10, 1929, authors' files.

4. *Houston Chronicle*, February 18, 1929; *San Antonio Express*, February 16, 1929; *San Antonio Express*, January 19, 1929; February 20, 1929; David Mauzy, draft of history of Texas women legislators, typescript, [1996], Senate Research Office, State of Texas, p. 43, Edith Wilmans Collection, Archives Division, Texas State Library, Austin; Jackson, "Petticoat Politics," pp. 514, 521. The Joint Legislative Council was a coalition of Progressive Era women's groups that formed in 1922 to lobby the legislature for reform legislation. It was also called the "Petticoat Lobby" by the press and legislators. See Sherilyn Brandenstein, "Joint Legislative Council," *NHOT*, 3:974–975.

5. *San Antonio Light*, [August 2?], 1928, authors' files; *Houston Chronicle*, February 18, 1929; *San Antonio Express*, March 2, 1929.

6. William Negley to Ruthe Winegarten, October 31, 1997; Laura Negley Gill, telephone interview by Ruthe Winegarten, January 10, 1998; *San Antonio Express*, January 25, 1973; copy of unidentified newspaper clipping, June [9, 1930?], authors' files.

HELEN EDMUNDS MOORE

HOUSE 41st, 42nd, and 44th Legislatures (1929–1933, 1935–1937)
Democrat, Texas City
DISTRICT 17
COMMITTEES Public Health; Education; Appropriations; Eleemosynary and Reformatory Institutions (Chair)

DATES January 3, 1881–September 20, 1968
BIRTHPLACE Black River Falls, Wisconsin
FAMILY Hugh Benton Moore; three adopted nieces
EDUCATION Unknown
OCCUPATION Nurse

"I decided to run for the legislature in 1929," said **HELEN MOORE**, "because I thought a woman could pass some good laws."[1] Moore was a nurse and suffragist before becoming the fourth woman to serve in the Texas Legislature. In 1905 she married Hugh Moore, one of her patients in Kansas City, Missouri, and they moved to Texas City that year. There she was the city's only medical practitioner until a doctor arrived in 1907. Hugh Moore developed much of the area's industry and transportation while Helen Moore was active in civic organizations, helping organize the Texas City Red Cross branch in 1916 and serving as its first president. She and her husband helped bring to the city incorporation, health laws, parks, and what became the Moore Memorial Public Library.[2]

Minnie Fisher Cunningham, president of the Texas Equal Suffrage Association (TESA), urged Moore to campaign for woman suffrage, saying, "I know your spirit and your fire, and they are irresistible." As a result, Moore toured the state in support of the 19th Amendment (woman suffrage). She later became a district chair of TESA and in 1923, with suffrage won, she became president of the Texas League of Women Voters. She was a delegate to the Democratic National Conventions of 1924 and 1928. In 1924 Moore supported Miriam A. "Ma" Ferguson's gubernatorial campaign because of Ferguson's stand against the Ku Klux Klan and for improved rural schools, reduced taxes, and prison reform. Moore also believed that Ferguson's husband, impeached former governor James Ferguson, would be of help to his wife and would not "advise anything which would cast a reflection on her administration." In 1928 Moore served on the Democratic Party campaign committee for Al Smith's presidential bid.[3]

After successful campaigns in 1928 and 1930, Moore was badly defeated in the 1932 Democratic primary. Her defeat, said the *Houston Post*, was caused by "a misunderstanding of her stand on prohibition."[4] She pledged to oppose prohibition and was reelected in 1934 as a New Deal Democrat, returning to the legislature for her third term. With the departures of both Carthage senator Margie E. Neal and Dallas representative Sarah T. Hughes in 1935, Moore was left as the only woman in the 44th Legislature. Her style was reportedly different from that of her former colleagues. "She makes no ringing aggressive speeches as did Mrs. Hughes," said a Houston newspaper, adding: "Neither does she weep when defeated as Miss Neal did." Quietly determined, Moore said she did not believe in "calling names or making wild charges. The merits or the faults of the bill I'm discussing are what counts."[5]

Moore focused on social reform legislation. She sponsored a bill to allow county commissioners to pay pensions to aged indigents instead of maintaining "poor farms," but it failed. In her first term she opposed bills supported by the Woman's Christian Temperance Union in response to the WCTU's opposition to Al Smith's failed 1928 presidential bid. She was opposed to a sales tax, supported state unemployment insurance, adequate support for all schools, raising the age of compulsory school attendance to fifteen, ratification of the child labor amendment, and a "living wage for all women workers." She succeeded in assuring that the mentally ill would be removed from jails and placed in asylums and that hospitals would be allowed to treat cancer, pellagra, and tuberculosis (and TB patients under fourteen for the first time); she mounted, on her own time and at her own expense, a personal investigation into the quality of state orphanages, prisons, and hospitals and was instrumental in obtaining increased funding for and maintenance of them as a result. She helped establish the first psychopathic hospital at University of Texas Medical Branch at Galveston and supported the creation of hospitals for the criminally insane to segregate them from the harmless mentally ill.[6]

She also sponsored legislation reconstituting the state board of education, requiring public school teachers to be U.S. citizens, adding U.S. and Texas government classes to the curriculum, and requiring education for penitentiary prisoners. She supported passage of a federal child labor amendment and protective legislation for women to reduce their weekly work hours from fifty-four to forty-eight. She also tried—and failed—to enact an eight-hour work day. In 1935 she and Dallas representative Sarah T. Hughes proposed a bill to legalize jury service for women, but it failed. She supported taxes on liquor instead of income and sales and the repeal of Prohibition. She also secured state approval for construction of the Texas City Dike as a permanent part of the Galveston Bay channel system.[7] At her retirement, near the close of a special session, the House passed a resolution honoring Moore for a career that "contributed invaluable service to the eleemosynary institutions of this state and to the underprivileged of our citizenship [and] . . . [e]stablished Mrs. Moore as a pioneer in the humanitarian history of our state."[8]

After her husband died in 1944, Moore moved to Houston, where she remained until her death.[9]

NOTES

1. *Houston Press*, April 19, 1935. Four women ran for the legislature in 1928 in addition to Moore and Laura Burleson Negley (San Antonio), who served with her: Mrs. C. W. Satterfield, San Antonio (House); Mrs. E. J. Anderson, Waxahachie (House); Mrs. R. E. Thompson, Amarillo (House); and Helen Viglini (Representative Edith Wilmans' sister), Dallas (House). All four lost. See Emma Louise Moyer Jackson, "Petticoat Politics: Political Activism among Texas Women in the 1920's" (Ph.D. diss., University of Texas at Austin, 1980), p. 571.

2. *Galveston Daily News*, September 23, 1968; Priscilla Myers Benham, "Helen

Edmunds Moore," *New Handbook of Texas* (Austin: Texas State Historical Association, 1996), 4:819 (hereafter *NHOT*).

3. *Galveston Daily News*, September 23, 1968; Benham, "Helen Edmunds Moore," p. 819; Jackson, "Petticoat Politics," pp. 283, 464.

4. Susie Moncla, Director, Moore Memorial Public Library, to Ruthe Winegarten, July 11, 1997; *Houston Post*, July 8, 1934.

5. *Texas City Sun*, July 20, 1934; *Houston Press*, April 19, 1935.

6. *Galveston Daily News*, September 23, 1968; *Houston Press*, April 19, 1935; *Texas City Sun*, July 20, 1934; Benham, "Helen Edmunds Moore," p. 819; Jackson, "Petticoat Politics," p. 471.

7. *Galveston Daily News*, September 23, 1968; *Houston Press*, April 19, 1935; *Texas City Sun*, July 20, 1934; Benham, "Helen Edmunds Moore," p. 819; Judie Karen Walton Gammage, "Quest for Equality: An Historical Overview of Women's Rights Activism in Texas, 1890–1975" (Ph.D. diss., North Texas State University, 1982"), pp. 106, 113–114. Jury service for women was not legalized in Texas until 1954.

8. *Texas City Sun*, [Summer] 1936, Helen Moore Collection, Moore Memorial Public Library, Texas City; Benham, "Helen Edmunds Moore," p. 819.

9. *Galveston Daily News*, September 23, 1968.

☆

FRANCES MITCHELL ROUNTREE

HOUSE 42nd Legislature (1931–1933)
Democrat, Bryan
DISTRICT 26
COMMITTEES Appropriations; Education; School Districts; Privileges, Suffrage, and Elections

DATES 1878?–December 5, 1956
BIRTHPLACE Llano County
FAMILY Lee J. Rountree (died); no children
EDUCATION Round Rock Institute; Southwestern University (graduated, 1900?)
OCCUPATION Newspaper publisher; columnist

FRANCES MITCHELL ROUNTREE was one of the first two widows of legislators elected to the Texas Legislature (the other was Cora Strong), and the first woman elected to represent Brazos County. She was also the first woman to head the Bryan chamber of commerce, the first female head of the Texas Editorial Association, and vice president of the National Editorial Association. In 1902 she married Lee J. Rountree, then the chief clerk of the Texas House of Representatives. They moved to Bryan where he established the *Bryan Daily News* in 1920 (later renamed the *Eagle*) and in 1922 was elected to the Texas House. He died of a stroke in 1923 while seated at his House desk. Although one source indicates that Frances Rountree was named to serve the remainder of her husband's term, there is no indication that she actually served in the House in the 36th Legislature. She was known throughout her married life by her husband's name, and many people did not know her given name.[1]

Frances Rountree had operated the *Daily News* while Lee Rountree was in Austin and continued to do so after his death, becoming one of the first women managing editors of a Texas newspaper (Margie Neal, Texas' first female state senator, published her own newspaper in the early 1900s). Rountree continued in this role until her death. During Prohibition she was once threatened by a bootlegger who told her not to print a story about him. She responded: "It's on the court records, and if I'm alive at four o'clock, it'll be printed." She was, and it was.[2] She once said that one could not be a journalist and grow old because the life was too exciting. But, she continued, the "rewards are . . . great, even though you don't make a lot of money. . . . I choose to get much more out of life." The newspaper made money for Rountree and its stockholders every year she managed it, even during the Depression. As an editor and columnist, Frances Rountree was regarded as both tenacious and fair. She wrote an editorial during the Depression, "Relief Work Need Grows," that described inadequate shelter and heat for indigent local families.[3]

Rountree was active in the Democratic Party, serving as a delegate to the Democratic National Conventions of 1928, 1936, and 1944. In 1930, as "Mrs. Lee J. Rountree," she ran for and won the chance to fill the seat her husband had held in the House, with the intention of finishing the work he had begun on the Brazos River Conservation and Reclamation District. She subsequently served on its board.[4] She sponsored five bills, two of which became law. One allowed the governor to exchange highway rights of way and the other established a training school for firemen at Texas A&M College. In addition, she supported the successful effort to assure that Texas A&M received one-third of oil royalties designated for the University of Texas, and she refused to support the repeal of "blue laws" (statutes that regulated commerce and entertainment) that would have allowed theaters in the state to operate on Sundays. She also served during four called sessions through the end of 1932, during which she sponsored an unsuccessful bill to repeal sections of the Highway Code. She ran for reelection in 1932 but was defeated.[5]

Frances Rountree returned to her life in Bryan, publishing the *Eagle* and writing a column called "Pavement Pick-ups," which was "feared and cherished" for its frank opinions. She remained an active Democrat and civic leader. She was a member of the executive board of the Texas Federation of Women's Clubs, and during her seventeen years as president of the local Carnegie Library board, Rountree established the Children's Education Foundation and created a children's department that became known as the library's Rountree Room for Children. She collapsed at her desk while typing the copy for her daily column and died of a stroke the following week.[6]

NOTES

1. *Bryan Daily Eagle*, December 5, 1956; *Texas Press Messenger*, January 1957; *Dallas Morning News*, June 25, 1940; Glenna Fourman Brundidge, ed., *Brazos County History: Rich Past, Bright Future* (Bryan: Family History Foundation, 1986), p. 334, claims Frances Rountree was named to finish her late husband's term in 1923. However, this assertion is not confirmed by *Members of the Texas Congress, 1836–1845, Members of the Texas Legislature, 1846–1992*, vol. 1 (Austin: Senate Engrossing and Enrolling and Senate Reproduction, 1992).

2. *Texas Press Messenger*, January 1957.

3. *Dallas Morning News*, June 25, 1940; *Bryan–College Station Eagle*, March 10, 1991; *Bryan Daily Eagle*, January 18, 1930.

4. Brundidge, ed., *Brazos County History*, p. 64.

5. David Mauzy, draft of history of Texas women legislators, typescript, [1996], Senate Research Office, State of Texas, pp. 49–50, Edith Wilmans Collection, Archives Division, Texas State Library, Austin.

6. *Bryan–College Station Eagle*, March 10, 1991; Dianna Evans, Reference Librarian, Bryan Public Library, telephone interview by Ruthe Winegarten, September 4, 1997; Brundidge, ed., *Brazos County History*, p. 166.

CORA GRAY STRONG

HOUSE 42nd Legislature (1931–1933)
Democrat, Slocum
DISTRICT 55
COMMITTEES Eleemosynary and Reformatory Institutions; Education; Engrossed Bills; Liquor Traffic; Public Health

DATES September 4, 1882–March 21, 1959
BIRTHPLACE Elkhart
FAMILY N. R. Strong (died)
EDUCATION Summer Hill Select School for Young Women; Metropolitan Business College (1900?)
OCCUPATION Teacher; farmer; business owner

CORA GRAY STRONG was one of the first two widows of legislators elected to the Texas Legislature (the other was Frances Mitchell Rountree). She taught one year at Day in Anderson County and another year at Bethel for thirty-five dollars a month. After graduating from business college in Dallas, she worked for Briggs Machinery Supply Company there. In 1905 she married Colonel N. R. Strong, one of the developers of Port Arthur and its first mayor, and they lived in Slocum, where she bought her father's mercantile store from him and operated it for several years. For twenty years she was also assistant postmaster.[1]

In 1928 N. R. Strong was elected to the Texas House, but ill health prevented him from serving much of his term, and he died during the fifth called session of the 41st Legislature. Cora Strong was elected to replace him. She sponsored a successful bill to provide for rural school supervisors in some counties and a joint resolution for a constitutional amendment to combine the positions of county tax assessor and tax collector, thereby making her the first woman in the House to propose a successful constitutional amendment resulting in economy and efficiency in county tax collection. During the second called session, Strong pushed the passage of a bill prohibiting the taking of fish for sale from freshwater streams in thirty-four counties.[2]

Strong returned to Slocum with the end of the session to operate the farms that she and her husband had acquired. She was a member of the Daughters of the Republic of Texas and an alternate delegate to the Democratic National Convention in 1944.[3]

NOTES

1. Pauline Buck Hohes, *A Centennial History of Anderson County, Texas* (San Antonio: Naylor Company, 1936), pp. 253–254.

2. Ibid.

3. Ibid.

☆

SARAH TILGHMAN HUGHES

HOUSE 42nd–44th Legislatures (1931–1935) Democrat, Dallas
DISTRICT 51
COMMITTEES Education; Game and Fisheries; Judiciary; Labor; Eleemosynary and Reformatory Institutions; Federal Relations; Public Lands and Buildings

DATES August 2, 1896–April 23, 1985
BIRTHPLACE Baltimore, Maryland
FAMILY George Ernest Hughes; no children
EDUCATION Goucher College (B.S., 1917); George Washington University (J.D., 1922)
OCCUPATION Police officer; teacher; attorney; state district and federal judge

SARAH T. HUGHES was, at age thirty-four, the youngest woman elected to the legislature at that time. She was an attorney, women's rights activist, supporter of the United Nations, and later Texas' first female state and federal judge. She taught science before becoming—at five feet tall—a policewoman in Washington, D.C. In 1922 she married a fellow law student, George Ernest Hughes, and they moved to Dallas, where she joined the firm of Priest, Herndon, and Ledbetter as one of only four women practicing law in the city. "We didn't want any children," she said. "It did not make any difference to George[,] and I . . . was interested in a career." Hughes soon became active in local politics, speaking out against a Dallas school board policy of excluding married women from teaching.[1]

In 1930, after spending three hundred dollars on the campaign, Hughes was elected to her first term in the Texas House. While campaigning for a second term, Hughes' opponent ridiculed her candidacy by saying, "We should slap her face and send her back to the kitchen." Hughes won, but during the 43rd Legislature she was the only woman in the House (Margie Neal was the sole woman in the Senate). The press voted Hughes Most Valuable Member of the House during this term.[2]

In the legislature Hughes became involved in such issues as penal reform, oil proration, and public school land use. She earned a reputation as an effective debater during fights over a measure supporting the completion of Buchanan Dam on the Colorado River, she supported an income tax while opposing sales taxes, and she was successful in getting the House to pass a corporate income tax, but the Senate rejected it.[3] In 1934, referring to state laws that prevented married women from controlling their own property, Hughes contradicted a House member on the floor who claimed Texas women had rights by saying, "It's a lot of bunk about women in Texas having rights. They don't even get a square deal." She tried unsuccessfully to introduce legislation requiring child support payments by noncustodial parents. (In the 1940s, she asked Representative Rae Files Still to carry similar legislation, but it also failed.) In 1935 she and Texas City representative Helen Moore sponsored a bill legalizing jury service for women, but Hughes would become a judge before she could become a juror. Texas women won that right in 1954.[4]

In 1935, at the start of Hughes' third legislative term, Governor James Allred repaid her for supporting his candidate for speaker of the House by appointing her to the 14th District Court in Dallas. She left the legislature on February 11 to accept that position. When a Dallas state senator objected to her appointment because she was married and declared that Hughes should stay home and wash dishes, she gained support from local women. Forty-five years later, she thanked him, saying, "I still credit Claude Westerfield for uniting Texas women."[5] Hughes thus became the state's first female district judge. One of her supporters, a Dallas attorney, declared, "I am for her because I know her qualifications, and I have had my ears knocked down in court when opposing her."[6] She was reelected seven times.

During World War II, Hughes gave Governor Coke Stevenson a cross-indexed list of forty-four Texas women—compiled by a committee of Dallas female professional and community leaders—who were qualified for appointment to state office. She ran for the U.S. Congress in 1946 on a platform that supported peace, jobs, collective bargaining, and drafting women into the military. In a bitter campaign, however, she lost to businessman J. Frank Wilson, who had characterized his opposition as "left wing political terrorists." In 1948 she campaigned in support of Lyndon B. Johnson's U.S. Senate race against Coke Stevenson, with whom Hughes had served in the legislature. "I was on the opposite side of everything he [Stevenson] wanted to do, and actually it wasn't very difficult for me to decide" to support Johnson, she said.[7]

In 1952, while national president of the National Federation of Business and Professional Women's Clubs, Hughes was nominated for the vice presidency on the Democratic Party ticket. She found a woman to second the nomination when she could not find a man to do so. However, the effort was only a gesture, because speaker of the House and Democratic Party chair Sam Rayburn, a fellow Texan, would not allow the nomination to occur unless Hughes immediately withdrew her name from consideration. "I'm glad it wasn't finally put to a vote, because I only had two and a half votes," she recalled.[8] In 1954 Hughes helped secure a successful amendment to the Texas Constitution allowing women to serve on juries. In 1958 she ran unsuccessfully for the Texas Supreme Court. She also served as president of the Dallas United Nations Association at a time when support for the U.N. was considered virtually subversive in Dallas. She was one of two U.S. representatives to the United Nations Educational, Scientific, and Cultural Organization (UNESCO) when it was under attack from conservative extremists.[9]

Hughes was part of the liberal or "loyal" wing of the Texas Democratic Party. In 1960 she was Dallas County co-chair of the Kennedy-Johnson presidential campaign. After the election, Hughes told Texas' U.S. senator, Ralph Yarborough, and Vice President Johnson that she wanted to be a federal judge. In 1961 President John F. Kennedy appointed her. Hughes thereby became Texas' first female federal judge, despite opposition to her selection from the American Bar Association and Attorney General Robert F. Kennedy, who thought that, at sixty-five, she was too old. (Rarely was anyone sixty-four or older selected as a federal judge.) Lyndon B. Johnson's press secretary, Liz Carpenter, recalled that House speaker Rayburn kept "losing" the appropriations bill for the Justice Department. "It's just these old hands, son," Rayburn reportedly told the attorney general when asked. "I just can't seem to find that bill with these old hands." Kennedy then dropped his opposition to Hughes.[10] After President Kennedy was assassinated in Dallas on November 22, 1963, Judge Sarah T. Hughes administered the presidential oath of office to Lyndon B. Johnson aboard *Air Force One*. She is the only woman to have officiated at the swearing in of a U.S. president.[11]

While serving on the federal bench, Hughes supported equal pay for equal work for women, ruled Texas abortion laws unconstitutional (in *Roe vs. Wade*, the case argued by Austin representative Sarah Weddington), and ordered Dallas County jail facilities improved. She ruled that Texas must increase aid to families with dependent children and presided over the Securities and Exchange Commission's stock fraud suit involving former Texas House speaker Gus Mutscher and former Texas attorney general Waggoner Carr, among others, that resulted from the Sharpstown banking scandals.[12] A Dallas political consultant who knew Hughes well said that she believed that government "is for the powerless and the poor. She was sympathetic to the poor but would often give jail time to white-collar criminals."[13]

At the end of her life, Hughes reflected on the challenges she had met as a woman in public life. "I believe women have to go after what they want," she said. "I didn't feel discriminated against in 1930. Of course, I knew that there were people who wouldn't vote for me because I was a woman. But that just made it necessary for me to work harder. I think you've got to ask for things. You can't wait to have things given to you."[14] She also valued her time in the Texas Legislature: "I thought that I was able to do more good for the community, and the state as well, in the legislature than in any other office I've ever had."[15]

Sarah T. Hughes took senior judge status in 1975, meaning she might sit in cases assigned by other judges and hear the remaining cases on her docket. She suffered a stroke in 1982 and, with her eyesight failing, retired after forty-six years on the bench. She was inducted into the first Texas Women's Hall of Fame in 1984.[16]

NOTES

1. Robert S. La Forte, "Sarah Tilghman Hughes," *New Handbook of Texas*, 3:774; Ann Fears Crawford and Crystal Sasse Ragsdale, "Sarah Tilghman Hughes: The Little Lady on the Big Bench," *Women in Texas: Their Lives, Their Experiences, Their Accomplishments*, pp. 286–287; Patricia Lasher and Beverly Bentley, "Sarah T. Hughes," *Texas Women: Interviews and Images*, p. 86; Sarah T. Hughes and Joe B. Frantz, "Oral History" [1968], Lyndon Baines Johnson Library, Austin, pp. 1–2; *Houston Post*, April 25, 1965; *Dallas Morning News*, October 24, 1971; Michael Drury, "The Woman Who Swore In President Johnson Recalls What Happened Aboard," *McCall's*, November 1966; *Dallas Times Herald*, April 25, 1985.

2. *Austin American-Statesman*, June 23, 1980; *Houston Chronicle*, September 30, 1934.

3. La Forte, "Sarah Tilghman Hughes," pp. 774–775; Crawford and Ragsdale, "Sarah

Tilghman Hughes," p. 287; Lasher and Bentley, "Sarah T. Hughes," p. 87; *Dallas Times Herald*, August 30, 1933, April 28, 1985.

4. *Fort Worth Press*, April 18, 1934; David Mauzy, draft of history of Texas women legislators, typescript, [1996], Senate Research Office, State of Texas, p. 88, Edith Wilmans Collection, Archives Division, Texas State Library, Austin; Judie Karen Walton Gammage, "Quest for Equality: An Historical Overview of Women's Rights Activism in Texas, 1890–1975" (Ph.D. diss., North Texas State University, 1982), p. 116.

5. Julie Anne Booty, "Sarah Hughes at 83," *Vision Magazine*, August 1979, p. 6; Lasher and Bentley, "Sarah T. Hughes," p. 87; *Dallas Morning News*, February 2, 1935; *Fort Worth Star-Telegram*, April 5, 1980.

6. Crawford and Ragsdale, "Sarah Tilghman Hughes," p. 288.

7. *Dallas Morning News*, October 31, 1944; George Norris Green, *The Establishment in Texas Politics: The Primitive Years, 1938–1957*, p. 98; Hughes and Frantz, "Oral History," p. 4.

8. La Forte, "Sarah Tilghman Hughes," p. 775. Hughes was not the first woman so nominated. India Edwards, vice chair of the Democratic National Committee, was nominated prior to Hughes at the same convention. She also withdrew her name from contention. See Hughes and Frantz, "Oral History," p. 15, and Eugenia Kaledin, *Mothers and More: American Women in the 1950s*, p. 85.

9. Cordye Hall, *"What Can One Person Do?" A Texas Woman Activist Answers* (Dallas: N.p., [early 1980s]), pp. 4, 14–15, 43.

10. Hughes and Frantz, "Oral History," pp. 10–11; *Dallas Morning News*, August 11, 1961, September 26, 1961; *Austin American*, March 8, 1962; *Texas Observer*, December 19, 1997.

11. Hughes and Frantz, "Oral History," pp. 4, 26–27; *Dallas Morning News*, October 24, 1971; *San Antonio Express*, August 23, 1981.

12. La Forte, "Sarah Tilghman Hughes," p. 775; *Houston Post*, August 10, 1975; Crawford and Ragsdale, "Sarah Tilghman Hughes," p. 290. Corpus Christi Representative Frances "Sissy" Farenthold was instrumental in bringing the scandal to light while she was in the Texas House in 1971.

13. *Dallas Morning News*, April 25, 1985.

14. Lasher and Bentley, "Sarah T. Hughes," p. 86.

15. Booty, "Sarah T. Hughes at 83," p. 7.

16. *Dallas Times Herald*, August 4, 1975, April 25, 1985; *Dallas Morning News*, May 19, 1982, April 25, 1985; *Fort Worth Star-Telegram*, April 25, 1985.

THE 1940s–1950s

MARGARET GREER HARRIS GORDON (AMSLER)

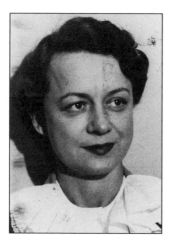

HOUSE 46th Legislature (1939–1941)
Democrat, Waco
DISTRICT 97-1
COMMITTEES Banks and Banking;
Judiciary; Public Health; Eleemosynary
and Reformatory Institutions
DATES June 15, 1908–
BIRTHPLACE Waco
FAMILY John Kenneth Gordon (di-
vorced); Sam H. Amsler, Jr.; one daughter
EDUCATION Baylor University (A.B.,
1929); Wellesley College (M.A., 1931);
Baylor University (L.L.B., 1937; L.L.B. to
Juris Doctorate, 1969)
OCCUPATION Teacher; attorney; professor

MARGARET GORDON decided she wanted to be an attorney, like her father, Nat Harris, a prominent judge and former associate of Governor Pat Neff. "Mostly, the clients who came to the house were Negroes," she recalled of her father's practice. He opposed the Ku Klux Klan and, she said, was "an Irish fighter who could not stand for anyone to be bullied. . . . We lived with a loaded shotgun in the front hall of the house because the family was always being threatened, but we never used the gun." Decades later, she served as attorney for some of her father's clients, in-cluding a ninety-year-old former Baylor University cleaning woman in danger of losing her home to urban renewal.[1]

In 1933 she married John Kenneth Gordon, but they divorced. She worked her way through Baylor Law School teaching French and raising a young daughter; she graduated with honors in 1937, the only female in her class. The following year she campaigned for a seat in the Texas House. "I was trading on being a woman," she said. "It was summer. I wore a pink dress. . . . I would get up and go to factories at six o'clock in the morning and . . . climb up in cotton gins." She defeated seven male opponents and, with Neveille Colson, became one of only two women in the 46th Legislature. "The opinion seemed to be that any woman who would get out and run for public office would have to be a sort of fish-wife type with a sharp tongue," she recalled. "They were so relieved to find that neither Mrs. Colson or I was that type, that we came to the legislature to be working members without any chips on our shoulder, or any special interests to serve. I think they were so relieved, that we were treated beautifully." When the Houston chamber of commerce held a "stag" party to which only male legislators were invited, Gordon and Colson took picket signs into the House declaring the organization unfair to women. "It was just fun. We were not seriously picketing," she said. "But the men apparently took it to heart." The following week the two women received flowers, candy, and perfume.[2]

Gordon was inexperienced in the culture of the legislature and in the procedures for drafting and passing legislation. Influential family friends, however, provided her with guidance. When former Governor Neff called her early in the session to tell her he wanted a bill passed to allow the transfer of Judge R. E. B. Baylor's court records to the Texas Collection at Baylor University, she sought assistance from Lieutenant Governor Coke Stevenson, a family friend. Stevenson, also a friend of Neff, explained to Gordon what Neff wanted, then drafted what became House Bill 2 and told her how to get it passed. After that success, Neff called Gordon again to see that five hundred dollars be added to the House appropriations bill for a well pump in Mother Neff Park. Although the bill had already passed both houses and was in conference, Gordon succeeded in getting the item added through the friendships she had developed and because her colleagues knew that Pat Neff was the source of the measure. She also learned how to negotiate the social aspects of House life. Aware that friction existed between factions over which brand of beer would be served at social functions, Gordon decided to drink only Dr. Pepper, which had been developed in Waco. When one representative promised to give her Brewster County if she would marry him, she considered the offer but declined. Unwilling to allow anyone else to win her, the suitor apparently promised to support a competitor's bill if the man would leave her alone. She did not, however, like Governor W. Lee "Pappy" O'Daniel, who referred to her only as "That Woman." Of him, Gordon said, "He was a flour salesman with a radio program who ran for Governor and won, and he had no idea of what government was all about." Gordon was one of the leaders of "The Immortal 56," a group of legislators opposed to O'Daniel's attempts to levy a sales tax by amending the state constitution. She made defeating O'Daniel's measure the focus of her work and repeatedly voted against it along with her cohorts. The Immortals succeeded, and the amendment never went to the voters.

Gordon believed her opposition to O'Daniel caused her to lose reelection to the House in 1940.[3]

After leaving the legislature, Gordon became the first female law professor in Texas when she joined the Baylor Law School faculty in 1940. "I do a lot of law practice for the faculty," she said. "They feel a woman is not a real lawyer, so they're not afraid to talk to her." She taught "the courses the men didn't want to teach"—contracts, agency and partnership, commercial transactions, and bills and notes. In 1942 she married Sam H. Amsler, Jr., and they opened a law practice in McGregor. That year she became the first female marshal of the Texas Supreme Court. During World War II Margaret Gordon Amsler was head of the Geography Department for the Army Specialized Training Program at Baylor University, supervising about five hundred soldiers. As a part of their study, they planned the invasion at Anzio, Italy, and some students later participated in that action, a turning point in the war.[4]

As a former legislator familiar with the lawmaking process, Margaret Gordon Amsler wrote many bills and lobbied sitting legislators to sponsor them. Most of these were designed to change corporate law and to improve the status of women. She was appointed to the State Bar of Texas Committee on Revision of Corporation Law in 1950 (later known as the Corporation Bank and Business Law Committee) and served as its chair from 1956 to 1966. She helped draft the Texas Business Corporation Act, passed by the 54th Legislature in 1955. In 1961, for her efforts to revise corporate statutes, Amsler was awarded the Bar Association's first President's Award, given to the outstanding attorney in the state.[5]

Margaret Gordon Amsler was a proponent of women's rights and spent much of her time lobbying the legislature for passage of bills to equalize women's status under the law. "Since laws protecting women's rights have to be passed in the male-dominated legislature," she said, "we have to depend on men to fight for our rights." In the 1960s she opposed the passage of the Texas Equal Legal Rights Amendment, siding with groups like the State Bar Association that believed such a measure would cause legal chaos. "When I went to the legislature and appeared to oppose the Equal Rights Amendment, they were just [so happy] to have a woman come down there and tell them this is a bunch of tripe," she recalled. "I remember Sarah T. Hughes never could understand why the lawyers loved me. I loved them. They never loved her. She was vicious. . . . It's not fair for a woman to attack a man, because he cannot say a word, . . . and I always recognized that, and I never allowed sex to intrude."[6]

Amsler preferred to change or eliminate individual statutes that discriminated against women. In cooperation with law professor Angus McSwain, Amsler drafted two bills that passed during the 58th Legislature in 1963. One of these gave married women the same rights as single women to enter into contracts. The other, the Texas Married Women's Act, removed the requirement that a married woman have her husband's signature on real estate transactions involving her own property. In addition, she succeeded in getting legislation passed to equalize the legal definition of adultery as it applied to women and men. Previous to this, she said, there were two definitions: "A man could get a divorce from his wife for one act of adultery, but for the wife to get a divorce on the same grounds she would have to prove she had been abandoned. If her husband came home for breakfast once in awhile, there was no proof of adultery on his part." Governor John Connally appointed her to the Governor's Commission on the Status of Women in 1967, and she chaired its committee on labor laws affecting women. In particular, she became interested in securing laws to allow women the benefit of collective bargaining through labor unions and to improve legal standards for women's working conditions. Of her lobbying, she said, "The legislature is supposed to be representing everybody."[7]

Amsler's opinions about race were apparently not as progressive as her views on women's rights. In 1965 she published "The True 'Advancement of Colored People': How Is It To Be Accomplished?" in which she suggested that the civil rights movement was unleashing anarchy by attempting to change law "in the streets" instead of in the courts, that "We Shall Overcome" was a song of hate, that the principal problem among "our negroes" was lax sexual mores, that literacy tests should be required in order to vote, and that school systems should provide "different types of education to their differing students."[8]

Amsler retired from teaching at Baylor University School of Law in 1972. After more than thirty years there, she had become known as "Lady A" to the students. In 1977 she was appointed by the Texas Supreme Court to the Texas Board of Law Examiners, a panel of nine attorneys who give and score sections of the bar examination. In 1987 Margaret Gordon Amsler was inducted into the Texas Women's Hall of Fame.[9]

NOTES

1. Margaret [Gordon] Amsler, "Oral Memoirs," [1972], Baylor University Project, Program for Oral History, pp. 19–20; Margaret Greer Harris Amsler, Texas Women's Hall of Fame Nomination Form, 1986, Woman's Collection, Texas Woman's University, Denton, p. 3; *Waco News-Tribune*, July 14, 1966.

2. Angela Dorau, "Oral History of Margaret Harris Amsler," Chronology Project, Women in the Law Section, State Bar of Texas, Austin, 1996, p. 30; Amsler, "Oral Memoirs," pp. 20, 70–71; *Waco Tribune-Herald*, June 26, 1978.

3. *Texas Parade*, February 1939; Amsler, "Oral Memoirs," pp. 20–21, 84; *Waco News-Tribune*, July 14, 1966; Nancy Beck Young and Lewis L. Gould, *Texas, Her Texas: The Life and Times of Frances Goff*, p. 24. The beer debate began because speaker of the House Emmett Morse had Houston friends who ran the Grand Prize brewery, and Grand Prize was therefore served at House functions. This caused "a good deal of distress" among members who did not like Grand Prize. See Amsler, "Oral Memoirs," p. 84.

4. Amsler, Nomination Form, p. 2; *Baylor Lariat*, October 20, 1965; *Waco Tribune-Herald*, June 26, 1978; Amsler, "Oral Memoirs," p. 15.

5. Amsler, Nomination Form, p. 4; *Baylor Lariat*, October 20, 1965; *Waco News-Tribune*, July 14, 1966.

6. Unidentified newspaper clipping, c. 1967, Texas Collection, Baylor University, Waco; Dorau, "Oral History," p. 59.

7. *Waco News-Tribune*, July 14, 1966; *Waco Tribune-Herald*, June 26, 1978; Hall of Fame Nomination Form, p. 2.

8. Margaret Harris [Gordon] Amsler, "The True 'Advancement of Colored People': How Is It To Be Accomplished?" *Baylor Line*, Summer 1965, pp. 2–4.

9. Dorau, "Oral History," p. 49; *Richardson News*, August 3, 1972; *Waco Tribune-Herald*, June 26, 1978, October 7, 1987.

ESTHER NEVEILLE HIGGS COLSON

HOUSE 46th–50th Legislatures (1939–1949)
SENATE 51st–59th Legislatures (1949–1967)
Democrat, Navasota
DISTRICT House, 27F; Senate, 5
COMMITTEES: House: Claims and Accounts (Chair); Insurance; Banking; State Affairs; Constitutional Amendments; Municipal and Private Corporations; Conservation and Reclamation; Education; Highways and Roads; Eleemosynary and Reformatory Institutions. Senate: Public Debts; Claims and Accounts (Chair); Penitentiaries (Chair); Engrossed Bills (Vice Chair); Enrolled Bills (Vice Chair); Agriculture; Finance (Chair); Insurance; Interstate Cooperation; Representative Districts; Senatorial Districts; Stock and Stock Raising; Commerce and Manufacturing; Congressional Districts; Educational Affairs (Chair); Aeronautics; Banking; Counties and County Boundaries; Federal Relations; Internal Improvements; Judicial Districts; Public Buildings and Grounds; Public Health (Chair); Public Lands; State Institutions and Departments (Chair); Privileges and Elections; Town and City Corporations; Military and Veterans Affairs; Oil and Gas

DATES July 18, 1902–March 3, 1982
BIRTHPLACE Bryan
FAMILY Nall Colson (divorced); no children
EDUCATION Baylor University; Agricultural and Mechanical College of Texas; Sam Houston State Teachers College; University of Texas at Austin (no degrees)
OCCUPATION Teacher; principal

NEVEILLE COLSON was the first woman to serve in both houses of the legislature and, with twenty-eight years of service, one of its longest-serving members. In 1932 her husband, Nall Colson, was elected to the first of two terms in the Texas House, where she served as his secretary. She also worked in the office of the secretary of state and for the Internal Revenue Service. They divorced, and in 1938, after his death, Neveille Colson ran successfully for the seat he had held. She defied a "gentleman's agreement" twice, first by getting elected in the year that it was another county's "turn" to select the legislator to represent District 27F, then by getting reelected rather than stepping aside after only one term. After listening to an angry male opponent criticize her for these "infractions," she explained that while gentlemen's agreements were fine things and gentlemen should observe them, voters should recognize that she was not a gentleman. She beat seven "gentlemen" that year and came within 1,000 votes of winning without a runoff. She was elected to five consecutive terms in the House.[1]

With reelection in 1946, Colson set a new record for a woman serving in the legislature, surpassing Margie Neal's eight years. In 1948 Colson ran successfully against the incumbent and four other challengers for the 5th District senatorial seat and became the first woman to serve in both houses of the Texas Legislature. She was the only woman in the Senate throughout her eighteen years there. Colson served in the legislature during what has been called "the doldrums" of the women's movement— after suffragists like Edith Wilmans, Margie Neal, Laura Burleson Negley, Helen Moore, and Sarah T. Hughes had left and before women inspired by either the civil rights or modern women's movements arrived. She left the Senate in 1967, the year that Barbara Jordan arrived.[2]

Throughout her career, Colson refused to sponsor bills specifically for women, fearing they would be referred to as "petticoat legislation," an acknowledgment of the derisive manner with which the press and legislators had greeted reform legislation supported by progressives and many of her predecessors.[3] Rather, her legislative efforts focused on agriculture, education, conservation of soil, water, and wildlife, roads, prison reform, and World War II veterans' affairs. During Colson's last term in the House, the *Dallas Morning News* described Colson, Waxahachie representative Rae Files Still, and Winnsboro representative Elizabeth Suiter as keeping "the welfare of their sex in mind, but none can be classified as ardent feminists. . . . Contrary to the reputation of women for talking, the three female legislators probably do less public speaking than the average male member. But all three are noted as capable advocates and effective sponsors for bills. Unlike some men in the Legislature, they sponsor few bills, and effectively work for their adoption." None of the women, the paper continued, "advocates the election of women to office unless they are better qualified than the male candidates."[4]

When she entered the Senate, Colson made a point of refusing favors offered by her colleagues because of her gender. She rejected a large office near the Senate floor because it was traditionally reserved for senior senators. Instead, she accepted an office with three flights of stairs (and no elevator) between it and the Senate chamber. She was careful with her appearance and once told a friend that she wanted her thirty male colleagues to know there was a lady present. One newspaper reported that Colson experienced no prejudice from male senators and speculated that this was probably because of her "attitude" on the Senate floor: "I say as little as I can on the floor," she said, perhaps revealing the reason she had also been relatively quiet in the House, "because the men always stop and listen when they hear a woman's voice." The *Dallas Morning News* described Senator Colson as acting like a lady and voting like a man.[5]

Colson passed a high percentage of her bills. In her first House term, she sponsored or co-sponsored eight bills, and seven became law. She had promised voters she would "get them out of the mud" by having county roads paved, and her greatest success in keeping this promise came in 1946 when she sponsored a joint resolution that became the "good roads amendment." It dedicated three-fourths of all motor fuel taxes and vehicle registration fees to constructing and maintaining highways and the remaining one-fourth to the state's Available School Fund for education. She became the first female representative to pass a constitutional amendment. In the Senate she was proud of her sponsorship of what became the Colson-Briscoe Act, which established the farm-to-market road system in Texas. In eighteen years in the Senate, sixty-seven of the eighty-three bills for which she was sole or primary sponsor passed, a rate of 81 percent.[6]

Colson sometimes served on a majority of the existing committees, as in the 54th Legislature, when she was on twenty of thirty-seven Senate committees. Senate colleagues unanimously elected her president pro tempore of the Senate in 1955, and, as third in succession, she was "governor for a day" five times. In 1959 Colson was appointed one of three Senate members to the Coordinating Commission for State Health and Welfare Services, a body created by a measure she had sponsored. In 1960 the *Progressive Farmer* named her "Woman of the Year."[7]

Colson took pride in being "the only full-time Senator in Texas," having no other employment. She once estimated she averaged driving 2,000 miles per month at a time when senators' pay was ten dollars per day. Colson was able to serve full time only because of her parents' financial support; her mother also managed all of Colson's campaigns except her last, in 1966, the only campaign Colson lost.[8] In response to a U.S. Supreme Court decision and civil rights legislation, the Texas Senate redistricted in 1965 to increase the proportion of urban districts to rural districts. As a result, Colson had to campaign against fellow senator Bill Moore the next year. She was concerned about her mother's health and was possibly too complacent because of her past margins of victory. But Colson's refusal to support a state Equal Legal Rights Amendment (ELRA) may have been the ultimate cause of her defeat. Supporters of an ELRA, under the leadership of attorney Hermine Tobolowsky and the Texas Federation of Business and Professional Women's Clubs (BPW) had first introduced it in the legislature in 1959, to a quick defeat. But the BPW continued to introduce it in every session and support for it had grown. By 1966, the BPW had developed a successful strategy for targeting and defeating legislators who opposed or ignored it. That year, Colson's stand came under their scrutiny. The BPW threw its support behind Moore; he won, ending Colson's twenty-eight-year legislative career. Her mother and father died within four months of her defeat.[9]

In 1967 Neveille Colson became curator of the Sam Houston Museum, for which she had often obtained funding. She retired in 1977, soon after her seventy-fifth birthday. Shortly thereafter, she entered a Bryan nursing home where she died. The longest girder bridge in Texas, near historic Washington-on-the-Brazos, was named the Neveille H. Colson Bridge in recognition of her contributions to Texas roads.[10]

NOTES

1. "Mrs. Neveille H. Colson," campaign biography, c. 1963, Woman's Collection, Texas Woman's University, Denton; David Mauzy, draft of history of Texas women legislators, typescript, [1996], Senate Research Office, State of Texas, pp. 57–58, Edith Wilmans Collection, Archives Division, Texas State Library, Austin; Sherilyn Brandenstein, "Esther Neveille Higgs Colson," *New Handbook of Texas*, 2:232.

2. For an analysis of "the doldrums," see Leila J. Rupp and Verta Taylor, *Survival in the Doldrums: The American Women's Movement, 1945 to the 1960s*.

3. Mauzy, draft, p. 63.

4. *Dallas Morning News*, February 2, 1947; Brandenstein, "Colson," p. 232.

5. Mauzy, draft, p. 63; *Houston Chronicle*, April 19, 1953; *Dallas Morning News*, January 11, 1949.

6. Mauzy, draft, pp. 59–70; "Mrs. Neveille H. Colson"; Brandenstein, "Colson," p. 233.

7. "Mrs. Neveille H. Colson"; Mauzy, draft, p. 70; *Navasota Examiner*, January 28, 1960; Brandenstein, "Colson," p. 233.

8. "Mrs. Neveille H. Colson"; Mauzy, draft, p. 64.

9. Mauzy, draft, pp. 75–76; Judie Karen Walton Gammage, "Quest for Equality: An Historical Overview of Women's Rights Activism in Texas, 1890–1975" (Ph.D. diss., North Texas State University, 1982), pp. 139–144, 165. Gammage credits the BPW with also helping to defeat Senator William Fly in 1960, Senator Wardlow Lane in 1962 (and preventing Senator Crawford Martin from becoming lieutenant governor), and Representative James Cotten in 1964.

10. Mauzy, draft, p. 77; "Mrs. Neveille H. Colson."

☆

RAE MANDETTE FILES (STILL)

HOUSE 47th–51st Legislatures (1941–1951)
Democrat, Waxahachie
DISTRICT 100-1, 101-1
COMMITTEES Agriculture; Banks and
Banking; Claims and Accounts; Federal
Affairs (Vice Chair); Constitutional
Amendments; Interstate Cooperation;
Education (Chair)

DATES 1907–April 8, 1991
BIRTHPLACE Hill County

FAMILY Forest Still; no children
EDUCATION University of Texas (B.A., 1934; M.A., 1949)
OCCUPATION Teacher

RAE FILES STILL's greatest legislative achievement was successfully sponsoring the massive educational reform measures known as the Gilmer-Aikin laws. She decided to run for the legislature in 1940 after a speech she made advocating U.S. neutrality in the event of war brought her wide public support. Using the slogan "Let a woman put your House in order," she campaigned against three male opponents, limiting her expenses to the three hundred dollars required by state law. Some voters supported her, but others opposed her candidacy because of her gender: "Woman's place is not in the legislature," said one male farmer, "woman's place is in the field." During the heat of summer Files spoke in a different town every night. She found that being a woman running against three men was an advantage; people listened to her out of curiosity. She went door to door; walked through plowed fields; rode hay balers, tractors, and thrashers; and visited numerous country stores. She defeated all of her opponents in the Democratic primary and then won the runoff by sixty votes. She ran unopposed in the general election.[1]

During her first term, Files and Neveille Colson were the only women in the House. There were never more than four women in the legislature at any one time while she served. Nevertheless, she quickly earned a reputation for speaking openly in the face of opposition, regardless of the opponent. As a freshman, she described Governor W. Lee (Pappy) O'Daniel as "a man who has forced me to despise him" for his unrelenting criticism of the legislature for what he perceived to be its unethical and unbusinesslike behavior. After O'Daniel used his weekly radio broadcast to tell elderly listeners that legislators were refusing to pay pensions, she wrote an open letter describing the governor's actions as a betrayal of the legislature. When one of the governor's supporters in the House described her actions as a spontaneous outburst, Files replied that it was "done deliberately and with malice aforethought. . . . I will never allow anyone to make disparaging remarks about the legislature without challenging them." During her second term, she was one of a minority of representatives to vote against inviting O'Daniel, then a U.S. senator, to address the legislature, saying, "There's no use wasting our time and his."[2]

As fear of communism spread in the 1940s and 1950s, Rae Files Still opposed a bill requiring teachers to take a loyalty oath and suspending them for teaching "theories of other governments" opposed to the U.S., calling it a "direct slap at the Americanism of Texas schoolteachers." She supported a measure, originally sponsored unsuccessfully by Dallas representative Edith Wilmans two decades earlier, to require women as well as men to be examined for venereal disease to receive a marriage license. She sponsored successful measures requiring the same fees for issuing birth and death certificates; providing credit within the Teacher Retirement System for educators' time served in the military, Red Cross, or war-related work; requiring care and upkeep of public cemeteries; increasing the tax rate that school districts could levy; regulating the process of bringing children into the state for adoption; and appropriating nearly $2 million for agricultural, home economics, and vocational education courses in public schools. One of the unsuccessful measures she sponsored required child support payments by the parent without custody. Judge Sarah T. Hughes, who had originally sponsored a similar bill while she was a representative, asked Still to sponsor the new bill because she believed Still would support it "more vigorously" than any member of her own Dallas delegation. Although all the women in the House supported the measure, it failed. Still also supported a law allowing women to serve as jurors in Texas, saying, "Women live under our laws, enjoy their privileges, and are punished by them. Their responsibility in maintaining our system of law is the same as any man's."[3]

Early in 1945, shortly after University of Texas regents fired university president Homer P. Rainey for supporting academic freedom and, in particular, for refusing to ban the John Dos Passos novel *U.S.A.* in English classes, Files introduced a bill to establish motion picture censorship boards throughout the state. It required at least three women to serve on each of thirty-one boards and empowered the Texas Rangers to close theaters that refused to remove films the boards censored. The bill was probably a facetious retort to university regent D. F. Strickland, a prominent attorney in the motion picture business. It incurred much debate that echoed the acrimonious battle between Rainey and the regents over censorship and was eventually killed in committee.[4]

Without question, Rae Files Still's most successful effort was the passage in 1949 of the Gilmer-Aikin laws, which replaced an elected state superintendent of public instruction with a commissioner of education appointed by an elected twenty-one-member State Board of Education (subject to confirmation by the state Senate); consolidated the state's 4,500 school districts into 2,900; authorized state funding, based on attendance instead of enrollment, to supplement and equalize local taxes; raised teacher salaries; guaranteed children access to twelve years of public schooling; and defined the length of the school year.[5]

The laws were the result of a study of the state of public education in Texas conducted by an interim committee on which Still served in 1947 and 1948. As the only House member who served on that committee, and as chair of the House Education Committee, Still assumed leadership for passing the Gilmer-Aikin bills. Longtime state superintendent L. A. Woods, who opposed them, marshaled support from among teachers, superintendents, and other educators to pressure House members to defeat the proposals. In a parliamentary maneuver that allowed Still to remain chair of the Education Committee while her own legislation was considered by it, and because the committee's vice chair opposed the

measures, she waited until the bills had passed the Senate before conducting a House hearing, then used Senate rather than House versions.
Hundreds of people attended the hearing of March 16, 1949, and it lasted
all night, apparently a first in the history of the legislature. Opponents
claimed the measures were communistic and a personal assault on Woods.[6]

Although ultimately successful, the Gilmer-Aikin fight and the influence of the lobby convinced Still that she did not want to return to the
House. Instead, the "Waxahachie bombshell," as she was called by the
Austin American, returned to teaching and completed her master's degree, writing a thesis that was published in 1950 as *The Gilmer-Aikin Bills:
A Study in the Legislative Process*. The book is still regarded as an important record of not only the battle that resulted in the most comprehensive
education reform in the state to that time, but also the inside workings of
the legislature. She taught in Waxahachie and Dallas and received an
award from the Texas State Teachers Association in 1956. In the 1960s
she taught in Germany and traveled through Europe. She retired in 1975
and died in 1991, as the Texas Legislature debated funding for public
education.[7]

NOTES

1. David Mauzy, draft of history of Texas women legislators, typescript, [1996], Senate Research Office, State of Texas, pp. 79–81, Edith Wilmans Collection, Archives Division, Texas State Library, Austin; *Austin American*, May 27, 1945. Rae Files married
Forest Still on May 27, 1945, at the end of the 49th Legislature. We refer to her as "Files"
for events occurring before her marriage and as "Still" after her marriage.

2. Mauzy, draft, pp. 83, 87.

3. Ibid., pp. 84–88; *Daily Texan*, May 16, 1946.

4. *Dallas Morning News*, January 30, 1945; *Austin American*, May 15, 1945.

5. Oscar Mauzy, "Gilmer-Aikin Laws," *New Handbook of Texas*, 3:172.

6. Mauzy, draft, pp. 90–93; *Austin American*, March 30, 1949.

7. Mauzy, draft, pp. 93–94; *Austin American*, May 24, 1950, January 11, 1951; *Dallas Morning News*, January 20, 1949.

FLORENCE FENLEY

HOUSE 48th–49th Legislatures (1943–1947)
Democrat, Uvalde
DISTRICT 77
COMMITTEES Common Carriers; Liquor
Regulation; Motor Transportation;
Public Health; Livestock and Stock
Raising; Penitentiaries; Examination of
Comptroller's and Treasurer's Accounts;
Appropriations

DATES December 19, 1898–May 27, 1971
BIRTHPLACE Uvalde
FAMILY Arthur Wilson (died); twice
divorced; seven children
EDUCATION College of Industrial Arts
(1916?)
OCCUPATION Folklorist; journalist

FLORENCE FENLEY was a folklorist and chronicler of ranching and ranch culture who supported herself as a writer for the *Uvalde Leader-News*, producing a column called "Old Trails" and countless other features. She also wrote feature stories for several magazines, including *The Cattleman*, *True West*, and *Frontier Times*. She spoke Spanish fluently, and she used her birth name Fenley throughout her life, adding a "Mrs.," she said, for her children's sake. Her early life was punctuated with death and disappointment. Her young mother died when Florence was a child, and Florence and her sister were raised by grandparents. Her father was shot to death when she was fourteen, and her first husband, Arthur Wilson, whom she married in 1916, was fatally shot during a range feud as Florence watched. Two more marriages ended in divorce, leaving her a single mother with seven children to raise during the Depression.[1]

Fenley first made a name for herself in the Uvalde area by recording the stories of area pioneers. First published in the *Leader-News*, the sketches were later collected in the book *Oldtimers* and published by the newspaper in 1939. Historian J. Frank Dobie reviewed it positively, contributing to Fenley's growing reputation as a folklorist.[2] An accomplished horsewoman, she rode the eighty-five miles from Uvalde to San Antonio and into the lobby of the Gunter Hotel in 1940, followed by a *Leader-News* photographer, to register for the Old Trail Drivers Association convention. The publicity stunt earned her election as Sweetheart of the Old Trail Drivers and the International Cowboy's Association.[3]

In 1942 she defeated the incumbent to became the first woman elected to represent District 77 in the Texas House, crediting elderly voters with her victory.[4] Her platform promised a businesslike approach to state government and assured voters that she had made no political promises other than working "in behalf of the aged people who helped to bring to you your present prosperity."[5] Three of her sons were serving in World War II at the time, and Fenley brought her two youngest children to Austin with her. She sponsored legislation that focused on rural and agricultural issues such as re-recording marks and brands, creating closed fishing seasons in her district, exempting counties in her district from the inspection of hides and animals, and making the killing of javelina illegal.[6]

At the end of her second term, Fenley returned to Uvalde and to writing, serving as president of the Texas Woman's Press Association (TWPA).[7] In 1957 the *Leader-News* published her second book, *Oldtimers of the Southwest*, with an introduction by former vice president John Nance Garner. The following year the book won a statewide award from TWPA.[8] After Fenley's death, U.S. representative O. C. Fisher read a tribute to her into the *Congressional Record*. A final book, *Heart Full of Horses*, a selection of stories she had collected from a variety of riders, was published posthumously in 1975.

NOTES

1. Lora B. Garrison, "Who Was Florence Fenley?" in *Oldtimers*, by Florence Fenley (Uvalde: Hornby Press, 1939; rpt., Uvalde: Sabinal Canyon Chapter of the Daughters of the American Revolution, 1991), excerpted in *Uvalde Leader-News*, September 12, 1991; *State Observer*, February 1, 1943.

2. Garrison, "Who Was Florence Fenley?"

3. *Uvalde Leader-News*, October 25, 1940.

4. *The Lasso*, November 27, 1942.

5. *Uvalde Leader-News*, June 5, 1942.

6. David Mauzy, draft of history of Texas women legislators, typescript, [1996], Senate Research Office, State of Texas, pp. 96–97, Edith Wilmans Collection, Archives Division, Texas State Library, Austin.

7. *Uvalde Leader-News*, April 11, 1957.

8. *Kinney County News*, April 11, 1958.

MARY ELIZABETH SUITER

HOUSE 48th–50th Legislatures (1943–1949)
Democrat, Winnsboro
DISTRICT 34
COMMITTEES Judicial Districts; Judiciary
(Vice Chair); Education; Rules; Federal
Relations; Uniform State Laws; Public
Health; Privileges; Suffrage and Elections

DATES October 6, 1911–October 14, 1964
BIRTHPLACE Unknown
FAMILY Single; no children
EDUCATION University of Texas at Austin
(B.A., 1934; J.D., 1934)
OCCUPATION Attorney

ELIZABETH SUITER, the first female attorney in Wood County, served
three terms in the legislature, following in the footsteps of her father,
Will Suiter, who served in the Texas Senate from 1915 to 1923. His reputation for opposing woman suffrage was based on his belief that the question should be put to a public vote. He did vote, however, to ratify the
19th Amendment (woman suffrage) to the U.S. Constitution. As his child,
Elizabeth spent many hours in the capitol and grew up feeling comfortable with the idea of going there herself. She later told people she had
grown up on the floor of the Senate. She served as a Senate clerk for the
State Affairs Committee in the called sessions of the 44th Legislature in
the mid-1930s. She also practiced law with her father in Winnsboro.[1]

After an unsuccessful bid for the House in 1940 (she lost the Democratic primary runoff by twenty-nine votes), Suiter ran again in 1942, on
a platform of economy in wartime, and won, defeating a teacher from
Alba. Although she supported Prohibition, as had her father, she was
apparently uninterested in resurrecting the state prohibition law he had
helped pass. She said she most enjoyed her work on the House Judiciary
Committee, of which she was vice chair. Legislation she sponsored successfully included measures to clarify the names of insured on insurance
policies, to regulate insurance companies, and to reorganize the Special
District Court of Smith County.[2]

With Florence Fenley and Rae Files (Still), Suiter co-sponsored a law
to ease statutory requirements on married women with property, but it
failed. She also tried unsuccessfully to abolish gender-based discriminatory wage rates and to require that an assault by an employee of a state

eleemosynary institution be defined as aggravated assault. The *Dallas Morning News* described her as believing that women should not be elected to office "unless they are better qualified than the male candidates." She said, "Women should take a greater interest in politics, but not necessarily as organized groups." The paper further described Suiter and her colleagues Still and Neveille Colson as women who "keep the welfare of their sex in mind, but none can be classified as ardent feminists."[3]

Suiter did not run for a fourth term. She returned to Winnsboro to resume her law practice and care for her invalid father. In 1963 she was elected mayor of Winnsboro.

NOTES

1. David Mauzy, draft of history of Texas women legislators, typescript, [1996], Senate Research Office, State of Texas, pp. 97–98, Edith Wilmans Collection, Archives Division, Texas State Library, Austin.

2. Ibid., p. 98; *Dallas Morning News*, August 9, 1942, February 2, 1947.

3. Mauzy, draft, p. 98; *Dallas Morning News*, February 2, 1947.

☆

MARIAN ISABEL (MARIBELLE) HAMBLEN STEWART (MILLS REICH)

SENATE 50th Legislature (1947–1948)
Democrat, Houston
DISTRICT 16
COMMITTEES None

DATES December 1, 1912–April 8, 1991
BIRTHPLACE Houston
FAMILY W. Lacy Stewart (died); W. J. Mills (died); Carl J. Reich; one son
EDUCATION Unknown
OCCUPATION Clerk of court of civil appeals

MARIBELLE STEWART was the second woman elected to the Senate, on April 19, 1947, in a special election to fill the seat left vacant when her husband, W. Lacy Stewart, died on March 22, early in his term.[1] When Neveille Colson was elected in 1948, it appeared that two women would serve in the Senate at the same time when the legislature convened in

119

January 1949.[2] Stewart could have served throughout 1950, when her husband's original term expired, but in December 1948 she married Houston attorney W. J. Mills and resigned the seat, citing "personal reasons." Because she served only six weeks and there was no special session, it is unlikely that Maribelle Stewart introduced any legislation or served on any committees. Governor Beauford H. Jester called a special election to fill the vacancy, and attorney Searcy Bracewell won the election, becoming the Senate's youngest member. Stewart later served as clerk of the first court of civil appeals in Harris County. Her last residence was in Seabrook.[3]

NOTES

1. Senate Concurrent Resolution 213, *72nd Legislature, Regular Session Resolutions*, p. 3348; *Houston Chronicle*, April 9, 1991.

2. *Dallas Morning News*, August 8, 1948.

3. *Dallas Morning News*, December 10, December 12, and December 19, 1948, May 6, 1949; Senate Concurrent Resolution 213, p. 3348; *Houston Chronicle*, April 9, 1991.

☆

PERSIS JONES HENDERSON

HOUSE 51st Legislature (1949–1951)
Democrat, Groesbeck
DISTRICT 61
COMMITTEES Public Health; Insurance; Game and Fish; Common Carriers; Liquor Regulation; Water Conservation

DATES June 20, 1895–May 25, 1972
BIRTHPLACE Roswell, New Mexico
FAMILY A. Robin Henderson (died); two children; two stepchildren
EDUCATION Unknown
OCCUPATION Insurance

PERSIS JONES HENDERSON was drafted by hundreds of supporters of her late husband, Representative A. Robin Henderson, to run for his House seat after he died suddenly in March 1949, early in his third term. She handily won the special election of April 11, 1949 (listed on the ballot as "Mrs. A. Robin Henderson"), and became the third woman in the 51st Legislature, joining Rae Files Still in the House and Neveille Colson, who had just begun her first term in the Senate after five terms in the House.[1] Prior to taking her seat, Henderson had served as president of the Representatives' Wives Club. She was greeted with gentlemanly concern by her colleagues, who urged her to "take it easy; and any time you want any help, you just call on us."[2]

Henderson regarded her purpose in the House as completing her husband's unfinished agenda, which included the financing of rural roads and state welfare assistance for those physically or mentally handicapped. "I will try my best to carry out his program," she said.[3] By the end of the session, Henderson reflected that roughly two-thirds of it had been completed. Because she knew A. R. Henderson had opposed the Gilmer-Aikin package of three education reform bills sponsored by Still, Persis Henderson voted against them. She also supported annual sessions of the legislature and an increase in legislative salaries. She assisted with the passage of a bill to remove disparities in two state retirement systems, perhaps in response to a female constituent who had worked for the state for twenty-two years and had difficulty obtaining an equitable pension.[4]

In her sixties, Henderson found the life of a representative "strenuous" and one that "requires rigid attention." Her most difficult lesson, she said, was not letting personalities take precedence over issues. Nevertheless, she enjoyed her brief time in the House and recommended that more women try it: "I recommend this service to other women. Politics aren't quite as dirty as dish washing. Also, it isn't as hard on my hands."[5] She added that women were more economically minded than men, a reference to the financial woes of the session just ending, and that government needed more women, perhaps in reference to her personal concern about the care of the mentally incapacitated and the need for remedial legislation. During the special session of 1950, the legislature passed a tax bill of one cent per cigarette pack to establish a permanent building fund for eleemosynary institutions and a 10 percent increase in appropriations to keep those institutions running.[6]

In January 1950 Henderson announced for re-election to a full term and drew three male opponents. Not quite four months later, she withdrew her candidacy. Citing low legislative pay and the high cost of living in Austin, Henderson said she had to use her time to add to her income. The same day, the editor of the local paper stressed Henderson's important role in the special session, particularly with regard to the state school at Mexia. Henderson moved to Alabama to live with her daughter, then lived in Minnesota.[7]

NOTES

1. *Austin American*, March 19 and April 14, 1949; David Mauzy, draft of history of Texas women legislators, typescript, [1996], Senate Research Office, State of Texas, p. 101, Edith Wilmans Collection, Archives Division, Texas State Library, Austin.

2. *Dallas Morning News*, April 14, 1949.

3. *Groesbeck Journal*, April 14, 1949; *Austin American*, March 18 and April 15, 1949.

4. *Groesbeck Journal*, May 8 and June 16, 1949.

5. *Austin American*, June 19, 1949.

6. *Groesbeck Journal*, March 2, 1950.

7. *Groesbeck Journal*, January 12 and April 27, 1950, June 1, 1972.

DOROTHY GILLIS GURLEY (CAUTHORN)

HOUSE 52nd–53rd Legislatures (1951–1955)
Democrat, Del Rio
DISTRICT 87
COMMITTEES Legislative Council; Congressional and Legislative Districts; Conservation and Reclamation (Chair); Game and Fish; Motor Traffic; State Affairs; Rules

DATES March 14, 1924–
BIRTHPLACE Del Rio
FAMILY Charles Robert Gurley (died); Virgil Cauthorn; two children
EDUCATION University of Texas (B.A., 1944)
OCCUPATION Rancher

DOROTHY GILLIS GURLEY was the first woman elected to the Texas House from her district. She attended law school but did not graduate because she married and her husband was transferred out of Texas. She said later that her experience in law school and running for various offices as a student stimulated her interest in serving in government. Her grandfather, father, and brother were also politically active, thus contributing to her sense that she had "always been political minded."[1]

Gurley wanted to run for the legislature in 1948, but said she was dissuaded by "some prominent Del Rio people," including a district judge who told her a woman could never be elected in that district.[2] With help from her father, she ran anyway in 1950, at age twenty-six, married, and with a baby. Conducting a hand-shaking campaign in one of the state's largest districts, 300 miles along the Rio Grande River, she beat two male opponents in the Democratic primary without a runoff. It may also have helped that she spoke Spanish.[3] "Of course, my opponents told people I should stay home with my husband and baby," she said after her victory. She ran for her second term without opposition.[4]

Despite her youth, Gurley was effective from the beginning of her legislative career. She said she was "not up here to champion women's rights. . . . I'm just interested in doing a good job." She stated that she intended to "take things as they come" and did not plan to sponsor any legislation.[5] But according to an article headlined "Pretty Young Ranch Wife Scores Legislative First," Gurley's bill to change the term of the court in her district was the second to pass in that session.[6] During her second term she chaired the Conservation and Reclamation Committee when it handled an unusually heavy load of sixty bills, including a successful one of her own to permit landowners to build 200-acre-feet ponds on their lands without a water board permit. She was also successful in passing legislation that changed the term of the 63rd District Court and that related to trapping "varmints." In a special resolution, the House commended Gurley for "the skillful leadership of [the] extremely capable chairman." During legislative sessions, Gurley brought her family and a Mexican American housekeeper to an Austin apartment and went home on weekends to run the ranch and see constituents.[7]

The *San Antonio Evening News* called her the "Legislature's Glamour Gal" and reported that legislators "gallantly swarm about her chair, whistle and applaud when she gets up to speak." As with other women in the legislature, newspapers frequently referred to Gurley's appearance and gender. The *Houston Chronicle* and the *Austin American* both ran an Associated Press story describing her as "a ranch girl . . . and a good-looking brunette." The *American* reported that she was the only one of four women in the House who was married and that her husband was sometimes teased about whether he would form a legislative husbands' club like the legislative wives' club.[8] Although Gurley said of her gender, "if women are capable, they should be able to show their capabilities on an equal basis with men," she assured reporters that she was not elected to "champion women's rights." Headlines often reflected this aspect of interviews with her, assuring readers that she was "No Feminist" and that she "Asks No Favor."[9] The *Chronicle* said that "like other women in the legislature,

Mrs. Gurley is . . . proud of the fact that she can stand on her own ability and wants no special consideration." She added that "there is no discrimination" in the House.[10] However, Anita Blair, with whom Gurley served during her second term, recalled that Gurley was "deliberately bedeviled by some of the legislators" over a water bill affecting her ranch. "She had to break down and cry before they would pass that bill," Blair said.[11]

Gurley contemplated a third term, but, possibly because of her daughter's young age, she decided not to seek one. After leaving the legislature, Gurley helped run the family ranch and remained active in local politics in Del Rio and Val Verde County, including service as chair of the Democratic Party. In the 1970s and 1980s, she sometimes cared for her grandson while his mother, Susan Gurley McBee, served in the House representing District 70.[12]

NOTES

1. *Houston Chronicle*, January 10, 1951, April 22, 1953; Dorothy Gillis Gurley Cauthorn, resume.

2. *Dallas Morning News*, January 10, 1951; *Austin Statesman*, March 17, 1954.

3. *Dallas Morning News*, January 10, 1951; *Houston Chronicle*, January 10, 1951; *Austin American*, January 10, 1951.

4. *Houston Chronicle*, January 10, 1951; *Austin American*, January 10, 1951; *San Antonio Evening News*, January 22, 1953.

5. *Houston Chronicle*, January 10, 1951; *Austin American*, January 10, 1951; *Dallas Morning News*, January 10, 1951.

6. *Dallas Morning News*, February 1, 1951.

7. *Austin American*, June 17, 1953; *Del Rio News Herald*, May 24, 1953; *San Antonio Evening News*, January 22, 1953; Susan Gurley McBee to Ruthe Winegarten, June 18, 1997.

8. *Austin American*, January 10, 1951; *Houston Chronicle*, January 10, 1951; *San Antonio Evening News*, January 22, 1953; *Austin American*, June 17, 1953.

9. *Austin American*, January 10, 1951.

10. *Houston Chronicle*, April 22, 1953.

11. Anita Blair, telephone interview by Ruthe Winegarten, July 14, 1995.

12. *Austin American*, June 17, 1953; McBee to Winegarten; *Del Rio News Herald*, October 3, 1976, June 25, 1978.

VIRGINIA ELIZABETH DUFF

HOUSE 52nd–57th Legislatures (1951–1963)
Democrat, Ferris
DISTRICT 100, 52
COMMITTEES Privileges; Suffrage and
Elections; State Hospitals and Special
Schools (Chair); Penitentiaries (Chair);
Traffic Safety

DATES August 26, 1920–
BIRTHPLACE Ferris
FAMILY Single; no children
EDUCATION Trinity University (B.A., 1942);
Southern Methodist University (J.D., 1948)
OCCUPATION Teacher; laboratory assistant

VIRGINIA DUFF, who characterized herself as "little, but loud," was the first woman to succeed a woman from the same district in the Texas House: she followed Rae Files Still, from Ellis County, in 1951. During her twelve years in campaigning for and serving in the legislature, Duff never accepted donations—she ran on her own money and used vacation time accrued on her job. She financed her first campaign for $192 and said that modern campaigns on TV and radio would be "out of reason with my pocketbook."[1] She knocked on doors throughout the county, put ads in newspapers, and made countless speeches, one of the most popular being "Our Laws and Statutes in Accord with the Ten Commandments."[2] She said no organized groups or staff helped her. Only Duff's mother went with her to campaign, and only snakes and dogs bothered her as she went from house to house. Once she almost stepped on a water moccasin, and another time a dog almost tore her dress off. In another instance, a voter offered her a dip of snuff.[3] Her only runoff was in her first campaign, which ended in victory on her thirtieth birthday. After that, she won comfortably until she lost in her seventh run for the House.[4]

Duff came from a political family. Both her grandfather, Hans Smith, who came to Texas in 1846, and her uncle, Bowd Farrar, served in the Texas Legislature.[5] There were fewer than half a dozen women in her evening law classes, but "nobody told me that it was odd that I wanted to do that. I just did it,"[6] she said. She taught fifth grade at Hutchins School in Dallas County and was a laboratory assistant for Magnolia (later Mobil) Oil Corporation in Dallas, but she never actively practiced law.[7] Much of her life she lived as a companion to her widowed mother on the family's blackland farm between Ferris and Waxahachie.[8]

At age twelve, Duff campaigned for her uncle, who was running for road commissioner. Her childhood ambition was to be in the legislature. When she took the Texas Bar Examination, which was held in the House chamber, Duff said, "I decided I wanted to come down and sit as a representative in one of those chairs." Duff ran unsuccessfully for justice of the peace in 1946 to gain experience and meet voters. In 1950 she campaigned strenuously in her first legislative race, giving speeches every night for three weeks and three speeches on July 4.[9] She defeated two men, one of whom campaigned against her with the slogan, "We don't need a petticoat in the legislature." During Duff's political career, she sometimes opposed as many as four men, but never another woman. One man ran against her four times, complaining that her work in the oil industry was a conflict of interest.[10]

On her first day on the House floor in 1951, Duff wore a black, two-piece suit, corsage, and a white felt hat. "We wore hats every day, she recalled." She and colleague Dorothy Gillis Gurley, the only other female representative, were "swamped with flowers" from lobbyists and other representatives. Duff said she intended simply to listen and learn during that session.[11] Although the chamber smelled of cigar smoke and spittoons dotted the floor, Duff said she did not notice "any difference being a woman serving in the legislature. I did not expect any special favors, and I do not know that any . . . were extended to me. I do know that we were very highly respected."[12] The *Austin Statesman* said she was probably the tiniest representative in the history of the Texas Legislature, standing just under five feet and weighing ninety-one pounds. Years later that paper called her "the Sweetheart of the House" and cautioned readers, "Don't let size, gentle look fool you. Virginia Duff fights mansize politically."[13]

Duff said she was "never a crusader for women's rights," explaining, "I had nothing against those who were crusading. But I was just here to represent my district." She recalled, however, that former representative Sarah T. Hughes "was somewhat of a crusader for women's rights. And I cooperated fairly well with . . . what they [Hughes and the League of Business and Professional Women] were asking for."[14] Duff was responsive to the needs of her constituents. She recalled visiting with senior citizens at local domino parlors where they compared old age assistance payments. "If one received more than another, then I was called upon to find out why." In one case, the cost of a man's large aspirin dosage had been eliminated from his pension. In another case, Duff was able to get a mentally retarded boy into an appropriate state school.[15]

Duff was particularly concerned about eleemosynary institutions as well as help for farmers and teachers. Her main legislative goal was to improve the mental hospital system, and she successfully sponsored a bill to grant state hospitals and special schools the power to create a special school for "the mentally retarded."[16] She also sponsored legislation that created the Denton State School and improved facilities in prisons, including an appropriation for a gymnasium for the Gainesville State School for Girls. She was especially proud of sponsoring the legislation that requires motor vehicles to stop rather than pass school buses taking on or letting off children. This came as a result of the deaths of two children in her district. In addition, her House Bill 159 required publication of annual financial statements for each school district and junior college. She also sponsored legislation aimed at stopping theft of oil and gas maps by imposing prison sentences and fines of up to ten years in prison and $5,000, but it failed in the House.[17]

After the Supreme Court's 1954 decision in *Brown vs. Board of Education of Topeka*, which outlawed school segregation of African Americans, Duff took a leading role in attempting to block their integration into public schools. "The people in the South have been in despair" since *Brown*, she said, and, at least in part because black students outnumbered whites in her own district, she sponsored a bill "to keep blacks out of our schools."[18] The bill was part of a pro-segregation package that resulted from recommendations by Governor Allan Shivers' Advisory Committee on Segregation in Public Schools, of which Duff was the vice chair.[19] The committee's 1956 report recommended that the state force local schools to establish (or reestablish) segregated schools, to prohibit the counting of whites in black schools (or blacks in white schools), and to deny student transfers. The same year, a number of Texas districts desegregated quietly, but at Mansfield, southeast of Fort Worth, mobs responded to desegregation with violence and signs reading, "A dead nigger is the best nigger." In a move that may have inspired Arkansas governor Orville Faubus, Governor Shivers sent the Texas Rangers to prevent integration.[20]

But Shivers was defeated by the more moderate Price Daniel that fall, and the 55th Legislature that convened in 1957 found itself embroiled in debates over segregation. The package of bills recommended by Duff's advisory committee was designed to preserve the state's dual school system or "strike a death blow at the NAACP," which many legislators believed was controlled by communists. Duff designed the "comprehensive bill" (House Bill 231) that featured a placement plan whereby pupils would be assigned on the basis of seventeen factors, excluding race, and segregationist parents would be allowed to withdraw their children from integrated schools. Another of Duff's bills would have allowed local school districts to do away with compulsory public education rather than desegregate. Other bills in the package would have required all people advocating integration to register with the secretary of state; denied state employment to members of the NAACP; allocated state funds for private schools receiving students who had left integrating schools; and withheld funding from integrated schools. Only three of the bills, including House Bill 231, passed, in part because of filibusters organized by the first Latino elected to the Texas Senate in the twentieth century, Henry B. Gonzalez of San Antonio. Daniel signed Duff's bill and the two others, but they were never carried out.[21]

During sessions, Duff lived in a room at the Stephen F. Austin Hotel for $3.15 a night during regular sessions and $5.00 during special sessions, all paid for from her legislative salary of $10 per day. She said she lost money while being a legislator because her employer, Magnolia Oil, did not pay her salary during sessions. Duff's 1962 campaign, her seventh and last, was unsuccessful. She described her opponent as a "very nice young man" who campaigned in his National Guard uniform and observed that her voters simply felt she had held the job long enough. After leaving the legislature, Duff was locally active in the Daughters of the American Revolution, served as regent and chair of the Good Citizen Committee, trustee and clerk of the Presbyterian Church, chair of the Ellis County Historical Commission, and state member of Delta Kappa Gamma. She retired from Mobil Oil in 1976. She lived with her mother until the 1970s when they moved to Ferris. Her mother, "a great stabilizer" for Duff, lived to be almost 102.[22]

NOTES

1. Virginia Duff, videotape interview by Ruthe Winegarten, May 25, 1995, Archives for Research on Women and Gender, University of Texas at San Antonio (hereafter ARWG); *Austin Statesman*, March 31, 1954.

2. "Personality of the Month: Miss Virginia Duff of Ferris," *Ellis County Woman Magazine*, October 1951, p. 11.

3. *Austin Statesman*, January 13, 1961.

4. Duff, interview, ARWG.

5. *Ellis County Woman Magazine*, p. 10; *Dallas Morning News*, January 10, 1951.

6. *Waxahachie Daily Light*, February 27, 1994.

7. Virginia Duff, "Questionnaire," prepared and administered by Nancy Baker Jones and Ruthe Winegarten, 1997.

8. *Ellis County Woman Magazine*, p. 10.

9. Duff, interview, ARWG; *Ellis County Woman Magazine*, p. 11.

10. *Fort Worth Star-Telegram*, January 9, 1951; Duff, interview, ARWG.

11. *Dallas Morning News*, January 10, 1951; *Waxahachie Daily Light*, February 27, 1994.

12. Duff, interview, ARWG.

13. *Austin Statesman*, March 31, 1954, January 13, 1961; *Waxahachie Daily Light*, February 27, 1994.

14. Duff, interview, ARWG.

15. Ibid.

16. *Dallas Morning News*, April 27, 1957.

17. Duff, interview, ARWG; *Texas Press Messenger*, February 1957; *Dallas Morning News*, February 21, 1957.

18. *Austin American*, March 14, 1957; *Dallas Morning News*, May 7, 1957; Duff, interview, ARWG.

19. *Austin American*, March 14, 1957; Duff, "Questionnaire."

20. George Norris Green, *The Establishment in Texas Politics: The Primitive Years, 1938–1957*, pp. 189–190.

21. *Austin American*, March 14 and April 9, 1957; *Dallas Morning News*, May 7, 1957; Green, *Establishment*, p. 190; *House Journal of Texas*, 55th Legislature, Regular Session, 1957, pp. 3777–3778; Ronnie Dugger, "The Segregation Filibuster of 1957," *Texas Observer*, December 27, 1974, pp. 46–47; Molly Ivins, "Listening to Henry B.," *Texas Observer*, September 26, 1997, p. 20. According to Dugger, the other senators who joined Gonzalez were Laredo's Abraham Kazen, Austin's Charles Herring, Corpus Christi's Bruce Reagan, Brownsville's Hubert Hudson, and El Paso's Frank Owen III.

22. Duff, interview, ARWG; *Waxahachie Daily Light*, February 27, 1994.

ANITA BLAIR

HOUSE 53rd Legislature (1953–1955)
Democrat, El Paso
DISTRICT 105
COMMITTEES Education; Public Lands
and Buildings; School Districts; State
Hospitals and Special Schools

DATES September 8, 1916–
BIRTHPLACE El Paso
FAMILY Divorced; no children
EDUCATION Texas College of Mines
(B.A., 1944; M.A., 1951)
OCCUPATION Consultant

ANITA BLAIR was probably the first blind woman elected to any state legislature.[1] As a representative she fought for safety legislation and rights for the disabled, supported the interests of students and teachers, and was among those who helped defeat anti-communist legislation during the Red Scare of the 1950s. With Maud Isaacks, she was one of the first two women to serve in the Texas House from the same district at the same time. It would be twenty years before two women served again from the same district at the same time (Houston's Kay Bailey [Hutchison] and Senfronia Thompson).

Blair was blinded in an auto accident in 1936. In 1940 she became the first person in El Paso to receive a guide dog, a German shepherd named Fawn. With three hundred dollars that she borrowed from a local banker, Blair embarked on a lecture tour that allowed her and Fawn to travel the country, speaking to schools and factories about traffic and employment safety. U.S. Steel Corporation eventually sponsored her efforts, allowing her to live independently, primarily in Chicago.[2] In 1946 Fawn led Blair through noise, smoke, and confusion down an eleven-flight fire escape to safety in a Chicago hotel fire in which over fifty people died.[3] The escape brought the pair national attention: Blair appeared on national radio and made a film called *A Day with Fawn*, which she used in her lectures.[4]

In 1948 the Cook County Republican Women's Committee in Chicago asked her to run for Congress, but she declined because she was a Democrat and because she believed she needed more education. In 1950 Blair set a precedent during a visit to the U.S. Senate when she successfully overcame objections to the presence of her dog in the gallery.[5] The publicity generated by that event resulted in attention from radio journalist Drew Pearson and the offer of an eye from a convict in Montana, which Blair refused. President Harry Truman appointed Blair as the only female member of the Presidential Safety Committee, and she conferred with White House staff about safety legislation pending in Congress.[6] She returned to Texas to attend graduate school and to run for the legislature, hoping ultimately to run for Congress from Texas. She ran unsuccessfully for the Texas House in 1950, then was elected in 1952. *Time* ran a story about her success called "Dark Victory."[7]

Blair brought Fawn to the House, where she sat near Blair's desk. Blair had an assistant who collected and read newspapers, bills, amendments, and mail to her. She made a Braille telephone directory and a diagram of the floor of the House and used a thirty-pound dictating machine that she carried with her.[8] Like Dorothy Gillis Gurley, Blair claimed she was not there "to crusade for women's rights," but she became co-author of an unsuccessful bill to allow women to serve on juries.[9] In addition, she sponsored bills to impose mandatory jail sentences for convicted drunk drivers and to set fixed student union fees at state universities, supported the establishment of a nursing school at Texas Western University, and succeeded in getting funds appropriated to remodel the State School for the Deaf. She also supported teacher pay raises, opposed state income and sales taxes, and helped defeat bills supporting the construction of toll roads in Texas.[10]

In her most public stand, and one that probably led to her defeat in 1954, Blair joined Dallas representative "Barefoot" Sanders, San Antonio representative Maury Maverick, Jr., and others to oppose several communist-hunting bills proposed by San Antonio representative Marshall O. Bell. Two of Bell's bills that the group succeeded in diluting or defeating sought to ban politically offensive textbooks from schools and to force school officials to identify books written by communists or "other subversives." "I'm strongly opposed to Communism," Blair said, and she apparently would have supported "an honest, fair law to control Communism," but she opposed the bills because they could not "prevent the persecution of innocent people for political reasons." In addition, she wanted to rebuke Governor Allan Shivers, who supported such Red Scare legislation, because she was convinced he had "helped whitewash" an investigation of corruption among El Paso public officials that she had requested.[11] She introduced a resolution seeking an investigation of the investigation, but the resolution was ordered expunged from the record by a House vote of 100 to 4. In an angry denunciation of Shivers and the investigation, which cleared everyone charged, Blair accused the governor of condoning corruption and her colleagues of not having the courage to stand up to him.[12]

El Paso boosters, including the mayor, attorneys, and the *El Paso Times*, were offended by the negative publicity the investigation caused and angry with Blair for having requested it. In retaliation, some of them created a fund to support an opponent for Blair in 1954. "I resent that some El Paso people do not want to listen to the truth," she said. "I will run for re-election on my record. . . . I have never waited to see how a vote was going to go and then vote in the House with the crowd."[13] In addition to this opposition, Blair suffered from having lost Fawn to cancer the previous year and from a lack of money. "I didn't feel like I was going to win," she said, and she did not. Malcolm McGregor defeated her.

Blair was devastated by the defeat and felt ostracized in El Paso for years afterward. She ran once again, against incumbent Maud Isaacks in 1956, but lost.[14] She continues to take an active interest in local government and often attends Commissioners Court meetings.[15]

NOTES

1. *Dallas Morning News*, January 28, 1953.

2. *El Paso Times*, May 3, 1956, April 19, 1940, December 26, 1985.

3. *El Paso Times*, June 5, June 6, and June 8, 1946.

4. *El Paso Herald-Post*, June 7, June 8, and June 15, 1946, December 5, 1946, February 3 and September 5, 1948; *El Paso Times*, June 14, 1946.

5. Anita Blair, telephone interview by Ruthe Winegarten, July 14, 1995; *El Paso Times*, January 6, 1950.

6. *El Paso Times*, February 21, May 29, 1950; June 3, 1952.

7. *El Paso Herald-Post*, April 25, 1950; *El Paso Times*, May 11, 1950; *Time*, September 8, 1952; *People Today*, March 11, 1953; Blair, interview.

8. *People Today*, March 11, 1953; *Houston Chronicle*, April 22, 1953.

9. *Dallas Morning News*, January 28, 1953.

10. *Houston Chronicle*, April 22, 1953; *Daily Texan*, March 19, 1953; *El Paso Times*, May 3, 1956; *El Paso Times*, December 26, 1985; Blair, interview.

11. Don E. Carleton, *Red Scare! Right-wing Hysteria, Fifties Fanaticism, and Their Legacy in Texas* (Austin: Texas Monthly Press, 1985), pp. 199–201; *El Paso Herald-Post*, April 16, 1954; *El Paso Times*, April 2, April 9, and April 17, 1954.

12. *El Paso Times*, April 17, 1954.

13. *El Paso Herald-Post*, April 15 and April 16, 1954; *El Paso Times*, February 12 and April 29, 1954.

14. *Austin American*, August 19, 1953; *El Paso Times*, December 26, 1985; *El Paso Times*, May 3, 1956.

15. Blair, interview.

☆

MAUD ISAACKS

HOUSE 53rd–59th Legislatures (1954–1967)
Democrat, El Paso
DISTRICT 150
COMMITTEES Education (Vice Chair);
Labor; Penitentiaries; Privileges; Public
Health; School Districts; State Hospitals
and Special Schools; Suffrage and
Elections; Congressional and Legislative
Districts; Common Carriers

DATES 1885?–January 22, 1980
BIRTHPLACE Near Austin
FAMILY Single; no children
EDUCATION University of Texas (B.A.,
1927; M.A., 1940)
OCCUPATION Teacher

Saying that she was tired of seeing women pushed around in Texas law, **MAUD ISAACKS** was the first female legislator to attempt to pass an amendment to the Texas Constitution assuring equal legal rights for women (ELRA). She said, "The times have passed when women should be discriminated against in any way. The old laws were to protect poor, uneducated women but now women can take care of themselves."[1] In 1961, during her fourth term, she and Representative Ben Atwell of Hutchins co-sponsored an amendment to render moot laws that discriminated against women, such as those that prevented married women from managing or selling their own property or going into business with their own funds without their husbands' consent. The movement for such an amendment in Texas had been initiated in 1959 by the Business and Professional Women's Clubs and its legal adviser and lobbyist, attorney Hermine Tobolowsky. Isaacks remained an avid supporter of the amendment throughout her legislative career, although she never succeeded in passing it. Given the reception Tobolowsky received in the legislature when she introduced the ELRA, it is not surprising that twenty-five years would pass before the ELRA had enough support to become law. "There's no woman who has sense enough to sign a deed or to convey her stocks without the advice and consent of her husband," one lawmaker told Tobolowsky. Another handed her a cigar and said, "Here. You want to be a man. Smoke it."[2] Maud Isaacks' vocal support of women's rights was unique among the cohort of women with whom she served. And for a woman who began her political career deferring to the judgment of her father (longtime representative Sam Jackson Isaacks, whose House seat she won after he resigned it in 1954), the activist role revealed that Isaacks had the ability to become an independent thinker and that vocal support for women's rights existed in Texas during what has been called "the doldrums" of the women's movement.[3]

The descendent of early Texas settlers who may have been among the first Jews to enter the region, Maud Isaacks was apparently raised a Christian. She taught English in El Paso junior and senior high schools from 1916 until 1954 and chaired a high school English department. She was also a member of the textbook committee. In 1954 she became the first woman to succeed a father and, with Anita Blair, one of the first two women to serve one district at the same time.[4]

As a former teacher, Isaacks' primary legislative concern was to improve public education. During the special session in 1954, she supported successful efforts to raise teacher salaries and later supported efforts to allow counties to decide whether they needed school superintendents.[5] Her most provocative reform effort, however, was her attempt in 1959 to allow college-educated people (she assumed these would be women) who lacked education degrees to teach in public schools. "I think a teacher's certificate should be issued to teach to anyone who has graduated from a first class college or university, regardless if he or she has had any education courses," she said. "Teachers should take more basic subjects than the education courses."[6] Her bill, House Bill 763, would have allowed provisional, renewable teaching certificates to be awarded to college graduates who would then agree to take a maximum of twelve hours of education courses. Despite vocal objection from the Texas State Teachers Association, the bill passed the House. It failed in the Senate, but the controversy forced the State Board of Education and the Board of Examiners for Teacher Education to examine teacher certification standards. In 1961 Isaacks was appointed to the House Special Interim Committee on Education to study teacher certification in consultation with the Texas Legislative Council.[7] Ultimately, certification standards were reduced.

Isaacks sponsored a successful bill to lengthen the waiting period for couples filing for divorce and supported efforts to require lobbyists to register with the state. She also advocated legislation to address juvenile delinquency, establish a paid parole system for prisons, tighten insurance controls, strengthen narcotics regulations, and establish soil and water conservation programs. She sponsored a law to repeal the poll tax. In 1957 Isaacks was asked how it felt to be one of only three women members of the legislature. The newspaper headlined her response, "Representative Maud Isaacks Wants More Women to Seek Public Office." She said, "There ought to be more women in government."[8]

In 1966 Maud Isaacks declined to seek another term. By then, she was in her eighties and was the only woman in the House, a situation that had not occurred since 1933. Nevertheless, Isaacks urged women to seek political office in spite of the possible hardships on their families and businesses. On her last day, House members, who called her "Miss Maud," presented her with a laudatory resolution, a standing ovation, and red roses. She retired to El Paso where she was chosen for inclusion in *Who's Who of American Women.*[9]

NOTES

1. *Austin Statesman*, January 12, 1961.

2. Ibid.; *El Paso Times*, March 16, 1965; *Dallas Morning News*, July 27, 1995; Judie Karen Walton Gammage, "Quest for Equality: An Historical Overview of Women's Rights Activism in Texas, 1890–1975" (Ph.D. diss., North Texas State University, 1982), pp. 133–139.

3. *El Paso Times*, March 7, 1954; *Austin American*, March 16, 1954. For an analysis of "the doldrums," see Leila J. Rupp and Verta Taylor, *Survival in the Doldrums: The American Women's Movement, 1945 to the 1960s.*

4. Judith N. McArthur, "Maud Isaacks," *New Handbook of Texas*, 3:876; Maud Isaacks, biographical information sheet, April 20, 1962, Maud Isaacks Vertical File, Library, Texas Woman's University, Denton.

5. *El Paso Times*, March 7 and March 16, 1954; *El Paso Herald-Post*, April 15, 1954, January 3 and November 18, 1955; *Austin American*, February 28, 1959.

6. *El Paso Herald-Post*, February 4, 1957.

7. *El Paso Herald-Post*, December 5, 1961.

8. *Daily Texan*, January 14, 1955; *El Paso Herald-Post*, February 4, 1957; *Austin Statesman*, April 4, 1959; McArthur, "Maud Isaacks," p. 876.

9. *El Paso Times*, January 19, 1965; *Dallas News*, February 23, 1966.

THE 1960s–1970s

MYRA DAVIS WILKINSON BANFIELD (DIPPEL)

HOUSE 57th–58th Legislatures (1961–1965)
Democrat, Rosenberg District: 30
COMMITTEES Constitutional Amendments; State Affairs; Labor; State Hospitals
and Special Schools (Vice Chair);
Conservation and Reclamation; Education; Interim Study (Vice Chair)

DATES August 3, 1918–
BIRTHPLACE Rosenberg
FAMILY John Robert Wilkinson (died);
N. O. Banfield (divorced); Herbert
William Dippel; two children
EDUCATION University of Houston (no degree)
OCCUPATION Nurse; rancher; newspaper editor; oil and gas producer

A supporter of states' rights, school segregation, and "Americanism,"
MYRA BANFIELD won her first campaign for the House in 1960 as a
write-in candidate who published her platform on matchbooks. "In those
days, everyone smoked. . . . My husband bought the matches, [but]
that's the only thing he would let me have. I had to borrow on every
insurance policy I had. I sold my kids' piano; I sold everything in the
house I could get by with that he wouldn't miss" to finance the campaign, she said. As editor of the *Rosenberg Herald*, Banfield was well known
in her community. She had gotten her feet wet in politics in 1957, driving around the state lobbying in favor of the stalled package of segregation bills sponsored in part by Ferris representative Virginia Duff.
Banfield's efforts so impressed San Angelo senator Dorsey Hardeman
that he urged her to run for the legislature.[1] With the help of Elizabeth
Daufet, an editor of the *Waller County Record*, Banfield won in a runoff
in which her male opponent claimed her place was in the home, not the
legislature. One of the campaign flyers Daufet wrote for Banfield listed
twenty women—including Joan of Arc, Madam Curie, Susan B. Anthony, Elisabet Ney, and Eleanor Roosevelt—who had improved the
world by not staying home.[2]

Once in the House, Banfield opposed the state Equal Legal Rights
Amendment to the Texas Constitution co-sponsored by Maud Isaacks.
In 1961, having won the support of the Texas Federation of Business and
Professional Women for her support of the ELRA, Banfield voted against

it. In House hearings about the amendment, she said she feared her husband would stop behaving like a gentleman if the ELRA passed. Banfield said women's anger for her stand was one reason she lost in 1965. "I'm all for women making equal wages," she said, "but I still think it's a man's world. . . . I would like to see women at home with the children."[3]

With a few exceptions, these beliefs kept Banfield quiet in the House, reluctant to speak at the floor microphone, and supportive of her male colleagues. The culture of the House at that time was pointedly masculine: new male legislators could expect lobbyists to provide them with "a case of liquor, a carton of cigarettes, and gorgeous call girls," she recalled. The men treated their female colleagues with courtly respect and on occasion invited her to join them rather than the wives with whom she sat at social occasions.[4]

One of her first responsibilities was to vote for the speaker of the House. In a hotly contested race between Gober representative James A. Turman and McAllen representative Wade Spilman, Banfield refused to commit to either until the vote, then supported Spilman on the advice of Virginia Duff. He lost, and Banfield likely lost any chance for choice committee assignments as a result. Banfield claimed the election was closely observed, if not controlled, by lobbyists, particularly those representing the Rural Electrification Administration (REA), which she said offered her and other legislators two hundred dollars early in her first term.[5]

Banfield supported a state sales tax but opposed a state income tax, saying it would fall hardest on women workers. She sponsored an unsuccessful bill to have "Vacation State" added to Texas license plates, and she secured a $3.5 million appropriation for the Richmond State School.[6] Her two most vocal efforts, however, were supporting "Americanism" and opposing legalized gambling. Banfield had been appointed State Americanism Chairman of the American Legion Auxiliary in 1961.[7] In 1962 she urged readers of the *Fort Bend Reporter* to attend House Textbook Committee meetings during the summer special session. "In my opinion," she said, "we are afforded an extraordinary opportunity to expose, and to publicize the left-wing ideology" in public school textbooks "presented with such cunning and subtlety."[8] The meetings of that committee made headlines as members heard conservatives from around the state—like gubernatorial candidate and former general Edwin A. Walker—testify to the need to purge communist ideology from textbooks and curricula.[9] In 1963 Banfield supported House Bill 164 to require that high schools teach a course entitled "Americanism vs. Communism" to reveal the "dangers, fallacies and false doctrines" of communism and prohibit teachers from presenting communism as "superior to our Constitutional form of government."[10] In a letter to her constituents, Banfield described the bill as the "most important legislation" of the session: "[Our youth] must understand the Communist philosophy! We cannot afford a repetition of the Brainwashing which occurred in Korea!"[11] The bill passed the House but did not become law.[12]

Banfield was instrumental in setting back efforts to expand REA loans to groups of Texas farmers for electrical cooperatives. The program began during President Franklin D. Roosevelt's administration in the 1930s to bring electricity to rural areas, where only 2.3 percent of Texas farmers had access to central electricity. Because existing power companies refused to build lines into rural areas, groups of farmers and ranchers who convinced the REA that they had a workable plan received loans to install their own power lines. By the 1960s these cooperative lines reached most rural areas, but some power companies opposed REA development and fought legislation to expand its activities. The issue was hotly contested in the Texas Legislature in 1961, and Banfield was pressured by both sides.[13] She said later she cast the deciding vote against the bill to expand REA activities and was proud that "Today Texans do not have to pay their light bill to the government."[14]

Initially, Banfield kept her views on legalized gambling quiet: "I never told anyone how I stood on it," she said of San Antonio representative "Red" Berry's bill to legalize horse racing. "I just laughed and went along with the boys." In 1961 she was placed on the Constitutional Amendments Committee because Berry's supporters believed she would go along with the measure. Given the opportunity during committee hearings to question Berry, however, Banfield revealed her strenuous objections to the bill. Colleagues passed her notes advising her, "Be Quiet" and "Silence is golden." Berry himself threatened Banfield, she said, assuring her that she would never be reelected. Banfield did not stop there, however, and—like her attempt to help school segregation laws pass—launched a campaign to write and visit Baptist ministers throughout the state to galvanize their opposition. She credits her efforts with defeating Berry, but she remained frightened of him.[15]

In an unsuccessful race for a third term in 1964, Banfield took out an ad in the *Fort Bend Reporter* with her list of qualifications. They included being "100 percent all-American . . . not supported by 'big' money, . . . opposed to a sales tax and income tax, a devout Christian woman, for state's rights, healthy and well-balanced (her opponent is ailing—all Myra had was mumps)." By this time, her two-county district had been reduced to one due to redistricting. She claimed to have saved the district from being absorbed altogether into A. R. "Babe" Schwartz' senatorial district by threatening to run for his Senate seat if this happened, but this success did not help in her campaign. District 30 had traditionally operated under a gentleman's agreement allowing representatives no more than two terms. That, in addition to her ex-husband's vocal and financial opposition to her, and the political enemies she had made, contributed to her defeat.[16]

After leaving the legislature, Banfield became a Christian Scientist and a nurse, lived in Boston, Houston, and finally Tyler. She later reflected about the difficulty of a woman entering politics, saying that "most men feel [it] is an invasion of their personal domain. Politics, and especially campaigning, is a job designed for and by men, and the obstacles of politics are harder for women to circumvent."[17] By 1997, Banfield had become unhappy with Republican leadership and considered herself neither a Republican nor a Democrat, but a believer in free enterprise. She organized Grandmothers for Honest Government in fifty states to repeal the North American Free Trade Agreement and the General Agreement on Trades and Tariffs, as well as the 17th Amendment (the direct election of U.S. senators).[18] To reform Congress, retire all lobbyists, and "save the country for our children, grandchildren, and our posterity," Banfield would have the nation return to a system whereby each state's legislature selected "two of its most honorable members" for the U.S. Senate, rather than be elected by popular vote, so a legislature could "recall and replace" a senator "at any time the senator stepped out of line."[19]

NOTES

1. Myra Banfield Dippel, videotape interview by Ruthe Winegarten, May 25, 1995, Archives for Research on Women and Gender, University of Texas at San Antonio (hereafter ARWG); Myra Banfield Dippel, telephone interview by Ruthe Winegarten, July 15, 1997.

2. Myra Banfield campaign flyer; Dippel, interview, ARWG.

3. Dippel, interview, ARWG; Judie Karen Walton Gammage, "Quest for Equality:

An Historical Overview of Women's Rights Activism in Texas: 1890–1975" (Ph.D. diss., North Texas State University, 1982), pp. 133–139.

4. Dippel, interview, ARWG.

5. Ibid.; Dippel, telephone interview.

6. *Fort Bend Reporter*, June 4, 1964; Dippel, interview, ARWG; *Houston Post*, July 1, 1961.

7. *Tri-County News* (Hempstead), October 19, 1961.

8. *Fort Bend Reporter*, January 18, 1962.

9. *Dallas Morning News*, June 1, 1962.

10. House Bill 164, authors' files.

11. Myra Banfield, letter to constituents, March 5, 1963, authors' files.

12. *House Journal of Texas*, 58th Legislature, Regular Session, March 4, 1963, pp. 1115–1116; Myra Banfield Dippel to Ruthe Winegarten, [July 13, 1997].

13. See Norris G. Davis, "Rural Electrification," *New Handbook of Texas*, 5:719–720.

14. Dippel to Winegarten; Banfield's inscription on a letter from Carl B. Sherman, Vice President of Houston Lighting and Power Company, to Banfield, March 9, 1961, copy in authors' files. On this letter Sherman hand-wrote his added praise for Banfield's vote on behalf of him and his associates: "*Real* nice work doll!"

15. Dippel, interview, ARWG.

16. Ibid.

17. Myra Banfield, typescript, n.d., copy in authors' files.

18. Dippel, telephone interview.

19. *Grandmothers for Honest Government*, newsletter, n.d., authors' files; *Tyler Morning Telegraph*, March 16, 1997; Dippel to Winegarten.

SUE BLAIR HAIRGROVE (MUZZY)

HOUSE 60th Legislature (1967–1969)
Democrat, Lake Jackson
COMMITTEES Common Carriers;
Congressional and Legislative Districts;
Parks and Wildlife; Penitentiaries; Public
Health

DATES October 1, 1922–
BIRTHPLACE Justin
FAMILY James A. Hairgrove (died);
Donald Ralph Muzzy; two children
EDUCATION Business college
OCCUPATION Business

SUE BLAIR HAIRGROVE won a special election in 1967 to take the place of her late husband, Representative James A. Hairgrove. She considered the election a tribute to her husband and planned to fulfill his legislative agenda. The president of radio stations in Freeport and Lake Jackson, she became the only woman in the House (following the 59th Legislature, in which no women served in the House). Because her election took place at the end of the regular session, however, Hairgrove served only during the special session in 1968, where she supported a sales tax and sale of liquor by the drink and did not introduce any bills of her own.[1] She declined to seek reelection, thereby making her a freshman and a lame duck at he same time. After leaving the legislature to resume the care of her family, Hairgrove remained active in community affairs. Although elected as a Democrat, she became a Republican in 1975. She was named Brazosport's Woman of the Year in 1970 and Washington County's Woman of the Year in 1991. She has worked as consumer awareness and education coordinator for a local beer distributor.[2]

NOTES

1. Sue Hairgrove Muzzy, telephone interview by Ruthe Winegarten, July 10, 1997.
2. *Houston Chronicle*, May 26, 1967; *Dallas Morning News*, May 30, 1967, June 13, 1968.

BARBARA CHARLINE JORDAN

SENATE 60th–62nd Legislatures (1967–1973)
Democrat, Houston
DISTRICT II
COMMITTEES Education; Environmental
Matters; Finance; Interstate Cooperation;
Jurisprudence; Labor and Management
Relations (Chair); Legislative, Congressional,
and Judicial Districts (Vice Chair); Military
and Veterans Affairs; Nominations; Privileges
and Elections (Vice Chair); Public Health;
State Affairs; State Departments and
Institutions; Youth Affairs

DATES February 21. 1936–January 17, 1996
BIRTHPLACE Houston
FAMILY Single; no children
EDUCATION Texas Southern University
(B.A., 1956); Boston University (J.D., 1959)
OCCUPATION Attorney; U.S. representative;
university professor

BARBARA CHARLINE JORDAN was born in Houston's Fifth Ward,
the third of three daughters. As a member of Texas Southern University's
debating team, which defeated or tied team after team of whites, including Harvard's, she realized that "some black people could make it in this
white man's world, and that those who could, had to do it." After graduating magna cum laude with a degree in political science, she left
her racially segregated world to attend Boston University Law School.
She was one of only six women, and only two black women, in her
400-member class. Of the women, only the black women graduated.[1]

Armed with a law degree, Jordan returned to Houston. In 1960 she
worked on the John F. Kennedy–Lyndon B. Johnson presidential campaign and was bitten by the political bug, as she put it. In 1962 and 1964
she ran for the Texas House of Representatives, but no black woman had
ever been elected to the legislature. Although she had run on a ticket
with liberal Democrats and campaigned vigorously for the whole ticket,
she was the only candidate who lost, and Jordan felt she had given her
candidate colleagues more support than she had received. She briefly
considered leaving Texas for a state that would elect a woman but de-

cided against it.[2] Her next campaign was a success, in part because of the passage of the 1964 Civil Rights Act (which strengthened the voting rights of people, particularly blacks, who had been denied the right to vote) and a U.S. Supreme Court ruling in which population overruled geography in determining legislative representation. The new single-member districts that resulted gave Harris County four state Senate seats instead of one. That, plus the 1966 ruling of the U.S. Supreme Court outlawing poll taxes, led to an overwhelming victory for Jordan when she ran for one of those seats.[3]

Jordan was the state's first black state senator since 1883 and its first African American woman legislator. She was the only female senator throughout her two terms, but she was not the first member of her family to serve there. Jordan's great-grandfather, Edward Patton, had served in the Texas House in the 22nd Legislature (1891–1893). He was the only black legislator that term. Jordan's election electrified her constituents. "Everybody in my district . . . was very excited, especially the black people, because they had never thought they would have a representative in the state capital of Austin," Jordan recalled. "And so they closed the town down to come to Austin to see me take the oath of office; as I looked up into the Senate gallery, there was a sea of black faces."[4]

Jordan's political strategy, once inside the Senate, stemmed from her conviction that blacks—in fact, all "minorities"—should join the system rather than challenge it and from her refusal to be identified by either her race or her gender. "I'm not a black politician," she said. "I'm not a female politician. I'm a politician. And a good one."[5] Although she was not known as an activist in the civil rights or women's movements, Jordan was committed to equal rights issues and was successful in passing significant legislation that enlarged or expanded the rights of minorities and women. She helped speed the process of school desegregation in Houston by negotiating with the district's school board on behalf of the local chapter of the National Association for the Advancement of Colored People, of which she was a longtime member. And along with Corpus Christi representative Frances "Sissy" Farenthold, she was instrumental in making Texas one of the first states in the South to ratify the federal Equal Rights Amendment and to propose and secure the Equal Legal Rights Amendment to the Texas Constitution. "All blacks are militant in their guts," she said in 1970, "but militancy is expressed in various ways. Some do it quite overtly while others try to work their way through 'the system.' . . . That's the way I like to work. Disruptive or divisive behavior is no help."[6]

Once she was a senator, Jordan's primary goal was to become the consummate insider, even though she was the only female among thirty males. "We are a macho state. We just are. . . . Those 30 men didn't know what to expect of me, and I certainly didn't know what to expect of them. . . . [But] I knew that the best way for me to operate as a player in the Senate was to become friends with my colleagues, and not to have them uncomfortable because there was a woman in their presence."[7] This approach earned Jordan criticism from some who thought her too conciliatory, but Jordan retained the respect of Houston's civil rights leaders, perhaps because they knew her as disciplined, practical, hardworking, and committed to representing their interests.

Jordan quickly taught herself the rules of the Senate and the art of compromise. Her strategy was so successful that Senator Dorsey Hardeman of San Angelo, who initially opposed her presence in the chamber, was later chief sponsor of a resolution naming Jordan outstanding freshman senator.[8] In 1972 she was unanimously elected the Senate's president pro tempore. In another measure of her popularity, she attended a politically based East Texas quail hunt at which she persuaded the primarily white male group to sing "We Shall Overcome" as she played it on her guitar.[9] During her second term, she served as governor for a day, leapfrogging eight senators with more seniority who were in line for the honor.[10] She thus became the first African American woman to serve as a state's chief executive.

Late in her life, Jordan assessed her primary success in the Senate as "the premier feat of taking a few hundred thousand people who felt that state government was an alien Other, and helping those people understand, 'you have a voice in that big Other, which has been alien to you. And I'm going to be that voice. And I'm going to speak.'"[11] Nearly half of the 150 bills she introduced passed. She supported the state's first minimum wage and civil rights laws and sponsored a bill to establish a state commission on fair employment practices. She also supported the equalization of public school funding and improvement of worker compensation. In addition, she called in political chips from her colleagues to block legislation that would have made voting and voter registration more difficult.[12]

While earning a reputation as a moderate, Jordan also supported some distinctly conservative issues for political reasons. As a delegate to the 1968 Democratic National Convention, she fought to maintain the Texas delegation's support for President Lyndon Johnson's Vietnam policies, despite having opposed the war just a few years earlier.[13] "That plank probably resulted in further killing and dying," she reportedly said, "but I felt it was important for Texans to be supportive of their man."[14]

In 1972 Jordan won the new U.S. House seat that she helped create as a result of redistricting following the 1970 census. Her opponent, a black activist and former Texas House member, Curtis Graves, challenged Jordan for the seat because he held her responsible for the destruction, during redistricting, of her old Senate seat, to which he believed he had a rightful claim. Jordan had more money, influence, and popular support than Graves, who attempted to picture her as a pawn of the powerful and moneyed, both black and white. In a hard campaign, Jordan stuck to her principal message: vote for the person who can get things done. She won an overwhelming victory. The Reverend Bill Lawson, active in the civil rights movement and friendly with Graves, later credited Jordan with having the ability to see "beyond the conflict to the enduring institutions, and she saw that most people, even black people, wanted to believe in them, if they could only be made to work."[15]

The victory made Jordan the first black woman from a southern state and the first black Texan ever to take a seat in Congress. She was also the first Texas woman elected to Congress in her own right. During her three congressional terms, Jordan co-sponsored bills establishing equal credit for women, freedom of information, home rule for the District of Columbia, a larger food commodities program for school lunches, tax credits for low-income workers, and several health programs. She opposed most of the Texas delegation, Governor Dolph Briscoe, and Secretary of State Mark White by supporting the extension of the 1965 Voting Rights Act to cover Mexican Americans in the Southwest, including Texas.[16]

In the House, as in the Texas Senate, Jordan continued to keep her own counsel. She was a member of the Congressional Black Caucus but took positions independent of it. When U.S. representative (and future House speaker) Tip O'Neill, assuming he had a new political friend, put his arm around her to guide her to a cluster of House liberals, she reportedly moved away. As one of five new female representatives elected in 1972, Jordan usually declined to join the other women's informal caucus and did not refer to herself as a feminist. Nevertheless, she worked with women to fight for and win a three-year extension of the period allotted to ratify the Equal Rights Amendment. Jordan wanted even more time. "I regret that 14 years is repugnant as a time frame. . . . [It] is not to me," she said.[17]

Her old friend and mentor, former president Lyndon B. Johnson, helped her get appointed to the House Committee on the Judiciary, one of the most influential committees in Congress, and in 1974, during the committee's televised hearings into the Watergate scandal, Jordan made a speech that turned her into a national icon: "When the Constitution of the United States was completed . . . , I was not included in that 'We the People.' . . . I have finally been included. . . . My faith in the Constitution is whole. It is complete. It is total. I am not going to sit here and be an idle spectator to the diminution, the subversion, the destruction of the Constitution."[18]

While Jordan rejected others' attempts to turn her into a symbol, she often used herself as one, as she did in this speech. Her life was full of such paradoxes, the principal one being her consciousness of and her ability to use her "difference" in surprising ways to gain what she wanted while at the same time refusing to describe herself in terms of her race and gender. Throughout Jordan's life, people attempted to fit her into categories, but she continued to resist while at the same time taking action. In a 1975 speech for the International Year of the Woman, for example, Jordan pointed out injustices done to women and their achievements in overcoming them. "There can be no slackening of effort," she asserted.[19]

In 1976, *U.S. News & World Report* declared Jordan the most prominent woman in the country. In July of that year, she became the first African American to address the Democratic National Convention. Her speech energized the delegates and sparked a brief movement to nominate her for vice president. Major newspapers across the country covered the speech. When presidential nominee Jimmy Carter asked for Jordan's help in his campaign, she agreed, and her speeches and public appearances helped turn out the black voters who provided a margin of victory for Carter in thirteen states. In Texas, one of the six states in which Jordan campaigned for him, Carter won 97 percent of the black vote. Jordan expected an appointment to Carter's administration, and she wanted to be named attorney general. But she and her supporters were disappointed. "No one named Jimmy Carter *ever* offered me any job," she said later.[20]

In 1977 Jordan announced she would not seek reelection. After more than a decade as an elected official, she wanted to try something different. Increasingly frustrated with President Carter, her colleagues in Congress, and obstacles to passing legislation, Jordan was also diagnosed with multiple sclerosis, which was hampering her mobility and draining her energy. After leaving Congress, Jordan was rumored a likely candidate for vice president, attorney general, and Supreme Court justice. Instead, in 1979, she went home to Texas, engaged in a book tour to promote her autobiography (written with Shelby Hearon), became a professor at the Lyndon Baines Johnson School of Public Affairs at the University of Texas at Austin, teaching courses in ethics and political values, and began living in Austin full time, in the house she had built and lived in with her long-time friend, Nancy Earl.[21]

Despite suffering from multiple sclerosis, hypertension, diabetes, and later leukemia, Jordan continued her busy schedule of teaching, speaking, traveling, and public service. She served as ethics adviser to Texas governor Ann Richards, was awarded over thirty honorary degrees, and was declared one of the twentieth century's most influential women by the National Women's Hall of Fame, into which she was inducted in 1993. The same year, President Bill Clinton appointed her to chair the U.S. Commission on Immigration Reform, but he declined to support her proposal for a worker identification system. In 1994 Clinton awarded Jordan the Presidential Medal of Freedom, the nation's highest civilian honor, for her work for civil rights.[22]

Shortly before her death, Jordan reflected on her career in the Texas Legislature and the fact that many groups of Texans were still not fully represented there. "We cannot stand to have, in a democracy, any significant portion of the people who do not have a voice in what happens to them," she said. "All I know is that we as a people, black, white, Asian, Hispanic, must keep scratching the surface until we get where we've got to be, and that's all inclusiveness for all people."[23] After Jordan died in 1996, her body lay in state at the Lyndon Baines Johnson Library and Museum in Austin. She is buried in the Texas State Cemetery.

NOTES

1. Paul Burka, "Major Barbara," *Texas Monthly*, March 1996, p. 111.

2. William Broyles, "The Making of Barbara Jordan," *Texas Monthly*, October 1976, p. 132.

3. *Austin American-Statesman*, January 20, 1996.

4. Mary Beth Rogers, *Barbara Jordan: American Hero*, pp. 7–10; Barbara Jordan, videotape interview by Nancy Baker Jones, September 12, 1995, Archives for Research on

Women and Gender, University of Texas at San Antonio (hereafter ARWG). Jordan served in three legislatures but was elected for only two terms: a two-year term in 1966 and a four-year term in 1968. See Rogers, *Barbara Jordan*, p. 374.

5. Jordan, interview, ARWG.

6. Shelby Hearon and Barbara Jordan, *Barbara Jordan: A Self Portrait*, p. 213; Broyles, "The Making of Barbara Jordan," p. 133; Burka, "Major Barbara," p. 110; Frances Farenthold, videotape interview by Ruthe Winegarten, June 12, 1995, ARWG.

7. Jordan, interview, ARWG.

8. *Austin American-Statesman*, January 18, 1996.

9. Burka, "Major Barbara," p. 111.

10. Ibid.

11. Jordan, interview, ARWG.

12. Ann Fears Crawford and Crystal Sasse Ragsdale, "Barbara Jordan: Congresswoman from Texas," *Women in Texas: Their Lives, Their Experiences, Their Accomplishments*, pp. 324–325; *Austin American-Statesman*, January 20, 1996; Jordan, interview, ARWG.

13. Broyles, "The Making of Barbara Jordan," p. 201.

14. *Dallas Morning News*, January 9, 1977.

15. Broyles, "The Making of Barbara Jordan," p. 198. Broyles says the campaign was difficult in part because of the spread of rumors about Jordan's sexual orientation. Jordan never discussed her personal life in public, and she resisted others' attempts to classify her in any way. Shortly after Jordan's death, *The Advocate* published a cover story claiming that she was a lesbian. See J. Jennings Moss, "Barbara Jordan: The Other Life," *The Advocate*, March 5, 1996.

16. Crawford and Ragsdale, "Barbara Jordan," pp. 326–329; *Austin American-Statesman*, January 20, 1996.

17. Walter Shapiro, "What Does This Woman Want?" *Texas Monthly*, October 1976, p. 203; Rogers, *Barbara Jordan*, pp. 177–179, 188–189; Hearon and Jordan, *Barbara Jordan*, pp. 114–115; Jack C. Plano and Milton Greenberg, eds., *American Political Dictionary*, 7th ed. (New York: Holt, Rinehart, and Winston, 1985), p. 71.

18. Rogers, *Barbara Jordan*, pp. 178–179; Hearon and Jordan, *Barbara Jordan*, pp. 186–187.

19. Hearon and Jordan, *Barbara Jordan*, pp. 215–216.

20. Mark Odintz, "Barbara Charline Jordan," *New Handbook of Texas*, 3:1001; *Austin American-Statesman*, January 18, 1996; Rogers, *Barbara Jordan*, pp. 270–272, 275–284.

21. Burka, "Major Barbara," p. 89; Rogers, *Barbara Jordan*, pp. 142–143, 250–254, 286–297, 316–321.

22. Odintz, "Barbara Charline Jordan," p. 1001; *Austin American-Statesman*, January 18, 1996.

23. Jordan, interview, ARWG.

FRANCES TARLTON (SISSY) FARENTHOLD

HOUSE 61st–62nd Legislatures (1969–1973)
Democrat, Corpus Christi
DISTRICT 45
COMMITTEES Oil, Gas, and Mining;
Labor; Governmental Affairs

DATES October 2, 1926–
BIRTHPLACE Corpus Christi
FAMILY George Farenthold (divorced); five
children, one stepchild
EDUCATION Vassar (A.B., 1946); University
of Texas (J.D., 1949)
OCCUPATION Attorney; professor; college
president; peace activist

"I was in the legislature about two weeks before I decided that reform
had to be my major concern. I went there knowing blacks weren't represented, knowing Mexican Americans weren't represented. I found that
Texans weren't even represented."[1] With characteristic sardonic humor,
FRANCES (SISSY) FARENTHOLD assessed the state of the Texas House
when she entered it in 1969 as its only female member. Her analysis had
not changed by the time she left to run for governor in 1972.

Sissy Farenthold was born to a prominent and politically active South
Texas family; the library at the University of Texas Law School is named
for her grandfather, Benjamin Dudley Tarlton, an attorney, state legislator, and law professor. Her father was also an attorney who opposed the
Ku Klux Klan and inculcated in his daughter a deep respect for the Constitution. One of her aunts, Lida Dougherty, was the first woman school
superintendent in Texas.[2] Her mother was often ill, and Farenthold lived
in Dallas with relatives to finish high school at Hockaday. She was one of
three women in her law class, an experience she remembers as "vicious.
There were bets on how long I would last."[3] She graduated with honors
and practiced law with her father until she married in 1950 and had five
children in five years.

Farenthold called her efforts at being a corporate wife a "disaster," but
it was the death in 1960 of one of her twin sons that finally propelled her
out of her home and into helping her cousin run for the legislature. She
later worked in John F. Kennedy's 1960 presidential campaign, then turned
her focus to the community, organizing mothers to promote playground

safety at her children's school and convincing the Corpus Christi city council to form a human relations commission, on which she served for five years. "Those were our naive days in civil rights. . . . I didn't know what 'public accommodation' meant," she said. In 1965 she became director of the Nueces County Legal Aid Program, in one of the nation's poorest counties. The experience left Farenthold with a gnawing anger and frustration with state policies that prevented her from significantly improving the lives of her poverty-stricken clients. She resigned in 1967.[4]

In 1968 Farenthold became the first woman to run for the House from her district. Despite the fact that, "for many considered knowledgeable in political matters, I was not a token, I was a joke," she believed she could change the policies that had frustrated her while working for Legal Aid. She also wanted to shake up the Democratic Party, which she thought pigeonholed women as volunteers rather than candidates. Shy and uncomfortable with selling herself, she started her campaign in a laundromat. Her husband then gave her 1,000 "pushcards," took her to a mall, and said he would not return for her until she had passed out every card. Concerned for the environment, she refused to advertise with billboards; instead she used donated coffin lids tied to campaign vehicles. Despite such idiosyncratic campaigning, she won against the Republican incumbent. The next day, a Corpus Christi voter told her proudly that he had voted for her husband. "Oh, it was I," Farenthold replied. "If I had known that," the man said, "I wouldn't have voted for you."[5]

As a new legislator, Farenthold defined herself as an advocate of civil rights, not women's rights. She initially opposed a state Equal Legal Rights Amendment (ELRA) because the state bar association did. "I was a dutiful daughter of the bar," she said. "That was just part of the tradition." She rejected Harris County representative Rex Braun's request that she cosponsor ELRA legislation with him, and when she drafted legislation to create a state human relations commission, she balked at the idea of including gender as well as racial discrimination as part of its purview.[6]

Although she termed herself "naive" during her first session, she did not ignore what she saw. Capitol guards, assuming she was not a legislator, told her she could not park where legislators parked, and they tried to prevent her from entering the House and Senate chambers. Fort Worth senator Don Kennard asked her whom she worked for. The sergeant-at-arms strode unannounced into her office and removed her male secretary. The more she observed the general climate for women staffers, the more she saw it as "an abomination. I wasn't bold enough to do it," she said, "but I would have liked to have led a march out of the place of all women employed [there], and this government would have stopped."[7]

Eventually she acted. When Governor Preston Smith told a conference on women's issues that he hoped a woman would be in the legislature someday, Farenthold delivered her calling card to his office. When House members declared her their valentine and read a poem, she was furious and rejected the offer. After the Constitutional Amendments Committee, of which she was a member, met for lunch at Austin's all-male Citadel Club and stood by as she was denied entry, the committee chair later brought her chocolates but did not tell her about the committee's discussions. Farenthold objected, and she was not barred from another meeting. And, after hearing testimony against the ELRA presented to the Constitutional Amendments Committee, she changed her mind. "The bar lost total credibility with me that night," she said, because it presented the same insubstantial arguments it had used fifteen years earlier to prevent women from sitting on juries. She then "went into the fray" and co-sponsored ELRA legislation with state senator Barbara Jordan.[8]

"In the beginning, I could have been a pet," she said. "There was a sort of pethood ordained for you, if you accepted it. . . . If I had quietly gone about what was expected of me, I probably would have had a few perks. . . . [But] I wasn't up here as a guest. I was up here as an elected representative." Farenthold attempted to join forces with the sole woman in the Senate, Barbara Jordan. "Nothing came of that," Farenthold said. "I used to smile and think, 'What's the story? The white woman's outside throwing rocks, and the black woman's inside working with the system.'" She later found a Senate ally in San Antonio's Joe Bernal.[9]

In addition to her efforts to support civil and women's rights, Farenthold attempted to protect beaches, bays, and estuaries from pollution and commercial development, supported efforts to make Mustang Island a state park, and tried to prevent noise pollution caused by the Supersonic Transport. She tried unsuccessfully to establish a governor's committee on children and youth, a family planning service, a public utilities commission, a committee to establish educational programs for preschool children, an additional three student seats on the University of Texas Board of Regents, and a reduction in the penalty for possession of marijuana from a felony to a misdemeanor. She supported requiring divorced parents to be current in child support payments before remarrying. She passed an antiquities bill giving the state a share of artifacts found along the Texas coast, and she sponsored a successful resolution reprimanding Land Commissioner Jerry Sadler for his relationship with a business that gained possession of gold treasure found off the coast. She proposed legislation to require making testimony before legislative committees public, supported the disclosure by state officials of their finances and by universities of their investments, and attempted to reform the procedures for electing the speaker of the House.[10]

Farenthold worked to defeat what she deemed an unconstitutional "anti-riot" bill that defined groups of three or more people as a potential riot, and she was the lone dissenter against a resolution praising former president Lyndon Johnson because she opposed the war in Vietnam. She also tried, and failed, to prohibit nuclear power plants from being built in Texas. In addition, she attempted to remove the ceiling on welfare spending and submitted an unsuccessful concurrent resolution allowing solicitation of private funds for emergency relief for needy children, making food stamp and commodities programs available regardless of whether counties sponsored such programs, and calling for a list of people whose welfare payments were rescinded or reduced as a result of the ceiling on welfare payments. She also voted against increases in consumer and gasoline taxes and supported a corporate profits tax. In an event that she credits with turning her into an activist, Farenthold opposed Governor Smith's support of efforts to expel Vista volunteers from Del Rio for registering Mexican Americans to vote. She angered Del Rio representative Hilary Doran when she entered his district to participate in a Palm Sunday march supporting the volunteers, which armed sheriff's deputies watched from the courthouse roof.[11]

Farenthold was called an "advocate of lost causes" by some, but during her second term she led a successful revolt that ended the political careers of the governor, lieutenant governor, and speaker of the House. She and a bipartisan group of representatives, called "those dirty thirty bastards" by an angry lobbyist, tried to uncover the roles Speaker Gus Mutscher and others had played in the Sharpstown stock fraud scandal, in which the Securities and Exchange Commission (SEC) charged that Houston banker Frank Sharp had bribed lawmakers to obtain beneficial legislation. In March 1971, Farenthold introduced a resolution to force an investigation of the legislative history of the bills at the heart of the scandal. Farenthold's House resolution, and a companion resolution requiring Mutscher to resign from the speakership during the SEC investigation, failed.[12]

The Dirty Thirty kept the issue alive for the entire session, however, infuriating Mutscher, who accused them of irresponsible, partisan politics. In return, they called him a dictator who was more concerned with private than public interests. Mutscher retaliated against Farenthold. She was told that none of her legislation would pass, and her district was eliminated during redistricting. Worse still, the House photographer informed Farenthold that Mutscher had instructed him to follow and photograph her son, who opposed the war in Vietnam. She told Mutscher that "as difficult as it was to raise children, I didn't need that kind of thing," and he finally gave her the negatives. Eventually Mutscher was found guilty and sentenced to five years' probation. Governor Smith was named an unindicted co-conspirator, and Lieutenant Governor Ben Barnes left politics.[13]

Farenthold and the Dirty Thirty hoped that revelation of the Sharpstown deals would usher in a thorough reform of Texas politics. They finished the session and took to the stump, informing their constituents of the need for cleaning Texas' political house. Hoping she could ensure lasting reform, Farenthold ran for governor in 1972 against Preston Smith, Ben Barnes, and rancher and former legislator Dolph Briscoe. Farenthold ran second in a field of seven in the Democratic primary, forcing Briscoe into a runoff, and defeating Smith and Barnes, who had been tainted by Sharpstown. Although Farenthold's campaign ignited high interest, especially among women and young voters, it was understaffed and poorly financed. In the runoff, despite garnering 884,000 votes, she lost to Briscoe, who succeeded in convincing voters that Farenthold was too liberal for Texas.[14]

Farenthold's experience with the Dirty Thirty and her gubernatorial campaign brought her national attention and helped galvanize women's interest in politics. In 1972, at the Democratic National Convention in Miami Beach, after U.S. representative Shirley Chisholm removed herself from consideration, Sissy Farenthold was nominated for vice president by a multiracial coalition led by the new National Women's Political Caucus (NWPC). She won 420 delegate votes, coming in second to the winner, Senator Thomas Eagleton. This made her the first woman ever to receive convention votes for vice president. "That was the first time I was supported because I was a woman. I had always been supported despite the fact," she said. She became the first chair of the NWPC in 1973. She ran for governor again in 1974, but the desire for reform, such as it had ever been, had passed, and Briscoe won easily.[15]

Farenthold did not seek political office again. "I could see where the reform movement was going—down the drain. I left politics because I was hitting my head against a brick wall, and I don't believe in personal destruction," she said. "That's why I left the legislature after only two terms. I'd have become either a legislative hack or a whine."[16] She taught law at Texas Southern University and in 1976 became the first female president of Wells College, a small women's school in New York. In 1978 she initiated a program in political leadership for women through the Center for the American Woman and Politics at Rutgers University.[17] She returned to Texas in 1980, opened her own law practice in Houston, taught law at the University of Houston, and became an activist in peace, nuclear disarmament, and nuclear waste disposal movements. She divorced in 1985. She supported Jesse Jackson's presidential campaign in 1988 but was irritated by the 1990 and 1994 gubernatorial campaigns of Ann Richards, saying they were more mood- than issue-driven. Nevertheless, Farenthold was sorry that Richards lost.[18]

Frances Farenthold was the only woman member of the House from 1969 through 1972. In 1972, the year she lost the governorship, five women were elected to the House and one to the Senate, making six in all. The legislature's class of 1973 had more women than had ever been seated in a single session. Farenthold's political life, despite its failures, contributed to this historic achievement.

NOTES

1. *Chicago Tribune*, February 18, 1973.

2. Frances Farenthold, videotape interview by Ruthe Winegarten, June 12, 1995, Archives for Research on Women and Gender, University of Texas at San Antonio (hereafter ARWG); Suzanne Coleman, "The Politics of Participation: The Emergent Journey of Frances Farenthold" (M.A. thesis, University of Texas at Arlington, 1973), p. 7.

3. Farenthold, interview, ARWG.

4. Coleman, "Politics of Participation," pp. 8–14.

5. Sissy Farenthold, "The Woman in Politics," *Saturday Evening Post*, March 1974, p. 14; Coleman, "Politics of Participation," p. 16; Farenthold, interview, ARWG.

6. Farenthold, interview, ARWG.

7. Ibid.

8. Ibid.

9. Ibid.

10. Coleman, "Politics of Participation," pp. 19–22.

11. Ibid.; "Notes and Cross References," Frances T. Farenthold Papers, Barker Texas

History Center, Center for American History, University of Texas at Austin; Frances Farenthold campaign brochures, Vertical Files, Barker Texas History Center, University of Texas at Austin; Farenthold, interview, ARWG.

12. Farenthold, interview, ARWG; Coleman, "Politics of Participation," pp. 24–27.

13. Farenthold, interview, ARWG; Coleman, "Politics of Participation," pp. 26–28; John G. Johnson, "Dirty Thirty," *New Handbook of Texas*, 2:653 (hereafter *NHOT*); Sam Kinch, Jr., "Sharpstown Stock-Fraud Scandal," *NHOT*, 5:998.

14. Coleman, "Politics of Participation," pp. 35–55; Ruthe Winegarten, *Governor Ann Richards and Other Texas Women: From Indians to Astronauts*, p. 139.

15. Elizabeth Frappollo, "The Ticket That Might Have Been," *Ms.*, January 1973, pp. 118–119; Farenthold, interview, ARWG.

16. *Houston Chronicle*, August 29, 1977.

17. *New Directions for Women*, Autumn 1978, p. 22.

18. *Fort Worth Star-Telegram*, March 6, 1988; *Austin American-Statesman*, March 8, 1990; Farenthold, interview, ARWG.

KATHRYN A. (KAY) BAILEY (HUTCHISON)

HOUSE 63rd–64th Legislatures (1973–1976)
Republican, Houston
DISTRICT 90
COMMITTEES Revenue and Taxation; Elections; Intergovernmental Affairs (Vice Chair); Rules; Constitutional Convention, 1974 (Delegate)

DATES July 22, 1943–
BIRTHPLACE Galveston
FAMILY Ray Hutchison; no children
EDUCATION University of Texas at Austin (J.D., 1967; B.A., 1992)
OCCUPATION Journalist; attorney; business owner

KAY BAILEY was the first Republican woman elected to the Texas House. The same year, fellow Republican Betty Andujar was elected to the Texas Senate. Although Bailey was one of just six women to enter the legislature in 1973, she was part of the largest group of women ever to have appeared there. Bailey won in part because of voters' desire to reform the legislature in the wake of the Sharpstown scandal and because the rising tide of the women's movement lifted the boats of many female candidates. In the legislature, indeed throughout her political career, she has maintained a seemingly paradoxical posture, contributing to the improvement of the legal status of women but also distancing herself from feminism. "I believe in equal rights for women," she said in 1971, "but I like being protected." Years later she observed, "My gender does not determine my ideology. Yet, as a woman in the Texas Legislature, I thought of, and pursued issues that men often would not think of pursuing."[1]

The daughter of a financially comfortable family in LaMarque, Bailey said she went to law school because "I hadn't found a husband by my junior year" in college. She earned her law degree in 1967 through a short-lived University of Texas program that allowed undergraduates to enter the law school without first earning an undergraduate degree. Unable then to get a job as an attorney because she was a woman, Bailey decided to change fields and in 1968 became the first woman to work as a television reporter in Houston, where she covered politics, particularly the Texas Legislature. After interviewing fellow Texan Anne Armstrong, then vice chair of the Republican National Committee, Bailey became Armstrong's press secretary and moved to Washington, D.C.[2]

In 1972 Bailey decided that Texas needed a stronger two-party system and ran for a seat in the House. She found fund-raising hampered by her gender. "Women couldn't get big checks from contributors. So I just worked hard getting lots of smaller checks, most of them from other women," she said.[3] During her two terms, Bailey worked across the aisle with Democrats to pass reform legislation improving the status of women. "The Democratic women could work the Democratic side of the aisle, and I could work the Republican side of the aisle," she said, "and because of that, we overwhelmingly passed a landmark piece of legislation for the victims of rape." The Bailey-Weddington law, co-sponsored with Sarah Weddington and considered Bailey's most significant legislative accomplishment, ensured fair treatment for rape victims. It "positioned Texas as a leader in the establishment of fair treatment for rape victims," she said.[4]

In addition, Bailey co-sponsored successful legislation to ensure equal credit rights for women and introduced an unsuccessful bill to alter the garnishment of wages for child support. "We did bring some new issues to the table, that because we were women we were uniquely able to address and able to bring to focus," she said of her two terms in the House. "I think some of our experiences were very important. A man wouldn't have been experienced in the trauma of rape or the discrimination in getting credit if you've been divorced, or if you're a young and single woman. So I think we did make a difference because we were women and because we were willing to work together for some of these common goals." She also co-sponsored legislation to provide mass transit authorities in Houston and San Antonio and to create county historical commissions. She opposed making Martin Luther King's birthday a state holiday.[5]

In 1976 President Gerald Ford appointed Bailey vice chair of the National Transportation Safety Board, so she resigned from the House in July. In 1978 she married Ray Hutchison, a bond attorney and former state legislator, and moved to Dallas where she was general counsel of the Republic Bank Corporation, founded McCraw Candies, and was a partner in Boyd-Levinson, a furniture company. In 1980 Kay Bailey Hutchison chaired Texas Women Leaders for Reagan/Bush and later served as a Republican National Committeewoman.[6] In 1982 Hutchison resumed her political life and ran unsuccessfully for the U.S. House of Representatives from Dallas County. In part, her loss was attributed to her stand on abortion as a private matter, which was regarded by Republican voters as too liberal.[7] In 1990 she ran for and won the state treasurer's job, becoming the first Republican woman elected to a statewide office. While treasurer, she enrolled again at the University of Texas at Austin to complete degree requirements for her undergraduate degree, which was awarded to her in 1992; this became public knowledge in the wake of highly publicized charges that railroad commissioner and former legislator Lena Guerrero had lied about her education.[8]

In a special election in 1993, Hutchison defeated Democrat Bob Krueger to fill the unexpired U.S. Senate term of Democrat Lloyd Bentsen, thus becoming the first woman senator from Texas. Later that year, she was indicted by a Travis County grand jury on felony charges of having used state employees for political and personal work, then covering it up, while she was treasurer. Hutchison maintained her innocence and accused Democratic district attorney Ronnie Earle of "sleazy politics." The indictments were dismissed on a technicality, but Hutchison was indicted again on similar charges. She was ultimately acquitted when Earle declined to pursue the case.[9] In 1994 she was easily elected to a full term as senator, asserting in her campaign that her gender would convince women voters that she could better represent them than her male opponent could.[10] In 1995 she became a deputy majority whip.

She has supported the expansion of funding for breast cancer research and passed one bill making stalking a federal crime and another allowing full-time homemakers to set aside money for retirement. While not a political rebel, she has differed from Republican positions on some issues: in 1996 her decision to oppose the state Republican Party's platform plank on abortion nearly cost her a delegate's chair at the national convention. She also joined the eight other female senators (Democrats and Republicans) to oppose President Bill Clinton's recommendation that Admiral Frank Kelso, chief of naval operations during the event that resulted in the Tailhook sexual harassment scandal, be allowed to retire with full rank. She is a member of the Senate Armed Services Committee, Appropriations Committee, and Commerce, Science, and Transportation Committee.[11]

NOTES

1. *Houston Chronicle*, October 17, 1971; Kay Bailey Hutchison to Ruthe Winegarten, March 13, 1997.

2. *Fort Worth Star-Telegram*, February 5, 1993; Jan Jarboe, "Sitting Pretty," *Texas Monthly*, August 1994, p. 103; Kay Bailey Hutchison, "Questionnaire," prepared and administered by Nancy Baker Jones and Ruthe Winegarten, 1997.

3. Jarboe, "Sitting Pretty," p. 104.

4. Kay Bailey Hutchison, videotape interview by Nancy Baker Jones, August 18, 1995, Archives for Research on Women and Gender, University of Texas at San Antonio (hereafter ARWG).

5. Hutchison, "Questionnaire"; Hutchison, interview, ARWG; Hutchison to Winegarten; Jarboe, "Sitting Pretty," p. 104.

6. Hutchison, "Questionnaire"; *Who's Who in American Politics 1981–1982* (Newark: R. R. Bowker & Co., 1981), p. 937.

7. *Fort Worth Star-Telegram*, May 16, 1993; Jarboe, "Sitting Pretty," pp. 104–105.

8. *Dallas Morning News*, January 3, 1991; *Austin American-Statesman*, January 3, 1991; *Fort Worth Star-Telegram*, February 5, 1993.

9. *Fort Worth Star-Telegram*, September 28 and December 17, 1993.

10. *Austin American-Statesman*, October 20, 1994.

11. Kay Bailey Hutchison, "Biography," January 24, 1997, in files of Nancy Baker Jones; Hutchison to Winegarten; *Austin American-Statesman*, June 23, 1996.

SARAH RAGLE WEDDINGTON

HOUSE 63rd–65th Legislatures (1973–1977)
Democrat, Austin
DISTRICT 37-2; 37b
COMMITTEES Appropriations; Criminal
Jurisprudence; Insurance; Elections;
Constitutional Convention, 1974
(Delegate)

DATES February 5, 1945–
BIRTHPLACE Abilene
FAMILY Ron Weddington (divorced); no
children
EDUCATION McMurry College (B.S.,
1964); University of Texas at Austin (J.D.,
1967)
OCCUPATION Attorney; professor; lobbyist

SARAH RAGLE WEDDINGTON is best known for having successfully argued *Roe vs. Wade* (which legalized abortion) before the U.S. Supreme Court just five years after she graduated from law school. The daughter of a Methodist minister and his wife, she went to public schools in Canyon and Vernon and attended McMurry College in Abilene to become a teacher. Weddington believes that the world into which she was born and grew up contributed to her desire to change society. It was "a time when social and legal restrictions forced women into narrower roles than we longed to occupy. We were told 'Women don't,' 'You can't,' 'That would be too strenuous for you.'"[1] Her parents, however, were simultaneously encouraging her to do whatever she wanted. She decided to become a lawyer and to work for equal legal rights for women.

At the University of Texas Law School, she was one of only 40 women among 1,600 students. She worked briefly as an assistant city attorney of Fort Worth, then opened her own practice and almost immediately joined with Dallas lawyer Linda Coffee on the *Roe* case, deciding to defend their client's right to have an abortion. Herself once "a scared graduate student in 1967 in a dirty, dusty Mexican border town to have an abortion, fleeing the law that made abortion illegal in Texas,"[2] Weddington was determined that other women would not be forced to face the same experience.

Throughout 1971 and 1972, Weddington worked on *Roe*, arguing it before the Supreme Court twice. She was also active in the women's movement, lobbying in the Texas Legislature for ratification of the Equal Rights Amendment (ERA) and becoming a founder of the Texas and the National Women's Political Caucuses. Her lobbying experience, during which she had difficulty finding legislators who cared about what she had to say,[3] convinced Weddington the best way to get women's issues translated into good law was to become a legislator herself. She had worked in the House in 1965 as a clerk-typist and had spent a lot of time watching the House in session. "The more I watched, the more I thought, 'I could do that.'"[4] In 1972 she waged a grassroots campaign directed by an experienced political activist named Ann Richards. Weddington became the first woman from Austin and Travis County elected to the Texas House of Representatives, defeating a runoff opponent who referred to her only as "that sweet little girl."[5] It was a watershed election year, for more women were sent to the legislature than ever before—one to the Senate and five to the House. Women legislators were such an unusual sight that when they were asked to official functions, the invitations suggested they bring their wives. During the first month of her first session, in January 1973, Weddington learned that she had won *Roe vs. Wade*.[6]

Not only was the women's movement "in the air," but so was a reform spirit in Texas politics. Voters, angered by the Sharpstown scandal and supportive of Weddington's work on *Roe* and for the ERA, elected her to make a difference. One of the first things Weddington did was to change the law that restricted women's ability to get credit cards in their own names. Being denied a card of her own had provoked Weddington: "I was a licensed attorney, my husband had come back from military service, I was putting him through law school, . . . and we were basically living on my salary, and I didn't think I ought to have to have his signature. . . . So I would not accept credit on that basis and passed the Equal Credit Bill and went back and got my credit card."[7]

As a legislator, Weddington co-sponsored the Kidney Health Bill, a $5 million appropriation to assure Texans access to kidney dialysis machines, and worked on legislation for historic preservation and the veterans' land program. She joined with the other women in the House—Kay Bailey (Hutchison), Eddie Bernice Johnson, Chris Miller, and Senfronia Thompson—to get other reform legislation passed. They passed bills to stop schools from firing pregnant teachers and to assure five-year-olds access to kindergarten. Weddington introduced a bill supporting alimony, but it would take another twenty years before Senfronia Thompson finally passed a bill providing for limited alimony. She joined with Republican Kay Bailey to pass House Bill 284 to provide compensation to rape victims, to protect their privacy, and to stop authorities from treating victims as if they were guilty. Weddington also opposed a separate presidential primary for Texas and supported increased benefits for state and university employees. She fought anti-abortion legislation, supported funding for the arts, and created a new district court for Travis County. After her first term, the Texas Student Lobby named her one of the top ten freshmen. In 1975 *Texas Monthly* named her one of the ten best legislators in the state. "They were wonderful years," Weddington recalled, "and part of what made it so wonderful was that the injustices involving women were so clear and that some of the women were Republicans and some of the women were Democrats, but any time all of the women in the Texas Legislature could agree on a piece of legislation, it passed."[8]

Making friends in the legislature was occasionally difficult, Weddington recalled, because the culture was unaccustomed to the presence of women as lawmakers. "There were situations when there were individual members, especially after late evenings when there was drinking, who had a hard time telling women who were the members from women who were not, so I just decided I wouldn't go to those late night activities."[9] In addition, doorkeepers occasionally prevented women members from entering the House because they assumed the women were not members. Weddington, however, did make lifelong friends there, and one of them was Bob Johnson, House parliamentarian, who served as a mentor. During this time, she also served as president of the National Abortion Rights Action League.[10]

In 1977, during her third term, Weddington worked part time under an executive appointment as a paid legal consultant to the Department of Agriculture in Washington, D.C., and published a book, with several co-authors, called *Texas Women in Politics*. After Jimmy Carter became president, Weddington resigned her seat in the legislature to become general counsel for the Department of Agriculture. In 1978 she became an adviser to the president on women's issues, during which time she fought for an extension of the time required to ratify the Equal Rights Amendment and provided Carter with names of women qualified for high-level appointments. Weddington was later promoted to the White House senior staff as a liaison to state Democratic parties during Carter's reelection campaign. She was named by *Time* magazine as one of the ten outstanding young American leaders in 1979.[11]

After Carter's loss in 1980, she taught at Wheaton College in Norton, Massachusetts, at the University of New Mexico School of Law, and at Texas Woman's University. In 1983 Governor Mark White appointed her director of the Office of State-Federal Relations in Washington, D.C. She resigned this position in 1985 under pressure from some state legislators who charged her with abusing state time and money. Weddington contended the charges were politically motivated.[12] She returned to Austin to her own law practice and taught at the University of Texas at Austin. In 1992 she published *A Question of Choice*, her account of winning *Roe vs. Wade*. She became a lobbyist for the Maine Yankee Atomic Power Company, among others, and moved increasingly into writing and public speaking, particularly about women and leadership.

NOTES

1. Sarah Weddington, *A Question of Choice*, p. 17.

2. Ibid., p. 11; *Fort Worth Star-Telegram*, September 1, 1978.

3. Sarah Weddington, Jane Hickie, Deanna Fitzgerald, Elizabeth W. Fernea, and Marilyn P. Duncan, "Sarah Weddington," *Texas Women in Politics*, p. 78.

4. Sarah Weddington, videotape interview by Nancy Baker Jones, June 18, 1995, Archives for Research on Women and Gender, University of Texas at San Antonio (hereafter ARWG).

5. Weddington et al., "Sarah Weddington," p. 78.

6. Ibid., p. 79.

7. Weddington, interview, ARWG.

8. Weddington et al., "Sarah Weddington," p. 81; Ann Fears Crawford and Crystal Sasse Ragsdale, "Sarah Ragle Weddington: Adviser to the President," *Women in Texas: Their Lives, Their Experiences, Their Accomplishments*, pp. 336–337; *Daily Texan*, May 11, 1973; Weddington, interview, ARWG.

9. Weddington, interview, ARWG.

10. Ibid.

11. Crawford and Ragsdale, "Sarah Ragle Weddington," pp. 337–341; Patricia Lasher and Beverly Bentley, "Sarah Weddington," *Texas Women: Interviews and Images*, pp. 186–187.

12. *San Antonio Express-News*, March 22, 1985.

DOROTHY J. CHRISMAN (CHRIS) MILLER

HOUSE 63rd–65th Legislatures (1973–1979)
Democrat, Fort Worth
DISTRICT 32-8; 32-I
COMMITTEES Human Resources; Health
and Welfare; Environmental Affairs;
Reapportionment; Constitutional Revision
(Vice Chair); Constitutional Convention,
1974 (Delegate); Joint Committee on
Prison Reform

DATES June 15, 1926–March 12, 1995
BIRTHPLACE Boston, Massachusetts
FAMILY Clarence Miller (divorced);
Dwayne Jose; two children
EDUCATION Mills College (no degree)
OCCUPATION Public relations

CHRIS MILLER was an advocate for women's rights who entered politics out of a desire to help others. She was the first woman elected to represent Tarrant County in the House (Betty Andujar was elected from that county in 1972 to the Texas Senate), defeating a three-term incumbent in 1972. She grew up in a Navy family. She and her first husband moved to Fort Worth in the late 1940s where she owned her own public relations agency, was moderator of the local television program *Voters' Digest*, and volunteered for a variety of nonprofit organizations such as the Human Relations Commission, League of Women Voters, and Minorities Cultural Arts Association.[1]

After her divorce in 1965, Miller found herself confronted with obstacles and increasingly aware of injustices against women.[2] Her interests in women's rights and politics coalesced in her work as a founder of the Texas Women's Political Caucus in 1971. She "never shied away from the 'women's lib' tag," said one newspaper, and she did not understand women who accepted benefits won for them by women's rights pioneers but who disavowed women's liberation. As a legislator, she was an outspoken advocate for women but also promised to represent all of her constituents. "We didn't carry just women's things," she said of herself and the women with whom she served. "I think we would have been very bad legislators if we had."[3]

In the House, Miller actively worked for reform of laws related to rape and was largely responsible for a constitutional amendment allowing single adults to get homestead exemptions. She supported the creation of the Texas Commission on the Status of Women and opposed efforts to rescind the state's ratification of the federal Equal Rights Amendment, pointing out that nothing bad had happened since Texans had approved a state equal rights amendment in 1972.[4] Miller was disappointed that the legislature did not deal with school financing or provide backing for day care, which she regarded as the only solution for getting women off welfare and into employment. She believed that these reform efforts would have succeeded had there been more women in the legislature because "the needs of children probably have a greater impact on women."[5]

Once approached by a lobbyist who implied he could help her get reelected if she would support a particular bill and, by putting her name on it, "purify" it, Miller refused, saying it was a bad bill. "Right now the lobbyists . . . don't know how to approach [women]," she said. "And they can't offer us the same things as they do men legislators—a girl somewhere." But she believed at some point lobbyists would learn, and women would respond. Women would not purify the political system of corruption, Miller believed, because "as more women are elected to public office, they will be confronted with as many pressures and temptations as men and will succumb."[6]

Miller was a pioneer in advocating water quality control; she also supported prison reform, favored restructuring the school financing system to include a corporate profits tax, and served on the Legislative Ad Hoc Committee on Utility Regulation. She authored bills that reduced several "taxes on taxes," provided penalties for hit-and-run accidents on water, made it possible for urban counties to obtain federal funds, and opposed a state income tax and an increase in sales taxes.[7]

As a member of the 63rd Legislature, Miller, along with all her colleagues, was a delegate to the Constitutional Convention of 1974. Spearheaded by the League of Women Voters, the convention was the first significant attempt to create a new state constitution since the Constitutional Convention of 1875. It was an effort Miller described as "more important than the next election or anything else" because it would determine "the next 100 years of Texas government." But after seven months of work, the delegates, distracted by an election year and divided by arguments over a right-to-work amendment that pitted union against anti-union forces, failed by three votes to produce a constitution to submit to voters. Miller had supported the document but finally voted against it.[8]

Shortly before the Democratic primary in May 1978 that could have brought Miller a fourth term, she and another incumbent, Fort Worth representative Gib Lewis, were unopposed in their respective districts. But the Supreme Court affirmed new court-ordered districts, and she and Lewis were thrown into a race against each other. Lewis was a conservative who was heavily supported by life insurance, banking, and medical interests as well as many wealthy individuals. Miller was supported by the United Auto Workers, the Fort Worth Police Association, and environmental and conservation groups. She lost by more than 2 to 1. Miller had supported the redistricting that cost her seat, but she said she had no regrets.[9]

After leaving the House, Miller remarried and remained active in civic and women's issues. A founding member of the Women's Center of Tarrant County, she provided the site of her Fort Worth legislative office to the new center and paid its rent for eight years. She also went into the travel business and started her own agency. Chris Miller died as a result of a stroke.[10]

NOTES

1. *Fort Worth Star-Telegram*, March 13, 1995; Sarah Weddington, Jane Hickie, Deanna Fitzgerald, Elizabeth W. Fernea, and Marilyn P. Duncan, "Chris Miller," *Texas Women in Politics*, p. 75.

2. *Dallas Morning News*, March 14, 1995.

3. *Dallas Morning News*, June 14, 1973.

4. *Fort Worth Star-Telegram*, October 21, 1974; Weddington et al., "Chris Miller," p. 75.

5. *Dallas Morning News*, June 14, 1973.

6. *Dallas Times Herald*, September 14, 1973.

7. Weddington et al., "Chris Miller," p. 75.

8. *Fort Worth Star-Telegram*, October 21, 1974.

9. *Dallas Times Herald*, May 10, 1978. Lewis became speaker of the House in 1983.

10. *Dallas Times Herald*, May 10, 1978; *Fort Worth Star-Telegram*, March 13, 1995.

EDDIE BERNICE JOHNSON

HOUSE 63rd–65th Legislatures (1973–1977)
SENATE 70th–72nd Legislatures (1987–1993)
Democrat, Dallas
DISTRICT House, 33-O; Senate, 23
COMMITTEES House: Labor (Chair);
Constitutional Amendments; Social Services,
Human Resources, Calendars, State Affairs;
Constitutional Convention, 1974 (Delegate);
Public Information (Vice Chair). Senate:
Education; Finance; Health and Human
Services; Nominations; Intergovernmental
Relations

DATES December 3, 1936–
BIRTHPLACE Waco
FAMILY Divorced; one child
EDUCATION University of Notre Dame (D.P.N., 1955); Texas Christian University
(B.S., 1967); Southern Methodist University (M.P.H., 1976)
OCCUPATION Nurse; federal administrator; business owner

EDDIE BERNICE JOHNSON was the first African American woman elected from Dallas to the Texas House, the first African American from Dallas in the Texas Senate, and only the second African American woman to represent Texas in the U.S. Congress. Active in both the civil rights and women's movements, she ran for office to secure social reform legislation. She grew up in Waco, the daughter of parents who registered African Americans to vote in the 1940s. Although her parents were Democrats, Johnson became a Republican to vote for Dwight Eisenhower. She became a Democrat in 1960.[1]

In the late 1950s Johnson moved to Dallas, where she endured "the most blatant, overt racism that I ever experienced in my life." As the first African American professional at the Dallas Veterans Administration Hospital, she became chief psychiatric nurse, despite overt discrimination, and wrote the hospital's equal employment opportunity guidelines to protect future minority employees. Before the 1964 Civil Rights Act, black women were not allowed to try on clothing or shoes in Dallas department stores. "People tried them on for you, or they would measure your foot and guess your size," Johnson said. She helped organize an economic boycott by black women, then became involved in getting blacks elected to public office. She was the founding president of a Dallas section of the National Council of Negro Women and, in cooperation with other women's and civil rights groups, worked to desegregate Dallas buses and public accommodations. She was also a charter member of the Texas Women's Political Caucus and joined the state board of the Women's Equity Action League.[2]

Johnson resigned from the VA hospital staff to run for the legislature in 1972. "I didn't have many mentors, but the ones I had were very good," she said, pointing to Sarah T. Hughes, Barbara Jordan, and Sissy Farenthold. Most of her support came from black men and white women. "Black females weren't sure that [this was] what a black woman should do," she said. Her campaign against Berlaind Brashear was underfinanced, but she was elected in a landslide in the Democratic primary by voters ready to reform the legislature after the Sharpstown stock fraud scandal. She had no opponent in the general election. Although in 1973 there were more women and blacks in the House than had served at one time before, the sight of both was still unusual. "This was the first time in Texas that we'd had that kind of diversity in the House," she recalled. "There was a great deal of questioning and suspicion and challenge we could see on the faces of those who had been there longer, because this was a new crop of people for a new era. And we ushered in that era, and we made a lot of changes." Early in that term, Johnson established her presence: she made headlines by criticizing Texas comptroller Robert Calvert for hiring women only for clerical jobs.[3]

She also set to work on legislation. "At that time, a woman couldn't get a bank loan or, often, a department store credit card without the signature of her husband or father," Johnson said. "So I cosponsored the credit act which finally eliminated discrimination against women." She also sponsored bills to guarantee job protection and equal benefits for pregnant teachers, prevent jurors from being fired by their employers for jury service, require schools to provide breakfast for needy children, prevent pregnant women from being denied unemployment compensation, help low-income citizens secure and retain housing, establish a fair housing commission to prevent discrimination, and prevent lending institutions from discriminating in making home loans. In addition, she sponsored child care legislation and supported Austin representative Sarah Weddington's efforts to make abortion and amniotic testing available. She was a vocal supporter of the Equal Rights Amendment, and when some legislators attempted to rescind the state's ratification of it in 1975, her membership on the Constitutional Amendments Committee allowed her to table the rescission legislation, thereby killing it. She ran unopposed for her second and third terms in the House.[4]

Johnson left the House in 1977 to become a regional director of the Department of Health, Education, and Welfare, a position to which she was appointed by President Jimmy Carter. She later moved to Washington, D.C., to work in the office of the surgeon general at HEW. After Carter's defeat, she served briefly as a consultant to a cable television franchise, then became vice president of the Visiting Nurses Association of Texas and opened her own consulting business. She postponed plans to run for office to care for her ailing parents.[5]

In 1986 Johnson entered politics again and won another decisive victory for a seat in the Texas Senate, winning the place formerly occupied by Oscar Mauzy. After ten years away from the legislature, she noted few changes. The "three B's" of lobbying—"booze, beefsteak, and broads"—had been replaced by hunting and golfing trips, but women were, for the most part, not included in them. "The trips are bad politics," she said, "but I don't even hear about them until I read about them in the papers." Women, she observed, were still not taken seriously. "When you look at the important huddles, the important power positions, the people the big legislation is taken to and who gets all the big [campaign] checks, they're all men."[6]

In the Senate, Johnson got a resolution passed asking the governor to issue an executive order to raise the number of state agency contracts with minority- and women-owned businesses. She also sponsored a successful bill to allow battered spouses accused of murdering their abusers to enter evidence of abuse into their trials.[7] However, she gained most attention for her role in redesigning Dallas' Congressional District 30, as Barbara Jordan had done in Houston, to secure a congressional seat. As chair of the Senate's subcommittee on congressional districts in 1991, Johnson challenged members of the Dallas delegation, primarily U.S. representatives John Bryant and Martin Frost, and achieved a district in which she, rather than either of them, would become the most likely winner of a congressional race. The effort earned her a mention on *Texas Monthly*'s list of worst legislators, but others felt Johnson simply had been underestimated by her colleagues and that she had outmaneuvered them.[8]

Race played a big part in the redistricting struggle, for black Dallas voters and politicians were suspicious of who would redesign the district and how they would fare as a result. Johnson and black state representative Fred Blair threatened to sue their opponents if the new district was not to their liking. When Lieutenant Governor Bob Bullock repaid Johnson's loyalty by throwing his considerable political weight behind her design—a 50 percent black district—the game was over and Johnson had won.

In 1992, twenty years after Barbara Jordan's election to the U.S. Congress, Johnson won 74 percent of the vote and her first term there, making her only the second African American woman to represent Texas in Congress. In 1996 the U.S. Supreme Court declared District 30 and two other Texas districts to have been unconstitutionally drawn on the basis of race. Johnson stood for election that year, after the district was redrawn, and won, defeating six opponents decisively. The redistricting process "is not one of kindness. It is not one of sharing. It is a power grab," Johnson said to her constituents, urging African Americans to act in their own political self-interest when redistricting occurred again. "It's a question of getting what you can when you can get it."[9]

Reflecting on the increasing number of women in the Texas Legislature and in the U.S. Congress, Johnson said, "When you think about it, this nation has come to where it is now with only half of its brain power. It's just beginning to get the additional brain power that women can bring to the table. Can you imagine what this nation would be if we had had all of this brain power at work . . . all these years that women were left out . . . of this process? Look at all the gray matter we have missed."[10]

NOTES

1. *Dallas Morning News*, February 1, 1987.

2. "Spotlight on . . . Eddie Bernice Johnson," *Texas Women's News*, March 1986, p. 24; *Dallas Morning News*, February 1, 1987; Sarah Weddington, Jane Hickie, Deanna Fitzgerald, Elizabeth W. Fernea, and Marilyn P. Duncan, "Eddie Bernice Johnson," *Texas Women in Politics*, pp. 70–71.

3. Eddie Bernice Johnson, videotape interview by Mike Greene, October 19, 1995, Archives for Research on Women and Gender, University of Texas at San Antonio (hereafter ARWG); *Fort Worth Star-Telegram*, June 29, 1990.

4. *Fort Worth Star-Telegram*, June 29, 1990; *Texas Women's News*, March 1986, p. 24; Weddington et al., "Eddie Bernice Johnson," pp. 70–71; "Biography" and resume, authors' files; *Austin Insight* (Eddie Bernice Johnson newsletter), [1977], authors' files.

5. 1985 Texas Women's Hall of Fame Nomination Form, p. 2, The Woman's Collection, Library, Texas Woman's University; *Dallas Times Herald*, November 5, 1986; *Dallas Morning News*, February 1, 1987.

6. *Fort Worth Star-Telegram*, June 29, 1990.

7. "Eddie Bernice Johnson: Congresswoman-Elect," [1992], authors' files; *Austin American-Statesman*, March 22, 1991.

8. *Fort Worth Star-Telegram*, February 11, 1992; "The Best and Worst Legislators," *Texas Monthly*, October 1991, p. 157.

9. *Dallas Times Herald*, September 1, 1991; "Congresswoman Eddie Bernice Johnson, Biography," January 27, 1997, p. 1, authors' files; *Dallas Morning News*, June 14 and November 7, 1996; *Austin American-Statesman*, January 15, 1997.

10. Johnson, interview, ARWG.

☆

ELIZABETH (BETTY) RICHARDS ANDUJAR

SENATE 63rd–67th Legislatures (1973–1983)
Republican, Fort Worth
DISTRICT 12
COMMITTEES State Affairs; Intergovernmental Relations; Human Resources; Constitutional Convention, 1974 (Delegate)

DATES November 6, 1912–June 8, 1997
BIRTHPLACE Harrisburg, Pennsylvania
FAMILY John J. Andujar; two children
EDUCATION Wilson College (B.A., 1934)
OCCUPATION Volunteer; political activist

BETTY ANDUJAR was the first Republican woman elected to the Texas Senate, the same year fellow Republican Kay Bailey (Hutchison) was elected to the Texas House. Andujar was the first Republican senator elected since Reconstruction. In the fallout from the Sharpstown bank fraud scandal, which involved a number of members of the legislature, Andujar defeated Representative Mike Moncrief, a Democrat, in 1972. The campaign was a bitter one in which Andujar accused Moncrief of being tied to the scandal through House speaker Gus Mutscher. "Why fire the ventriloquist and keep the dummy?" she asked voters.[1] Andujar was the only woman and one of three Republicans in the Senate during her first term. She remained the only woman throughout her four terms.

The daughter of a Pennsylvania chief justice, Andujar married a physician who became president of the World Association of Pathology. Before her own political career, she was active in many civic and community organizations and volunteered in political campaigns, including Dwight Eisenhower's 1952 presidential race. But she credited two things—a desire to achieve something separate from her husband's professional prominence and a 1960 trip to Moscow—as notable influences on her decision to become politically active. "I became more interested in the freedoms we have, our concepts of free enterprise and the freedom from too much government interference and harassment," she said of the trip to the USSR. She became a Republican National Committeewoman in 1964 and was a delegate to the Republican National Convention in 1968. The party drafted her to run for the Texas House in 1970, which she did unsuccessfully, and then again for the Senate race in 1972.[2]

Called a consummate politician who "never quit being a lady," Andujar the senator was conscious of her identity as a woman, a physician's wife, and the lone female in the Senate.[3] "Women always have been important in politics because they are the transmission, oil, and gas of any political machine," she said. "We are having something to say about the direction in which the vehicle moves, and in some areas we are being asked to drive it. It finally dawned on our fine men that women do vote and that we have minds that are worth listening to." She hoped that women would bring new ideas about welfare, education, budgeting, and "responding to voters as individuals" to public life.[4] Once in the Senate, she said, her fellow senators' treatment of her was "gentlemanly," but she never became accustomed to their practice of reneging on promises to support bills she favored. She also said she was denied the chance to become a committee chair in the Democrat-controlled Senate because she was a Republican.[5]

She supported the creation of the Texas Commission on the Status of Women as a clearinghouse and complaint center about legal and economic rights of women, advocated the creation of service centers for displaced homemakers, and dealt with issues of rape and lowering the legal marriage age to fourteen under some circumstances. She also worked for sales tax reduction and penalizing possession of marijuana and supported a bill to grant immunity from lawsuits to people testifying about public school textbooks.[6] One of Andujar's major interests was legislation affecting the medical profession. She favored requiring county coroners to be qualified pathologists as well as increasing the membership of the State Board of Health; she was instrumental in the expansion of the Texas

College of Osteopathic Medicine, now the North Texas Health Science Center. On the last day of the 66th Legislature, she was embroiled in a controversy when, apparently at the request of the counsel of the Texas Hospital Association, she killed Austin representative Gonzalo Barrientos' bill to increase penalties for denying emergency treatment to non-English-speaking indigents. Andujar said the bill needed more study. When asked how to solve the problem of the language barrier between patients and hospital personnel, Senator Andujar replied: "My solution is they had better learn English. If I were sick in Hong Kong, I would be in trouble."[7]

In 1977 she was elected president pro tem of the Senate, making her third in line for succession to the governorship. Later that year she became the first Republican woman to serve as governor for a day, a ceremonial honor previously given to Neveille Colson and Barbara Jordan. She called that day the most memorable in her career. She was also proud to have encouraged the legislature to return to obeying its own rules and to have opened committee hearings by posting their meeting times and places.[8]

In December 1980, Andujar suffered a heart attack and was not able to resume her duties for several months. In the interim she missed opportunities to vote on two issues as she would have liked: for a pay raise for state employees and against allowing individuals who quit their jobs from receiving unemployment benefits.[9] Andujar retired in 1982. During the last twenty-six years of her life, she battled leukemia. In 1992 the Texas Medical Association hung her portrait in its headquarters. In 1996 the Texas Association of Pathologists honored her as the first layperson to receive its Citation of Merit. She died in her Fort Worth home.[10]

NOTES

1. *Fort Worth Star-Telegram*, June 9, 1997. The Republican senator who preceded Andujar was an African American, Walter Moses Burton (1874–1883).

2. Betty Andujar, "Questionnaire," prepared and administered by Nancy Baker Jones and Ruthe Winegarten, 1997; *Who's Who in American Politics* (New York: R. R. Bowker and Co., 1981), p. 919; *Fort Worth Star-Telegram*, August 8 and 31, 1972, June 9, 1997.

3. *Fort Worth Star-Telegram*, June 9, 1997.

4. *Fort Worth Star-Telegram*, August 8, 1972.

5. Andujar, "Questionnaire"; *Who's Who in American Politics*, p. 919.

6. *Senate Journal of Texas*, 65th Legislature, Regular Session, February 7, 1977, p. 2401;

Sarah Weddington, Jane Hickie, Deanna Fitzgerald, Elizabeth W. Fernea, and Marilyn
P. Duncan, "Betty Andujar," *Texas Women in Politics*, p. 55; *Dallas Morning News*, April
10, 1975, January 21, 1977.

7. Andujar, "Questionnaire"; *Dallas Times Herald*, June 7, 1979; *Austin American-Statesman*, May 29, 1979. English was the predominant language of Hong Kong at the time.

8. *Dallas Morning News*, January 11, 1977; Andujar, "Questionnaire."

9. *Fort Worth Star-Telegram*, February 7, 1981.

10. *Fort Worth Star-Telegram*, June 9, 1997.

SENFRONIA PAIGE THOMPSON

House 63rd Legislature– (1973–)
Democrat, Houston
District 89, 141
Committees Judicial Affairs (Chair);
Judiciary (Chair); Rules and Resolutions
(Chair); Constitutional Revision;
Appropriations; Business and Industry;
Education; Environmental Affairs; Higher
Education; Insurance; Labor; Local and
Consent Calendars; Redistricting;
Retirement and Aging; Rules; Urban
Affairs; Ways and Means; Constitutional
Convention, 1974 (Delegate)

DATES January 1, 1939–
BIRTHPLACE Booth
FAMILY Jobie Thompson (died); W. M. Carrington (divorced); three children
EDUCATION Texas Southern University (B.S., 1961); Prairie View A&M University
(M.Ed., 1964); Texas Southern University (J.D., 1977); University of Houston
(L.L.M., 1997)
OCCUPATION Teacher; attorney

SENFRONIA THOMPSON carries the honor of "dean" of women legislators, having served longer in the House than any other woman. In 1997
she became the longest-serving African American as well. She arrived in
the House in 1973 and, with Eddie Bernice Johnson, became one of the
first two black women ever to serve there. Early in her career, Thompson
wanted to be vice president, certain that the country was not ready for a
black female president. Eventually, however, she decided being a state rep-

resentative suited her well. Her constituents have reelected her twelve times. Prior to running for office, she taught mathematics, biology, physiology, and special education in Houston junior and senior high schools. One of eight children, she is the first in her family to have earned a high school diploma. She credits the atmosphere of 1972 with motivating her to go into politics. It was "the Year of the Woman," she said. "We had Barbara Jordan running for the U.S. Congress and Sissy Farenthold running for governor . . . and I just wanted to be part of this big harvest, so I ran. And I won."[1]

As a legislator, Thompson has focused on issues related to women, minorities, labor, consumers, victims of domestic violence, the elderly, teachers, and the protection of civil liberties. Saying she was not in the legislature "to window dress," she killed a bill her first term that would have given free tuition to Nicaraguan students attending state-supported colleges. She supported efforts to award legal counsel to juveniles before and after incarceration, pay state employees twice monthly, allow the public to sue polluting industries, protect the elderly from home repair fraud, support bilingual and early childhood education, reform child support enforcement, simplify probate proceedings and judicial elections, foster economic independence for blacks and other minorities, and observe "Juneteenth" statewide (celebrating June 19, 1865, the day the Emancipation Proclamation was declared in effect in Texas). She also worked to create a progressive corporate profits tax that she said would allow the state to increase homestead exemptions from school taxes, double elderly and disabled exemptions, and abolish the corporate franchise tax. She supported legalizing horse racing and compensation for farm workers. She authored and passed the Durable Power of Attorney Act, the Uniform Interstate Family Support Act, the Sexual Assault Program Fund, and the Family and Juvenile Justice Codes.[2]

Over the years, Thompson saw change in the way male legislators treated her. In her first term, after a white representative jokingly called her his mistress, she delivered a scathing personal privilege speech on the floor of the House. "I felt compelled that I had to put everyone on notice that I was a duly elected official, just like they were; I was always going to respect them, and I was going to demand respect from them," she said. Many of the men "felt that I had really offended them, that I should have ignored it. But it never happened again. Not to me and not to any other woman I'm aware of." In the early years, when there were few blacks, Thompson heard racist comments from time to time. "There were some legislators who used to walk around the House talking about how niggers ought to be back in the field chopping cotton," she said. As the numbers of blacks grew, those attitudes began to change, or at least were not openly voiced, sometimes because whites simply needed the votes. On one occasion, when Thompson and white Springlake representative Billy Clayton were both headed for the microphone at the same time, side by side, he "jumped like a leapfrog" when he realized he was walking next to her. The next session, as Clayton mounted his race for speaker, "he was begging me for my vote."[3]

Thompson's reputation evolved over the years as well. In the beginning, she was frequently noted for her beauty more than her ability. Twenty years later, she was regarded as a presence, pugnacious, determined, and straight-talking. "She's like a Gila monster" on issues she supports, said Beaumont representative Mark Stiles. "When she has her teeth sunk in, no amount of thunder can shake her loose. But she is everyone's friend because she doesn't hold a grudge." When asked to define her personal style, she said simply, "I don't take shit."[4]

In 1995, in what may have been her most satisfying victory, Thompson succeeded, after twelve years, in passing her bill legalizing a limited form of alimony, thereby ending Texas' claim as the only state in the nation without it. Only two years earlier, she had blasted the ten men on the House Calendars Committee for keeping the bill bottled up. "When the Almighty, in her infinite wisdom, shatters sexist economics in one miraculous blow, may the shards of that glass ceiling pierce those cold-hearted men whose greed has held us down for far too long," she declared. Intended to assist spouses who had spent their time raising families and then found themselves without marketable job skills after a divorce, the bill became palatable, she said, when the conservative push for welfare reform overtook the House. Thompson was able to argue, at last successfully, that providing alimony in these cases would reduce the welfare rolls. "It was hard to argue against that," she said.[5]

NOTES

1. *Houston Chronicle*, November 12, 1972, February 12, 1973; Senfronia Thompson, resume, 1997; Senfronia Thompson, videotape interview by Nancy Baker Jones, May 26, 1995, Archives for Research on Women and Gender, University of Texas at San Antonio (hereafter ARWG).

2. *Houston Chronicle*, February 12, 1973; Thompson resume; *Houston Chronicle*,

May 21, 1980; Senfronia Thompson, "Taxing Corporate Profits: A Proposal," *Texas Observer*, December 10, 1982, pp. 19–21; Senfronia Thompson fact sheet, 1985.

3. *Houston Post*, April 13, 1973; Thompson, interview, ARWG; *Beaumont Enterprise*, May 6, 1985.

4. *Houston Chronicle*, May 9, 1995; Thompson, interview, ARWG.

5. *Houston Post*, March 30, 1993; *Houston Chronicle*, May 9, 1995.

☆

SUSAN GURLEY MCBEE

HOUSE 64th–67th Legislatures (1975–1983)
Democrat, Del Rio
DISTRICT 70
COMMITTEES Agriculture and Livestock;
Calendars (Chair); Elections (Chair)

DATES December 9, 1946–
BIRTHPLACE Del Rio
FAMILY James Larry McBee; one child
EDUCATION Texas A&M University (B.A.,
1969); Sul Ross State University (M.Ed.,
1989)
OCCUPATION Rancher; teacher

SUSAN MCBEE is the first woman to follow her mother in the Texas Legislature. The daughter of Dorothy Gillis Gurley (Cauthorn), McBee credited a family history of political activity and her own interest in politics with spurring her to run for the House. Frequently asked if she were a supporter of "women's lib," McBee said no. "People were very interested in whether I was going to continue keeping house and maintaining our family unit if I was elected to serve in Austin," she said.[1] It was the same question asked of her mother twenty-four years earlier. People seemed "especially glad" to see McBee's husband campaigning with her. "Somehow, they needed his approval to establish my credibility as a serious candidate."[2] She was twenty-eight when she won her first term.

McBee saw the overriding issue of her first session as public school finance reform—specifically, increased funding for needy rural schools. She had firsthand knowledge of these needs, having spent two years teaching in the speech therapy department in San Felipe before it was consoli-

179

dated with Del Rio's school district. She also taught in the special education department of the consolidated district. In her vast nine-county district in South Texas, agriculture and tourism were primary interests, but she recognized other interests there, including oil and gas, spinach, and the Raza Unida Party, which had been created in the district in 1970 to champion the interests of Mexican Americans and had fielded candidates for governor in 1972 and 1974.[3]

During her first session, McBee sponsored a bill to allow sparsely populated rural counties to establish precincts with fewer than one hundred voters. She also co-sponsored a bill to require payment to ranchers within twenty-four hours of the sale of cattle. She worked for passage of a bill requiring state agencies, including prisons and educational agencies, to buy only domestic beef, excluding imported meats in an effort that *Independent Cattleman* magazine called "one of the year's greatest assists to livestock producers in Texas." McBee was named Del Rioan of the Year by the *Del Rio News-Herald* in 1977.[4]

McBee was disappointed at the end of her second session when the legislature failed to pass a tax reduction bill and bills to increase teacher salaries and education funding for her district and other rural schools. She introduced seven bills and co-sponsored several others; five passed and went to the governor. Two of these dealt with election code changes to give counties more flexibility in registration and election procedures. Her other successful bills included one to solve some junior college problems, one to make federal funds available for cattle tick eradication, and one that favorably affected wool and mohair lenders, including those in her district. In 1980 McBee became the first woman to be named Man of the Year by the Texas County Agricultural Agents Association for outstanding leadership in agriculture and related industries. In 1982 she became the first woman recipient of the Fred T. Earwood Memorial Award by the Texas Sheep and Goat Raisers Association.[5]

Notable aspects of McBee's legislative career were three of her appointments—to the legislature's Ethics Advisory Committee (EAC), to the Legislative Council, and as chair of the powerful Committee on Calendars. The EAC was created in 1981 by House speaker Billy Clayton (after he was found innocent of bribery charges in connection with campaign contributions) to recommend guidelines and standards of conduct on how politicians obtain and spend campaign contributions. One reporter observed that McBee's appointment to the committee revealed that Clayton intended it to be effective. Lobbyists, who knew McBee not only as a conservative, business-oriented team player, but also as someone with a reputation for honesty and independent thought, were reportedly disappointed by her selection.[6]

McBee's membership on the Legislative Council gave her oversight of the staff office that researches and writes bills, thus setting their tone. As chair of the powerful Calendars Committee, McBee controlled when and if the House would consider bills. In July 1981, *Texas Monthly* selected McBee as one of the ten best legislators of the year, partly because of the way she reformed the Committee on Calendars. She "brought democracy to a fiefdom that . . . has known only tyranny," the magazine said. Prior to her tenure, any member could arbitrarily scuttle any bill "for reasons wholly unrelated to merit: personal enmity for the sponsor, opportunity for deal-making, [or] whim." McBee imposed majority rule on the committee, making it impossible for one person to kill a bill. Next to Clayton, *Texas Monthly* concluded, McBee was most responsible for creating a "spirit of rapprochement that pervaded the House this session." Additionally, she showed her mettle by casting a swing vote in committee for a Republican challenger against a conservative Democrat, "one of the most courageous and independent acts" of the session, her fourth.[7]

McBee had considered not running for a third term in 1979 but decided to continue so she could protect her district from being divided by redistricting. By the end of her fourth term, however, McBee had decided not to run for reelection, saying she was exhausted and that someone else deserved the honor. The most satisfying part of her service, she said, was the overwhelming support of her constituents. After a year of retirement, however, McBee was in Austin again, as newly elected governor Mark White's legislative liaison. She called it a unique opportunity to serve as a link between the governor and the legislature.[8]

After leaving politics, McBee returned to her family's 32,000-acre ranch and resumed teaching special education. She remains active in community affairs.

NOTES

1. Kellyn Murray, "'Like Mother Like Daughter'. . . Or So the Saying Goes," *Steering Wheel*, January 1975, pp. 16–17; "Lady, Rancher, Lawmaker," *Ranch Magazine*, April 1975, p. 13.

2. *Houston Chronicle*, January 10, 1951; Dorothy Gillis Gurley Cauthorn, resume; "Gillis Family History," typescript, n.d., authors' files; Murray, "'Like Mother Like Daughter,'" p. 16.

3. Murray, "'Like Mother Like Daughter,'" p. 17; McBee defeated La Raza Unida candidates in at least one of her races (Susan Gurley McBee to Ruthe Winegarten, September 1997).

4. "Homemaking, Ranching and Lawmaking Come Together at the McBee Place," *Independent Cattleman*, April 1976, pp. 26, 28; *Del Rio News-Herald*, January 2, 1977.

5. *Del Rio News-Herald*, June 9, 1977; *Sanderson Times*, July 17, 1980; Susan Gurley McBee, resume.

6. Unidentified clipping, September 20, 1981, Susan Gurley McBee's files.

7. "The Best and Worst Legislators," *Texas Monthly*, July 1981, p. 104.

8. Press release, campaign office of [Governor-elect] Mark White, January 12, 1983; *San Angelo Standard Times*, December 15, 1981, February 13, 1983.

☆

WILHELMINA RUTH FITZGERALD DELCO

HOUSE 64th–73rd Legislatures (1975–1995)
Democrat, Austin
DISTRICT 31-1; 37-D; 50
COMMITTEES Constitutional Revision; Rules (Vice Chair); Health and Welfare; Liquor Regulation; Constitutional Amendments; State, Federal, and International Relations; Business and Commerce; Science and Industry; Corrections (Vice Chair); General Investigating (Chair); Public Education (Vice Chair); Higher Education (Chair)

DATES July 16, 1929–
BIRTHPLACE Chicago, Illinois
FAMILY Exalton Delco; four children
EDUCATION Fisk University (B.A., 1952)
OCCUPATION Civic and educational affairs

WILHELMINA DELCO experienced many "firsts" in her life: first African American elected to the school board of the Austin Independent School District, first African American elected to represent Travis County in the Texas House, and first woman appointed speaker pro tempore of the House. Her career there lasted twenty years—through three speakers and four governors. She introduced more than one hundred bills.

Delco's interest in the community started when her children were small. She was active in the Girl Scouts and PTA, but in 1968 decided to run for the school board of the Austin public schools to have wider influence. Delco's impressive ideas and speaking ability, combined with the timing of the election two days after the assassination of Dr. Martin Luther King, Jr., resulted in voters' awakening to the need for diversity. She won. "People expressed their sorrow for Martin Luther King, then said they were going right out to vote for Wilhelmina Delco," said Ada Anderson, an Austin businesswoman and civic leader.[1]

Delco committed herself to representing the interests of her multiethnic East Austin district. She helped speed the school desegregation process and in 1969 was named one of Austin's outstanding women of the year. Serving on the school board took time from caring for the home, but she turned that into a family lesson. "Mother is not a maid," Delco told her children, and she and her husband created a "work wheel" to assign chores to themselves and each child.[2]

Delco continued to pursue educational equity and access for the poor and minorities. In 1973 she was a founder of Austin Community College and was elected to its first board of trustees. Delco said ACC offered people of limited financial means the opportunity to get a college education or training and to "lift themselves up and seize careers and education." Believing she would have even more influence over the quality of education if she were a state representative, Delco ran for a seat in the Texas House. In 1974 she and her primary fund-raiser, Ann Richards, raised enough money to support Delco's campaign. Again she won.[3]

During Delco's years in the legislature, the number of women elected to serve there grew steadily. In the 64th Legislature, her first term in 1975, she was one of nine women in the House and one woman in the Senate. By the 73rd Legislature, her final term, there were twenty-seven women in the House and four women in the Senate. In the early years especially, Delco believed a measure of accommodation to the House's male culture was necessary; she prepared herself by "doing my homework" so that no one could accuse her of being unprepared or ill informed.[4] On the other hand, she was not willing to change everything. In those years she wore her hair in an Afro, much as many black activists did. "Angela Davis wore her hair that way. So lots of legislators felt very threatened. And that was okay," Delco said.[5] Nor was she ready to do whatever it took to become part of the speaker's inner circle, where real power lay. "My devotion to family cost me politically," she said. "In Texas, power politics often is played out away from the public eye—in back room, after-hour meetings. . . . I wasn't one to sit around and sip coffee and drink a beer. . . . When I went to functions in the evenings, my husband went with me."[6]

Maintaining a balance between her personal and political lives remained one of Delco's challenges. "A lot of women choose to do it the same way that men do, . . . decide it's more important to be up at the House, or be with the group," she recalled. "I chose to try to accommodate both. I would come to the legislature at seven in the morning if it was necessary, but . . . I would always go home for lunch because I felt that was the time for me to step back from a high pressure position and get some sense of myself. . . . When members are elected to public office, it generates a high divorce rate. . . . I don't think it would have added to my effectiveness as [a committee] chair if I'd played golf, or if I'd gone hunting."[7]

Delco pursued such issues as child welfare, the licensing of day care facilities, support for displaced homemakers, a grievance procedure for state employees, and protection against child abuse. She also passed legislation to force Austin either to move its airport or to soundproof buildings in its flight path. However, her priorities remained focused on the quality of education. She was once the only representative to vote against allowing silent prayer in the schools. She supported dropout prevention and the reduction of class size to twenty-two students; she set a state standard for kindergarten through fourth grade, and she continually supported school finance reform, an issue she claimed was no nearer resolution when she retired than when she arrived. As chair of the House Higher Education Committee from 1979 to 1991, Delco oversaw one of the largest budgets in the state. Among her accomplishments was the bill establishing the Texas Academic Skills Program to identify college freshmen in need of remedial academic assistance, and House Bill 72, known popularly as "No Pass, No Play," which prevented students who were not succeeding academically from participating in sports.[8]

The accomplishment of which she was proudest was the passage of House Joint Resolution 19 in 1983 (after six years of trying), which proposed a constitutional amendment to alter the Permanent University Fund (PUF), the multibillion-dollar endowment funded by West Texas gas and oil royalties, to which only the University of Texas at Austin and Texas A&M University had access. The subsequent passage of that amendment by voters made the PUF accessible to all UT and A&M system schools and established the Higher Education Assistance Fund for the colleges that did not qualify for PUF money. One of the poorest campuses to benefit from Delco's efforts was the historically black university, Prairie View, which became part of the A&M system and gained access to the PUF. "Black is beautiful," she liked to say, "but not when it's poor and dumb." The school later named a building in her honor. In 1990 Delco chaired the South Africa Task Force of the National Conference of State Legislatures, toured South Africa with thirteen state legislators, and convinced conference delegates to continue economic sanctions against South Africa to help defeat apartheid.[9]

Delco's relationship with speaker of the House Gib Lewis was uneven. She refused to serve on a conference committee Lewis asked her to chair because he assigned his own allies to it in place of the members Delco had requested. "I told him I would not preside over a charade if I didn't have the votes to prevail," she said.[10] In 1991, despite misgivings about what he was about to do, Lewis named Delco speaker pro tempore, making her the first woman to hold the powerful "temporary speaker" position. As such, Delco served as the eyes and ears of the speaker, gauging the mood of the House membership on legislation and taking Lewis' place in his absence. "I realized how important it was for women and children, particularly, to walk in that House and see a woman in charge," she said about her reason for accepting the job. But she knew, too, that she was not a member of Lewis' inner circle. "I expect that he didn't get very much comfort from including somebody who would be in a decision-making role who was not part of that group," she recalled.[11]

Delco eventually violated Lewis' team ethic when she and other minority House members staged a walkout to stop a growing steamroller of opposition to educational funding. Lewis was outraged. "I appointed you Speaker and I can unappoint you," Delco remembered his saying. She replied, "You've gotta do what you've gotta do. And I've gotta do what I've gotta do." Delco believed that this was the defining moment in their relationship: he "clearly understood that I wasn't giving up my sex or my ethnicity or my principles for the honor of being Speaker *Pro Tem*." Lewis left her alone, and she served until 1993.[12]

Delco later decided that twenty years in the House were enough and that she wanted to step aside to let younger leaders take their place in public life. She retired from elective politics in 1995. Upon reflection, Delco noted what she believed to be a change in women and their relationship to politics. "In the past, women came out of . . . a setting as volunteers—as issue oriented rather than office oriented. We were always the helpers and the supporters. We didn't mind writing the speeches . . . until we realized, 'Hey, the speeches we're writing are better delivered by us than they are by those other folks,'" she said. Now she sees more women for whom political office is an end rather than a means to an end, as it was for her. "If something comes up where I could best address my issue by running or serving, I'm perfectly willing to do that. But to run for the sake of running . . . is not my interest at all."[13] Delco was succeeded in office by Dawnna Dukes.

NOTES

1. Wilhelmina Delco, resume, 1978; Wilhelmina Delco, fact sheet, 1991; *Austin American-Statesman*, November 3, 1993.

2. *Austin American-Statesman*, February 23, 1983.

3. Alberta Brooks, "No More House Work," *Our Texas*, Winter 1995, p. 21; Ken Martin, "Call Me *Madam*: Austin's Gift to Education," *Good Life*, February 1998, p. 16. Ann Richards later won three elections of her own to become county commissioner (1976), state treasurer (1982), and governor (1990).

4. *Austin Sun*, September 9, 1977.

5. Brooks, "No More House Work," p. 21.

6. Ibid., p. 22.

7. Wilhelmina Delco, videotape interview by Ruthe Winegarten, July 20, 1995, Archives for Research on Women and Gender, University of Texas at San Antonio (hereafter ARWG).

8. *Daily Texan*, March 6, 1975; *Dallas Morning News*, May 28, 1989; *Austin American-Statesman*, November 3, 1993; Brooks, "No More House Work," p. 22.

9. *Austin American-Statesman*, February 23, 1983, January 25, 1989, November 3, 1993; *Villager*, October 5, 1990; *NOKOA*, October 5–11, 1990; Delco, interview, ARWG.

10. Brooks, "No More House Work," p. 22.

11. Delco, interview, ARWG.

12. Ibid.

13. Ibid.

LOU NELLE CALLAHAN SUTTON

HOUSE 64th–70th Legislatures (1976–1989)
Democrat, San Antonio
DISTRICT 57-E, 120
COMMITTEES Appropriations; Retirement
and Aging (Vice Chair); Reapportionment;
Human Services; House Administration

DATES December 20, 1905–July 1, 1994
BIRTHPLACE Livingston
FAMILY Garlington Jerome Sutton (died);
one stepchild
EDUCATION Sam Huston College (Honorary LL.D., 1980s)
OCCUPATION Business owner

At age sixty-six, **LOU NELLE SUTTON** became the second woman to represent Bexar County in the Texas House. She was elected without opposition to fill the unexpired term of her husband, who died in office in 1976. She attended segregated public schools in San Angelo, and because she could not attend the segregated San Angelo Junior College (later Angelo State University), she moved to Austin to attend Sam Huston College.[1]

In 1939 she moved to San Antonio, where she became a church and civic leader and successful beauty salon operator. She worked with various groups to end discrimination and helped desegregate the San Antonio YWCA board. She was also active in politics, registering voters through the Organized Voters League. After her marriage into the prominent Sutton family, she became co-owner, with her husband, of the Sutton-Sutton Mortuary. Her mother-in-law, Lillian Viola Sutton, was a church and club leader; her sister-in-law, Dr. Thelma Sutton Brooks, was one of the first African American women in Texas to earn a medical degree; and her brother-in-law, attorney Percy Sutton, is an owner of Harlem's famous Apollo Club and a number of media enterprises. Her husband, G. J. Sutton, a civil rights activist, was the first black person from the South to win public office in the twentieth century when, in 1948, he became a member of the San Antonio Union Junior College District Board of Trustees. He was elected to the Texas House in 1972 and 1974. Hers was the only name on the ballot of the special election August 7, 1976, to fill his unexpired term, and she was reelected in November 1976 to a full term.

She won her 1978 Democratic primary election by a 4-1 majority and was unopposed in the November general election.[2]

Speaker of the House Billy Clayton appointed Lou Nelle Sutton to the same committees on which her husband had served, thereby making her a member of the powerful House Appropriations Committee. She pledged to finish a number of projects started by her husband, including establishing the first state office building outside Austin (the G. J. Sutton Building) and completing the St. Paul's Square renovation, both in her district. She was the only legislator not to introduce a bill in the 65th Legislature because, she said, she did not have time both to introduce bills and to attend to legislation she wanted funded by the Appropriations Committee. Nevertheless, Clayton praised her for having "brought home the bacon to San Antonio." Governor Bill Clements vetoed the funding for the Sutton Building, but she persuaded legislators to override the veto. Her critics called the building an expensive boondoggle, but she said it would be "a one-stop building," providing a valuable service to her poor constituents. Another of her accomplishments was funding for a mental health facility where retarded San Antonio children could stay near their families. Later she secured state funding for San Antonio's New Braunfels Street Bridge.[3]

Sutton's other legislative interests included upgrading St. Philips and San Antonio colleges, equalizing tuition grants for higher education, special education, and compulsory liability insurance. She voted for legalizing horse racing and opposed the death penalty because "it discriminates against blacks, browns, and poor whites."[4]

According to an African American columnist in San Antonio, many of Sutton's constituents thought she should not run for reelection in 1985 because her "best days as a legislative representative have passed." Nevertheless, she was reelected. Near the end of the next session, reporters for the same newspaper said she would soon announce her retirement to devote more time to civic affairs. She ran once again and was reelected. Sutton decided not to run again in 1988, and she was replaced by another African American woman, Karyne Jones Conley. Sutton's health began to decline in 1990, and she died in San Antonio at age eighty-eight.[5]

NOTES

1. *San Antonio Express*, August 8, 1976; Roy Burley, telephone interview by Ruthe Winegarten, August, 13, 1997; *San Angelo Standard Times*, February 12, 1984.

2. *San Antonio Light*, July 25, 1976; Leonard Murphy, "Sutton, Garlington Jerome (G. J.) (1909–1976)," typescript, [c. 1984], Sutton Family Collection, Institute of Texan Cultures, University of Texas at San Antonio, p. 2; *San Antonio Light*, July 25, 1976.

3. *Corpus Christi Caller*, May 20, 1977; *San Antonio Express*, August 14, 1976, October 29, 1977; *San Antonio Express-News*, May 6, 1984, July 3, 1994.

4. *San Antonio Express-News*, May 28, 1987; Files, Legislative Reference Library, Austin.

5. *San Antonio Express-News*, June 5, 1985, May 28, 1987, July 3, 1994; *Austin American-Statesman*, July 3, 1994.

MARY JANE GOODPASTURE BODE

HOUSE 65th–66th Legislatures (1977–1981)
Democrat, Austin
DISTRICT 37-B
COMMITTEES Transportation; Government Organizations; Constitutional Amendments; Rules

DATES July 28, 1926–September 23, 1998
BIRTHPLACE Chicago, Illinois
FAMILY Amadeo Carmignani (died); Winston Bode (divorced); four children
EDUCATION University of Houston; Incarnate Word College (no degrees)
OCCUPATION Journalist

A veteran member of the Austin Capitol Press Corps and press secretary for Texas attorney general John Hill, **MARY JANE BODE** launched her first campaign for the Texas House in 1968 with the slogan, "We need a woman in the House." Although she did not want to be elected simply to vote for women's issues, Bode understood the significance of women's presence in the legislature. "Three out of every five persons who work in Travis County are women," she said, but if she were not elected, she predicted, the House would remain 100 percent male. "The vital and significant point of view of women should be voiced and demonstrated in the legislature," she wrote in a campaign letter to a group of women in communication. Her platform focused on "the 'human things'—education, mental health and retardation, public health, air, water, and land pollution control, halfway houses for juveniles . . . [and] economy and efficiency in state government." Bode lost this election, but she ran again in a December 1977 special election to replace Austin representative Sarah Weddington. When she won by 66 votes, her supporters nicknamed her "Landslide Bode."[1]

As a legislator, Bode served in the July 1978 special session on taxation. In her only full session, she worked for children, the disabled, and state employees. She said her most memorable moment occurred on the last day of the session when Speaker Billy Clayton let her preside, and she held onto the gavel long enough to save one bill raising pay for state workers and others passed by her Government Organizations Committee. Clayton was "too much of a gentleman to have me thrown off" the dais, she said. As chair of the Select Committee on State Employee Productivity, she produced legislation that brought "serious improvements," but only because "some high-powered corporate stars on my committee conned Governor Clements into backing my recommendations."[2]

She helped pass a school finance package providing more equitable funding and allowing teachers and administrators to maintain more effective discipline. She also helped enact legislation that restructured property taxation, providing more equity between urban and rural taxpayers. She served on a statewide Child Abuse Study Committee and helped create a separate probate court for juveniles, authored a constitutional provision to exempt permanently disabled homeowners from property taxes, won passage of her bill to extend parking privileges to disabled veterans, authored legislation to remove stigmatizing language from the Texas Drivers License Code, and co-sponsored bills to reform group auto insurance and increase benefits for retired teachers and state workers. She tried unsuccessfully to end automatic relicensing of elderly drivers and to eliminate the state sales tax on commercial utilities. In addition, she supported a bill to remove the sales tax from household utilities, worked for accountability for highway expenditures, supported a rapid transit rail system to connect Austin with other major cities, preserved low-cost married-student housing at the University of Texas at Austin, and helped defeat efforts to abolish faculty tenure. She supported neighborhood associations, the use of state funds to buy and maintain state parks, and the prohibition of discrimination in insurance and hiring.[3]

Bode said many of her successes resulted from "killing or de-fanging some bad legislation" and from her ability to "write amendments quickly and correctly—on the spot."[4] In 1980 she was defeated by Terral Smith, claiming she was a victim of the Republican landslide that elected Ronald Reagan president. After leaving the legislature, she resumed her journalism career in Corpus Christi, Del Rio, and San Antonio, where she retired in 1989. Afflicted with ill health throughout her life, Bode overcame lockjaw, polio, Guillain-Barre Syndrome, and back surgery. She died of thyroid cancer in 1998, in a Chicago suburb, and was remembered for her journalistic ethics, lovely singing voice, and ebullient spirit. She was buried in the Texas State Cemetery.[5]

NOTES

1. Mary Jane Bode to members of Theta Sigma Phi, March 6, 1968, Mary Jane Bode, Vertical File, Barker Texas History Center, Center for American History, University of Texas at Austin; Mary Jane Bode, "Questionnaire," prepared and administered by Nancy Baker Jones and Ruthe Winegarten, 1997; *Austin American-Statesman*, December 20, 1977.

2. Bode, "Questionnaire."

3. Ibid.; campaign brochure, [1980]; Mary Jane Bode press release, January 1980.

4. Bode, "Questionnaire."

5. Bode, "Questionnaire"; *Austin American-Statesman*, September 24 and 27, 1998.

☆

LANELL COFER

HOUSE 65th–67th Legislatures (1977–1983) Democrat, Dallas
DISTRICT 33-O
COMMITTEES Criminal Jurisprudence (Vice Chair); Elections; Labor; Liquor Regulation

DATES 1950?–
BIRTHPLACE Dallas
FAMILY One child
EDUCATION East Texas State University (B.A., 1971); Texas Southern University (J.D., 1974)
OCCUPATION Attorney

Attorney **LANELL COFER** won a special election in November 1977 to replace state representative Eddie Bernice Johnson, who resigned to become a regional director of the Department of Health, Education, and

Welfare in the Carter administration. Cofer won in a runoff and won reelection for full terms in 1978 and 1980. The second of seven children of a truck driver and vocational nurse, Cofer decided in elementary school to be a lawyer after Judge Sarah T. Hughes spoke at the school. Her political inspiration came when she heard Barbara Jordan in a commencement address.[1]

Cofer's introduction to the legislature, during a special session that convened in July 1978 to consider tax relief, left her disappointed in her colleagues, who were shooting rubberbands and throwing paper airplanes. A Dallas newspaper columnist assessed Cofer at this time as "young and often shy. She hasn't come across as an articulate public speaker." But Cofer replied that "experience and exposure will take care of that."[2]

Cofer supported redistricting to give minorities more representation, regulation of animal shelters, allowing heirs to retain defaulted property, increased funding for Prairie View and Texas Southern universities, requiring sprinkler systems in nursing homes, and establishing January 15 as Martin Luther King, Jr., Day in Texas. She also advocated sending Texas Rangers and state funds to Atlanta, Georgia, to help solve a series of child murders, although Governor Bill Clements reportedly told her that he could not send rangers out of the state uninvited. A final newsletter from her office leaves unclear whether she supported or opposed appropriations for additional school financing and the Department of Corrections or for "War on Drugs" proposals such as wiretapping. *Texas Monthly* reported that she adamantly opposed wiretapping.[3]

At the end of Cofer's first session, colleagues called her performance "less than remarkable and nothing special." One said it was hard to predict what she would oppose or support. But the *Dallas Morning News* commended her for looking after her constituents and being in the vanguard of planning a protest of a Ku Klux Klan rally and march. During this first session, Cofer let it be known that she was tired of being referred to as the successor of Eddie Bernice Johnson, perhaps because Johnson had endorsed one of Cofer's opponents in the special election. In 1981 she caused the death of a bill to assure selection of women and minorities as masters to assist judges in criminal cases because Dallas County officials would not make certain compromises about it. "They have got to take me seriously, not manipulate me," she said.[4]

After Cofer's second session, *Texas Monthly* listed her as one of the term's ten worst legislators for her role as head of a special subcommittee

on wiretapping of suspected drug dealers. Speaker Billy Clayton reportedly named her to head the subcommittee only if she promised she would
not use the position to kill a bill legalizing wiretapping. Once appointed,
she tried to kill the bill. In 1982 she ran in the Democratic primary in the
redesigned District 111 against Jesse Oliver. Oliver won, with 2,175 votes
to Cofer's 1,414.[5]

NOTES

1. *Dallas Morning News*, April 2 and June 25, 1978.

2. *Dallas Morning News*, October 23, 1977; June 25, July 17, April 2, 1978.

3. Lanell Cofer, brochure to voters of District 33-O after the 67th Legislative Session
[1981], authors' files; *Texas Monthly*, July 1981, pp. 107–108.

4. *Dallas Morning News*, April 2, 1978, November 1, 1979, May 30, 1981.

5. *Texas Monthly*, July 1981, pp. 107–108; Marvin Thurman, Office of the Secretary of
State, to Ruthe Winegarten, November 7, 1997.

☆

ERNESTINE VIOLA GLOSSBRENNER

HOUSE 65th–72nd Legislatures (1977–1993)
Democrat, Alice
DISTRICT 58, 44
COMMITTEES Elections (Chair); Public
Education (Chair); Business and Com-
merce; Business and Industry; Health and
Welfare; Rules (Vice Chair)

DATES November 1, 1932–
BIRTHPLACE Troup
FAMILY Single; no children
EDUCATION Kilgore College (A.A., 1952);
University of Texas (B.A., 1954); Texas A&I
University (M.A., 1971)
OCCUPATION Teacher

ERNESTINE GLOSSBRENNER rose from what she calls a "long line
of oil-field trash" in East Texas to become one of the most respected legislators in the state. One of six children of an oil gauger and his wife, she
grew up in a home with "four rooms and a path to the privy." But books

and education were priorities, and her parents expected the children to go to college. She became a teacher, assuming she would "teach myself around the world." She planned to teach in Alice only two years but fell in love with the rich cultural mix and the humility of the people she met in the poverty-stricken area and stayed. She ran for the Alice city council in 1975 and came in fifth of nine candidates (the first four were elected). But she was the only candidate whose support was racially balanced.[1]

Glossbrenner desperately wanted to increase educational opportunity for her students, but was stymied by her district's representative, who had the highest absentee rate in the legislature and consistently voted—when he voted—against educational improvement. After attending a meeting of the new Texas Women's Political Caucus (TWPC) and hearing former representative and gubernatorial candidate Sissy Farenthold speak, Glossbrenner decided to run against the incumbent.[2] She ran in 1974 and lost, primarily because of voting irregularities in Duval County, long the fiefdom of father-son political bosses Archer and George "Duke of Duval" Parr. Glossbrenner's campaign workers reported that Duval County voters were afraid to talk with them or take her card. Because a state law required voters who did not use voting machines to sign their ballots, George Parr could easily learn how people voted. Glossbrenner brought fraud charges, but the grand jury indicted no one.[3]

By 1976, however, George Parr had committed suicide in the wake of mounting investigations into his part in three local murders, and Glossbrenner won the Democratic primary runoff. After Parr's death, she said, campaigning in Duval County was fun. "It's like people were saying 'Free at last!' and there were lots of candidates for every office." She jokes about her entry into politics: "What I did was go to town and teach until I'd taught a majority of the voters, and then I ran for office." The first time, she said, "I miscalculated, and they made me go back and teach two more years. Then I won by a landslide of 136." Because she could not accept two public salaries, Glossbrenner quit teaching and learned to live on a legislator's monthly salary of six hundred dollars. "Luckily," she said, "I'd been a teacher all my life and never had any money anyway." She was one of the poorer citizens in one of the poorest districts in the state.[4]

Glossbrenner was genuinely thankful to her constituents for her victory. Given her district's political history, and the possibility that she won the first uncontrolled race for representative there since the 1920s,

Glossbrenner felt especially aware of her responsibility to her constituents, whom she characterized as "humble people." She promised them that she would represent them rather than herself, remain accessible and accountable, fight to improve education, and try to reform the welfare system, "letting people feel again that they have a handle on their lives." When a lobbyist told her, "Nobody pays any attention to what you do when you get [here]," she responded, "Well, they may not have paid attention to you when you were in the legislature, but I have to answer to my voters."[5]

Glossbrenner supported equalization of state taxes across counties, closer supervision of elections by the secretary of state and attorney general, financing the purchase of newspapers for use in schools, improving safety for workers in trench digging, a state income tax, raising legislators' pay, raising the legal drinking age to twenty-six, and making the probate code conform to the state's Equal Legal Rights Amendment. Early in her legislative career, Glossbrenner used her wit during a rancorous redistricting debate to get her colleagues to listen to her and to end the debate. "You've all heard the saying: 'It ain't over till the fat lady sings.' Well, here she is." She then sang "Lead Kindly Light." The legislators laughed, the debate continued, and Glossbrenner's side lost. But she was asked to sing at the end of the session, and a tradition was born marking the end of subsequent sessions with her singing. One of her notable performances was "Thank God and Greyhound, We're Gone."[6]

Glossbrenner did not consider herself "just a women's candidate," saying, "I personally think women's liberation is human liberation." Everyone is affected by such "women's issues," she observed, as funding good education, medical care, getting people off welfare, helping families where both parents have to work, and focusing on unwed fathers as well as unwed mothers. She opposed parental notification of abortions for minors. In the 1987 session, when it became apparent that a bill to limit teenagers' access to abortion would pass, she made a final plea against it, delivering "one of the most memorable floor speeches in recent years to a stunned and silent House." Glossbrenner said: "I'm a fat, old-maid schoolteacher. I've never been pregnant, and I'm never going to be pregnant. But I have a concern here for those who will. . . . I believe what we are doing here today will mean that some of the abortions that are being performed in clinical places now will be performed in back alleys and dirty motels. And some young girls when they are old enough to be mothers will have been, if not killed, probably disfigured."[7]

Glossbrenner is probably best known for her work on the Public Education Committee that she chaired from 1989 until she retired. Her appointment to that committee by Speaker Gib Lewis was widely praised by educators, and Glossbrenner viewed the responsibility as her best opportunity to make a lasting difference in public schools. The Texas Supreme Court had ordered reform of school finance in 1989. Glossbrenner led efforts in 1990 and 1991 to approve revised plans, but each was rejected by the courts. She was ultimately disappointed when, during her last session, legislators failed to approve a funding plan during a special session, even though faced with a court-ordered deadline. Saying she had lost her enthusiasm for the job, Glossbrenner decided not to run again. She declined to sing at the end of her final session.[8]

Glossbrenner credited several influences on her as a legislator, including her parents, teaching and caring for children, belief in equality of opportunity for everyone, a belief in input into policymaking from many sources, including lobbyists, and the need for women in the legislature to raise the issues that men usually did not. Without women's views, she said, there were often "unintended consequences" to children and the family.[9]

Although she believed "the women of the house were just as diverse as the house itself," Glossbrenner and other women organized a successful network. Democrats and Republicans, they met at weekly lunches to exchange views, information, and ideas. To keep their meetings informal and avoid divisiveness, they did not call themselves a caucus. They did have a name, however; at one time their letterhead read "Ladies' Marching, Chowder, Terrorist, and Quasi-Judicial Society." Such meetings and collegial mentoring were more important to women than men in the legislature, she said, because men had already had more opportunities to get policymaking experience and because "there are things you have the nerve to ask a woman that you wouldn't . . . ask a man." She added, "That's probably true of men, too." She praised Sarah Weddington, Senfronia Thompson, and Susan McBee for helping her learn the ropes. In addition, she credits the TPWC with galvanizing her move into public life.[10]

After leaving the legislature, Ernestine Glossbrenner returned to Alice. She became president of the TWPC and remains active in it.

NOTES

1. *Corpus Christi Caller*, December 27, 1992; *Houston Chronicle*, November 2, 1989; Ernestine Glossbrenner, videotape interview by Ruthe Winegarten, July 7, 1995, Archives for Research on Women and Gender, University of Texas at San Antonio (hereafter ARWG); Sarah Weddington, Jane Hickie, Deanna Fitzgerald, Elizabeth W. Fernea, and Marilyn P. Duncan, "Ernestine Glossbrenner," *Texas Women in Politics*, p. 68.

2. Glossbrenner, interview, ARWG.

3. *Corpus Christi Caller*, December 27, 1982.

4. Evan Anders, "George Berham Parr," *New Handbook of Texas*, 5:70; Glossbrenner, interview, ARWG; Ernestine Glossbrenner, "Questionnaire," prepared and administered by Nancy Baker Jones and Ruthe Winegarten, 1997; *Houston Chronicle*, November 2, 1989.

5. Weddington et al., "Ernestine Glossbrenner," p. 70; Glossbrenner, "Questionnaire."

6. *Corpus Christi Caller*, December 26, 1976, June 8, 1987, December 27, 1992; *San Antonio Express*, February 16, 1983; *Houston Chronicle*, November 2, 1989; Glossbrenner, interview, ARWG; Glossbrenner, "Questionnaire."

7. *Corpus Christi Caller*, December 26, 1976; *Fort Worth Star-Telegram*, November 30, 1991.

8. *Corpus Christi Caller*, December 27, 1992; Glossbrenner, "Questionnaire."

9. *Corpus Christi Caller*, December 26, 1976.

10. Glossbrenner, interview, ARWG; Glossbrenner believed in the TWPC because of its commitment to legislation that has a positive impact on women and children, such as issues related to work and child care. The TWPC was founded in 1971 to galvanize women as voters and to help them become candidates. It also helps elect men with the same values and goals. Glossbrenner, interview, ARWG.

ANITA DORCAS CARRAWAY HILL

HOUSE 65th–72nd Legislatures (1977–1993)
Democrat until 1979, then Republican,
Garland
DISTRICT 33-D, 101
COMMITTEES Business and Commerce
(Vice Chair); Government Organization;
Local and Consent Calendars; Business and
Industry; Judicial Affairs (Vice Chair);
Cultural and Historical Resources (Vice
Chair); State, Federal, and International
Relations

DATES August 13, 1928–
BIRTHPLACE Chatfield
FAMILY Harris Hill (died); two children
EDUCATION Texas Woman's University
(B.A., 1950)
OCCUPATION Journalist; chemist

ANITA HILL was the first female legislator in Texas to change parties
while in office. In 1979, predicting a Republican sweep of her district in
the 1980 presidential election and contending that the Democratic Party
had become too liberal for her conservative views, Hill switched to the
GOP. Her husband, then secretary of the Dallas County Democratic Party,
resigned his post to help her campaign. The move was symptomatic of
the inevitable shifts across party lines that occurred in Texas during the
1970s and 1980s as the Republican Party gained ground, providing a home
for conservatives who formerly had no choice but the Democratic Party.
Although Anita Hill had been a Democrat since 1966, she had supported
Barry Goldwater's presidential campaign in 1964.[1]

Hill was first elected to the House as a Democrat on August 5, 1977, in
a special election runoff to fill the unexpired term of Representative Kenneth Vaughan, for whom she had worked as a legislative aide.[2] She ran
advocating the repeal of state taxes on utilities and remained interested in
utilities legislation throughout her tenure. Her first experience as a legislator was the 1978 summer special session, called to consider a variety of
tax issues, during which she and fellow Dallas County representative Lanell
Cofer observed legislators playing with paper airplanes and firing
rubberbands at one another.[3]

Hill introduced legislation regarding penalty and sentencing alternatives for those convicted of sexual abuse of children; fire safety and building standards for nursing and convalescent homes; funding for gifted and talented students; punishment for bad check writers; restrictions on the sale of motor fuel in places where alcohol was served or sold; types of behavior by public school students that could result in expulsion; and sealed-bid procedures for acquisition of property by counties. She also supported seat belt and child safety seat regulations; job safety regulations; retaining "blue laws" that prohibited stores from opening on Sundays; worker compensation; sunset legislation; and a minimum wage. She opposed availability of abortion services, horse racing, and a state lottery. After she and her brother took responsibility for an aged aunt with few financial resources, Hill was inspired to sponsor legislation making more low-income people eligible for Medicaid. After retiring from the legislature, Hill said one of her major achievements was regulation that toughened standards in nursing homes.[4]

In 1981 Hill experienced discrimination for the first time in her life, she said, when the private Citadel Club in Austin's Driskill Hotel ejected her after she entered for a lunch with Garland officials and her legislative delegation. "We're just not set up to handle women at noon," said attorney and club president Clint Small. Besides, he added, "a gaggle" of women sound like "magpies" and are distracting to males. Hill said the experience made her angry, embarrassed, and more sympathetic to the experiences of blacks and Mexican Americans. "I'm just upset enough to look at things very differently," she said.[5]

In contrast to the silence that greeted the Citadel's preventing Corpus Christi representative Sissy Farenthold from entering a decade before, this event stirred up public discussion: the ten other women in the legislature, led by Wilhelmina Delco, quickly passed a resolution stating that no member of the House would attend a function excluding another member, thereby starting a boycott against the Driskill. "This business of determining admission by race, sex, and ethnic background has to stop," said Alice representative Ernestine Glossbrenner. "It's deplorable," said Susan McBee of Del Rio. Senator Betty Andujar, a Fort Worth Republican, refused to get involved, however. Hill herself, saying she did not believe in boycotts, did attend one luncheon in the Driskill's regular dining room. She then said she would not return until the Citadel was gone. She later wrote about the experience for the *Dallas Morning News*, saying that any facility that allowed nonmembers to enter for a fee relinquished the right to discriminate against other nonmembers. "State government should not conduct business with a business that supports discrimination," she concluded. When the Senate sergeant-at-arms, assuming Hill was not a legislator, attempted to remove her from the Senate floor a month later, Hill laughed. Although she did not describe herself as a feminist and identified more with African Americans and Mexican Americans than with women as a result of the Citadel incident, Hill nevertheless concluded years after leaving the House that women members were more sensitive to the needs of individuals than to special interest groups.[6]

The death of Hill's husband in 1989, combined with her desire to spend more time with her children and grandchildren, led to her decision not to run for reelection in 1992.[7]

NOTES

1. *Dallas Morning News*, September 13, 14, 1979; *Dallas Times Herald*, September 13 and 14, 1979; Anita Hill, "Questionnaire," prepared and administered by Nancy Baker Jones and Ruthe Winegarten, 1997.

2. Hill, "Questionnaire."

3. *Dallas Morning News*, August 6, 1977, July 17, 1978.

4. *House Journal of Texas*, 69th Legislature, Regular Session, 1985, pp. 244–245; *House Journal of Texas*, 70th Legislature, Regular Session, 1987, p. 53; *Dallas Times Herald*, December 23, 1981; Hill, "Questionnaire."

5. *Dallas Times Herald*, February 10 and 12, 1981.

6. Ibid.; *San Antonio Light*, February 15, 1981; *Dallas Morning News*, March 11, 1981; Hill, "Questionnaire."

7. *Dallas Times Herald*, October 25, 1991.

BETTY DENTON

HOUSE 65th–73rd Legislatures (1977–1995)
Democrat, Waco
DISTRICT 35a, 56, 57
COMMITTEES Appropriations; Agriculture;
Criminal Jurisprudence; Aging and Retire-
ment; Business and Commerce; Financial
Institutions; Public Safety; Judiciary (Chair)

DATES August 19, 1946–
BIRTHPLACE McClennan County
FAMILY Lane Denton; one child
EDUCATION Baylor University (B.A., 1964;
M.A., 1971; J.D., 1980)
OCCUPATION Teacher; attorney

BETTY DENTON was one of McLennan County's longest-serving legislators, winning nine consecutive elections with little or no opposition
from either party. She was elected to her first term in 1976 to fill the seat
left by her husband, Lane Denton, to make an unsuccessful bid for the
Texas Railroad Commission.[1]

Betty Denton supported employee assistance for displaced homemakers, mandatory homestead exemptions for the elderly, funding for the
Waco State Home (an orphanage), interpreters for deaf students, increased
benefits for retired teachers, funding for cancer research through cigarette taxes, simplification of state agency regulations, making divorce less
expensive, and basing auto insurance rates on driving records instead of
age and gender. She also supported allowing Texas-produced nuclear waste
to be dumped in Texas and forbidding the dumping of non-Texas waste,
making generic drugs available, preventing utilities from passing fuel costs
on to consumers, automatically adding five years to the sentence of anyone using a gun to commit a crime, raising teacher pay, installing igni-
tion interlock systems on the cars of drivers convicted of drunk driving,
easing financial eligibility requirements for nursing home admission,
improving health care for senior citizens, creating a state elections and
ethics commission, producing drug-free zones around schools, and stiffening penalties for selling drugs near schools.[2]

In 1983 Speaker Gib Lewis announced that he had appointed Denton
to the powerful House Appropriations Committee for the legislature's

special session, making her one of only three women, and the only Anglo woman, on the twenty-nine-member body. In 1991 she made an unsuccessful race for the Texas Senate seat vacated when Chet Edwards won election to the U.S. Congress. She was defeated by Republican David Sibley, a former mayor of Waco.[3]

Lane and Betty Denton's business and political finances were investigated a number of times during her House career and ultimately caused her only defeat. In 1978 state medical and education authorities questioned the couple's placement service, Doctors for Rural America (DRA), which guaranteed placement in a foreign medical school for a $1,500 fee from prospective students, then asked graduates to consider practicing in rural Texas. Betty Denton maintained that DRA's practices were cleared by state regulatory boards and the Office of the Attorney General. In 1991 her annual fund drive for the residents of the Mexia State School was investigated for having awarded an excessive amount of the proceeds to the telephone sales company, associated with Lane Denton, that conducted the drive. Although the campaign raised nearly $20,000, less than $2,500 went to the school that year. While the Dentons denied having done anything wrong, the incident upset many of her constituents. Nevertheless, she won another decisive victory in her 1992 reelection campaign, defeating Republican Barbara Rusling.[4]

Shortly after that election, the press revealed that the Dentons were being sued by the Federal Deposit Insurance Corporation for failure to repay a $435,000 loan. Betty Denton said she was surprised by the action; she explained that she thought the bank's earlier foreclosure on collateral property had already resolved the problem and suggested that Republican politics had motivated the suit. In 1993 both Betty and Lane Denton were indicted by Travis County grand juries, she for felony and misdemeanor charges of campaign fraud during her 1991 Texas Senate race and he for felony charges of misapplying over $67,000 raised while he was director of the Texas Department of Public Safety Officers Association (TDPSOA). Prosecutors alleged that Betty Denton had listed over $146,000 in fictitious campaign donations on her finance reports to intimidate her opponents. She claimed they were legitimate pledges and, as a member of a House appropriations subcommittee overseeing the budgets of public safety agencies, began her own investigation into Travis County district attorney Ronnie Earle's office (through which grand juries had indicted the Dentons). The charges had not been resolved by the

1994 election, and Denton lost to Barbara Rusling, who campaigned against "scandals and politicians who abuse their offices." In 1995 Betty Denton pleaded no contest to reduced charges of a Class A misdemeanor and was sentenced to six months' deferred adjudication and fined $2,000. Her record was cleared after the sentence ended, and she resumed practicing law in Waco. In 1998 the Third Court of Appeals rejected Lane Denton's appeal for his conviction of theft from TDPSOA.[5]

NOTES

1. *Waco Citizen*, November 9, 1990; *Austin American-Statesman*, September 17, 1978.

2. *Denton Report*, [1977 or 1978] and Fall 1991; *Waco Tribune-Herald*, January 19, 1979, March 4 and 8, 1981, July 8, 1981, January 13 and February 27, 1983, February 3, 1987, November 9, 10, December 5, 1990, March 19, 1991; *Houston Post*, April 1, 1979.

3. *Waco Tribune-Herald*, May 6 and November 1, 1983, November 10 and December 5, 1990; *Ennis News*, January 17, 1991; *Austin American-Statesman*, September 9, 1995. Lou Nelle Sutton and Senfronia Thompson were the other two women who served on the Appropriations Committee with Denton during the special session ("Exhibit 1: Standing Committees, Special Session, House of Representatives," *Guide to the Texas Legislature: 68th Session* [Austin: Legislative Reference Library, 1983]).

4. *Austin American-Statesman*, September 17, 1978, November 24, 1991; *Waco Tribune-Herald*, October 20, 1978, March 11, 1992.

5. *Waco Tribune-Herald*, November 7, 1992; *Austin American-Statesman*, March 10, 1993, August 15 and September 9, 1995, August 14, 1998; Barbara Rusling, campaign flyer, [1994].

IRMA RANGEL

HOUSE 65th Legislature– (1977–)
Democrat, Kingsville
DISTRICT 49, 37, 35
COMMITTEES Higher Education (Chair);
Pensions and Investments; Joint Select
Committee on Historically Underutilized
Businesses; International and Cultural
Relations (Vice Chair); General Investigat-
ing; Judicial Affairs (Vice Chair); House
Administration; Urban Affairs (Vice
Chair); Judiciary; Transportation; Security
and Sanctions; Business and Industry;
Social Services

DATES May 15, 1931–
BIRTHPLACE Kingsville
FAMILY Single; no children
EDUCATION Texas A&I University (B.B.A., 1952); St. Mary's University (J.D., 1969)
OCCUPATION Teacher; attorney

The daughter of field workers who became business owners and political activists, **IRMA RANGEL** became, in 1976, the first Mexican American woman elected to the Texas House. Before entering politics, Rangel taught in Venezuela and California, wrote a Spanish textbook, then went to law school, where she began to realize the importance of Mexican Americans' participation in public life. After law school, she accepted a job as assistant district attorney in Corpus Christi, but only after insisting that she be paid what her male counterparts earned.[1]

Rangel later opened her own law office in Kingsville and became inter-ested in local politics. In 1975 she attended a conference on women in public life at the Lyndon Baines Johnson School of Public Affairs in Aus-tin, and members of the Mexican American Women's Caucus and the Texas Women's Political Caucus (TWPC) encouraged her to run for the legislature. Although Rangel received some seed money from the TWPC, she gives the most credit for fund-raising to the women farm workers who donated to her campaign before they left to work the "migrant stream" north out of Texas picking other people's crops. "They knew I had been involved with the farm workers' march in 1966 and that I was compas-sionate toward their problems and their concerns," Rangel said. With such grassroots support, advice from her politically active father, and assistance from members of the local League of United Latin American Citizens and the American G.I. Forum, she defeated Jean K. Hines, an Anglo woman who had the political and financial support of the powerful King Ranch.[2]

Rangel was unaware that her election had made her the first Mexican American female in the history of the House. When she found out, she felt an obligation to "show them that a Mexican American woman could do as well as or better than any other legislator." Rangel has made the concerns of women, children, and the poor the focus of her work. As a freshman, she opposed Governor Dolph Briscoe's bill to finance the state highway system, saying the funds should be spent instead on education and human welfare. She authored two bills, co-authored five, and co-signed another ten that session. She has passed legislation to provide educational and employment programs to mothers on welfare, create centers for victims of domestic abuse, help grocers and wholesalers donate food to the elderly poor, extend the absentee voting system, increase funding for South Texas colleges and universities by over $400 million, and improve her district's highways and roads.[3]

Although a Catholic, Rangel supports abortion rights. During her seventh term, she and nineteen of the twenty-five women in the House helped defeat an effort to criminalize abortion. She took this position as the result of having once investigated the death of a Nueces County woman from an abortion self-induced with a coat hanger. In 1993, after receiving threatening telephone calls for advocating a change in name for Texas A&I University, Rangel voted for an anti-stalking bill.[4]

President Jimmy Carter appointed her to the Judicial Nominating Panel for the U.S. Court of Appeals for the Fifth Circuit. In 1993 Rangel became the first female to chair the House Mexican-American Legislative Caucus. In 1994 she was elected to the Texas Women's Hall of Fame. She succeeded Wilhelmina Delco as chair of the Higher Education Committee in 1995, and in 1997 House speaker Pete Laney assigned the committee the task of studying the effects of the *Hopwood* decision banning the consideration of race in university admissions. The same year, Rangel became the first female or Mexican American legislator to be awarded the G. J. Sutton Award from the Legislative Black Caucus, for passing a bill ensuring that students in the top 10 percent of their high school classes be guaranteed admission to Texas colleges.[5]

Rangel seeks opportunities for hiring Latinas on her staff, and San Antonio representative Christine Hernández credits Rangel with serving as a role model. "She has taken most of the Hispanic women [legislators] under her wing, advises us, gives us moral support, tells us we're doing a good job, and always has a complimentary word for us. She's been a real morale booster."[6]

NOTES

1. Irma Rangel, resume, 1997; Sarah Weddington, Jane Hickie, Deanna Fitzgerald, Elizabeth W. Fernea, and Marilyn P. Duncan, "Irma Rangel," *Texas Women in Politics*, pp. 75–76; Ann Fears Crawford and Crystal Sasse Ragsdale, "Irma Rangel: First Chicana Legislator," *Women in Texas: Their Lives, Their Experiences, Their Accomplishments*, pp. 331–332; Irma Rangel, videotape interview by Nancy Baker Jones, May 25, 1995, Archives for Research on Women and Gender, University of Texas at San Antonio (hereafter ARWG).

2. Crawford and Ragsdale, "Irma Rangel," pp. 333–334.

3. Ibid., pp. 335–336; Rangel, interview, ARWG.

4. *Corpus Christi Caller*, March 9, 1993, January 30, 1994; *San Antonio Express-News*, January 23, 1993.

5. Rangel, resume; *Kerrville Record*, April 20, 1977; *Austin American-Statesman*, September 20, 1997; *Corpus Christi Caller*, June 7, 1997.

6. Christine Hernández, videotape interview by Nancy Baker Jones, May 26, 1995, ARWG; Rangel, interview, ARWG.

MARY J. MCCRACKEN POLK

HOUSE 66th–68th Legislatures (1979–1984) Democrat, El Paso
DISTRICT 71, 73
COMMITTEES Human Services (Chair); Select Committee on Teenage Pregnancy (Chair); Energy Resources; Ways and Means; Judicial Affairs; Local and Consent Calendars; State, Federal, and International Relations; House Administration

DATES September 13, 1928–
BIRTHPLACE Gasoline
FAMILY D. Wade Polk (died); three children
EDUCATION North Texas State College; University of Texas at El Paso (B.B.A., 1967)
OCCUPATION Teacher; accountant

MARY POLK entered politics after raising a family, being widowed, and achieving success as an accountant and a teacher. Interested in people and issues, she wanted to be a legislator to put her experience to use representing constituents.[1] In 1977, after years of activism in educational associations and lobbying the legislature for higher teacher salaries and educational reform, she ran in a special election to fill an unexpired House term, but lost to Republican Shirley Abbott. In 1978, to the surprise of political insiders, she defeated Abbott by a margin of some 300 votes. She won again in 1980 by some 3,000 votes and was elected to her third and last term in 1982.[2]

Although some assumed Polk would focus only on education, she became a productive legislator informed about many areas. In her first term, she researched and developed a plan for indirect initiative—allowing citizens to propose changes to state laws—that was partially incorporated into a proposed constitutional amendment. She was also successful at changing the taxation rate for interstate carriers; requiring state agencies providing human services to have volunteer programs; creating mass transit authorities in El Paso and Austin; and mandating competency examinations for teachers and basic skills tests for education majors. In addition, she sponsored successful legislation to create the Texas Low Level Radioactive Waste Disposal Authority; encourage the development of the domestic rubber industry; give low-income families access to affordable loans for improving home energy conservation; coordinate the work of state agencies delivering direct human services; and authorize the state land commissioner to make long-term leases.[3]

Polk was unsuccessful in several efforts, including those to secure funding for research in solar energy and other alternative energy sources; integrate displaced homemakers into the job market; establish a committee of medical professionals to draw up guidelines allowing nurses to dispense medication under standing orders from physicians; exempt school publications from sales taxes; create state regulation of foster care facilities for senior citizens; exempt rural school districts without kitchens from mandatory participation in the school breakfast program; and repeal Texas "blue laws," banning the sale of certain goods on Sundays.[4]

Her two greatest achievements, she said, were chairing the Select Committee on Teenage Pregnancy, whose recommendations earned national recognition and became models for other states; and sponsoring the bill that created and funded the Family Violence Shelter Fund (FVSF), which helped support thirty nonprofit shelters around the state.[5] Polk's success in passing the FVSF was a result of a conscious strategy. Before introducing the bill, she organized a statewide network that contacted and educated all legislators about the issues. When she introduced it, most House members co-sponsored it, and it passed both houses without opposition. In order to achieve such legislative goals, Polk said, one must "know the issue—pro and con, who supports it, who opposes. Be honest with your colleagues and constituents; be accessible; know the system and work within [it]."[6] Although she was a progressive politically, Polk decided early, in opposition to political friends, to back the conservative House speaker Billy Clayton. An El Paso newspaper said her alliance with him "allowed her influence as a legislator to increase more rapidly than would normally have been possible."[7]

Happy to be labeled a feminist, Polk believed women in the legislature make a difference because "we are exceptional in our stubbornness, but our intelligence and awareness enable us to recognize the human side of the issue when voting on legislation and budgets." She saw the necessity for more women to be in government at all levels because "so many decisions are made affecting the lives of women." In order to have access to more male representatives about these issues, Polk asked to be on committees not considered to be traditionally "women's committees."[8]

Although Polk contemplated running for Congress, she resigned her seat in 1984, before the end of her third term, for financial reasons—to become executive assistant for legislative relations in the Texas Department of Human Resources in Austin. She remained in that position until she retired in 1990. She was replaced in the House by Nancy McDonald.[9]

NOTES

1. Mary Polk, "Questionnaire," prepared and administered by Nancy Baker Jones and Ruthe Winegarten, 1997.

2. *El Paso Times*, June 22, 1979; *El Paso Weekly/Journal*, November 24, 1981.

3. *El Paso Times*, June 22, 1979; *Polk 'n Austin* (constituent newsletter), August 1979, January 1982, [1983], Mary Polk's files.

4. *Polk 'n Austin*, August 1979; *El Paso Times*, June 22, 1979, January 25, 1984.

5. Polk, "Questionnaire"; "Mary Polk," fact sheet, [1983], Mary Polk's files.

6. Polk, "Questionnaire."

7. *El Paso Weekly/Journal*, November 24, 1981.

8. Polk, "Questionnaire"; *El Paso Weekly/Journal*, November 24, 1981.

9. *El Paso Weekly/Journal*, November 24, 1981; Polk, "Questionnaire"; *El Paso Times*, January 25, 1984.

THE 1980s–1990s

DEBRA DANBURG

HOUSE 67th Legislature– (1981–)
Democrat, Houston
DISTRICT 79, 137
COMMITTEES Calendars; Elections (Chair);
State Affairs; Appropriations; Cultural and
Historical Resources (Vice Chair);
Criminal Jurisprudence; Rules and
Resolutions; Environmental Affairs (Vice
Chair); Business and Industry

DATES September 25, 1951–
BIRTHPLACE Houston
FAMILY Single; no children
EDUCATION University of Houston (B.A.,
1974; J.D., 1979)
OCCUPATION Attorney

DEBRA DANBURG is the first woman in the Texas House to groom herself for a legislative career rather than to arrive there as a citizen legislator. In addition, she is the first vocal feminist to have secured the confidence of influential insiders *before* her first term, thereby enabling her to become an immediately productive representative. Education, family connections, timing, tact, and communication skills, combined with Danburg's ability and the mutual respect with which she and her constituents apparently regard each other, have resulted in her becoming both a reformer and an insider—and successful at both.

Danburg entered college at the start of the modern women's movement; she was active in campus politics at a time when women were increasing their numbers in the legislature. After graduating, she became assistant director of Texans for an Equal Rights Amendment, a coalition that lobbied the legislature for passage of the ERA, and met Austin representative Sarah Weddington, who encouraged her to seek political office. Advised by another mentor to "learn the ropes as an insider," Danburg worked for four years as a legislative aide to Houston representative Ron Waters, during which time she "did everything a legislator does except push the button to vote." She also became an attorney and worked as an intern with the legal team that successfully defended speaker of the House Billy Clayton against federal charges implicating him in an insurance kickback and bribery scheme, commonly referred to as "Brilab."[1]

During Danburg's first campaign, Clayton helped her raise $60,000, probably more money than any woman had ever raised for her first legislative race. She was the only woman candidate in that campaign and confidently championed feminist, civil rights, and other traditionally liberal issues in Montrose, one of the most politicized districts in the state, an inner-city Houston area peopled with strong contingents of feminists, gays and lesbians, environmentalists, and an involved older population.[2] In Danburg's first session, Clayton appointed her to choice committees, allowing her "to be taken more seriously," she said, than most freshmen. Her experience as an attorney and as an aide enabled her to write bills and fight for them from her first day on the job. She has won every Democratic Party primary election since without a runoff.[3]

Danburg passed more legislation than any other Harris County freshman and made friends in the process. Local press reported that "people who were expecting a fire-breathing feminist liberal were surprised to encounter a low-key, personable rep who assiduously did her homework and adopted the Dale Carnegie approach to relationships." She protected tenant rights without offending landlords and co-sponsored the Family Violence Shelter Fund (establishing thirty nonprofit shelters around the state), the first comprehensive revision of campaign finance laws, and a bill giving assistance to Vietnam veterans suffering from exposure to Agent Orange. She also passed a bill to protect endangered plants.[4]

She rewrote the sexual assault laws of Texas by attaching 159 pages of revised wording to a small bill sponsored by Representative Charles Evans, then chair of the powerful Calendars Committee. When the bill came before the House, Evans turned discussion over to Danburg, she explained it, and the bill passed. "Texas had some of the most backward laws in the nation" at the time, Danburg said, including allowing sexual assault against a spouse. "People were making jokes like 'if you can't rape your spouse. . . .'" She has continued to revise those laws, including definitions of spousal assault, classifying rape and sexual abuse as acts of violence rather than of sexuality, and deleting requirements that victims prove a degree of resistance against their attackers.[5]

In subsequent sessions Danburg has secured a "bill of rights" for elderly people in health care settings, a Texas Trails System to coordinate use and development of nature trails, regulations governing billboards, regulations allowing victims of family violence to get protective orders against their attackers more quickly, funding for the arts, legalization of breast feeding in public, and, for the first time in Texas history, the right of homeowners to secure loans using their home equity as collateral.[6] In a floor fight to pass the bill of rights for the elderly, Danburg was opposed by a legislator who objected to her inclusion of sexual orientation as a classification protected against discrimination. The debate stalled her bill and 140 others until Danburg called Speaker Gib Lewis from his office to decide whether one representative could keep her bill from being considered. Her bill passed.[7] She has been similarly tenacious about such issues as protecting spouses and children from family violence, protecting endangered species, supporting urban parks, controlling toxic materials, supporting the arts, assisting individuals with AIDS, and stiffening penalties against drunken drivers. In 1995, 79 percent of the bills she sponsored passed.[8]

The women's caucus, "to the extent that we have one," Danburg says, has often acted on gender-based agreement during her tenure. She says women are the broadest-based group in the legislature—rural, urban, old, young, black, Hispanic, Anglo—"we run the gamut." Danburg has collaborated with even the most conservative members on legislation to license abortion clinics, give preference to historically underutilized businesses, permit breast feeding of infants in public, and reduce sexual violence. "It's interesting to watch," she said in 1995. "Where people considered me to be somewhat strident or radical on sexual assault legislation 15 years ago, now every guy and his dog is ready to sign on as a joint author; some even try to be the primary author." But the steady *work*, she added, "the year-in, year-out research, working with coalitions, working with the women who are actual victims of violence, has been done almost entirely by the women in the legislature."[9]

Over time, however, Danburg has seen the variety among female legislators increase as their numbers have grown. One result of this diversity has been a decrease in female camaraderie, of women's identifying with each other as women. "It's really gotten to be a strange dynamic, because if something is pegged as a feminist issue, it will lose more votes [if a feminist carries it] than if a woman who is seen as more traditional is seen carrying the identical issue. [Then] it is considered kind of obvious. I've seen that with Senator Kay Bailey Hutchison's legislation on the homemaker's retirement program. That's clearly a feminist issue, but she is not considered to be a feminist. Now when she and I worked together on Texans for an Equal Rights Amendment issues years ago, she was a feminist. I'm not quite sure what happened."[10]

Danburg advises young people considering politics to follow the route she took. "I don't think you can just look at this system from the outside and expect to go in and be effective," she says. "It's absolutely critical to learn the ropes. There is a big difference in the new legislators who come in if they have experience. You learn by doing in politics more than any other area."[11]

NOTES

1. *Dallas Times Herald*, February 17, 1980; *Fort Worth Star-Telegram*, February 11, 1980.

2. Debra Danburg, videotape interview by Ruthe Winegarten, May 26, 1995, Archives for Research on Women and Gender, University of Texas at San Antonio (hereafter ARWG).

3. *Houston Chronicle*, April 19, 1980; Danburg, interview, ARWG.

4. Danburg, interview, ARWG; *State Representative Debra Danburg* (constituent newsletter), [1982], p. 1; *State Representative Debra Danburg's Legislative Report* (constituent newsletter), [1983].

5. Danburg, interview, ARWG; *State Representative Debra Danburg*, p. 1; *Legislative Report*, [1983].

6. *Legislative Report*, [1983, 1985]; Danburg, interview, ARWG; *Austin American-Statesman*, May 13, 1997.

7. *Houston Post*, May 14, 1983.

8. *San Antonio Express,* February 17, 1983; Gary Halter and Harvey Tucker, *Texas Legislative Almanac*, p. 373.

9. Danburg, interview, ARWG.

10. Ibid. Danburg was a lobbyist for Texans for an Equal Rights Amendment when she worked with Kay Bailey (Hutchison) to pass the federal amendment.

11. Danburg, interview, ARWG.

JAN MCKENNA

HOUSE 68th–69th Legislatures (1983–1987)
Republican, Arlington
DISTRICT 94
COMMITTEES Urban Affairs; Financial
Institutions; Retirement and Aging

DATES June 15, 1949–
BIRTHPLACE Nashville, Tennessee
FAMILY Gordon McKenna (divorced); five
children
EDUCATION Texas Christian University (B.A.,
1973; M.A., 1979); Texas Wesleyan University
(J.D., 1995)
OCCUPATION Business owner; attorney

JAN MCKENNA was elected from a conservative district to the Texas
House as a Reagan Republican who supported the president's "New Federalism" plan to transfer federal programs to the states. The vice president
of a public relations firm and owner of an employment agency, she worked
in Bill Clements' 1978 gubernatorial campaign and narrowly lost a 1980
race for the House before succeeding Representative Bob McFarland,
whom she had served as legislative aide.[1]

McKenna opposed tax increases and favored increasing teacher salaries, but only if the funding came from cuts in social programs and other
"wasteful spending." She opposed abortion, horse racing, an appointed
state board of education, and a child safety seat law because it "just allows
the state to come in and tell us what we can do in the privacy of our
automobile." She also objected to a kindergarten program for four-year-
olds as "a tax-payer funded baby-sitting service." She supported raising
the drinking age to twenty-one, banning open alcohol containers in automobiles, enacting stiffer penalties for parents who kidnap their children, publishing the names of prisoners being released, pardoned, or paroled, and mandating penalties for certain crimes so judges "[won't] have
so much leeway."[2]

McKenna told Fort Worth voters to oust their school board, including
Republicans, because it had adopted a volunteer pilot sex education class.
Shortly thereafter she introduced an unsuccessful bill that would have
exempted children from compulsory school attendance based on their
religious beliefs and allowed parents to educate children at home instead.

As a freshman, McKenna angered influential Dallas senator Oscar Mauzy when she convinced Brownsville representative Rene Oliveira to tack an amendment onto Mauzy's election code bill allowing some legislators to take the bar examination without attending law school. Her intent was to allow lawmakers without law degrees to get credit for their legislative experience. Mauzy had the amendment killed in committee.[3]

After McKenna's first term, the Young Conservatives of Texas rated her one of only seven representatives to receive its 100 percent approval rating for her voting record: she had opposed extending worker compensation to farm workers, strengthening state antitrust laws, and creating a state human rights commission, and she had supported requiring child welfare recipients to get job training and exempting certain businesses from the Texas Deceptive Trade Practices Act. Nevertheless, she was criticized at home for having passed only two bills, one allowing police to destroy obscene materials after a conviction and the other allowing retired judges to hear civil cases. Colleagues in the House referred to her as "gullible," "green," and "naive." After her second term, during which she had passed none of the eleven bills she authored, including a lengthy anti-abortion bill, *Texas Monthly* magazine included her—for the second time—on its list of the ten worst legislators. She threatened to sue but apparently did not.[4]

Influential Arlington Republicans agreed with the magazine's assessment, however, because many of them, including most of the Arlington city council and Eddie Chiles, owner of the Texas Rangers baseball team, threw their support behind Kent Grusendorf, a former member of the State Board of Education. McKenna lost to him in a 1986 Republican primary, and he ran unopposed for the seat in the general election. After leaving the legislature, McKenna became an attorney.[5]

NOTES

1. *Fort Worth Star-Telegram*, March 4, 1982.

2. *Arlington Citizen-Journal*, October 28 and November 18, 1984; *Fort Worth Star-Telegram*, March 4, 1982, June 5, 1983, October 15, 1984, March 20, 1985.

3. *Fort Worth Star-Telegram*, June 5, 1983, January 25, 1985; *Arlington Citizen-Journal*, February 10, 1985.

4. *Fort Worth Star-Telegram*, June 5, 1983, February 14 and May 1, 1984, June 15 and March 20, 1985, May 4, 1986.

5. *Arlington Citizen-Journal*, October 27, December 11, and December 19, 1985, April 30, 1986; *Fort Worth Star-Telegram*, December 14, 1985, May 1 and 4, 1986.

PATRICIA ELLEN PORCELLA HILL

HOUSE 68th–71st Legislatures (1983–1991)
Republican, Dallas
DISTRICT 102
COMMITTEES Judicial Affairs (Chair);
Government Organization; Redistricting;
State Affairs (Vice Chair); Select Commit-
tee on the Judiciary; Sunset Advisory
Commission (Vice Chair); State, Federal,
and International Relations

DATES December 10, 1945–
BIRTHPLACE Lima, Ohio
FAMILY Lee Abbit (divorced); Robert Hill (died); three stepchildren
EDUCATION Virginia Polytechnic Institute (B.A., 1967); University of Houston (J.D.,
1970)
OCCUPATION Teacher; attorney

On her second day in the House, **PATRICIA HILL** wrote a letter to the
Austin American-Statesman objecting to political cartoonist Ben Sargent's
depiction of the 68th Legislature as clowns and wastrels. Sargent "was
calling us idiots before we had a chance to prove it," she said later. After
three months as a legislator, Hill wrote that she was beginning to understand why so many Texas statutes were "convoluted" and "poorly worded."
Bills, she explained, are carefully drafted by the Legislative Council, but
they undergo metamorphosis in committee and on the floor, where many
representatives see them for the first time, and amendments from the
floor may even contradict each other. Nevertheless, she was not agreeing
with Sargent. "I have found the members of the legislature to be a group
mostly thoughtful, hardworking, and doing a pretty good job of governing the state. . . . I have never been involved in an endeavor that moves so
quickly, involves so many varied and important issues, or demands so
many decisions . . . . I find it stimulating, enjoyable and only occasionally
frustrating."[1]

As a young woman, Hill said, she planned to become a teacher and get
married. She turned to a career in law after a disappointing year as a high
school English teacher. "I taught the average students," she said. "The
problem with it was, there were no leaders." While pursuing her law degree, she met, married, and divorced another law student. After complet-

ing her law degree in 1970, Hill could not find a job with a Dallas law firm. "Being a woman was a factor," she said. She took a job clerking for U.S. district judge Robert Hill, whom she later married. He was a widower with three grown children. After serving as one of two lawyers representing the Republican Party in a state redistricting case, she became interested in running for the legislature. Her upper-income district included Highland Park and University Park.[2]

Hill describes herself as a "generalist." Most of her legislative accomplishments were in the fields of environmental, criminal, and consumer law. She lists among her achievements reenacting the Air Control Board (the agency responsible for implementing the federal Clean Air Act); restoring Interstate River Compact Commission laws that provide for the protection and sharing of Texas waters with other states; helping "to get billboards down in big cities"; creating legislation defining obscenity to allow for criminal punishment; amending the capital murder statute to provide for the death penalty in cases of mass or serial murder; creating new felony courts across the state; supporting the re-creation of the Adult Probation Commission; requiring insurance companies to pay for mammogram screening for women over thirty-five; keeping AT&T a regulated utility; and reforming worker compensation laws.[3]

For her environmental record, Hill received a Sierra Club Legislative Award in 1985. For work against cancer, she received the Susan G. Komen Award for Excellence in Legislation in 1987 as well as the Texas Cancer Council's Gibson D. Lewis Award for Excellence in Cancer Control in 1989. She was recognized for her family law reforms on the *Dallas Morning News* Honor Roll in 1989.[4]

Hill said she decided not to run for reelection in 1991 because she "got tired of it; same issues every session." Instead she made an unsuccessful run for attorney general of Texas, an office that, under Texas law, handles almost no criminal cases. Hill based much of her campaign on getting legislative approval to fight crime and drugs. Since 1990, Hill has been a partner in the Houston firm of O'Quinn, Kerensky, McAnich & Riebschlager. During 1992–1993, she served as an alternate municipal judge in Houston.[5]

NOTES

1. *Houston Post*, [May or June], 1983, Legislative Reference Library, Austin; *Dallas Morning News*, May 2, 1983.

2. *Houston Post*, [May or June], 1983; *Dallas Morning News*, July 10, 1983; Patricia Hill,

"Questionnaire," prepared and administered by Nancy Baker Jones and Ruthe Winegarten, 1997.

3. Patricia Hill, resume; Hill, "Questionnaire."

4. Hill, resume.

5. Hill, "Questionnaire"; *Dallas Times Herald*, August 22 and September 1, 1989; Hill, resume.

☆

PHYLLIS ROBINSON

HOUSE 68th–71st Legislatures (1983–1991)
Democrat, Gonzales
DISTRICT 31
COMMITTEES Insurance; Agriculture and Livestock (Vice Chair); County Affairs; Local and Consent Calendars

DATES September 11, 1946–
BIRTHPLACE Gonzales
FAMILY Thomas Miller; two children
EDUCATION Southwest Texas State University (B.A., 1967); St. Mary's University (M.A., 1972)
OCCUPATION School counselor; teacher

Running as a conservative who would be a full-time legislator, **PHYLLIS ROBINSON** said she saw an opportunity to make some improvements for her rural constituency. On the road campaigning sixteen hours a day for five months in her large district, she promised voters that education would be her top priority, with tax relief, the state's drug problem, and incentives for farmers, ranchers, and oil and gas development not far behind. She got 63 percent of the vote and beat three men without a runoff in the Democratic primary. With no Republican opposition in the general election, Robinson became the first woman to represent District 31. Robinson served four terms before announcing she would not run again. Of her forty-four bills, twenty-three passed.[1]

She supported giving rural commissioners' courts more powers of appointment and co-sponsored a bill to remedy chronic river logjams considered partially to blame for flooding in Victoria County. She co-sponsored a constitutional amendment to restructure the Permanent University Fund and supported creation of a housing assistance program for veterans. She also approved of encouraging Congress to eliminate some authority of the Internal Revenue Service and supported exempting learning-disabled students from grade requirements for participation in extra-curricular activities.[2]

Robinson endorsed a legislative package to reform the civil justice system of lawsuits and general liability insurance. "Everyone wants to sue everyone else," she said. "Even children in elementary grades are caught up in the same psychology-of-entitlement game that demands good housing, good diet, good jobs, and good health. . . . It is sickening that even ministers are being forced to carry liability insurance. The hurts of people are not going to be solved by money." She pledged, however, not to push reform so far that it would limit a person's access to the courtroom or deprive injured people of just rewards. She authored a bill memorializing Congress to increase Medicare compensation to rural hospitals as well as several bills to reform rural health care systems, particularly in her district. She also authored a bill addressing the liability of people who harvest or allow their fields to be harvested for free distribution to the needy.[3]

The Texas Association of Business honored Robinson for her "strong stand for reform of the [Texas worker compensation] system" that was "victimizing injured workers as well as employers and costing jobs for our state." She declined to seek a fifth term, saying she wanted to give someone else the opportunity to represent the district.[4]

NOTES

1. *San Antonio Express*, February 16, 1983; *Victoria Advocate*, January 12 and June 6, 1982, November 18, 1989.

2. *Victoria Advocate*, February 9 and 20, 1983, February 7, 1987; "Legislative Master List by Author," 69th Regular Session, 1985, p. 437.

3. *Victoria Advocate*, March 6, 1986, February 21, 1987; "Author/Sponsor List of Bills," 71st Regular Session, 1989, pp. 638–639.

4. *Victoria Advocate*, August 5 and November 18, 1989.

GWYN CLARKSTON SHEA

HOUSE 68th–72nd Legislatures (1983–1993)
Republican, Irving
DISTRICT 98
COMMITTEES Administration; Insurance
(Vice Chair); Urban Affairs (Vice Chair);
Ways and Means

DATES August 3, 1937–
BIRTHPLACE Iraan
FAMILY John Shea; three children
EDUCATION North Texas State University
(no degree); Dallas Baptist University Police
Academy (Graduate, 1994)
OCCUPATION Legislative aide; constable

GWYN SHEA built on knowledge she gained as office manager to U.S. representative Jim Collins and administrative assistant to Irving representative Robert Davis to wage four successful campaigns for a House seat representing a conservative district. She stressed her promise to fight to prevent state government from expanding "into areas that are not necessarily the function of government"; to increase criminal penalties; to protect the right-to-work law against labor unions; to study the cost of importing water from neighboring states and conserving subsurface water; to cut federal programs that cost almost five times more to administer than they provide to people who need help; and to foster excellence in education through properly skilled, adequately compensated educators with classroom discipline.[1]

In her five terms Shea focused much of her attention on issues related to insurance and insurers (such as legislation instructing the State Board of Insurance to reassign furniture stores to more accurate classifications). She proposed a constitutional amendment to control the authority of the courts to require the state or local governments to increase the level of funding for the judicial branch. In addition, she supported marriage as a defense in rape and opposed horse racing, the lottery, and worker compensation for farm workers.[2]

In 1991 she was surprised by the appearance, on a bill revising the alcoholic beverage code, of an amendment that legalized liquor sales in Texas Stadium, effectively overturning an Irving ordinance prohibiting such sales. The bill passed the House 140-0, and Shea tried unsuccessfully to get Speaker Gib Lewis to retrieve the legislation. Later that year she contemplated running for the Texas Senate but decided not to do so. Fort Worth representative Anna Mowery later credited Shea as advising her, "A woman can do anything down here in the House of Representatives a man can except have her shoes shined in the men's restroom."[3]

The Young Conservatives of Texas recognized Shea for her conservative record during two terms. In 1992 she was defeated by Republican representative Will Hartnett after the two were paired against each other following redistricting. After leaving the legislature, Shea became the first female constable in Dallas County. She received the Texas Chamber of Commerce Legislative Leadership Award as well as the Red Ribbon Award from the Texas Association of Concerned Taxpayers, and she was named one of the top ten legislators by the Free Market Committee for promoting limited government, free enterprise, and conservative principles. In 1995 she was appointed to the governing committee of the Texas Worker's Compensation Insurance facility by Governor George W. Bush.[4]

NOTES

1. *Dallas Times Herald*, October 24 and 30, 1982; Gwyn Shea, biography, typescript, January 1992, copy in authors' files.

2. "Bills Passed by the Legislature," 68th Regular Session, 1983, p. 149; "List of Bills by Author," 68th Regular Session, 1983, p. 273; "Legislative Master List by Author," 69th Regular Session, 1985, p. 480; "Bills Passed by Author," 69th Regular Session, 1985, p. 91; "Author-Ordered List of Bills Passed," 70th Regular Session, 1987, p. 98; "Author/Sponsor List of Bills," 70th Regular Session, 1987, p. 556; "Author/Sponsor List of Bills," 71st Regular Session, 1989, p. 666.

3. Anna Mowery, videotape interview by Nancy Baker Jones, May 29, 1995, Archives for Research on Women and Gender, University of Texas at San Antonio (hereafter ARWG).

4. *Fort Worth Star-Telegram*, May 26 and July 30, 1991, April 16, 1992; *Dallas Morning News*, February 26, 1993; Shea, biography.

NANCY HANKS MCDONALD

HOUSE 68th–74th Legislatures (1984–1997)
Democrat, El Paso
DISTRICT 73, 76
COMMITTEES Appropriations (Vice Chair);
Administration; Public Health; Calendars;
Labor and Employment Relations; Higher
Education; Ways and Means; Rules and
Resolutions; State, Federal, and International Relations

DATES October 21, 1934–
BIRTHPLACE Bowling Green, Kentucky
FAMILY Willis B. McDonald; ten children
EDUCATION St. Thomas School of Nursing
(B.S., 1954)
OCCUPATION Nurse

Early in **NANCY MCDONALD**'s career as a registered nurse, she realized that there were no women representing nursing on El Paso's public health board. Increasingly aware of the importance of citizen involvement in government, she urged nurses to participate in public life. McDonald took her own advice and, at the urging of her husband, ran for the Texas House when Mary Polk resigned her seat. She was supported not only by her husband but by the children at her son's high school and by the other members of her family.[1]

McDonald survived five elections in 1984 to fill an open seat in a special election to replace Polk (the first four elections occurred in only three months). She served in the second called session of the 68th Legislature, then defeated Republican Pearl Calk to return for a full term in the 69th and was not challenged in any subsequent election. She was the first registered nurse since Eddie Bernice Johnson to serve in the House. She felt that her experience as a nurse and mother of ten prepared her for politics because both required skills in teaching, persuasion, negotiation, and arbitration. She had also been active in neighborhood and nurses' associations.[2]

McDonald ran primarily because of her interest in public policy regarding access to health care and financing for public education. She was also concerned about the effects of the federal Gramm-Rudman deficit reduction act on Texas. Although not Latina, McDonald joined the Mexican American Legislative Caucus because 63 percent of her constituents were Mexican American. While the women did not have a formal caucus, McDonald said they met regularly and supported each other as they discussed issues across party lines. "There seemed to be that connection there, that we met as women legislators. We talked about issues, all issues. . . . Women seem more eager to share and support each other," she said. "Men tend to keep their legislative agendas to themselves and work in a more competitive environment."[3]

Getting women into leadership positions in the House was one issue around which the female representatives united. "Women are not represented as much in the leadership [although] we're certainly as qualified as the men. . . . I myself was the first woman who was a member of the Calendars Committee for a long time. We're very similar to women in other fields. We get so high up on the executive ladder, but we don't get quite [high enough] up and break that glass ceiling." During Pete Laney's campaign for speaker of the House, the women of the House made their desires for leadership roles a key issue. Laney won, and McDonald said he tried to promote more women. "We have chairmanships," she said, "which is a great step forward. But the powerful chairmanship [of major committees] is going to be the next step" in the process of seeing a woman become speaker. A woman brings different life experiences and styles of leadership to the House, McDonald maintains. "Most women are more sensitive to issues concerning family needs and discrimination [against] minorities."[4]

McDonald helped pass legislation for a statewide water plan, improved health care for the poor, increased immunizations for children, prevention of family violence, and improvement of the court system for foster children. She also supported increased state enforcement of hazardous waste laws and repeal of Sunday "blue laws." She sponsored legislation to give farm workers information about their exposure to pesticides and supported raising legislators' pay to $25,000. One of McDonald's sons served as a deputy press secretary to Governor Ann Richards and lobbied his mother unsuccessfully for Richards' "Fair Share" school finance plan. "I've had a lot of experience saying 'no' to my children," she said. In 1991 McDonald was appointed by Richards to the Texas Health Policy Task Force and by Supreme Court justice Oscar Mauzy to the Gender Bias Task Force. In 1994 she was appointed by the speaker to the Commission on Children and Youth.[5]

McDonald retired from politics in 1997. She and her husband settled in Austin.

NOTES

1. Nancy McDonald, videotape interview by Ruthe Winegarten, May 29, 1995, Archives for Research on Women and Gender, University of Texas at San Antonio (hereafter ARWG); *El Paso Herald Post*, February 25, 1985.

2. Nancy McDonald, resume; McDonald, interview, ARWG; *El Paso Times*, June 14, 1984, April 26, 1987.

3. McDonald, interview, ARWG.

4. *El Paso Herald-Post*, May 26, 1984; *El Paso Times*, January 26, 1986; McDonald, interview, ARWG; Nancy McDonald, "Questionnaire," prepared and administered by Nancy Baker Jones and Ruthe Winegarten, 1997.

5. *El Paso Times*, January 26, 1986, April 26, 1987, November 18, 1992, September 5, 1995; McDonald, interview, ARWG; Nancy McDonald, biography, typescript, n.d., copy in authors' files.

MARGARET ANNE BECKER COOPER

HOUSE 69th–70th Legislatures (1985–1989)
Republican, San Marcos
DISTRICT 47
COMMITTEES Human Services (Vice Chair); Public Health; Retirement and Aging; Rules and Resolutions

DATES February 28, 1935–
BIRTHPLACE Marshalltown, Iowa
FAMILY Bob A. Cooper; four children
EDUCATION Iowa State College (B.S., 1957)
OCCUPATION Teacher; community volunteer

ANNE COOPER's first election was unexpected because she, her opposition, and her own party believed she would lose. She ran for the legislature because she thought the Democratic incumbent was not representing the philosophy of most of the people in the district. Her legislative goal was "to be well-informed, helpful to constituents, and to be respectful to constituents and other members." Cooper came from a family of lawyers, and her parents were both interested in politics. Her maternal grandfather was an attorney and a Republican. Her great-great-uncle was

225

Congressman J. B. Grinnell, for whom Grinnell College in Iowa is named. Her father, the son of immigrants and a Roosevelt Democrat who solicited party funds from packinghouse workers in Detroit, ran for office in Iowa. "If you have a family of lawyers," she said, "you are naturally interested in government and the law and feel like you have a perfect right to run for office if you want to . . . that you have a God-given right to run."[1]

Cooper's main interest was education, but in the wake of the sweeping education reforms of House Bill 72, which passed the year before her election, she had no major agenda other than "fine-tuning" that bill. To help accomplish this, she visited the seven school districts in District 47 to gain more insight into educational issues. To preserve her independence and avoid lobbyists' pressure, Cooper refused money from special interests. Even when lack of these funds meant she could not afford a hoped-for radio program, she said she had made the right decision.[2]

The first bill Cooper authored would have required all businesses that sold alcoholic beverages to post the penalties of conviction for driving while intoxicated. It did not pass. She was successful in obtaining an additional county court for Hays County. She was concerned with protecting water quality, water rights, bays and estuaries, and regulating groundwater.[3]

Cooper was defeated in her 1988 race for a third term, she said, because the demographics of the Austin part of her district changed, and her opponent, Libby Linebarger, ran a well-financed and sophisticated campaign. "It took a woman to beat me," said Cooper. As a woman in the legislature, Cooper said she served as a reminder that "government is a citizen responsibility, not just a male responsibility." After leaving, she served on the Guadalupe-Blanco River Authority Board and on the Council on Alcohol and Drug Abuse for Hays and Caldwell counties.[4]

NOTES

1. Margaret Anne Becker Cooper, "Questionnaire," prepared and administered by Nancy Baker Jones and Ruthe Winegarten, 1997; Margaret Cooper, interview by Ruthe Winegarten, September 15, 1997.

2. Cooper, "Questionnaire"; *San Marcos Daily Record*, [January?], 1985, San Marcos Public Library.

3. *San Marcos Daily Record*, [January?], 1985.

4. Cooper, "Questionnaire; Cooper, interview.

MARÍA ELENA (LENA) GUERRERO

HOUSE 69th–71st Legislatures (1985–1991)
Democrat, Austin
DISTRICT 51
COMMITTEES Rules and Resolutions (Vice
Chair); State Affairs (Vice Chair); Govern-
ment Organization; Human Services;
Sunset Commission (Vice Chair)

DATES November 27, 1957–
BIRTHPLACE Mission
FAMILY Lionel Aguirre; one child
EDUCATION University of Texas at Austin
(B.J., 1993)
OCCUPATION Communications; business
owner

LENA GUERRERO became one of the most effective legislators in the
House despite serving there only three terms. The child of low-income
parents who, with their children, worked agricultural fields in summer,
she attended the University of Texas in the 1970s where she became active in student politics and in Austin's Democratic political scene. She
worked on Carol Keeton McClellan's and Ron Mullen's mayoral races,
for Mary Jane Bode's winning 1976 campaign for the Texas House, for
Ann Richards' successful race for Travis County commissioner, and on
Bob Armstrong's failed gubernatorial campaign. She later became executive director of the Texas Women's Political Caucus and president of the
Texas Young Democrats.[1]

Interested in civil rights and women's issues, Guerrero decided in 1984
to run for the seat representing District 51 when Gonzalo Barrientos left
it to run for the Texas Senate. She won and, at twenty-six, became one of
the youngest women and only the second Mexican American woman
ever elected to the House. She was pregnant throughout her second session and brought her young son to the floor frequently during her third.[2]

As a state representative, Guerrero wanted to be a voice for the average person. She supported, sponsored, and passed bills to provide increased retirement benefits for state employees, strengthen child abuse
enforcement, require "truth in taxation" to regulate property tax increases,
and promote recycling. She also passed legislation to prohibit exploitation of minors by topless and nude bars, create the Edwards Aquifer

Underground Water District, and protect state institutions in Austin from being relocated. She supported mass transit and got a minimum wage for field workers, but her bill to provide longer tools for these workers, thereby ending "stoop" labor, was vetoed by Governor Bill Clements. She authored a bill prohibiting discrimination against AIDS patients and got a child care system for employees of the Capitol complex. She also defeated a bill to weaken strip-mining regulations and helped facilitate the end of a feud between Governor Clements and Texas agriculture commissioner Jim Hightower over pesticide regulation. By the end of her last term, she had become the third most successful representative in the passage rate of her bills.[3]

Guerrero entered the legislature as a hothead but soon changed. "I learned that pulling grenade pins out of grenades and throwing them into a crowd . . . wasn't wise," she said. Hale Center representative Pete Laney, later speaker of the House, said of his first encounter with her, "I thought she was a bomb-throwing liberal" because she opposed a hunting bill by accusing the man who wrote it of "killing Bambi." Laney became her mentor, however. "She learned relatively quickly that if she worked within the system, she could do more," he said. Guerrero was soon playing golf, hunting, fishing, and telling jokes with her male colleagues.[4] In addition, Guerrero learned the importance of the committee structure for getting legislation passed. She began using her position on committees to trade favors with other legislators, thereby getting attention and support for her legislation. She also learned how to write a bill that would pass. "I always go talk to her, even though I know she won't vote with me," said a lobbyist, "because she tells me how to fix my bad ol' bills."[5]

Guerrero understood the importance of women working together as well. "That male-dominated system often made us fly off to lunch with each other just to have some sense of 'is it me, or what?'" she said. She looked forward to the day when "there are so many women on the floor of the Texas House and Senate that we're not counting any more, . . . that we're looking at substance and character and personalities." When that day comes, Guerrero thinks it will no longer be politically unpopular to label issues as women's issues, as it was when she served. "Why are [men] so quick to judge on their own perspective what the issue is, but will not allow us to identify an issue as a woman's issue because we are women?" As an example, she pointed to the attitudes she and Debra Danburg encountered when trying to define rape as a reality within marriage. Guerrero believed many males objected to the bill because, instead of thinking about protecting women from the reality of spousal rape, they worried about the less likely possibility of women crying rape falsely against innocent men. She and Danburg educated legislators' wives about the issue, and many of these women convinced their husbands of its merits.[6]

In 1989 *Texas Monthly* named Guerrero one of the ten best legislators in the House, one of the few women it had so praised. "Guerrero was able to pass legislation on child care, ground water management, and teenage pregnancy by winning the confidence of the people most likely to oppose her," the magazine said. "She worked with the governor's staff to eliminate their objections to her plan to help battered-women's centers." She was also praised for her legislative ability by the *Texas Observer* and a coalition of environmental and consumer groups.[7]

In 1990 *Newsweek* named Guerrero one of the up-and-coming Hispanic leaders in the United States. In 1991 Governor Ann Richards appointed Guerrero to the Texas Railroad Commission, one of the most powerful agencies in the state, regulating oil and gas and other industries. She was the first woman and the first minority to serve there and was chair for two years. Later that year, *USA Today* listed Guerrero as one of several women with the potential to become the first female president of the United States. When she ran for reelection in 1992, a presidential election year in which Democrats hoped her race would also gain votes for presidential candidate Bill Clinton, Guerrero was accused of lying on her resume about having graduated with honors from the University of Texas. In reality, she had left the university several hours short of a diploma, with a C average. She maintained that she did not know she had not graduated, but voters did not believe her, and she lost to Republican Barry Williamson. "I am angry at myself. I am embarrassed. And I am terribly sorry. I think you should know that I have learned a very hard lesson," she said at the time. Guerrero later said she believes the press and the public hold women and minorities to a higher standard for behavior than they do white males. "They expected me to be better than perfect," she said. She opened her own lobbying firm, Lena Guerrero and Associates, and completed her university degree in 1993. In 1996 she reported earnings as a lobbyist of between $170,000 and $370,000. She does not anticipate seeking public office again.[8]

NOTES

1. Lena Guerrero, videotape interview by Nancy Baker Jones, August 11, 1995, Archives for Research on Women and Gender, University of Texas at San Antonio (hereafter ARWG); *Austin American-Statesman*, October 1, 1990; *Images*, February 21, 1991.

2. Guerrero, interview, ARWG.

3. Guerrero campaign flyer, [1988]; *Images*, February 21, 1991; Guerrero, interview, ARWG; *Dallas Morning News*, February 5, 1993.

4. *Dallas Morning News*, September 1, 1991; interview, ARWG.

5. Guerrero, interview, ARWG; "The Best Legislators," *Texas Monthly*, July 1989, p. 88.

6. Guerrero, interview, ARWG.

7. "The Best Legislators," p. 88; *Austin American-Statesman*, December 1, 1990.

8. *Austin American-Statesman*, December 1, 1990, September 12, 1992, November 3, 1996, January 27, 1998; Lori Rodriguez, "Lena Guerrero," *Houston Chronicle Magazine*, November 24, 1991; *Houston Chronicle*, September 12, 1992; Guerrero, interview, ARWG; *Dallas Morning News*, February 5, 1993.

☆

CYNDI TAYLOR KRIER

SENATE 69th–72nd Legislatures (1985–1992)
Republican, San Antonio
DISTRICT 26
COMMITTEES Finance; Education; Natural Resources; Criminal Jurisprudence; Health and Human Services

DATES July 12, 1950–
BIRTHPLACE Beeville
FAMILY Joseph R. Krier; no children
EDUCATION University of Texas at Austin (B.J., 1971; J.D., 1975)
OCCUPATION Journalist; attorney; county judge

CYNDI TAYLOR KRIER was the sixth woman elected to the Senate and the only female senator during her first session. In her second session (1987–1989), she was joined in the Senate by Judith Zaffirini and Eddie Bernice Johnson, making the 70th Legislature the first in Texas history to have more than one woman senator. She was Bexar County's first Republican and its first female senator. She surprised many when she upset longtime Democratic senator Bob Vale to win the seat. Krier arrived in the Senate after working on U.S. senator John Tower's legislative staff and for Anne Armstrong, then a counselor to President Gerald R. Ford. After her first election, Krier surprised her constituents and political insiders when she returned over $16,000 in unsolicited donations from political action committees that had not contributed to her until after she won. Krier said she had no campaign debt to retire. "It is critical to me that I go up to Austin without any question of whether I am indebted to anybody but the people of Bexar County," she said.[1]

Krier differed from Republican Party leaders, notably President Ronald Reagan, in that she supported the Equal Rights Amendment and a woman's right to choose whether to have an abortion. She encountered two early reminders of her singularity as the Senate's only woman. On her first day, she learned that the Senate dress code required that women wear bras, a regulation apparently directed at female journalists. "I want to know," she asked, "if male senators are required to wear any particular type of underwear." Krier obtained a reinterpretation of the code. Less than a week later, she was refused entry into the House chamber to hear Governor Mark White's State of the State address because the assistant sergeant-at-arms did not realize that she was a senator. She listened to the speech from the gallery, and the Senate later presented her with a poster-size identification badge. Krier discounted both events, saying she had more important issues to get to work on.[2]

Krier had yet another hurdle to jump, however. Early in her first session, her bill to establish appointive municipal courts of record in San Antonio was greeted with a surprisingly large amount of debate and defeated 25 to 3. Krier soon realized that this was an initiation rite performed by her fellow senators, and Lieutenant Governor Bill Hobby overrode the vote to allow its legitimate passage 27 to 1.[3]

Krier went on to introduce fifty-one more bills and to see twenty-seven of them pass that session. Upon reflection, she considered her most significant legislative accomplishments measures to improve the collection of child support; address problems of child abuse and family violence; establish a juvenile court for Bexar County; reform the worker compensation system; create the Texas Alternative Dispute Resolution Act, promoting arbitration and mediation; create the Texas Literacy Council; restrict children's access to tobacco products and inhalants; protect the water supply; collect medical, dental, and other health care costs from inmates; promote volunteerism; improve children's health care; and repeal archaic statutes that discriminated against women. Even so, she said her most memorable moments as a senator were not passing or defeating legislation but helping constituents—"the mother who needed mental retardation services for her disabled son who years later sent me his graduation picture; the owner of a small business which was about to close until the workers' compensation system was reformed."[4]

Krier said that women belong in the legislature because it is important that the body reflect the Texas population. "Without women, important perspectives would be missing," she said. Krier resigned her seat in 1992 to run for Bexar County judge. She won, becoming the first Republican and female to hold that position.[5]

NOTES

1. *San Antonio Express-News*, December 5, 1984; Jim Davis, "Newly Elected Senator Isn't Playing Political Games," unidentified clipping, December 9, 1984, Legislative Reference Library, Austin; *Austin American-Statesman*, December 25, 1984.

2. *San Antonio Express-News*, January 16, 1985; *Austin American-Statesman*, December 25, 1984, January 17, 1985; *San Antonio Light*, January 10, 1985.

3. *San Antonio Light*, March 15, 1985.

4. Martha Sheridan, "Cyndi Krier: Learning Her Legislative ABCs," *San Antonio Express-News*, April 26, 1987; Cyndi Taylor Krier, "Questionnaire," prepared and administered by Nancy Baker Jones and Ruthe Winegarten, 1997.

5. Krier, "Questionnaire"; *San Antonio Express-News*, December 9, 1992.

JUDITH LEE PAPPAS ZAFFIRINI

SENATE 70th Legislature– (1987–)
Democrat, Laredo
DISTRICT 21
COMMITTEES Health and Human Services
(Chair); Finance; Education; General
Investigating; Natural Resources; Intergov-
ernmental Relations; Appropriations;
Conference

DATES February 13, 1946–
BIRTHPLACE Laredo
FAMILY Carlos M. Zaffirini; one son

EDUCATION University of Texas at Austin (B.S., 1967; M.A., 1970; Ph.D., 1978)
OCCUPATION Educator

JUDITH ZAFFIRINI was the first Latina elected to the Texas Senate and
the first woman elected to the Texas Legislature from Laredo. "My opponents and their supporters and the people who opposed me were just laugh-
ing themselves to death," she recalled, "thinking that a woman from South
Texas could be elected. And a Mexican American woman at that." Along
with Cyndi Taylor Krier and Eddie Bernice Johnson, Zaffirini made the
70th Legislature the first in Texas history to have more than one female
senator. When Lieutenant Governor Bob Bullock appointed Zaffirini chair
of the Health and Human Services Committee, she became the first woman
since Barbara Jordan to chair a Senate committee. Each of Zaffirini's senate campaigns resulted in landslide victories in her large district, which at
one time included not only Laredo but also parts of El Paso and Bexar
County, making it larger than many states.[1]

Zaffirini has earned a reputation as one of the hardest-working senators
in the chamber. She arrives at her office before five o'clock in the morning
and rarely socializes. As of the end of the 74th Legislature (1995–1997), she
was the only senator with 100 percent attendance and voting records. During the 75th Legislature (1997–1999), she cast her 15,000th consecutive
vote, a record not likely to be broken. "It doesn't matter to me that I was
the first Mexican American woman elected to the Texas Senate," she said
in 1995. "What matters to me is that since 1987 I have passed 215 bills. . . .
We who are trailblazers have to also show others that we cannot only get
here, but we can accomplish." Her legislative efforts have included bills to
immunize all Texas children; suspend the licenses of drunk drivers; keep

radioactive waste dumps out of her district; stop the spread of *colonias* (substandard housing areas inhabited primarily by low-income Mexican Americans and Mexican immigrants); and reform Medicaid and the welfare system. She has also supported drug abuse education, toughening open container laws, regulating abortion, improving dropout prevention, increasing compensation to crime victims, establishing an office for developmental disabilities, and establishing Texas A&M International University at Laredo. She has worked to strengthen anti-stalking laws, stop domestic violence, mandate the reporting of child abuse, establish a sex-offender registration program, and restrict minors' access to tobacco products.[2]

Zaffirini has been a vocal champion of what she calls a "momma agenda," focusing on issues that she views from her role as a mother. Zaffirini realized this perspective was sometimes different from that of her colleagues when she debated the dangers of alcohol content in candy with a male senator who thought the issue was unimportant. "You know, Senator, I finally understand why you and I disagree about so many issues," she concluded. "Because you study legislation from the perspective of Bubba. I study legislation from the perspective of Momma." His laughter reminded Zaffirini of the importance of humor, a tool she finds valuable for handling attitudes about her identity as the first Latina senator. In her first campaign, Zaffirini responded in Spanish to a voter who said in Spanish he thought women belonged at home cleaning house instead of running for office with, "Yes, sir, that is exactly what I'm doing. I dusted off in May, I swept up in June, and I'm going to mop up in November." In 1993, when Lieutenant Governor Bullock told Zaffirini that if she "cut her skirt off about six inches and put on some high heels she could pass anything she wants," Zaffirini laughed it off and praised Bullock's record for hiring, promoting, and paying women. And when a fellow senator congratulated her for passing her bill about radioactive waste 28-2 by saying, "You have to understand what that means coming from me, because . . . for me, the only purpose for women is to entertain men between wars," she simply thought, "Twenty-eight to two—who cares what he thinks?"[3]

Zaffirini credits some of her success as a senator to her upbringing in Laredo, where Mexican Americans are not a minority but "the dominant population. We are bilingual, bicultural, binational . . . and proud of it." She is similarly confident and vocal about the need for more women in the Senate. "Cumulatively, women comprise half of the population and, cumulatively, we are mothers of the other half. We are in a perfect position of influence. . . . We need a population in the Legislature that reflects the population in the state, just like we need a population in Congress that reflects the population of our nation. We must be as diverse as the population we represent." In 1997 Zaffirini was elected president pro tempore of the Senate and served as governor for a day. She was named one of the 75th Legislature's ten best legislators by *Texas Monthly*.[4]

NOTES

1. Judith Zaffirini, videotape interview by Molly Dinkins, October 1995, Archives for Research on Women and Gender, University of Texas at San Antonio (hereafter ARWG); "Sen. Judith Zaffirini Profile," typescript, January 30, 1997, authors' files; *San Antonio Express-News*, January 24, 1993.

2. Zaffirini, interview, ARWG; *Laredo Morning Times*, January 14 and June 6, 1987, January 15 and July 24, 1994; *San Antonio Express-News*, June 25, 1989; *Houston Chronicle*, August 6, 1989; "Sen. Judith Zaffirini Profile"; *Austin American-Statesman*, August 10, 1996, February 28, 1997; "The Best," *Texas Monthly*, July 1997, p. 97.

3. *San Antonio Express-News*, June 25, 1989; Zaffirini, interview, ARWG; *El Paso Times*, January 22, 1993; *Houston Post*, January 22, 1993.

4. Zaffirini, interview, ARWG; "The Best," p. 97.

☆

ANNA RENSHAW MOWERY

HOUSE 71st Legislature– (1989–)
Republican, Fort Worth
DISTRICT 97
COMMITTEES Elections (Vice Chair); Labor and Employment Relations; Appropriations (Vice Chair); Business and Industry (Vice Chair); Administration; Land and Resource Management (Vice Chair)

DATES January 4, 1931–
BIRTHPLACE Decatur
FAMILY Wesley Mowery; four children
EDUCATION Baylor University (B.A., 1951); Central State University (M.T., 1967)
OCCUPATION Political consultant

Calling herself a Jeffersonian who believes in limited government, **ANNA MOWERY** sees her primary purpose in the House to be killing bills she considers bad rather than introducing legislation. Her constituents, up-per-income conservatives ("I have every . . . doctor and lawyer in the area"), prefer the government to stay out of their lives, she says. "I hate to call them law libertarians, she explains, "but they do not like government regulation and limits on their activities. . . . They are offended at having to pay taxes."[1]

Mowery credits her father with shaping her early interest in politics. She and her husband were Democrats until 1960 when they became Re-publicans to oppose the election of John F. Kennedy as president. In 1975 she was the first woman elected chair of the Tarrant County Republican Party. In 1976 she was a Ronald Reagan delegate to the Republican Na-tional Convention and chaired his Tarrant County campaign in 1984. She also chaired Kay Bailey Hutchison's local campaign for state treasurer. She considered Fort Worth state senator Betty Andujar her mentor. Mowery lost the first race she ran (for Tarrant County commissioner) in 1982. In 1988 she won her first attempt for a seat in the Texas House.[2]

In addition to her focus on killing legislation, Mowery has never been interested in following the traditional route to power and influence in the House—chairing committees. "I didn't expect to be made chairman of a committee for the simple reason that I knew with chairmanship you be-came part of [the speaker's team] and your independence was gone. . . . If you're needed on an issue, you may be expected to go one way when you and your constituents may not want to go that way." As a result of these strategies, Mowery has not expected an easy time passing the occasional bills she does introduce. In her first attempt, she picked what she imag-ined to be a noncontroversial issue, removing librarians' liability for dam-ages arising from the use of information contained in a library's materials. She sent the bill to a committee chaired by her friend, Dallas representa-tive Patricia Hill, thinking she would help. However, Hill, an attorney, did not like the bill and, supported by "the trial lawyers [who] lined up clear down the hall to speak against it," buried the bill in committee.[3]

Mowery learned from this early embarrassment and improved her suc-cess rate. Aspects of seven of her welfare reform measures were included in the final version of one bill, and she succeeded in changing the way ac-counting is done for state employees' social security. Although she de-scribed her bill as "very tough" and disliked by state employees, she be-lieved they would like it "once they get their paychecks and find they've not lost a penny and gained retirement money." She has also authored or sponsored bills related to water quality, primary election dates, political conventions, absentee voting, recycling of solid waste, and rescinding the law setting the speed limit for trucks ten miles per hour below that for cars.[4]

Mowery is hesitant about calling anything a woman's issue "because I think all issues are women's issues." She supported Houston representative Senfronia Thompson's efforts to provide some level of spousal support (alimony), however, and said she and the other women of the legislature "worked together for a long, long time on spousal support, which finally passed [in 1995]." Although Mowery generally does not have strong feelings about feminism, "because my dad always talked to me as an equal and my husband does, too," she also acknowledges that her 101-year-old mother didn't have the right to vote for many years and "was probably somewhat a suffrage advocate." She admits that as "the only child of a mother like that," she "can't say . . . that I was not influenced" by the women's movement. As a college student interested in becoming a representative, Mowery was unaware that women were already serving in the Texas Legislature, so she chose men as role models. After several sessions in the House, Mowery sees the existence of a "certain amount of some good ol' boy networks." But, she adds, "women have the advantage that they don't play golf. They've got about four hours every day to do some detail work that nobody else is doing. I think it balances." She concluded: "I've really not found any prejudices because I'm a woman. Maybe I don't look for it."[5]

NOTES

1. Anne Mowery, videotape interview by Nancy Baker Jones, May 29, 1995, Archives for Research on Women and Gender, University of Texas at San Antonio (hereafter ARWG); *Fort Worth Star-Telegram*, August 17, 1975.

2. Mowery, interview, ARWG; *Fort Worth Star-Telegram*, August 17, 1975.

3. Mowery, interview, ARWG.

4. Ibid.; "Author/Sponsor List of Bills," 71st Regular Session, 1989, pp. 593–594; "Master List of Bills by Author/Sponsor," 72nd Regular Session, 1991, pp. 603–604; "List of Bills Passed by Author/Sponsor," 72nd Regular Session, 1991, pp. 313–314; *Austin American-Statesman*, June 28, 1997.

5. Mowery, interview, ARWG; *Fort Worth Star-Telegram*, August 17, 1975.

ELIZABETH ANN (LIBBY) ANDREWS LINEBARGER

HOUSE 71st–73rd Legislatures (1989–1995)
Democrat, Manchaca
DISTRICT 47, 46
COMMITTEES Human Services; County
Affairs; Public Education (Chair); Local
and Consent Calendars

DATES November 29, 1947–
BIRTHPLACE Gregory
FAMILY Dale Linebarger; six children
EDUCATION Texas A&I University (B.S.,
1970; M.S., 1975)
OCCUPATION Teacher; business owner

During three terms in the House, **LIBBY LINEBARGER** earned a reputation among Republicans as well as Democrats as an intelligent, hardworking, progressive "new guard" legislator who had the potential to become the first female speaker of the House. The daughter of a school superintendent and a former teacher herself, Linebarger wanted to be in the legislature to solve the school finance crisis and improve human services and county affairs. She defeated Republican Anne Cooper in 1988, a presidential election year when Ronald Reagan's victory was expected to mean success for Cooper.[1]

As a three-term legislator, Linebarger repealed mandatory retirement for tenured faculty, supported ethics reform for the legislature, opposed efforts to restrict a woman's right to an abortion, defended Edwards Aquifer water reserves and quality, helped restrict smoking in hospitals, and filed many bills dealing with child care, such as funding a child care information clearinghouse, providing liability insurance for state child care programs, and allowing the use of federal money to train child care workers. Linebarger was also a key player in an effort to prevent weakening of the education reforms of 1984 and to provide spousal support (limited alimony) for Texans, a measure that did not pass until after she left the House.[2]

Reforming education financing remained her primary focus, however, and promised to be more difficult to achieve than several of her other successes. During her first two sessions, Linebarger was unable to persuade Speaker Gib Lewis to appoint her to the Public Education Committee. Linebarger refused to give up; she made herself an "ex officio" member of the committee, attended its meetings, absorbed its issues, and played key roles in the school debate. "I was always in the school finance fight," she said. A Republican member of the Education Committee said Linebarger's name was "always associated with leadership" in education even though she was not a committee member.[3]

In 1993, when Hale Center representative Pete Laney was elected speaker, he rewarded Linebarger's support by making her chair of the Education Committee. Within two weeks she accomplished what many thought impossible—negotiating the political tightrope of getting a bill passed that would not only satisfy the Texas Supreme Court but also win the support of disparate political interests. The House passed by the required two-thirds majority a proposed constitutional amendment to fund Texas public schools by redistributing funds from wealthy to poor districts. The *Austin American-Statesman* said: "Although the bill was far from perfect, it was better than it might have been—a testimony to Linebarger's patience, determination, and diplomacy." She said later that her most memorable moment in the legislature was getting 100 votes on school finance because "it's almost impossible to get 100 votes to take a lunch break in the House." Even Republican opponents of the amendment praised Linebarger's leadership. As one said, "It was a hard-fought battle. But it never got personal. That's a credit to her." A political ally of Linebarger's put it more strongly: "When it comes to issues dealing with children, she's as hard as penitentiary steel. She's unwavering in wanting to make sure there is a good education system in the state." Ultimately the amendment Linebarger fought for was defeated by voters in early May, and the legislature hurriedly passed Senate Bill 7, another "share the wealth" plan, that met the Supreme Court's June 1 deadline.[4]

Linebarger said her strategy in the House was to compromise to get the most she could and to "know your stuff." But she also understood the difficulties of working within the system: "Sometimes it's easier to be on the outside throwing bombs in. It's harder being the one trying to build a coalition." As a woman in the legislature, she said, "You have to work harder, think smarter, and run faster. Fortunately, that's not too difficult for most of us women." Although she looked forward to the time when she could walk down the floor of the House and "not be called 'little lady, sugar, or darlin',' " Linebarger also said it was important to "learn to pick your fights" and was happy to build coalitions with what she called the "Bubbas" of the House.[5]

As a close ally of Speaker Laney and respected by her colleagues as a serious and hardworking legislator, Linebarger was one of the legislature's rising stars. Debra Danburg described her desk mate as one "of the best and brightest" who had what it took to become the first female speaker. But for some time Linebarger had been torn between family and legislative duties. On the day her daughter turned ten, Linebarger was out corralling votes for the school finance bill and missed her daughter's party. This brought her to tears. "When you miss significant events in your children's lives that you can never relive, maybe it's time to rethink your priorities," she said. Linebarger decided not to run again so that she could become a full-time mother. "She sat in my office and read me a letter her daughter wrote her," recalled Speaker Pete Laney. "I think that's when she made the decision that she was going to spend more time with her children. . . . I would have liked for her to have made the other decision; she was a very, very important part of my leadership team."[6] Linebarger did not rule out a return to public office.

NOTES

1. *Austin American-Statesman*, November 10, 1988, April 17, 1989, October 11, 1993; Libby Linebarger, "Questionnaire," prepared and administered by Nancy Baker Jones and Ruthe Winegarten, 1997.

2. *Austin American-Statesman*, November 10, 1988, April 17, 1989, September 3, 1991, September 11, 1993.

3. *Austin American-Statesman*, February 17, 1993.

4. Linebarger, "Questionnaire"; *Austin American-Statesman*, February 17 and September 11, 1993.

5. *Austin American-Statesman*, April 17, 1989, February 17, 1993; Linebarger, "Questionnaire"; Libby Linebarger to Ruthe Winegarten, [September 1997]. Senate Bill 7 did not require voter approval across the state; it gave voters in the districts it affected the opportunity to approve or reject it in local elections.

6. *Austin American-Statesman*, September 11, 1993; Pete Laney, videotape interview by Nancy Baker Jones, May 29, 1995, Archives for Research on Women and Gender, University of Texas at San Antonio; Libby Linebarger, "The Miracle Worker: Libby Linebarger on the Art of Compromise," address to 1994 class of Leadership Texas, Austin, February 24, 1994.

KARYNE JONES CONLEY

HOUSE 71st–74th Legislatures (1989–1996)
Democrat, San Antonio
DISTRICT 120
COMMITTEES Urban Affairs (Vice Chair);
Appropriations (Vice Chair); Corrections;
Administration; Judiciary; State, Federal,
and International Relations; Local and
Consent Calendars

DATES August 14, 1953–
BIRTHPLACE San Antonio
FAMILY Jim Conley; four children
EDUCATION Clark University (B.A., 1975);
Northern Illinois University (M.P.A.,
1977); Harvard University (M.A., 1995)
OCCUPATION Congressional aide; college
instructor

In 1988 **KARYNE JONES CONLEY** defeated Ruth Jones McClendon, another African American, to replace longtime representative Lou Nelle Sutton. Because District 120 was considered San Antonio's only opportunity to send a black representative to the legislature, the fight for the seat was heated and occasionally bitter, with Sutton and most Democratic insiders, including San Antonio mayor Henry Cisneros, backing McClendon. Conley had had considerable experience in public affairs before her surprising victory, however, having worked as a congressional aide to U.S. representative Andrew Young in Washington, D.C., and as his public affairs officer when he was ambassador to the United Nations. She also served two terms on San Antonio's East Central school district board and taught at San Antonio College.[1]

Conley ran as an advocate for improved education and economic development for her district, which included black, Mexican American, and white constituents in low- and upper-income areas. She considered an important aspect of her job as a legislator to be "an irritant, . . . to make sure that positions of those that don't have voices are heard." She gained a reputation as a "tiger" for her commitment to improving the economy on the East Side and was a catalyst for getting bankers to make loans to local entrepreneurs. "My solution is not building more prisons, but to make sure we build communities," she said. Conley earned both praise and criticism for her vocal insistence that contaminated soil at the site of the Alamodome, San Antonio's sports arena, be cleaned up. She supported establishing minority contracts for state services and a college fund for low-income students, and she was also credited with leading legislative efforts to eliminate state policies discouraging interracial adoptions. When the legislature passed a bill, over her objection, allowing an appointed rather than an elected board to govern the Edwards Aquifer, San Antonio's only water supply, Conley warned the speaker and other supporters that "the Justice Department is going to have a problem with this. You've got a voting rights problem here." The Justice Department did file suit, and the legislature started over.[2]

Being a legislator forced Conley to face the reality affecting women more often than men—how to balance her private and political lives. She put 135,000 miles on her car commuting daily between Austin and San Antonio so that she could be at home with her children each day. "I have been married for 18 years. I have four children. . . . And I made the decision that it doesn't make any sense to go out and save the rest of the world and have four nuts growing up at home," she said. Because legislative sessions do not begin until ten o'clock, Conley was able to get her children up and off to school before leaving for Austin. "I decided that's what I'm going to do, so for four and a half months, I am dead tired."[3]

Although Conley recognized that challenges such as this were related to her gender, at other times she found herself "defending the issue of being an African American more so than being a woman." In part, she said, that was because women in the House had no formal caucus, and, consequently, women did not discuss or strategize about issues related to women and the family. She also felt that her male colleagues tended to "look at me as a black female rather than as an equal." During Conley's first term, a prominent senator asked her to visit him in the Senate. Thinking that he wanted to discuss a bill, she hurried to the chamber, only to discover that he wanted to go out to dinner with her. She declined, but his invitations continued. "I had a choice," she said. "I could embarrass him and make an enemy in the Senate forever and never get a bill out, or I could tell him that . . . I'm just not interested, but I do want to be [your] friend." She chose the latter, but not without anger. "Women make those decisions a million times a day, but it takes away any dignity that you have. He would never look at me as a legislator who is here to do a job, . . . the same way he was."[4]

Conley is convinced that such attitudes have helped maintain a glass ceiling in the House, an invisible barrier that prevents women from reach-

ing positions of real power and influence as chairs of important committees. "We are still in token positions where they have us placed; . . . you
can go hunting with them, and you can go golfing with them, . . . but
there's still a role for women. They say they [make appointments] by
seniority, but they really don't. It's who the speaker decides he wants, and
I guess that none of us as women have met his criteria." Such bluntness is
characteristic of Conley and her approach to representing her constituents. "All of my votes are cast on what I believe in. I don't care who [I'm]
going to piss off and whose bill this is, . . . if it's something I feel I can't
defend when I go back home, . . . I vote against it. When you do that,
though, you run the risk of not being a player, which means you're not
always included at the table, you can't play ball." Conley believes her
convictions precluded her from being made a committee chair because
she was not willing to compromise her principles to please the House
leadership. "Principle always outweighed popularity, which is why you
never get to be in the good old boys' club," she concluded.[5]

Similarly, Conley is frank about the role lobbyists play: "Lobbyists still
run this process," she says. "[They] write the bills and give them to us,
and we just perfect them. . . . So you've got to work with them. In 1996
Conley left the legislature during her fourth term to become director of
federal relations for SBC Communications, the parent firm of Southwestern Bell Telephone Company, in Washington, D.C. Although the
media characterized her new job as "lobbyist," Conley said it involved
education and outreach to national organizations to define issues and
craft legislative solutions.[6] Her House seat was filled by Ruth Jones
McClendon, whom Conley had defeated in 1988.

NOTES

1. *San Antonio Express-News*, December 26, 1988; "Biographical Sketch of State Representative Karyne Jones Conley," typescript, copy in authors' files; Karyne Jones Conley,
videotape interview by Molly Dinkins, May 26, 1995, Archives for Research on Women
and Gender, University of Texas at San Antonio (hereafter ARWG).

2. *San Antonio Express-News*, January 11, 1989; *San Antonio Business Journal*, December 17, 1993; *San Antonio Express-News*, June 20, 1996; Conley, interview, ARWG.

3. Conley, interview, ARWG.

4. Ibid.

5. Ibid.; Karyne Jones Conley, "Questionnaire," prepared and administered by Nancy
Baker Jones and Ruthe Winegarten, 1997.

6. Conley, interview, ARWG; *San Antonio Express-News*, June 20, 1996.

MARY CAROLYN BEDGOOD PARK

HOUSE 71st–74th Legislatures (1989–1997)
Republican, Euless
DISTRICT 92
COMMITTEES Public Health; Rules and
Resolutions (Vice Chair); Urban Affairs;
Appropriations; Human Services

DATES July 16, 1932
BIRTHPLACE Bloomberg
FAMILY John Park; five children
EDUCATION East Texas State University
(B.S., 1958); Texas Woman's University
OCCUPATION Teacher; speech pathologist

CAROLYN PARK endured five campaigns (a special election and run-off, the Republican primary and runoff, and the general election) within eleven months in 1988 to win her first term in the House. She had no opposition for her second term, but by her third, some constituents and her Democratic opponent, Bill Burkhart, criticized her for inaction. "She has not done anything," Burkhart said. "She just votes against." Park said voters liked her conservatism; she opposed the lottery, taxes, abortion, the "Robin Hood" school finance plan, and the state budget. Although her district included more Democrats after it was redrawn, it kept a Republican majority, and she remained in the legislature through 1996, when she decided not to run again. Her legislative goals involved welfare, education, tort reform, and a balanced state budget.[1]

A member of the Texas Conservative Coalition, a bipartisan group of legislators, Park generally opposed new taxes or tax increases, although she filed bills to implement a "crime tax" district in her area, to fund crime-fighting with increased sales taxes, and to increase sales taxes to benefit industrial development. She also wanted to establish drug-free zones around schools and playgrounds and enforce a ten-year minimum term for anyone convicted of selling or making drugs within the zones, with no time off for good behavior. She supported efforts to enhance the penalties for hate crimes and sponsored a bill to allow the death penalty for committing "drive by" killings or shooting at buildings or vehicles. In a debate over the bill to legalize the carrying of concealed handguns, she failed to win approval for her amendment to keep gun application records confidential.[2]

Although Park said she believed that neither the state nor federal government should have a role in resolving school violence, she introduced a bill to expel any student committing rape or arson in a public school. She was instrumental in establishing courts of record in her district, thereby increasing city revenues from traffic fines; she sponsored a bill to end promiscuity as a defense against sexual assault, and she supported home equity lending. In her last session, she joined twenty-nine others, including four women, to co-sponsor a bill requiring minors to obtain parental or judicial consent before getting an abortion and requiring abortion clinics to follow the same medical standards as day surgery centers. She asserted that the latter provision was necessary because clinics were not required to sterilize their instruments, a charge called "absurd" by the head of the Texas Family Planning Association. Her efforts to improve education included a bill to free instructors to teach the U.S. Constitution "like it's written." Park maintained that instructors were hesitant to use the Constitution because it contained words like "religion" and "God." Area teachers reported that they did not need Park's bill to teach effectively.[3]

The Sierra Club included Park on its "Worst List," contending that she and other legislators promoted industry and agriculture at the expense of the environment; the Texas Federation of Teachers gave her an "F" for her votes against taxes for school funding.[4] Park also drew conservative criticism when she supported acceptance of federal funds for local schools through the Goals 2000 program. Initially she had sided with those who said the program was a "Trojan horse" that would lead to mandated health classes, giving condoms to schoolchildren, and federal intrusion into local control of schools. After Governor George W. Bush appointed Park to chair the panel planning the state's role in the program, however, Park changed her mind, saying her earlier views were "coming from a very narrow perspective. . . . I had not done research for myself. Now I have."[5]

Although Park had no announced opposition in 1996, conservative opposition to her was growing. She declined to run for reelection, saying she had had enough of the time-consuming legislature and wanted to spend more time with her family.[6]

NOTES

1. *Fort Worth Star-Telegram*, January 14 and 20, February 14, April 10, 1988, January 7, 1990, October 7, 1992, February 26, 1993; Carolyn Park, "Questionnaire," prepared and administered by Nancy Baker Jones and Ruthe Winegarten, 1997.

2. *Fort Worth Star-Telegram*, January 29, 1991, March 26, April 22, and May 7, 1993, April 29, 1994, March 16 and May 2, 1995.

3. *Fort Worth Star-Telegram*, January 29, 1991, February 23, June 6 and 23, 1993, November 24, 1994, January 8 and 26, March 3, 1995.

4. *Fort Worth Star-Telegram*, August 14, 1991, November 24, 1992, February 10, 1993, May 5, 1993, June 4, 1993, April 26, 1995, August 21, 1996.

5. *Fort Worth Star-Telegram*, July 8, 1994, July 7, 1995, September 3, 1995; Park, "Questionnaire."

6. *Fort Worth Star-Telegram*, October 13, 1995.

☆

SUE ANN SMITH SCHECHTER

HOUSE 72nd–73rd Legislatures (1991–1995)
Democrat, Houston
DISTRICT 134
COMMITTEES Human Services (Vice Chair); Judicial Affairs; Redistricting

DATES November 11, 1952–
BIRTHPLACE Granbury
FAMILY Richard Schechter; two children
EDUCATION University of North Texas (B.B.A., 1974); South Texas College of Law (J.D., 1981)
OCCUPATION Claims adjuster; attorney

SUE SCHECHTER ran for the legislature to pursue her interests in education and worker compensation law and, as a pro-choice Democrat, to unseat the anti-choice incumbent. It was her first experience in politics. In her two terms, she focused on mental health and children's issues and passed legislation to make school volunteers immune from liability, allow the Texas lottery to be privatized, allow judges to consider sexual abuse of a child in emergency placement hearings, extend the Friend of the Court program for enforcing child support and visitation, waive college tuition and fees for children in foster care, raise the age for topless dancing, and allow the Department of Protective and Regulatory Services access to the criminal history of people being investigated for abuse.[1]

Schechter was equally proud of her push for legislation that was defeated, notably her attempts to deny unsupervised visitation with children by a convicted child abuser, expand the hearsay exception for children testifying in abuse cases, require mental health professionals to have a duty to all parties involved in an abuse case, and limit legislators' terms. She also failed in her attempts to "undedicate" the gasoline tax and Public University Fund so that more money would be available for human services; retain a council on teenage pregnancy; pass a "children's firearm prevention act" to protect children from access to firearms; allow courts to remove adult perpetrators rather than children from their homes in emergencies; and reform the financing of judicial campaigns.[2]

Schechter recalls a number of memorable legislative moments, such as when she presented a "no gifts" amendment to an ethics bill and heard a colleague laugh, "You mean I can't keep my fur coat?" or when another member, who supported a horse theft bill, asked that it provide for printing 1-800-CALL MR ED notices on milk cartons. She believed female legislators generally did not accept "that's the way it has always been" thinking "because generally women and children weren't included in those prior situations." Schechter decided not to run for a third term because of the stress of juggling parental and public responsibilities. "Parenting by phone doesn't work," she said.[3]

NOTES

1. "Representative Sue Schechter," typescript, n.d., p. 1, copy in authors' files; "Schechter: 73rd Legislative Session," typescript, n.d., p. 1, copy in authors' files; Sue Schechter, "Questionnaire," prepared and administered by Nancy Baker Jones and Ruthe Winegarten, 1997.

2. "Representative Sue Schechter," n.d., p. 2; "Schechter: 73rd Legislative Session," n.d., p. 2; Schechter, "Questionnaire."

3. Schechter, "Questionnaire"; *Austin American-Statesman*, November 21, 1993.

MARGARET ANN (PEGGY) MULRY ROSSON

SENATE 72nd–74th Legislatures (1991–1997)
Democrat, El Paso
DISTRICT 29
COMMITTEES State Affairs (Vice Chair);
Finance; Economic Development;
Intergovernmental Relations; International
Relations, Trade, and Technology;
Redistricting; Ethics and Elections; Natural
Resources

DATES April 11, 1935–
BIRTHPLACE Indianapolis, Indiana
FAMILY Joe L. Rosson; no children
EDUCATION George Washington High
School (1952)
OCCUPATION Homemaker; public utilities

PEGGY ROSSON defeated longtime incumbent senator Tati Santiesteban to become the ninth female Texas state senator. She ran because
she believed Santiesteban had had eighteen years to make a difference,
and it was time for a change. "El Paso was the fourth largest city in Texas,
yet it was virtually unknown in Austin," she said. "State agencies rou-
tinely ignored the district, funding was limited to the pet projects of a
select few, the community was on the threshold of becoming the gateway
to Texas under NAFTA, and we had Third World health and housing
conditions." These factors, added to the existence of underfunded schools,
limited access to higher education, and high unemployment resulted,
she said, "in no sense of connection to Texas and no voice in the decision
making process." Prior to becoming a senator, Rosson was appointed to
the state Public Utilities Commission by Governor Mark White. She
served there from 1983 to 1987 and was chair for two years.[1]

In the Senate, Rosson concentrated on border issues, including affordable housing, water and sewer services for *colonias* (substandard housing areas populated primarily by low-income Mexican Americans and
Spanish-speaking immigrants), health care, job training, and economic
and infrastructure development. She was a member of the Senate Hispanic Caucus and of the Border Working Group, which increased funding and expanded degree programs for colleges and universities along the
border. "While Austin is the capital of Texas, El Paso is the capital of the

border," Rosson said, "and has a very major contribution to make to the economic recovery of Texas."[2]

Rosson co-sponsored constitutional amendments to create a Texas Ethics Commission, increase money available for *colonias* to get water and sewer services, and finance low-interest loans to low- and middle-income families. She sponsored bills to improve vocational education, penalize employers who fail to pay employees (this was to aid El Paso garment workers), allow cities on either side of the U.S.-Mexican border to contract with each other for health and water needs, protect *colonia* residents from having property seized for attempting to improve it with utilities, and increase penalties for illegal dumping of refuse in the desert. Her threat to become the first woman in Texas history to filibuster a bill— which would have allowed utilities to change rates without posting hearing notices—postponed debate. In 1992 a coalition of consumer and environmental groups praised Rosson for what they viewed as her pro-consumer voting record.[3]

Lieutenant Governor Bob Bullock appointed Rosson to the new Senate Committee on International Relations, Trade, and Technology, which was created to deal with the increasing number of border-related bills. In Rosson's final term, Bullock appointed her to the powerful Senate Finance Committee, which shapes the state's budget. Rosson disappointed many constituents by voting to legalize concealed handguns and to prohibit cities from passing antismoking ordinances, but she was the only senator to oppose Southwestern Bell Telephone Company's telecommunications bill in the 74th Legislature, an act called "courageous" by some. She also opposed anti-choice legislation proposed that session.[4]

Rosson decided three terms were enough. "I retired from my job as a paralegal in 1977 to be a full-time wife," she said. "I left the Public Utility Commission of Texas in 1987 with the intention of being a full-time wife. I retired from the Senate in 1997 with the intention of being a full-time wife. This time I think I mean it." Upon reflection, she said the Senate is still a man's world but "it's getting better." She learned early that a woman in the legislature "fares better if she keeps her voice pitched low and takes a nonconfrontational approach." She also offered three pieces of advice for new legislators. First, "you must prepare, prepare, prepare. If you don't know as much or more about what you're trying to do than anyone else, it's easy to lose on what should be easy issues." Second, she recommended working with opponents in advance of votes, "otherwise [your] bill will simply die, and you'll never know why." And third, Rosson said, "It is mandatory to remain civil. The last thing you want to do is be branded a 'hot-dog' or 'showboater,' . . . by personally attacking or guilt-tripping colleagues on the floor or in the press. You must understand that there are no permanent friends or enemies in politics."[5]

NOTES

1. Peggy Rosson, "Questionnaire," prepared and administered by Nancy Baker Jones and Ruthe Winegarten, 1997; *El Paso Herald-Post*, February 16, 1983.

2. "Sen. Peggy Rosson Biography," typescript, n.d., p. 1, copy in authors' files; *El Paso Times*, December 20, 1990.

3. *Sen. Peggy Rosson Reports* (newsletter), October 1991, pp. 2, 4; *El Paso Times*, May 10, 1991, February 21, 1992.

4. *El Paso Times*, January 14, 1993, February 22, 1995, August 22, 1995.

5. Rosson, "Questionnaire."

YOLANDA NAVARRO FLORES

HOUSE 73rd Legislature (1993–1995)
Democrat, Houston
DISTRICT 148
COMMITTEES International and Cultural Relations; Urban Affairs

DATES 1949?–
BIRTHPLACE Houston
FAMILY Larry Flores; two children
EDUCATION Texas Southern University (B.A., 1975); University of Houston (J.D., 1981)
OCCUPATION Attorney

YOLANDA NAVARRO FLORES used her degree in radio and television communications from Texas Southern University to further her career in Houston television, where she moderated her own public affairs program. Her civic leadership with the YWCA, Houston Council on Human Relations, Houston Metropolitan Ministries, and Mental Health Association helped her win her first race for state representative in 1992. She was also co-chair of Imagine Houston; a board member of the

Guadalupe Social Services and the University of Houston Alumni Association; a president of Mexican American Democrats of Houston; and the recipient of the Rising Star Award from the Harris County Democrats in 1992. Flores was known as a quiet but hardworking grassroots campaigner. As a result, in the Democratic primary election she caught her opponent off guard and won with 60 percent of the vote.[1]

Flores introduced legislation dealing with elections, liability of public transportation, secondary and higher education, and alcoholic beverage restrictions in city parks. She also gained a reputation for independence in the House, although some of her colleagues defined this as a refusal to consult or work with them before taking action. The Mexican American Legislative Caucus and business constituents were repeatedly critical of her style.[2]

In 1994 Flores ran for the new Texas Senate District 6 seat (whose residents were 63 percent Mexican American) instead of running for a second House term. She lost the Senate race to Representative Mario Gallegos. Her House seat was won by Jessica Farrar, an architect. Flores ran for the House again in 1996 in an effort to retake the District 148 seat she had left. She lost to incumbent Farrar amid charges that Flores had misrepresented herself as the incumbent. Flores denied the charges, saying, "I would never identify myself as state representative if I'm not. At no time after my last day in office did I ever present myself as state representative." She continued in her law practice in Houston.[3]

NOTES

1. *Houston Chronicle*, March 3, 1996; *Houston Post*, December 3, 1993.
2. *Houston Post*, December 3, 1993.
3. *Houston Chronicle*, January 13, 1996.

SUSAN COMBS

HOUSE 73rd–74th Legislatures (1993–1996)
Republican, Austin
DISTRICT 47
COMMITTEES Natural Resources; Criminal
Jurisprudence; Administration; Land and
Resource Management; Natural Resources

DATES February 26, 1945–
BIRTHPLACE San Antonio
FAMILY Joe Duran; three children
EDUCATION Vassar (B.A., 1966); University
of Texas at Austin (J.D., 1976)
OCCUPATION Rancher; attorney; State
Commissioner of Agriculture

SUSAN COMBS is a fourth-generation Texan who runs a cow-calf operation on a ranch in Brewster County. The ranch was established by her
great-grandfather, one of Texas' original frontier trail drivers. Combs was
the only Republican in Travis County's delegation in the 73rd Legislature. She was reelected in 1994 without opposition. She campaigned as a
pro-business conservative, but her support for abortion rights separated
her from many of her Republican colleagues. Holding both positions,
she said, was consistent with her philosophy that government should have
limited ability to control people's behavior.[1]

As a legislator, Combs often did the unexpected, alternately pleasing
and irritating both progressives and conservatives. Like many ranchers,
Combs considered the federal Endangered Species Act an intrusion on
private property rights. She used it successfully, however, to block the
construction of a power line across her property and joined with the Sierra Club and other environmental groups to do so. In 1996 environmentalists found themselves fighting Combs' Private Real Property Rights
Preservation Act, which permitted private property owners to collect dam-
ages from state agencies and local governments, including schools, if environmental regulations reduced property values. She considered this act
one of her major legislative achievements.[2] Combs angered her own delegation when she introduced a bill to require Austin to obtain prior approval from voters within areas to be annexed. The president of a nonprofit creek-protection group said the bill would "force the city to soften

its rules or pay developers. I voted for her. It's time we started asking her just who she is representing." The bill lost to arguments that such legislation would curtail any urban area's ability to protect its water supply and environment. To the surprise of some and to the delight of consumer activists, Combs sponsored a bill to amend the state's "lemon law" to increase protection for car buyers.[3]

Combs also co-sponsored legislation to pay tort claims against state agencies out of agency budgets, create the Texas Incentive and Productivity Commission to pay state employees for successful cost-cutting ideas, make murder of a child under six a capital offense, provide limited access to information about jurors, make stalking a crime, and provide parents with school performance "report cards." She was also a co-author of a revision of the state's juvenile justice laws; she wrote and passed laws curbing the power of government to enter private land to gather information for public use without the owner's consent; and she supported a constitutional amendment to permit landowners to retain ad valorem exemption if they wished to engage in conservation activities. She believed that being a woman in the legislature made no significant difference. "The key is not your sex but your ability to persuade others of your view or to achieve consensus," she said.[4]

In 1990 Combs published *A Perfect Match*, an erotic melodrama. When Austin state senator Gonzalo Barrientos considered reading from it during a 1995 filibuster, he quickly reconsidered. "My glasses started getting steamed up, so instead I read Richard Nixon's resignation speech," he said.[5]

Environmentalists targeted Combs for defeat in her third term, but she surprised observers and resigned her seat a year before her second term ended to become state office director for U.S. senator Kay Bailey Hutchison. After working less than a year for Hutchison, Combs quit to run for a statewide office. In the 1998 elections, she was a member of the Republican landslide that swept top offices, and she became the state's first female commissioner of agriculture.[6]

NOTES

1. *Austin American-Statesman*, April 23 and May 21, 1992, May 14, 1995.

2. *Austin American-Statesman*, June 13, 1995; Susan Combs, resume; Susan Combs, "Questionnaire," prepared and administered by Nancy Baker Jones and Ruthe Winegarten, 1997.

3. *Austin American-Statesman*, May 14, 1995.

4. *State Rep. Susan Combs* (newsletter), [1993], Legislative Reference Library, Austin; Combs, "Questionnaire"; Combs, resume.

5. *Texas Observer*, July 4, 1997; *Austin American-Statesman*, May 28, 1995.

6. *Austin Amer.-Stat.*, June 7, 1995, January 20, 1996, July 4, 1997, January 12, 1999.

☆

SYLVIA ROMO

HOUSE 73rd–74th Legislatures (1993–1996)
Democrat, San Antonio
DISTRICT 125
COMMITTEES Financial Institutions; Ways and Means; Business and Industry; Investments and Banking

DATES December 27, 1942–
BIRTHPLACE San Antonio
FAMILY Divorced; four children
EDUCATION University of Texas at San Antonio (B.B.A., 1976; M.P.A., 1981)
OCCUPATION Certified public accountant

SYLVIA ROMO ran for the legislature because she believed her voice as a Latina CPA would make a difference. There were not enough women and minorities in government, Romo observed, and those who were there focused on human services and education more than economic empowerment. "My stand . . . has always been to reinvent government," she said, adding that economic development would lead to improved human services and education.[1]

During her two terms, she sponsored over ninety pieces of legislation. One successful act prevented exploitation of child labor. She also has two constitutional amendments to her credit. The first one, eliminating $500 million of unused bond debts, likely made her the first freshman legislator to sponsor a major amendment. The second provided funding for women and minorities to start their own businesses. Much of her other legislation related to banking and finance, such as establishing security standards at automated teller machines and requiring full cost disclosure on bond financing. During her second term, Romo was named to the powerful Ways and Means Committee and was its only female member.[2]

Romo became vice chair of the Mexican American Legislative Caucus but was disappointed that a formal women's caucus did not exist. She tried to form one as a freshman, but felt that senior women in the House were unhappy with a junior member taking on such a role, so she stopped trying. As a freshman, Romo also noticed that there was no women's restroom restricted to legislators' use, as there was for the men of the House. She complained and succeeded in getting a private restroom. She also recalled a male senior member's patronizing her that year by telling her, "Don't you worry, little lady. Don't expect to do anything great this session. Just sit back and learn." Romo considered that poor advice. "My first session, I passed a major constitutional amendment, and I filed 27 bills and passed a third of them. I think I did more than just sit back and learn," she said. In another instance, Romo recalled that during a debate over a program to help women start their own businesses, a male colleague who was hoping to enact similar legislation for veterans argued his case by asserting, "Veterans have done a lot for this country. You tell me, what have women done for this country?"[3]

In 1994 Romo was selected by the National Federation of Women Legislators to chair the Texas celebration of the 100th anniversary of the election of the first woman to a state legislature (Colorado, 1895).[4] Working with the Center for the Study of Women and Gender at the University of Texas at San Antonio, Romo raised private funds to produce *Getting Where We've Got To Be*, a video history of women in the Texas Legislature. The video, which premiered in 1995, was designed for use in high schools and colleges and for community groups.

Romo had planned to run for a third term but resigned her House seat in 1996 after deciding to run for Bexar County tax assessor-collector instead. In 1997 Romo became the first female tax assessor-collector in Bexar County history.[5]

NOTES

1. Sylvia Romo, videotape interview by Ruthe Winegarten, July 12, 1995, Archives for Research on Women and Gender, University of Texas at San Antonio (hereafter ARWG); *San Antonio Express-News*, November 16, 1995.

2. Sylvia Romo, resume, [1997].

3. Romo, interview, ARWG.

4. Romo, resume.

5. *San Antonio Express-News*, November 16, 1995.

BARBARA RUSLING

HOUSE 74th Legislature (1995–1997)
Republican, China Spring
DISTRICT 57
COMMITTEES Agriculture and Livestock;
State, Federal, and International Relations

DATES November 27, 1945–
BIRTHPLACE St. Louis, Missouri
FAMILY Robert B. Rusling; four children
EDUCATION Vanderbilt University (B.A.
1966)
OCCUPATION Teacher; business owner;
General Services Commissioner

In 1992 **BARBARA RUSLING** ran against longtime Waco representative Betty Denton, a Democrat, and lost. In 1994 Rusling tried again and, with 52 percent of the vote, earned the distinction of carrying a district with the highest concentration of Democrats ever won by a Republican in the history of the legislature. An experienced real estate broker and president and co-owner of Coldwell-Banker Hallmark Realty, Rusling said she did not want to spend as much time filing bills as she did serving constituents, killing bad bills, and amending bills with potential. She was interested in economic development, tax reform, effective government, and "education to prepare Texans for jobs of the future." She also said that providing constituent services would be a high priority.[1]

Rusling was pleased that House speaker Pete Laney appointed her to two of her top committee assignment requests—Agriculture and Livestock as well as State, Federal, and International Relations. She believed the two committees would work together well to increase trade and develop more aggressive ways to market the state's farm products. Rusling, who speaks Spanish and French, said that the intergovernmental relations assignment would give her a chance to deal with issues affecting Texas' relationship with Washington, explaining, "Officials from Texas and other states have complained that many federal laws have imposed a too-expensive burden on states and their taxpayers." She said, "Defining a lot of these issues and determining what the federal government will be in control of . . . and what the states should have the ability to determine for themselves is going to be more and more important." She also advocated passage of an equity lending amendment to provide certain protections and allow more freedom of choice for Texans to use the equity invested in their homes.[2]

Rusling, who lives on eighty-seven acres in China Spring, brought considerable business and civic experience to her legislative position. She was recognized in 1979 as Salesman of the Year by the Waco Board of Realtors. She has held many community leadership positions, including being president of the YWCA and serving on the board of United Way of Waco/McLennan County, Family Counseling Services, the Family Abuse Center, and the Waco Chamber of Commerce. In 1995 she was named Legislator of the Year by the Texas Warehouse Association for economic development and was chair of the Interim Committee on Value Added for Texas agricultural products. She was defeated in a 1996 race for a second term by Democrat Jim Dunnan. In 1997 Governor George W. Bush appointed her as general services commissioner for a six-year term.[3]

NOTES

1. Barbara Rusling to Ruthe Winegarten, November 7, 1997; *Waco Tribune-Herald*, November 28, 1994.

2. *Waco Tribune-Herald*, January 27, 1995; Rusling to Winegarten.

3. Barbara Rusling, biography, 1997; Rusling to Winegarten.

SNAPSHOTS

DIANNE WHITE DELISI

HOUSE 72nd Legislature– (1991–)
Republican, Temple
DISTRICT 55
COMMITTEES Appropriations (Vice Chair);
Public Health (Vice Chair); Rules and
Resolutions; Public Safety; State, Federal,
and International Affairs

SHERRI GREENBERG

HOUSE 72nd Legislature– (1991–)
Democrat, Austin
DISTRICT 48
COMMITTEES Appropriations; Jurispru-
dence; Economic Development; Natural
Resources (Chair); Science and Technology

PEGGY HAMRIC

HOUSE 72nd Legislature– (1991–)
Republican, Houston
DISTRICT 126
COMMITTEES Corrections; County Affairs;
Cultural and Historical Resources; House
Administration; Land and Resource
Management; Licensing and Administra-
tion Procedures; Redistricting; Urban
Affairs

CHRISTINE HERNÁNDEZ

HOUSE 72nd–75th Legislatures (1991–1999)
Democrat, San Antonio
DISTRICT 124
COMMITTEES Appropriations; Calendars;
Elections; Local and Consent Calendars;
Public Education; Science and Technology;
Legislative Budget Board

LETICIA SAN MIGUEL VAN DE PUTTE

HOUSE 72nd Legislature– (1991–)
Democrat, San Antonio
DISTRICT 115
COMMITTEES Insurance (Vice Chair);
Economic Development; International
and Cultural Relations; Juvenile Justice
and Family Issues; Human Services; Labor
and Employment

PATRICIA GRAY

HOUSE 72nd Legislature– (1992–)
Democrat, Galveston
DISTRICT 23
COMMITTEES Civil Practices (Chair);
Corrections (Vice Chair); General
Investigating; Appropriations; Environ-
mental Regulation

DIANA DÁVILA

HOUSE 73rd–75th Legislatures (1993–1999)
Democrat, Houston
DISTRICT 145
COMMITTEES Human Services; Urban
Affairs; Local and Consent Calendars;
Public Health

YVONNE DAVIS

HOUSE 73rd Legislature– (1993–)
Democrat, Dallas
DISTRICT 111
COMMITTEES International and Cultural
Relations; Rules and Resolutions;
Appropriations; Economic Development;
Energy Resources; Local and Consent
Calendars

MARY DIANE CARVER DENNY

HOUSE 73rd Legislature– (1993–)
Republican, Denton
DISTRICT 63
COMMITTEES Agriculture and Wildlife
Management; Elections; Human Services;
Rules and Resolutions; County Affairs

HELEN GIDDINGS

HOUSE 73rd Legislature– (1993–)
Democrat, De Soto
DISTRICT 109
COMMITTEES Business and Industry;
Investments and Banking; Financial
Institutions; Redistricting

VILMA LUNA

HOUSE 73rd Legislature– (1993–)
Democrat, Corpus Christi
DISTRICT 33
COMMITTEES Economic Development;
Public Safety; House Administration
(Vice-Chair); Judicial Affairs

NANCY J. JONES MOFFAT

HOUSE 73rd–75th Legislatures (1991–1999)
Republican, Southlake
DISTRICT 98
COMMITTEES Energy Resources; Natural
Resources; Civil Practices; Economic
Development; Higher Education

JANE GRAY NELSON

SENATE 73rd Legislature– (1993–)
Republican, Double Oak
DISTRICT 9
COMMITTEES Criminal Justice; Health
Services (Chair); State Affairs; Education;
Finance

ELVIRA REYNA

HOUSE 73rd Legislature– (1993–)
Republican, Mesquite
DISTRICT 101
COMMITTEES Higher Education; Public
Safety; State, Federal, and International
Relations

FLORENCE MURIEL DONALD SHAPIRO

SENATE 73rd Legislatures– (1993–)
Republican, Plano
DISTRICT 8
COMMITTEES Economic Development;
Education; Intergovernmental Relations;
Administration; Criminal Justice (Vice
Chair); Nominations (Vice Chair); State
Affairs (Chair)

DAWNNA DUKES

HOUSE 74th Legislature– (1995–)
Democrat, Austin
DISTRICT 50
COMMITTEES Environmental Regulation;
State, Federal, and International
Relations; Business and Industry

HARRYETTE EHRHARDT

HOUSE 74th Legislature– (1995–)
Democrat, Dallas
DISTRICT 107
COMMITTEES Elections, Rules, and
Resolutions; Urban Affairs; Financial
Institutions

JESSICA CRISTINA FARRAR

HOUSE 74th Legislatures– (1995–)
Democrat, Houston
DISTRICT 148
COMMITTEES Corrections; Criminal
Jurisprudence; Rules and Resolutions

JUDY HAWLEY

HOUSE 74th Legislature– (1995–)
Democrat, Portland
DISTRICT 31
COMMITTEES Agriculture and Livestock;
Energy Resources (Vice Chair); House
Administration; Transportation

ARLENE WOHLGEMUTH

HOUSE 74th Legislature– (1995–)
Republican, Burleson
DISTRICT 58
COMMITTEES County Affairs; Human
Services; Urban Affairs

BEVERLY WOOLLEY

HOUSE 74th Legislature– (1995–)
Republican, Houston
DISTRICT 136
COMMITTEES Local and Consent
Calendars; State Recreational Resources;
Urban Affairs; Business and Industry;
Pensions and Investments (Vice Chair)

NORMA CHAVEZ

HOUSE 75th Legislature– (1997–)
Democrat, El Paso
DISTRICT 76
COMMITTEES Human Services; Rules and
Regulations; State, Federal, and International Relations

CAROLYN GALLOWAY

HOUSE 75th Legislature (1997–1999)
Republican, Dallas
DISTRICT 108
COMMITTEES Criminal Jurisprudence;
Elections

TERRI HODGE

HOUSE 75th Legislature– (1997–)
Democrat, Dallas
DISTRICT 100
COMMITTEES Elections

SUZANNA GRATIA HUPP

HOUSE 75th Legislature– (1997–)
Republican, Lampasas
DISTRICT 54
COMMITTEES Agriculture and Livestock;
Corrections

RUTH JONES MCCLENDON

HOUSE 75th Legislature– (1997–)
Democrat, San Antonio
DISTRICT 120
COMMITTEES Juvenile Justice and Family
Issues; Public Safety

DORA OLIVO

HOUSE 75th Legislature– (1997–)
Democrat, Stafford
DISTRICT 27
COMMITTEES Insurance; Public Safety

SUE PALMER

HOUSE 75th Legislature– (1997–)
Republican, Fort Worth
DISTRICT 89
COMMITTEES Rules and Resolutions;
State, Federal, and International Rela-
tions; Recreational Resources

APPENDICES

APPENDIX A

THE HONORABLE WOMEN
OF THE TEXAS LEGISLATURE

The following women served in the 38th–75th Legislatures (January 1923–January 1999). Boldface denotes a senator.

Edith Eunice Therrel Wilmans (D) Dallas 1923–25
Mary Elizabeth (Margie) Neal (D) Carthage 1927–35
Laura Burleson Negley (D) San Antonio 1929–31
Helen Edmunds Moore (D) Texas City 1929–33; 1935–37
Frances Mitchell Rountree (D) Bryan 1931–33
Cora Gray Strong (D) Slocum 1931–33
Sarah Tilghman Hughes (D) Dallas 1931–35
Margaret Greer Harris Gordon (Amsler) (D) Waco 1939–41
Esther Neveille Higgs Colson (D) Navasota 1939–49 (House); 1949–67
   (Senate)
Rae Mandette Files (Still) (D) Waxahachie 1941–51
Florence Fenley (D) Uvalde 1943–47
Mary Elizabeth Suiter (D) Winnsboro 1943–49
Marian Isabel (Maribelle) Hamblen Stewart (Mills Reich) (D) Houston
   1947–48
Persis Jones Henderson (D) Groesbeck 1949–51
Dorothy Gillis Gurley (Cauthorn) (D) Del Rio 1951–55
Virginia Elizabeth Duff (D) Ferris 1951–63
Anita Blair (D) El Paso 1953–55
Maud Isaacks (D) El Paso 1954–67
Myra Davis Wilkinson Banfield (Dippel) (D) Rosenberg 1961–65
Sue Blair Hairgrove (Muzzy) (D) Lake Jackson 1967–69
Barbara Charline Jordan (D) Houston 1967–73
Frances Tarlton (Sissy) Farenthold (D) Corpus Christi 1969–73

Kathryn A. (Kay) Bailey (Hutchison) (R) Houston 1973–76
Sarah Ragle Weddington (D) Austin 1973–77
Dorothy J. Chrisman (Chris) Miller (D) Fort Worth 1973–79
Eddie Bernice Johnson (D) Dallas 1973–79 (House); 1987–93 (Senate)
Elizabeth (Betty) Richards Andujar (R) Fort Worth 1973–83
Senfronia Paige Thompson (D) Houston 1973–
Susan Gurley McBee (D) Del Rio 1975–83
Wilhelmina Ruth Fitzgerald Delco (D) Austin 1975–95
Lou Nelle Callahan Sutton (D) San Antonio 1976–89
Mary Jane Goodpasture Bode (D) Austin 1977–81
Lanell Cofer (D) Dallas 1977–83
Ernestine Viola Glossbrenner (D) Alice 1977–93
Anita Dorcas Carraway Hill (R) Dallas 1977–93
Betty Denton (D) Waco 1977–95
Irma Rangel (D) Kingsville 1977–
Mary J. McCracken Polk (D) El Paso 1979–84
Debra Danburg (D) Houston 1981–
Jan McKenna (R) Arlington 1983–87
Patricia Ellen Porcella Hill (R) Dallas 1983–91
Phyllis Robinson (D) Gonzales 1983–91
Gwyn Clarkston Shea (R) Irving 1983–93
Nancy Hanks McDonald (D) El Paso 1984–97
Margaret Anne Becker Cooper (R) San Marcos 1985–89
María Elena (Lena) Guerrero (D) Austin 1985–91
Cyndi Taylor Krier (R) San Antonio 1985–92
Judith Lee Pappas Zaffirini (D) Laredo 1987–
Anna Renshaw Mowery (R) Fort Worth 1988–
Elizabeth Ann (Libby) Andrews Linebarger (D) Manchaca 1989–95
Karyne Jones Conley (D) San Antonio 1989–96
Mary Carolyn Bedgood Park (R) Bedford 1989–97
Sue Ann Smith Schechter (D) Houston 1991–95
Margaret Ann (Peggy) Mulry Rosson (D) El Paso 1991–97
Dianne White Delisi (R) Temple 1991–
Sherri Greenberg (D) Austin 1991–
Peggy Hamric (R) Houston 1991–
Christine Hernández (D) San Antonio 1991–99
Leticia San Miguel Van de Putte (D) San Antonio 1991–
Patricia Gray (D) Galveston 1992–

Yolanda Navarro Flores (D) Houston 1993–95
Susan Combs (R) Austin 1993–96
Sylvia Romo (D) San Antonio 1993–96
Diana Dávila (D) Houston 1993–99
Yvonne Davis (D) Dallas 1993–
Mary Diane Carver Denny (R) Aubrey 1993–
Helen Giddings (D) Dallas 1993–
Vilma Luna (D) Corpus Christi 1993–
Nancy J. Jones Moffat (R) Southlake 1993–99
Jane Gray Nelson (R) Flower Mound 1993–
Elvira Reyna (R) Mesquite 1993–
Florence Muriel Donald Shapiro (R) Plano 1993–
Barbara Rusling (R) China Spring 1995–97
Dawnna Dukes (D) Austin 1995–
Harryette Ehrhardt (D) Dallas 1995–
Jessica Cristina Farrar (D) Houston 1995–
Judy Hawley (D) Portland 1995–
Arlene Wohlgemuth (R) Burleson 1995–
Beverly Woolley (R) Houston 1995–
Norma Chavez (D) El Paso 1997–
Carolyn Galloway (R) Dallas 1997–99
Terri Hodge (D) Dallas 1997–
Suzanna Gratia Hupp (R) Lampasas 1997–
Ruth Jones McClendon (D) San Antonio 1997–
Dora Olivo (D) Stafford 1997–
Sue Palmer (R) Fort Worth 1997–

NOTE

As a result of the 1998 elections, female membership in the 76th Legislature (January 1999–January 2001) changed slightly in the House. Christine Hernández, Diana Dávila, Nancy Moffat, and Carolyn Galloway left. Betty Brown (R, Terrell), Geanie W. Morrison (R, Victoria), and Vicki Truitt (R, Keller) arrived. Female membership in the Senate remained unchanged.

APPENDIX B

STATISTICAL SUMMARIES

TOTAL NUMBER OF WOMEN
38TH–75TH LEGISLATURES 86
(January 1923–January 1999)

PARTY AFFILIATION
DEMOCRAT 62
REPUBLICAN 24

ETHNICITY
ANGLO/WHITE 61
LATINA 13
AFRICAN AMERICAN 12

CHAMBER
SENATE ONLY 9
HOUSE ONLY 75
SENATE AND HOUSE 2

FIRSTS
HOUSE MEMBER Edith Wilmans, 1923
SENATE MEMBER Margie E. Neal, 1927

AFRICAN AMERICANS
HOUSE Senfronia Thompson,
    Eddie Bernice Johnson, 1973
SENATE Barbara Jordan, 1967

LATINAS
HOUSE Irma Rangel, 1977
SENATE Judith Zaffirini, 1987

REPUBLICANS
House: Kay Bailey, 1973
Senate: Betty Andujar, 1973

COUNTIES OF RESIDENCE
BEXAR, DALLAS, HARRIS, TARRANT,
    TRAVIS 49
OTHER 37

ANDERSON Strong
BELL Delisi
BEXAR Negley, Sutton, Krier, Conley,
    Hernández, Van de Putte, Romo,
    McLendon
BRAZORIA Hairgrove
BRAZOS Rountree
COLLIN Shapiro
DALLAS Wilmans, Hughes, Johnson,
    Cofer, A. Hill, P. Hill, Davis,
    Giddings, Ehrhardt, Galloway,
    Hodge, Reyna, Shea

DENTON Denny, Nelson

EL PASO Blair, Isaacks, Polk, McDonald, Rosson, Chavez

ELLIS Duff, Still

FORT BEND Banfield

GALVESTON Moore, Gray

GONZALES Robinson

GRIMES Colson

HARRIS Stewart, Jordan, Thompson, Bailey, Danburg, Schechter, Hamric, Flores, Dávila, Farrar, Woolley, Olivo

HAYS Cooper

JIM WELLS Glossbrenner

KLEBERG Rangel

LAMPASAS Hupp

LIMESTONE Henderson

MCLENNAN Gordon, Denton, Rusling

NUECES Farenthold, Luna, Hawley

PANOLA Neal

TARRANT Miller, Andujar, McKenna, Mowery, Palmer, Moffat, Park, Wohlgemuth

TRAVIS Weddington, Delco, Bode, Guerrero, Linebarger, Greenberg, Combs, Dukes

UVALDE Fenley

VAL VERDE Gurley, McBee

WEBB Zaffirini

WOOD Suiter

CITIES OF RESIDENCE

URBAN

ARLINGTON McKenna

AUSTIN Weddington, Delco, Bode, Guerrero, Greenberg, Combs, Dukes

BRYAN Rountree

CORPUS CHRISTI Farenthold, Luna

DALLAS Wilmans, Hughes, Johnson, Cofer, A. Hill, P. Hill, Davis, Giddings, Ehrhardt, Galloway, Hodge

EL PASO Blair, Isaacks, Polk, McDonald, Rosson, Chavez

FORT WORTH Miller, Andujar, Mowery, Palmer

GALVESTON Gray

HOUSTON Stewart, Jordan, Thompson, Bailey, Danburg, Schechter, Hamric, Flores, Dávila, Farrar, Woolley

LAREDO Zaffirini

SAN ANTONIO Negley, Sutton, Krier, Conley, Hernández, Van de Putte, Romo, McLendon

SAN MARCOS Cooper

TEMPLE Delisi

WACO Gordon, Denton

SUBURBAN

BEDFORD Park

BURLESON Wohlgemuth

CHINA SPRING Rusling

FLOWER MOUND Nelson

MANCHACA Linebarger

IRVING Shea

MESQUITE Reyna

PLANO Shapiro

SOUTHLAKE Moffat

RURAL

ALICE Glossbrenner
AUBREY Denny
CARTHAGE Neal
DEL RIO Gurley, McBee
FERRIS Duff
GONZALES Robinson
GROESBECK Henderson
KINGSVILLE Rangel
LAKE JACKSON Hairgrove
LAMPASAS Hupp
NAVASOTA Colson
PORTLAND Hawley
ROSENBERG Banfield
SLOCUM Strong
STAFFORD Olivo
TEXAS CITY Moore
UVALDE Fenley
WAXAHACHIE Still
WINNSBORO Suiter

PERSONAL INFORMATION*

OCCUPATIONS
ATTORNEY 18
BUSINESS/RANCHING 14
EDUCATOR 10
GOVERNMENT 3
HOMEMAKER/VOLUNTEER 4
NURSE 3
WRITER/PUBLISHER 6

MARITAL STATUS AT ELECTION
MARRIED 29
DIVORCED 6
NEVER MARRIED 12
WIDOWED 9 (6 of the 9 widows
    followed their husbands in office:
    Rountree, Strong, Stewart,
    Henderson, Hairgrove, and
    Sutton)
UNKNOWN 2

CHILDREN OR OTHER DEPENDENTS 38
AVERAGE AGE AT ELECTION 41
AVERAGE NUMBER OF TERMS 3.9

REELECTION
WON SECOND TERM 46
DEFEATED FOR SECOND TERM 5
RAN FOR OTHER OFFICE 1
DID NOT RUN AGAIN 6

*Includes only the fifty-eight women for
whom biographies appear in this volume.

APPENDIX C

NUMBER OF FEMALE MEMBERS OF THE TEXAS LEGISLATURE BY LEGISLATIVE SESSION JANUARY 1923–JANUARY 1999

LEGISLATURE	YEARS	SENATE	HOUSE	TOTAL
38	1923–25	0	1	1
39	1925–27	0	0	0
40	1927–29	1	0	1
41	1929–31	1	2	3
42	1931–33	1	4	5
43	1933–35	1	1	2
44	1935–37	0	2	2
45	1937–39	0	0	0
46	1939–41	0	2	2
47	1941–43	0	2	2
48	1943–45	0	4	4
49	1945–47	0	4	4
50	1947–49	1	3	4
51	1949–51	1	2	3
52	1951–53	1	2	3
53	1953–55	1	4	5
54	1955–57	1	2	3
55	1957–59	1	2	3
56	1959–61	1	2	3
57	1961–63	1	3	4
58	1963–65	1	2	3
59	1965–67	1	1	2
60	1967–69	1	1	2
61	1969–71	1	1	2
62	1971–73	1	1	2
63	1973–75	1	5	6

LEGISLATURE	YEARS	SENATE	HOUSE	TOTAL
64	1975–77	1	8	9
65	1977–79	1	13	14
66	1979–81	1	11	12
67	1981–83	1	11	12
68	1983–85	0	14	14
69	1985–87	1	15	16
70	1987–89	3	15	18
71	1989–91	3	16	19
72	1991–93	4	20	24
73	1993–95	4	27	31
74	1995–97	4	29	33
75	1997–99	3	30	33

NOTE

As a result of the 1998 elections, female membership in the 76th Legislature (January 1999–January 2001) dropped from 30 to 29 in the House. The number of female senators remained unchanged. The total number of women in both houses became 32.

APPENDIX D

FEMALE MEMBERS OF THE
TEXAS LEGISLATURE BY LEGISLATIVE SESSION,
JANUARY 1923–JANUARY 1999

LEGISLATURE	YEARS	GOVERNOR	SENATE	HOUSE	TOTAL
38	1923–25	Neff		Wilmans	1
39	1925–27	Ferguson (MIRIAM)			0
40	1927–29	Moody	Neal		1
41	1929–31	Moody Sterling	Neal	Moore, Negley	3
42	1931–33	Sterling	Neal	Moore, Hughes, Rountree, Strong	5
43	1933–35	Ferguson (MIRIAM)	Neal	Hughes	2
44	1935–37	Allred		Hughes, Moore	2
45	1937–39	Allred			0
46	1939–41	O'Daniel		Colson, Gordon	2
47	1941–43	Stevenson		Colson, Still	2
48	1943–45	Stevenson		Colson, Still, Fenley, Suiter	4
49	1945–47	Stevenson		Colson, Still, Fenley, Suiter	4
50	1947–49	Jester	Stewart	Colson, Still, Suiter	4
51	1949–51	Shivers	Colson	Still, Henderson	3
52	1951–53	Shivers	Colson	Duff, Gurley	3
53	1953–55	Shivers	Colson	Duff, Gurley, Blair, Isaacks	5
54	1955–57	Shivers	Colson	Duff, Isaacks	3
55	1957–59	Daniel	Colson	Duff, Isaacks	3
56	1959–61	Daniel	Colson	Duff, Isaacks	3
57	1961–63	Daniel	Colson	Duff, Isaacks, Banfield	4
58	1963–65	Connally	Colson	Isaacks, Banfield	3
59	1965–67	Connally	Colson	Isaacks	2
60	1967–69	Connally	Jordan	Hairgrove	2
61	1969–71	Smith	Jordan	Farenthold	2
62	1971–73	Smith	Jordan	Farenthold	2

LEGISLATURE	YEARS	GOVERNOR	SENATE	HOUSE	TOTAL
63	1973–75	Briscoe	Andujar	Bailey, Johnson, Miller, Thompson, Weddington	6
64	1975–77	Briscoe	Andujar	Bailey, Johnson, Miller, Thompson, Weddington, Delco, McBee, Sutton	9
65	1977–79	Briscoe	Andujar	Johnson, Miller, Thompson, Delco, Weddington, McBee, Sutton, Bode, Cofer, Denton, Glossbrenner, A. Hill, Rangel	14
66	1979–81	Clements	Andujar	Thompson, Delco, McBee, Sutton, Bode, Cofer, Denton, Glossbrenner, A. Hill, Rangel, Polk	12
67	1981–83	Clements	Andujar	Thompson, Delco, McBee, Sutton, Cofer, Denton, Glossbrenner, A. Hill, Rangel, Polk, Danburg	12
68	1983–85	White		Thompson, Delco, Sutton, Denton, Glossbrenner, A. Hill, Rangel, Polk, Danburg, P. Hill, McDonald, McKenna, Robinson, Shea	14
69	1985–87	White	Krier	Thompson, Delco, Sutton, Denton, Glossbrenner, A. Hill, Rangel, Danburg, P. Hill, McDonald, McKenna, Robinson, Shea, Cooper, Guerrero	16
70	1987–89	Clements	Krier, Johnson, Zaffirini	Thompson, Delco, Sutton, Denton, Glossbrenner, A. Hill, Rangel, Danburg, P. Hill, McDonald, Robinson, Shea, Cooper, Guerrero, Mowery	18
71	1989–91	Clements	Krier, Johnson, Zaffirini	Thompson, Delco, Denton, Glossbrenner, A. Hill, Rangel, Danburg, P. Hill, McDonald, Robinson, Shea, Guerrero, Mowery, Conley, Linebarger, Park	19
72	1991–93	Richards	Krier, Johnson, Zaffirini, Rosson	Thompson, Delco, Denton, A. Hill, Glossbrenner, Rangel, Danburg, McDonald, Shea, Mowery, Conley, Linebarger, Park, Delisi, Greenberg, Hamric, Hernández, Schechter, Van de Putte, Gray	24

LEGISLATURE	YEARS	GOVERNOR	SENATE	HOUSE	TOTAL
73	1993–95	Richards	Zaffirini, Rosson, Shapiro, Nelson	Thompson, Delco, Denton, Rangel, Danburg, McDonald, Mowery, Conley, Linebarger, Park, Delisi, Greenberg, Hamric, Hernández, Schechter, Van de Putte, Gray, Combs, Dávila, Davis, Denny, Flores, Giddings, Luna, Moffat, Reyna, Romo	31
74	1995–97	Bush	Zaffirini, Rosson, Shapiro, Nelson	Thompson, Rangel, Danburg, McDonald, Mowery, Conley, Park, Delisi, Greenberg, Hamric, Hernández, Van de Putte, Gray, Combs, Dávila, Davis, Denny, Giddings, Luna, Moffat, Reyna, Romo, Dukes, Ehrhardt, Farrar, Hawley, Rusling, Wohlgemuth, Woolley	33
75	1997–99	Bush	Zaffirini, Shapiro, Nelson	Thompson, Rangel, Danburg, Mowery, Delisi, Greenberg, Hamric, Hernández, Van de Putte, Gray, Dávila, Davis, Denny, Giddings, Luna, Moffat, Reyna, Dukes, Ehrhardt, Farrar, Hawley, Wohlgemuth, Woolley, Chavez, Galloway, Hodge, Hupp, McClendon, Olivo, Palmer	33

NOTE

As a result of the 1998 elections, female membership in the 76th Legislature (January 1999–January 2001) decreased from 33 to 32. George W. Bush was reelected governor. The female senators returned. In the House, Christine Hernández, Diana Dávila, Nancy Moffat, and Carolyn Galloway left, and three women arrived: Betty Brown (Republican, District 4), who replaced Democrat Keith Oakley; Geanie W. Morrison (Republican, District 30), who replaced Republican Steve Holzheauser; and Vicki Truitt (Republican, District 98), who replaced Republican Nancy Moffat. The number of Republican, black, and Latina women legislators increased. The 76th Legislature included 18 white women, 6 black women, and 8 Latinas. Of the 32, there were 18 Democrats and 14 Republicans. Thirteen of the 14 Republicans were Anglo/white, 1 was Latina. Five of the 18 Democrats were Anglo/white, 7 were Latina, and 6 were African American. See "Members-Elect: House of Representatives, 76th Legislature," November 12, 1998, Chief Clerk's Office, Legislative Reference Library, Texas State Capitol, Austin.

COMPOSITION OF THE 76TH LEGISLATURE
(JANUARY 1999–JANUARY 2001)

NAME	YEAR ELECTED	PARTY		ETHNICITY		
		DEMOCRAT	REPUBLICAN	WHITE	BLACK	LATINA
Senfronia Thompson	1972	X			X	
Irma Rangel	1976	X				X
Debra Danburg	1980	X		X		
Judith Zaffirini	1986	X				X
Anna Mowery	1988		X	X		
Dianne Delisi	1990		X	X		
Sherri Greenberg	1990	X		X		
Peggy Hamric	1990		X	X		
Letitia Van de Putte	1990	X				X
Patricia Gray	1992	X		X		
Yvonne Davis	1992	X			X	
Mary Denny	1992		X	X		
Helen Giddings	1992	X			X	
Vilma Luna	1992	X				X
Jane Nelson	1992		X	X		
Elvira Reyna	1992		X			X
Florence Shapiro	1992		X	X		
Dawnna Dukes	1994	X			X	
Harryette Ehrhardt	1994	X		X		
Jessica Farrar	1994	X				X
Judy Hawley	1994	X		X		
Arlene Wohlgemuth	1994		X	X		
Beverly Woolley	1994		X	X		

NAME	YEAR ELECTED	PARTY		ETHNICITY		
		DEMOCRAT	REPUBLICAN	WHITE	BLACK	LATINA
Norma Chavez	1996	X				X
Dora Olivo	1996	X				X
Terri Hodge	1996	X			X	
Suzanna Hupp	1996		X	X		
Ruth McClendon	1996	X			X	
Sue Palmer	1996		X	X		
Betty Brown	1998		X	X		
Vicki Truitt	1998		X	X		
Geanie W. Morrison	1998		X	X		
TOTALS		18	14	18	6	8

NOTE

Boldface type denotes senators.

TIME LINE

1868 At the request of a small group of women, a woman suffrage resolution is introduced at the Texas Constitutional Convention but is rejected. The 14th Amendment to the U.S. Constitution is ratified, extending citizenship to blacks.

1870 The 15th Amendment to the U.S. Constitution gives black males the vote but excludes women.

1872 The American Woman Suffrage Association petitions the Texas Legislature, asking for the enfranchisement of women.

1875 Millie Anderson wins suit in federal district court against the Houston and Texas Central Railroad for denying her admission to the first-class "ladies car" reserved for white women.

1877 Black Galveston laundresses strike for higher wages.

1882 Two Texas chapters of the Woman's Christian Temperance Union (WCTU), one for blacks and one for whites, are organized in Paris, Texas.

1888 The Texas WCTU is the first organization in Texas to endorse woman suffrage.

1893 The Texas Equal Rights Association (TERA) is founded in Dallas.

1897 The Texas Federation of Women's Clubs (TFWC) is organized.

1905 The Texas Association of Colored Women's Clubs (TACWC) is organized.

1908 Mrs. P. P. Tucker and Mrs. E. P. Turner are elected to the Dallas school board, long before women win the vote.

1909 The National Association for the Advancement of Colored People (NAACP) is organized.

1911 Jovita Idar is elected president of La Liga Femenil Mexicanista (the League of Mexican Women) in Laredo.

1913 Texas women join other women from all over the United States to march in Washington, D.C., for suffrage on the eve of Woodrow Wilson's inauguration.

1917 TACWC endorses woman suffrage. Galveston women organize the Negro Women Voters' League.

1918 Women are one-third of the founding members of the Dallas NAACP. The Texas Equal Suffrage Association (TESA) leads a successful campaign to gain women's right to vote in primary elections; 386,000 women register in seventeen days. Women help elect Annie Webb Blanton state superintendent of public instruction. Christia Adair and other black women work with white women in Kingsville on petitions demanding the vote in the Democratic primary election. Mrs. E. P. Sampson, on behalf of the El Paso Colored Woman's Club, applies for membership to TESA. The matter is referred to the National American Woman Suffrage Association, which refers it back to state (the action taken is not known). Texas women win the right to vote in primary elections.

1919 The Texas League of Women Voters is founded. TESA is dissolved. Texas voters reject a woman suffrage amendment to the state's constitution by 25,000 votes.

1920 Texas leads the nation in lynchings (eleven). The Ku Klux Klan is very active in Texas during this period. The 19th Amendment gives women the vote. Three Houston women run for office on the Republican Party's "Black and Tan" ticket. Mrs. R. L. Yocome, candidate for state representative, may be the first Texas woman to run for a legislative position. She loses.

1921 The National Maternal and Infant Health Program passes the legislature. The National Woman's Party introduces the idea of a federal Equal Rights Amendment (ERA).

1922 Edith Wilmans, a Dallas attorney, becomes the first woman elected to the Texas Legislature (House of Representatives).

1923 Jane Y. McCallum organizes the Joint Legislative Council, known as the Petticoat Lobby, to drive through progressive legislation. The legislature passes a White Primary law. Throughout the 1920s, the Women's Division of the Texas Council of the Commission on Interracial Cooperation is active around the state, with Georgetown suffragist Jessie Daniel Ames serving as council director.

1924 Miriam A. "Ma" Ferguson is elected Texas governor on an anti-Klan ticket. She appoints Emma Meharg as Texas' first female secretary of state. The Texas Supreme Court rules that a married woman's identity is submerged in her husband's.

1925 A special three-person All-Woman Supreme Court is appointed by Governor Pat M. Neff because all three presiding male justices are members of the fraternal organization involved in the case to be heard, and a conflict of interest is feared. No women serve in the 39th Legislature.

1926 Margie Neal, a Carthage newspaper publisher, is the first woman elected to the Texas Senate.

1927 Responding to pressure by TACWC and a few white allies, the Texas Legislature authorizes a state training school for delinquent black girls. Jane Y. McCallum is appointed Texas secretary of state by Governor Dan Moody for having supported his candidacy. The League of Women Voters and other women's groups win a statute giving wives authority to dispose of community property.

1928 Oveta Culp, House parliamentarian, codifies the state's banking laws.

1929 State representative Laura Negley sponsors a successful married persons' property rights bill that defines rent and revenues from separate properties of a married couple as community property.

1930 Jessie Daniel Ames founds the Association of Southern [White] Women for the Prevention of Lynching in Atlanta, Georgia.

1932 Women lobbyists gain passage of the Texas Division of Child Welfare Act. Miriam Ferguson wins a second term as governor.

1935 State representatives Helen Moore and Sarah T. Hughes propose a bill to legalize jury service for women, but it fails. Hughes is voted most valuable member of legislature during this second term. She resigns when Governor James Allred appoints her the state's first female district court judge. All seven gubernatorial candidates (including Miriam Ferguson) pledge to end lynching; she loses a bid for another term. Citing low legislative pay, state senator Margie Neal moves to Washington, D.C., to work for the National Recovery Administration. Charlotte Graham and other strike leaders of Dallas garment workers are jailed.

1936 Minnie Flanagan and other black Dallas women lead a voter registration campaign for the Progressive Voters League. The National Federation of Business and Professional Women (B&PW) supports the ERA campaign.

1938 Emma Tenayuca leads a strike of 12,000 San Antonio pecan shellers, mostly Mexican American women. No women serve in the 45th Legislature. Lulu B. White becomes acting president of the Houston NAACP. Later she is the NAACP's first full-time female salaried executive and builds her branch to become largest in South. In the 1930s and 1940s, White and her coworker, Juanita Craft of Dallas, organize dozens of local branches.

1941 With the nation's declaration of war, women enter the armed forces, defense factories, and other jobs formerly done by men while men are away.

Colonel Oveta Culp Hobby of Houston is commander of Women's Army Corps.

1942 Women's Airforce Service Pilots (WASPS) begin training at Avenger Field in Sweetwater. Thelma Paige Richardson, a teacher, files suit against the Dallas school district seeking equal pay for black teachers. The action is settled out of court the following year with a judgment that grants pay raises to black teachers and leads to similar actions in Galveston and Houston. The B&PW supports ERA.

1944 In *Smith vs. Allright*, the U.S. Supreme Court outlaws Texas "White Primaries." By 1947, black voter registration in the state triples. Minnie Fisher Cunningham runs for governor against incumbent Coke Stevenson in a Democratic Party fight between liberals and conservatives over support for President Franklin D. Roosevelt. She comes in second among nine.

1945 Chapters of the National Council of Negro Women are organized in Texas. Minnie Fisher Cunningham and Jane Y. McCallum form the Women's Committee for Educational Freedom to demand reinstatement for University of Texas president Homer P. Rainey, who had been fired by the conservative board of regents.

1946 Sarah T. Hughes loses the race for U.S. Congress. The U.S. Senate debates the ERA seriously for the first time, but fails to generate the majority required to send the amendment to states for ratification.

1947 Lulu B. White is accused of being a communist by the House Un-American Activities Committee. Erma LeRoy of Houston, a black woman, runs unsuccessfully as an independent for the state legislature. *The Lost Sex*, invoking Freudian psychology, declares that feminists are neurotics responsible for the country's problems.

1949 Former state representative Neveille Colson becomes a state senator and thus the first woman to have served in both chambers of the Texas Legislature.

1950 The U.S. Supreme Court rules in *Sweatt vs. Painter* that segregation in higher education is unconstitutional. Christia Adair leads the Houston NAACP in integrating department store fitting rooms, the airport, and the library. Throughout the 1950s, popular magazines like *Collier's* and *Ladies' Home Journal* call activism dangerous and urge women to devote themselves to home and family.

1951 The National Women's Party shrinks drastically in numbers, falling to only 200.

1952 Both Republicans and Democrats nominate women for vice president.

President Dwight D. Eisenhower adds women to his administration, including Texan Oveta Culp Hobby as the first secretary of the Department of Health, Education, and Welfare.

1954 The U.S. Supreme Court rules that "separate but equal" public schools are unconstitutional in *Brown vs. Board of Education*. The U.S. Senate censures Senator Joseph McCarthy. Texas women gain the right to serve on juries, largely through efforts of the League of Women Voters. Hermine Tobolowsky, Dallas attorney and legal counsel to B&PW, and later Texas B&PW president, leads an eighteen-year fight to pass the state Equal Legal Rights Amendment (ELRA).

1956 The attorney general of Texas tries to outlaw the Texas NAACP on charges of barratry, putting Christia Adair, Houston NAACP executive secretary, on the stand for seventeen days.

1957 Texas B&PW supports the ERA.

1958 Hattie Mae (Mrs. Charles E.) White is first black woman in Texas ever to hold office when she is elected to the Houston school board.

1959 Blanche Mae Preston McSmith of Marshall is appointed to the Alaska legislature to fill an unexpired term. The ELRA is introduced in the Texas Legislature for the first time but fails.

1960 Sit-ins in support of the civil rights movement spread to several Texas cities.

1961 State representative Maud Isaacks co-sponsors a constitutional amendment supporting equal rights for women in Texas, but it fails. Her efforts receive national attention. President John F. Kennedy creates the President's Commission on the Status of Women; it supports equal legal rights for women without taking a position on the ERA. District judge Sarah T. Hughes is appointed to the federal bench, the first Texas woman to serve.

1963 The Federal Equal Pay Act requires that women and men be paid equally for performing the same job. Publication of Betty Friedan's *The Feminine Mystique* serves as a lightning rod for a widespread mood of personal dissatisfaction among white, middle-class women.

1964 The 24th Amendment to the U.S. Constitution outlaws the poll tax as a requirement for voting. The U.S. Civil Rights Act outlaws racial discrimination in public accommodations and employment.

1965 U.S. Voting Rights Act passes, extending suffrage to more blacks and Hispanics.

1966 Barbara Jordan of Houston is elected to the Texas Senate, the first black to serve in legislature since 1899. Betty Friedan organizes the National

Organization for Women (NOW). The U.S. Supreme Court upholds the poll tax ban.

1967 Dallas attorney Louise Raggio spearheads the reform of limited property rights of Texas women, leading to passage of the Married Women's Property Rights Act. For first time, women can buy and sell their own real property and securities. Governor John Connally establishes Texas' first Commission on the Status of Women.

1968 Wilhelmina Delco is first black to win election to the Austin school board.

1969 Anita Martinez of Dallas is the first Mexican American woman elected to a city council in Texas. President Richard M. Nixon's Presidential Task Force on Women's Rights and Responsibilities urges Nixon to persuade the U.S. Congress to pass the ERA.

1970 The first hearings on the ERA since 1956 are held after NOW's disruption of U.S. Senate proceedings. The Women's Bureau celebrates its fiftieth anniversary; the Labor Department reverses its opposition to the ERA. La Raza Unida, a new political party, is founded. Virginia Musquiz is first Mexican American woman to run for the state legislature under the banner of La Raza Unida, of which she is a founder.

1971 The National Women's Political Caucus and the Texas Women's Political Caucus are founded. State senator Barbara Jordan and state representative Sissy Farenthold co-sponsor the ELRA. Sissy Farenthold is leader of a bipartisan group called "Dirty Thirty," which tries to investigate the Sharpstown stock fraud scandal and reform the legislature.

1972 Barbara Jordan is elected to the U.S. House of Representatives, the first black ever to represent Texas there. A protracted strike of Hispanic garment workers in El Paso leads to the winning of union representation and a national boycott. Six women are elected to the Texas Legislature (one to the Senate and five to the House), the most ever; they include two Republicans, Betty Andujar and Kay Bailey (Hutchison), two black women, Senfronia Thompson and Eddie Bernice Johnson, and two Anglo women, Sarah Weddington and Chris Miller. Title IX of the Federal Educational Amendment prohibits sex discrimination in institutions receiving federal funds. Frances "Sissy" Farenthold runs unsuccessfully for governor; she is nominated as the Democratic Party candidate for vice president. Alma Canales runs for lieutenant governor on the La Raza Unida ticket. The percentage of female delegates to the Democratic and Republican National Conventions increases dramatically, to 40 and 30 percent respectively. Phyllis Schlafly forms a national group, Stop ERA. Texas voters approve an equal legal rights amendment to the state constitution by 4-1 majority.

1973 In *Roe vs. Wade*, argued by Austin attorney Sarah Weddington, the U.S. Supreme Court establishes a woman's constitutional right to an abortion. Lucy Patterson is first black woman elected to the Dallas city council. The Texas chapter of NOW is founded, and chapters spread across the state. Democratic and Republican women in the Texas House spearhead passage of the Equal Credit Opportunity Act, prohibiting discrimination based on gender, race, national origin, and age. Women get credit in their own names for the first time. Congress passes the Women's Educational Equity Act to provide nonsexist teaching materials. The ERA passes both houses of Congress, with wide margins of support.

1974 Kathlyn Gilliam, a black woman, is elected to the Dallas school board. Wilhelmina Delco is first black woman elected to the Texas House from Austin. The federal minimum wage law extends benefits to 1.5 million domestic workers. Sissy Farenthold is defeated in a second race for governor. Maria Jimenez and Orelia Hisbrook Cole run for state representative on the La Raza Unida ticket, the first Hispanics to run for this office.

1975 Lila Cockrell of San Antonio becomes the first woman elected mayor of a large city in Texas. The state's antifeminists try to get a state resolution to rescind the ERA introduced in the legislature, but a coalition of pro-ERA groups defeats it. The United Nations declares 1975 the International Year of the Woman.

1976 Anne Armstrong is appointed U.S. ambassador to Great Britain, the first Texas woman to hold an ambassadorship. Irma Rangel of Kingsville becomes the first Latina elected to the Texas Legislature (House of Representatives). Liz Carpenter becomes chair of the newly formed ERA America. Austinite Azie Taylor Morton is appointed U.S. treasurer. Adlene Harrison becomes interim Dallas mayor. Ann Richards is elected Travis County commissioner.

1977 The International Women's Year National Conference in Houston hosts 2,000 delegates. Carole Keeton McClellan is elected Austin's first woman mayor. President Jimmy Carter appoints state representative Eddie Bernice Johnson as regional director of the Department of Health, Education, and Welfare. The number of women in the Texas Legislature reaches double digits (14) for first time.

1978 State representative Sarah Weddington becomes adviser to President Carter on women's issues.

1979 Gabrielle McDonald, a black woman, is appointed federal district judge in Houston. Time runs out for ratification of the ERA.

1980s Texas women legislators organize an informal caucus, the Ladies' Marching, Chowder, Terrorist, and Quasi-Judicial Society.

1980 Kathlyn Gilliam is the first woman and the first black to be elected president of the Dallas school board.

1981 Sandra Day O'Connor, El Paso native, becomes the first female U.S. Supreme Court justice.

1982 Ann Richards is the first woman elected Texas state treasurer.

1983 The National Political Congress of Black Women is founded. Elma Salinas of Laredo is the first Latina in the nation to be appointed to a district court bench; she is elected to a full term in 1984.

1984 Geraldine Ferraro is the vice presidential candidate on the Democratic Party ticket. Leslie Benitez is the first Latina to be appointed by a governor as chief legal counsel.

1986 Judith Zaffirini of Laredo becomes the first Latina elected to the Texas Senate.

1987 Annette Strauss is elected Dallas' first female mayor. With the election of Eddie Bernice Johnson and Judith Zaffirini, the Texas Senate, for first time, has more than one woman serving.

1990 Ann Richards is elected governor of Texas. Kay Bailey Hutchison is elected state treasurer, becoming the first Republican woman elected to statewide office in Texas.

1991 Wilhelmina Delco is appointed speaker pro tempore of the Texas House, the first woman to hold this position. Nelda Wells Spears is the first black woman in Texas elected a county tax assessor-collector (Travis County). She wins a full term in 1992.

1992 State senator Eddie Bernice Johnson is elected to the U.S. House of Representatives. More women than ever before are elected to the U.S. Congress—six senators and forty-seven representatives. Rose Spector of San Antonio is elected to the Texas Supreme Court.

1993 Kay Bailey Hutchison wins special election to the U.S. Senate, the first female senator from Texas. She wins a six-year term in 1994.

1994 Governor Ann Richards loses a bid for second term to George W. Bush. Houstonian Sheila Jackson Lee (D) is elected to the U.S. House of Representatives. Priscilla Owen is elected to the Texas Supreme Court. Alma

Lopez is elected to the Fourth Texas District Court of Appeals, Bexar County. Nelda Rodriguez is elected to the Thirteenth Court of Appeals, Nueces County.

1996 Kay Granger (R) of Fort Worth is elected to the U.S. House of Representatives.

1997 The Texas Legislature has thirty-three women serving in both chambers, more than ever before but not yet 20 percent of the total. By the end of the 75th Legislature's first year (1997), eighty-six women had served since 1923. Deborah Hankinson is appointed to the Texas Supreme Court by Governor George W. Bush to fill an unexpired term. State district judge Hilda Tagle is nominated by President Clinton to a federal Southern District judgeship, the first Latina selected to the federal bench in Texas; she is confirmed in 1998. Former state representative Sylvia Romo is elected Bexar County tax assessor-collector, the county's first woman to hold this position.

1998 Former state representative Susan Combs is elected Texas' first female agriculture commissioner. Races for seats in the Texas Legislature result in a net loss of one female member.

1999 The 76th Texas Legislature opens with thirty-two female members, three in the Senate and twenty-nine in the House.

BIBLIOGRAPHY

ARCHIVAL AND PRIMARY SOURCES

Amsler, Margaret Gordon. "Oral Memoirs of Margaret [Gordon] Amsler." Transcript, 1972. Baylor University Project, Baylor University Program for Oral History, Waco.

Andujar, Betty. Papers. Library, University of Texas at Arlington.

Bernal, Joe. Videotape interview by Ruthe Winegarten, July 12, 1995. Archives for Research on Women and Gender, University of Texas at San Antonio.

Blair, Anita. Vertical File. El Paso Public Library.

Bode, Mary Jane. Papers. Travis County Historical Society, Austin.

———. Vertical File. Barker Texas History Center, Center for American History, University of Texas at Austin.

Colson, Neveille. Campaign Biography. The Woman's Collection, Library, Texas Woman's University, Denton.

Conley, Karyne Jones. Videotape interview by Molly Dinkins, May 28, 1995. Archives for Research on Women and Gender, University of Texas at San Antonio.

Danburg, Debra. File. Houston Metropolitan Research Center, Houston Public Library.

———. Videotape interview by Ruthe Winegarten, May 26, 1995. Archives for Research on Women and Gender, University of Texas at San Antonio.

Dávila, Diana. Videotape interview by Nancy Baker Jones, May 26, 1995. Archives for Research on Women and Gender, University of Texas at San Antonio.

Delco, Wilhelmina. Collection. Library, Prairie View A&M University.

———. Videotape interview by Ruthe Winegarten, July 20, 1995. Archives for Research on Women and Gender, University of Texas at San Antonio.

Delisi, Dianne White. Videotape interview by Nancy Baker Jones, May 26, 1995. Archives for Research on Women and Gender, University of Texas at San Antonio.

Denton, Betty. Biographical File. The Texas Collection, Baylor University, Waco.

Dorau, Angela. "Oral History of Margaret Harris Amsler," 1996. Chronology Project, Women in the Law Section, State Bar of Texas, Austin.

Dippel, Myra Banfield. Videotape interview by Ruthe Winegarten, May 25, 1995. Archives for Research on Women and Gender, University of Texas at San Antonio.

Duff, Virginia. Vertical File. Barker Texas History Center, Center for American History, University of Texas at Austin.

———. Videotape interview by Ruthe Winegarten, May 25, 1995. Archives for Research on Women and Gender, University of Texas at San Antonio.

Farenthold, Frances T. Papers. Barker Texas History Center, Center for American History, University of Texas at Austin.

———. Vertical File. Barker Texas History Center, Center for American History, University of Texas at Austin.

———. Videotape interview by Ruthe Winegarten, June 12, 1995. Archives for Research on Women and Gender, University of Texas at San Antonio.

———. "The Woman in Politics." *Saturday Evening Post*, March 1974.

Farrar, Jessica Cristina. Videotape interview by Nancy Baker Jones, May 26, 1995. Archives for Research on Women and Gender, University of Texas at San Antonio.

Fenley, Florence. Vertical File. Barker Texas History Center, Center for American History, University of Texas at Austin.

Glossbrenner, Ernestine. Collection. Archives for Research on Women and Gender, University of Texas at San Antonio.

———. Videotape interview by Ruthe Winegarten, July 20, 1995. Archives for Research on Women and Gender, University of Texas at San Antonio.

Guerrero, Lena. Vertical File. Barker Texas History Center, Center for American History, University of Texas at Austin.

———. Videotape interview by Nancy Baker Jones, August 11, 1995. Archives for Research on Women and Gender, University of Texas at San Antonio.

Gurley, Dorothy Gillis. Papers. Library, Texas A&M University, College Station.

Hawley, Judy. Videotape interview by Nancy Baker Jones, May 26, 1995. Archives for Research on Women and Gender, University of Texas at San Antonio.

Hernández, Christine. Videotape interview by Nancy Baker Jones, May 26, 1995. Archives for Research on Women and Gender, University of Texas at San Antonio.

Hill, Anita. Vertical File. The Woman's Collection Library, Texas Woman's University, Denton.

Hughes, Sarah T. Collection. Library, University of North Texas, Denton.

———. Correspondence. Lyndon Baines Johnson Library, Austin.

———. Correspondence. White House Correspondence Files, John F. Kennedy Library and Museum, Boston, Massachusetts.

———. Oral History Interviews. Archives, University of North Texas, Denton.

Hughes, Sarah T., and Joe B. Frantz. "Oral History" [1968]. Lyndon Baines Johnson Library, Austin.

Hutchison, Kay Bailey. Videotape interview by Nancy Baker Jones, August 18, 1995. Archives for Research on Women and Gender, University of Texas at San Antonio.

Isaacks, Maud. Papers. Library, University of Texas at El Paso.

———. Vertical File. Barker Texas History Center, Center for American History, University of Texas at Austin.

———. Vertical File. Library, Texas Woman's University, Denton.

Johnson, Eddie Bernice. Oral Interview. Oral History Collection, Library, University of North Texas, Denton.

———. Videotape interview by Mike Greene, October 19, 1995. Archives for Research on Women and Gender, University of Texas at San Antonio.

Jordan, Barbara. Collection. Texas Southern University, Houston.

———. "How I Got There: Staying Power." The Atlantic, March 1975, pp. 38–39.

———. Oral History Interview, July 7, 1970. Library, Oral History Collection, University of North Texas, Denton.

———. Videotape interview by Nancy Baker Jones, September 12, 1995. Archives for Research on Women and Gender, University of Texas at San Antonio.

Laney, Pete. Videotape interview by Nancy Baker Jones, May 29, 1995. Archives for Research on Women and Gender, University of Texas at San Antonio.

McBee, Susan Gurley. Papers. Library, Texas A&M University, College Station.

McCallum, Jane Y. Papers. Austin History Center, Austin Public Library.

McDonald, Nancy. Collection. El Paso Public Library.

———. Videotape interview by Ruthe Winegarten, May 29, 1995. Archives for Research on Women and Gender, University of Texas at San Antonio.

Miller, Chris. Vertical File. Barker Texas History Center, Center for American History, University of Texas at Austin.

Moore, Helen. Collection. Moore Memorial Public Library, Texas City.

Mowery, Anna. Videotape interview by Nancy Baker Jones, May 29, 1995. Archives for Research on Women and Gender, University of Texas at San Antonio.

Neal, Margie E. "Brief of the Women's Section, NRA." Eleanor Roosevelt Papers. Franklin D. Roosevelt Library and Museum, Hyde Park, New York.

———. Correspondence with Eleanor Roosevelt. Eleanor Roosevelt Papers. Franklin D. Roosevelt Library and Museum, Hyde Park, New York.

———. File. President's Secretary's File. Franklin D. Roosevelt Library and Museum, Hyde Park, New York.

———. File. Records of the Democratic National Committee Women's Division, 1933–1936. Franklin D. Roosevelt Library and Museum, Hyde Park, New York.

———. Papers. Barker Texas History Center, Center for American History, University of Texas at Austin.

Negley, Laura Burleson. Papers. Negley Family, San Antonio.

Polk, Mary. File. The Woman's Collection Library, Texas Woman's University, Denton.

Rangel, Irma. Vertical File. Barker Texas History Center, Center for American History, University of Texas at Austin.

———. Videotape interview by Nancy Baker Jones, May 25, 1995. Archives for Research on Women and Gender, University of Texas at San Antonio.

Richards, Ann. Videotape interview by Ruthe Winegarten, July 10, 1995. Archives for Research on Women and Gender, University of Texas at San Antonio.

Romo, Sylvia. Videotape interview by Ruthe Winegarten, July 12, 1995. Archives for Research on Women and Gender, University of Texas at San Antonio.

Shapiro, Florence. Videotape interview by Ruthe Winegarten, May 29, 1995. Archives for Research on Women and Gender, University of Texas at San Antonio.

Still, Rae Files. Vertical File. Barker Texas History Center, Center for American History, University of Texas at Austin.

Sutton, Lou Nelle. Collection. African American Museum, Dallas.

———. Family Collection. Institute of Texan Cultures, University of Texas at San Antonio.

"Texas Women: A Celebration of History" Archives. Library, Texas Woman's University, Denton.

Thompson, Senfronia. Videotape interview by Nancy Baker Jones, May 26, 1995. Archives for Research on Women and Gender, University of Texas at San Antonio.

Weddington, Sarah. Oral History Interview, July 8, 1973, and July 11, 1977. Oral History Collection. Library, University of North Texas, Denton.

————. Oral Interview, March 30, 1973. Institute for Oral History, Baylor University, Waco.

————. Papers. Library, Texas Woman's University, Denton.

————. Vertical File. Barker Texas History Center, Center for American History, University of Texas at Austin.

————. Videotape interview by Nancy Baker Jones, June 18, 1995. Archives for Research on Women and Gender, University of Texas at San Antonio.

Willis, Doyle. Videotape interview by Nancy Baker Jones, May 29, 1995. Archives for Research on Women and Gender, University of Texas at San Antonio.

Wilmans, Edith Eunice. Collection. Archives Division, Texas State Library, Austin.

————. Vertical File. Barker Texas History Center, Center for American History, University of Texas at Austin.

Zaffirini, Judith. Videotape interview by Molly Dinkins, October, 1995. Archives for Research on Women and Gender, University of Texas at San Antonio.

SECONDARY SOURCES

Allred, Opah H. "Sarah T. Hughes: A Case Study in Judicial Decision-Making." Ph.D. diss., University of Oklahoma, 1987.

Anderson, Kristi. *After Suffrage: Women in Partisan and Electoral Politics before the New Deal.* Chicago: University of Chicago Press, 1996.

Baker, Paula. "The Domestication of Politics: Women and American Political Society, 1780–1920." *American Historical Review* 89 (1984): 620–647.

Barnes, Lorene T. "A Comparison/Contrast of Two Black Women in Politics: Shirley Chisholm and Barbara Jordan." M.A. thesis, Governors State University, 1979.

Biographical Files. Legislative Reference Library, State Capitol, Austin.

Boles, Janet K. "Advancing the Women's Agenda within Local Legislatures: The Role of Female Elected Officials." In *Gender and Policymaking: Studies of Women in Office.* Ed. Debra L. Dodson. New Brunswick, N.J.: Center for the American Woman and Politics, Eagleton Institute of Politics, Rutgers University, 1991.

———. "The Texas Woman in Politics: Role Model or Mirage?" *Social Science Journal* 21, no. 1 (January 1984): 78–89.

Brandenstein, Sherilyn. "*Sepia Record* as a Forum for Negotiating Women's Roles." In *Women and Texas History: Selected Essays.* Ed. Fane Downs and Nancy Baker Jones. Austin: Texas State Historical Association, 1993.

Brogan, Mary Rice, and Pat Hyatt. "Our Lady Legislators: Two Women, 179 Men," *Texas Magazine (Houston Chronicle),* March 21, 1965, pp. 14–15.

Brooks, Alberta. "No More House Work," *Our Texas,* Winter 1995.

Brown, Carol. "Women in Texas Politics." In *Public Policy in Texas.* Ed. Wendell M. Bedichek and Neal Tannahil. Glenview, Ill.: Scott Foresman, 1986.

Brown, Dorothy. *Setting a Course: American Women in the 1920s.* Boston: Twayne, 1987.

Brown, Norman D. *Hood, Bonnet, and Little Brown Jug: Texas Politics, 1921–1928.* College Station: Texas A&M University Press, 1983.

Broyles, William. "The Making of Barbara Jordan." *Texas Monthly,* October 1976, pp. 129–133, 197–202.

Carroll, Susan J. *Women as Candidates in American Politics.* 2nd ed. Bloomington: Indiana University Press, 1994.

Castleberry, Vivian Anderson. *Daughters of Dallas: A History of Greater Dallas through the Voices and Deeds of Its Women.* Dallas: Odenwald Press, 1994.

Clark, Lee. "The Most Powerful Women in Dallas and Ft. Worth," *D Magazine,* March 1977, pp. 65–71.

Coleman, Suzanne. "The Politics of Participation: The Emergent Journey of Frances Farenthold." M.A. thesis. University of Texas at Arlington, 1973.

Cook, Elizabeth Adell, Sue Thomas, and Clyde Wilcox, eds. *The Year of the Woman: Myths and Realities.* Boulder: Westview Press, 1994.

Cott, Nancy F. *The Grounding of Modern Feminism.* New Haven: Yale University Press, 1987.

Cottrell, Debbie Mauldin. *Pioneer Woman Educator: The Progressive Spirit of Annie Webb Blanton.* College Station: Texas A&M University Press, 1993.

Cottrell, Debbie Mauldin, and Nancy Baker Jones. *Women and Texas History: An Archival Bibliography.* Austin: Texas State Historical Association, 1990.

Cox, Elizabeth M. *Women State and Territorial Legislators, 1895–1995.* Jefferson, N.C.: McFarland and Co., 1996.

Crawford, Ann F., and Crystal Ragsdale. *Women in Texas: Their Lives, Their Experiences, Their Accomplishments*. Austin: State House Press, 1992.

Cunningham, Patricia Ellen. "Bonnet in the Ring: Minnie Fisher Cunningham and Her Race for Governor of Texas, 1944." M.A. thesis, University of Texas at Austin, 1985.

Darcy, R., Charles D. Hadley, and Jason F. Kirksey. "Election Systems and the Representation of Black Women in American State Legislatures." *Women and Politics* 13, no. 2 (1993): 73–89.

Darcy, R., Susan Welch, and Janet Clark. *Women, Elections, and Representation*. 2nd ed. Lincoln: University of Nebraska Press, 1994.

Davenport, Zeak. "Petticoat Lobbyist." *Texas Historian*, November 1991, 11–14.

Davidson, Chandler. *Race and Class in Texas Politics*. Princeton: Princeton University Press, 1990.

De Hart, Jane Sherron. "Rights and Representation: Women, Politics, and Power in the Contemporary United States." In *U.S. History as Women's History: New Feminist Issues*. Ed. Linda K. Kerber, Alice Kessler-Harris, and Kathryn Kish Sklar. Chapel Hill: University of North Carolina Press, 1995.

Dodson, Debra L. *Gender and Policymaking: Studies of Women in Office*. New Brunswick, N.J.: Center for the American Woman and Politics, Eagleton Institute of Politics, Rutgers University, 1991.

Dodson, Debra L., and Susan J. Carroll. *Reshaping the Agenda: Women in State Legislatures*. New Brunswick, N.J.: Center for the American Woman and Politics, Eagleton Institute of Politics, Rutgers University, 1991.

Downs, Fane, and Nancy Baker Jones, eds. *Women and Texas History: Selected Essays*. Austin: Texas State Historical Association, 1993.

Draper, Robert. "The Blood of the Farentholds." *Texas Monthly*, February 1992, pp. 138–141, 164–170.

Dudley, Mary. "Our Woman in Austin: Polishing the Female Stars of Texas." *Texas Woman Magazine*, November 1979, pp. 18–19.

Enstam, Elizabeth York. *Women and the Creation of Urban Life: Dallas, Texas, 1843–1920*. College Station: Texas A&M University Press, 1998.

Evans, Eola Adeline. "Activity of Black Women in the Woman Suffrage Movement, 1900–1920," M.A. thesis, Lamar University, 1987.

Evans, James R., Jr. "An Exceptional Legacy: The 1925 All Female Texas Supreme Court." *Heritage*, Spring 1998, pp. 12–15.

Flexner, Eleanor, and Ellen Fitzpatrick. *Century of Struggle: The Woman's Rights Movement in the United States*. Enlarged ed. Cambridge: Harvard University Press, 1996.

Freeman, Jo. "From Protection to Equal Opportunity: The Revolution in Women's Legal Status." In *Women, Politics, and Change*. Ed. Louise A. Tilly and Patricia Gurin. New York: Russell Sage Foundation, 1990.

Gammage, Judie Karen Walton. "Quest for Equality: An Historical Overview of Women's Rights Activism in Texas 1890–1975." Ph.D. diss., North Texas State University, 1982.

Gill, LaVerne McCain. *African American Women in Congress*. New Brunswick, N.J.: Rutgers University Press, 1997.

Giddings, Paula. *When and Where I Enter: The Impact of Black Women on Race and Sex in America*. New York: Bantam Books, 1985.

Gooch, Jane P. "Barbara C. Jordan: Her First Forty Years: A Rhetorical Analysis." M.A. thesis, Baylor University, 1977.

Gould, Lewis L. *Progressives and Prohibitionists: Texas Democrats in the Wilson Era*. Austin: University of Texas Press, 1973.

Graham, Sara Hunter. *Woman Suffrage and the New Democracy*. New Haven: Yale University Press, 1996.

Green, George Norris. *The Establishment in Texas Politics: The Primitive Years 1938–1957*. Westport Conn.: Greenwood Press, 1979. Reprint. Norman: University of Oklahoma Press, 1984.

Greenleaf, Gale Robin. "Print Media Coverage of the Frances Farenthold and Ann Richards Campaigns: A Comparative Case Study," M.A. thesis, University of Texas at Austin, 1991.

Hall, Jacquelyn Dowd. *Revolt against Chivalry: Jessie Daniel Ames and the Women's Campaign against Lynching*. New York: Columbia University Press, 1979.

Hall, Sue M. "The 1925 All-Woman Supreme Court of Texas." Unpublished ms., The Woman's Collection Library, Texas Woman's University, 1978.

Halter, Gary, and Harvey Tucker. *Texas Legislative Almanac*. College Station: Texas A&M University Press, 1997.

Hamner, Laura Vernon. "Cow Carols and Windmill Music: They Are the Sweetest Sounds on Earth to Writer Florence Fenley." *Cattleman,* March 1960, pp. 42–43, 62.

Harris, Walter Lawrence. "The Life of Margie E. Neal." M.A. thesis, University of Texas at Austin, 1955.

———. "Margie E. Neal: First Woman Senator in Texas." *East Texas Historical Journal* 9, no. 1 (Spring 1973): 40–50.

Hartmann, Susan M. *The Home Front and Beyond: American Women in the 1940s*. Boston: Twayne, 1982.

Hearon, Shelby, and Barbara Jordan. *Barbara Jordan: A Self Portrait.* New York: Doubleday, 1979.

Henton, Moses. "Miss Margie Neal: A First for the Texas State Senate." *Texas Historian,* May 1985, pp. 1–4.

Higgenbotham, Evelyn Brooks. "In Politics to Stay: Black Women Leaders and Party Politics in the 1920s." In *Women, Politics, and Change.* Ed. Louise A. Tilly and Patricia Gurin. New York: Russell Sage Foundation, 1990.

Hinding, Andrea. *Women's History Sources: A Guide to Archives and Manuscript Collections in the United States.* New York: R. R. Bowker, 1979.

Hohes, Pauline Buck. *A Centennial History of Anderson County, Texas.* San Antonio: Naylor Company, 1936.

Humphrey, Janet G. *A Texas Suffragist: Diaries and Writings of Jane Y. McCallum.* Austin: Ellen C. Temple, 1988.

Ivins, Molly. "Rep. Frances Farenthold: A Melancholy Rebel." *Texas Observer,* April 9, 1971, pp. 1–4.

Jackson, Emma Louise Moyer. "Petticoat Politics: Political Action among Texas Women in the 1920s." Ph.D. diss., University of Texas at Austin, 1980.

Jarboe, Jan. "Sitting Pretty." *Texas Monthly,* August 1994, pp. 81–83, 100–105.

Johnson, Linda Carlson. *Barbara Jordan: Congresswoman.* New York: Blackbirch Press, 1990.

Kaledin, Eugenia. *Mothers and More: American Women in the 1950s.* Boston: Twayne, 1984.

Kathleen, Lyn, Susan E. Clarke, and Barbara A. Fox. "Ways Women Politicians Are Making a Difference." In *Gender and Policymaking: Studies of Women in Office.* Ed. Debra L. Dodson. New Brunswick, N.J.: Center for the Ameri-can Woman and Politics, Eagleton Institute of Politics, Rutgers University, 1991.

Keever, Cynthia Pendergrass. "The Election of Miriam Ferguson as Governor, 1924." M.A. thesis, University of Texas at Austin, 1971.

Kerber, Linda K. *Women of the Republic: Intellect and Ideology in Revolutionary America.* Chapel Hill: University of North Carolina Press, 1980.

Kerber, Linda K., Alice Kessler-Harris, and Kathryn Kish Sklar, eds. *U.S. History as Women's History: New Feminist Issues.* Chapel Hill: University of North Carolina Press, 1995.

Kingston, Mike, Sam Attlesey, and Mary G. Crawford. *The Texas Almanac's Political History of Texas.* Austin: Eakin Press, 1992.

Kirk, Rita G. "Barbara Jordan: The Rise of a Black Woman Politician." M.A. thesis, University of Arkansas, 1978.

Klatch, Rebecca. "The Two Worlds of Women of the New Right." In *Women,*

Politics, and Change. Ed. Louise A. Tilly and Patricia Gurin. New York: Russell Sage Foundation, 1990.

Kraditor, Aileen. *The Ideas of the Woman Suffrage Movement, 1890–1920.* New York: Doubleday, 1971.

LaForte, Robert, and Richard Himmel. "Sarah T. Hughes, John F. Kennedy, and the Johnson Inaugural, 1963." *East Texas Historical Journal* 27, no. 2 (1989): 35–41.

Lasher, Patricia. *Texas Women: Interviews and Images.* Austin: Shoal Creek Publishers, 1980.

Lazarou, Kathleen. *Concealed under Petticoats: Married Women's Property and the Law of Texas.* New York: Garland, 1986.

Linden-Ward, Blanche, and Carol Hurd Green. *Changing the Future: American Women in the 1960s.* New York: Twayne, 1993.

Lucko, Paul. "The Next 'Big Job': Women Prison Reformers in Texas, 1918–1930." In *Women and Texas History: Selected Essays.* Ed. Fane Downs and Nancy Baker Jones. Austin: Texas State Historical Association, 1993.

McArthur, Judith N. *Creating the New Woman: The Rise of Southern Women's Progressive Culture in Texas, 1893–1918.* Urbana: University of Illinois Press, 1998.

———. "Motherhood and Reform in the New South: Texas Women's Political Culture during the Progressive Era." Ph.D. diss., University of Texas at Austin, 1992.

———. "Saving the Children: The Women's Crusade against Child Labor, 1902–1918." In *Women and Texas History: Selected Essays.* Ed. Fane Downs and Nancy Baker Jones. Austin: Texas State Historical Association, 1993.

McElhaney, Jacquelyn. *Pauline Periwinkle and Progressive Reform in Dallas.* College Station: Texas A&M University Press, 1998.

Martin, Ken. "Call Me *Madam*: Austin's Gift to Education." [Wilhelmina Delco] *The Good Life,* February 1998, pp. 15–19.

Moss, J. Jennings. "Barbara Jordan: The Other Life." *The Advocate,* March 5, 1996, pp. 39, 42–43, 45.

New Handbook of Texas. 6 vols. Austin: Texas State Historical Association, 1996.

Offen, Karen. "Defining Feminism: A Contemporary Historical Approach," *Signs: Journal of Women in Culture and Society* 14 (Autumn 1988): 119–157.

Patenaude, Lionel V. *Texans, Politics, and the New Deal.* New York: Garland, 1983.

Phillips, Anne. *Engendering Democracy.* University Park: Pennsylvania State University Press, 1991.

Reinier, Burns. "Florence Fenley." In *A Proud Heritage: A History of Uvalde County, Texas Written by the People*. Uvalde: El Progresso Club, n.d.

Richards, Ann, with Peter Knobler. *Straight from the Heart: My Life in Politics and Other Places*. New York: Simon and Schuster, 1989.

Riddlesperger, James W. "Sarah T. Hughes: Biography of a Federal District Judge." M.A. thesis, North Texas State University, 1980.

Rodriguez, Lori. "Lena Guerrero." *Houston Chronicle Magazine*, November 24, 1991.

Rogers, Mary Beth. *Barbara Jordan: American Hero*. New York: Bantam Books, 1998.

Rogers, Mary Beth, ed. *Texas Women: A Celebration of History*. Austin: Foundation for Women's Resources, 1981.

Rogers, Mary Beth, Sherry A. Smith, and Janelle D. Scott. *We Can Fly: Stories of Katherine Stinson and Other Gutsy Texas Women*. Austin: Ellen C. Temple, 1983.

Rosen, Ruth. "The Female Generation Gap: Daughters of the Fifties and the Origins of Contemporary American Feminism." In *U.S. History as Women's History: New Feminist Issues*. Ed. Linda K. Kerber, Alice Kessler-Harris, and Kathryn Kish Sklar. Chapel Hill: University of North Carolina Press, 1995.

Rupp, Lelia J., and Verta Taylor. *Survival in the Doldrums: The American Women's Rights Movement 1945–1960s*. New York: Oxford University Press, 1987.

Ryan, Mary P. *Women in Public: Between Banners and Ballots, 1825–1880*. Baltimore: Johns Hopkins University Press, 1990.

Scharf, Lois, and Joan M. Jensen. *Decades of Discontent: The Women's Movement 1920–1940*. Westport, Conn.: Greenwood Press, 1983.

Scott, Anne Firor. *Natural Allies: Women's Associations in American History*. Urbana: University of Illinois Press, 1991.

———. *The Southern Lady: From Pedestal to Politics 1830–1930*. Chicago: University of Chicago Press, 1970.

Scott, Anne Firor, and Andrew MacKay Scott. *One Half the People: The Fight for Woman Suffrage*. Urbana: University of Illinois Press, 1982.

Seaholm, Megan. "Earnest Women: The White Women's Club Movement in Progressive Era Texas 1880–1920." Ph.D. diss., Rice University, 1988.

Shapiro, Walter. "What Does This Woman Want?" [Barbara Jordan]. *Texas Monthly*, October 1976, pp. 134–135, 202–208.

Sklar, Kathryn Kish. *Florence Kelley and the Nation's Work: The Rise of Women's Political Culture, 1830–1900*. New Haven: Yale University Press, 1995.

Snapp, Elizabeth, and Harry F. Snapp. *Read All About Her! Texas Women's*

History: A Working Bibliography. Denton: Texas Woman's University Press, 1995.

Stanley, Jeanie R., and Diane D. Blair. "Gender Differences in Legislative Effectiveness: The Impact of the Legislative Environment." In *Gender and Policymaking: Studies of Women in Office.* Ed. Debra L. Dodson. New Brunswick, N.J.: Center for the American Woman and Politics, Eagleton Institute of Politics, Rutgers University, 1991.

Stark, Michael G. "Sarah T. Hughes: Her Early Public Career as Attorney, Legislator, and Judge." M.A. thesis, Baylor University, 1980.

Still, Rae Files. *The Gilmer-Aikin Bills: A Study in the Legislative Process.* Austin: Steck Publishers, 1950.

Stivers, Camilla. *Gender Images in Public Administration.* London: Sage Publications, 1993.

Strickland, Kristi Throne. "Sarah T. Hughes: Activist for Women's Causes." M.A. thesis, Tarleton State University, 1989.

Thomas, Sue. *How Women Legislate.* New York: Oxford University Press, 1994.

———. "Women in State Legislatures: One Step at a Time." In *The Year of the Woman: Myths and Realities.* Ed. Elizabeth Adell Cook, Sue Thomas, and Clyde Wilcox. Boulder, Colo.: Westview Press, 1994.

Tilly, Louise A., and Patricia Gurin, eds. *Women, Politics, and Change.* New York: Russell Sage Foundation, 1990.

Tolleson-Rinehart, Sue, and Jeanie R. Stanley. *Claytie and the Lady: Ann Richards, Gender, and Politics in Texas.* Austin: University of Texas Press, 1994.

Trillin, Calvin. "U.S. Journal: Texas Reformer." [Sissy Farenthold] *New Yorker,* June 17, 1972, pp. 78–81.

Tucker, Harvey J. "Bill Authors and Bill Sponsors in the 74th Texas Legislature." Paper presented to the annual meeting of the Western Political Science Association, San Francisco, March 1996.

———. "Bill Authors, Bill Sponsors, and Bill Passage in the Texas Legislature." Paper prepared for delivery at the annual meeting of the Midwest Political Science Association, April 10–12, 1997.

Turner, Elizabeth Hayes. *Women, Culture, and Community: Religion and Reform in Galveston, 1880–1920.* New York: Oxford University Press, 1997.

Wandersee, Winifred D. *On the Move: American Women in the 1970s.* Boston: Twayne, 1988.

Ware, Susan. "American Women in the 1950s: Nonpartisan Politics and Women's Politicization." In *Women, Politics, and Change.* Ed. Louise A. Tilly and Patricia Gurin. New York: Russell Sage Foundation, 1990.

————. *Beyond Suffrage: Women in the New Deal*. Cambridge: Harvard University Press, 1981.

————. *Holding Their Own: American Women in the 1930s*. Boston: Twayne, 1982.

Weddington, Sarah. *A Question of Choice*. New York: G. P. Putnam's Sons, 1992.

Weddington, Sarah, Jane Hickie, Deanna Fitzgerald, Elizabeth N. Fernea, and Marilyn P. Duncan. *Texas Women in Politics*. Austin: Texas Foundation for Women's Resources, 1977.

Welch, Susan, and Sue Thomas. "Do Women in Public Office Make a Difference?" In *Gender and Policymaking: Studies of Women in Office*. Ed. Debra L. Dodson. New Brunswick, N.J.: Center for the American Woman and Politics, Eagleton Institute of Politics, Rutgers University, 1991.

Winegarten, Ruthe. *Black Texas Women: A Sourcebook*. Austin: University of Texas Press, 1996.

————. *Black Texas Women: 150 Years of Trial and Triumph*. Austin: University of Texas Press, 1995.

————. *Finders Guide to the 'Texas Women: A Celebration of History' Exhibit Archives*. Denton: Texas Woman's University, 1984.

————. *Governor Ann Richards and Other Texas Women: From Indians to Astronauts, A Pictorial History*. Austin: Eakin Press, 1993. First published as *Texas Women: A Pictorial History from Indians to Astronauts*. Austin: Eakin Press, 1985.

————. *Texas Women's History Project Bibliography*. Austin: Texas Foundation for Women's Resources, 1980.

Winegarten, Ruthe, and Judith N. McArthur, eds. *Citizens at Last: The Woman Suffrage Movement in Texas*. Austin: Ellen C. Temple, 1987.

Winegarten, Ruthe, and Cathy Schechter. *Deep in the Heart: The Lives and Legends of Texas Jews, A Photographic History*. Austin: Eakin Press, 1990.

Young, Nancy Beck. "Margaret Carter and Texas Politics: Women and the Battle for Control of the Democratic Party." Paper presented at the Fourth Southern Conference on Women's History, Southern Association for Women Historians, Charleston, South Carolina, June 1997.

Young, Nancy Beck, and Lewis L. Gould. *Texas, Her Texas: The Life and Times of Frances Goff*. Austin: Texas State Historical Association, 1997.

PHOTO CREDITS

Edith Wilmans. Courtesy Texas State Library and Archives Commission. 77

Mary Elizabeth (Margie) Neal. Courtesy John Neal, Carthage; print from Mrs. Neal Cook. 81

Laura Burleson Negley. Courtesy University of Texas Institute of Texan Cultures, *San Antonio Light* Collection. 85

Helen Edmunds Moore. Courtesy University of Texas Institute of Texan Cultures. 89

Frances Mitchell Rountree. Courtesy Center for American History, University of Texas at Austin; print from Women in Texas Government Exhibit Collection, Archives for Research on Women and Gender, University of Texas at San Antonio. 92

Cora Gray Strong. Print from Texas House of Representatives Photography Department. 95

Sarah Tilghman Hughes. Courtesy University of Texas Institute of Texan Cultures, print from Women in Texas Government Exhibit Collection, Archives for Research on Women and Gender, University of Texas at San Antonio. 96

Margaret Greer Harris Gordon (Amsler). Courtesy Texas Collection, Baylor University, Waco. 103

Esther Neveille Higgs Colson. Courtesy University of Texas Institute of Texan Cultures, *Houston Chronicle*, 1955. 108

Rae Mandette Files (Still). Courtesy *Daily Texan*, May 15, 1946. 112

Florence Fenley. Print from Center for American History, University of Texas at Austin, copied from *Old Timers: Frontier Days in Uvalde Section of Southwest Texas* (Uvalde: Hornby Press, 1939). 116

Mary Elizabeth Suiter. Courtesy East Texas Bureau of the *Dallas Morning News*, August 9, 1942. 118

Marian Isabel (Maribelle) Hamblen Stewart (Mills Reich). Sketch by Beauford Anderson, print from Women in Texas Government Exhibit Collection, Archives for Research on Women and Gender, University of Texas at San Antonio. 119

Persis Jones Henderson. Sketch by Mary Ann Ambray Gonzales, San Antonio, print from Women in Texas Government Exhibit Collection, Archives for Research on Women and Gender, University of Texas at San Antonio. 120

Dorothy Gillis Gurley (Cauthorn). Courtesy Susan Gurley McBee. 122

Virginia Elizabeth Duff. Courtesy Virginia Duff, photo by Christianson-Leberman, Austin. 125

Anita Blair. Courtesy Anita Blair. 130

Maud Isaacks. Courtesy Texas House of Representatives Media Services, print from Women in Texas Government Exhibit Collection, Archives for Research on Women and Gender, University of Texas at San Antonio. 133

Myra Davis Wilkinson Banfield (Dippel). Courtesy Myra Davis Banfield Dippel, photo by Christianson-Leberman, Austin. 139

Sue Blair Hairgrove (Muzzy). Courtesy Sue Hairgrove Muzzy, photo by Christianson-Leberman, Austin. 144

Barbara Charline Jordan. Courtesy Texas Senate Media Services. 145

Frances Tarlton (Sissy) Farenthold. Courtesy Frances Farenthold (campaign brochure). 152

Kathryn A. (Kay) Bailey (Hutchison). Courtesy Texas House of Representatives Media Services, print from Women in Texas Government Exhibit Collection, Archives for Research on Women and Gender, University of Texas at San Antonio. 158

Sarah Ragle Weddington. Courtesy Office of Sarah Weddington. 162

Dorothy J. Chrisman (Chris) Miller. Courtesy Texas House of Representatives Media Services, print from Women in Texas Government Exhibit Collection, Archives for Research on Women and Gender, University of Texas at San Antonio. 166

Eddie Bernice Johnson. Courtesy Texas Senate Media Services. 169

Elizabeth (Betty) Richards Andujar. Courtesy Betty Andujar, print from Women in Texas Government Exhibit Collection, Archives for Research on Women and Gender, University of Texas at San Antonio. 173

Senfronia Paige Thompson. Courtesy Texas House of Representatives Media Services, print from Women in Texas Government Exhibit Collection, Archives for Research on Women and Gender, University of Texas at San Antonio. 176

Susan Gurley McBee. Courtesy Susan Gurley McBee. 179

Wilhelmina Ruth Fitzgerald Delco. Print by Danna Byrom, © 1991. 182

Lou Nelle Callahan Sutton. From the private collection of Ruthe Winegarten. 187

Mary Jane Goodpasture Bode. Courtesy Mary Jane Bode. 189

Lanell Cofer. From the private collection of Ruthe Winegarten. 191

Ernestine Viola Glossbrenner. Courtesy Texas House of Representatives Media Services, print from Women in Texas Government Exhibit Collection, Archives for Research on Women and Gender, University of Texas at San Antonio. 193

Anita Dorcas Carraway Hill. Courtesy Anita Hill, print by Jeanne Deis Studio. 198

Betty Denton. Courtesy Texas House of Representatives Media Services, print from Women in Texas Government Exhibit Collection, Archives for Research on Women and Gender, University of Texas at San Antonio. 201

Irma Rangel. Courtesy Office of Irma Rangel. 204

Mary J. McCracken Polk. Courtesy Mary Polk. 206

Debra Danburg. Courtesy Office of Debra Danburg. 211

Jan McKenna. Courtesy Texas State Library and Archives Commission. 215

Patricia Ellen Porcella Hill. Courtesy Patricia Hill, print by Woodallen Photographers, Inc., Houston. 217

Phyllis Robinson. Courtesy Texas State Library and Archives Commission. 219

Gwyn Clarkston Shea. Courtesy Office of Gwyn Shea. 221

Nancy Hanks McDonald. Courtesy Texas State Library and Archives Commission. 223

Margaret Anne Becker Cooper. Courtesy Texas House of Representatives Media Services, print from Women in Texas Government Exhibit Collection, Archives for Research on Women and Gender, University of Texas at San Antonio. 225

María Elena (Lena) Guerrero. Courtesy Lena Guerrero, photo by Lucia Uhl. 227

Cyndi Taylor Krier. Courtesy Texas Senate Media Services. 230

Judith Lee Pappas Zaffirini. Courtesy Texas Senate Media Services. 233

Anna Renshaw Mowery. Courtesy Office of Anna Mowery. 235

Elizabeth Ann (Libby) Andrews Linebarger. Courtesy Libby Linebarger, print by Texas House of Representatives Photo Department. 238

Karyne Jones Conley. Courtesy Office of Karyne Jones Conley. 241

Mary Carolyn Bedgood Park. Courtesy Carolyn Park, photo by Gilstrap Portraits. 244

Sue Ann Smith Schechter. Courtesy Sue Schechter, photo by Evin Thayer. 246

Margaret Ann (Peggy) Mulry Rosson. Courtesy Peggy Rosson. 248

Yolanda Navarro Flores. Courtesy Texas House of Representatives Media Services, print from Women in Texas Government Exhibit Collection, Archives for Research on Women and Gender, University of Texas at San Antonio. 250

Susan Combs. Courtesy Susan Combs, photo by Bill Records Photography, Austin. 252

Sylvia Romo. Courtesy Texas House of Representatives Media Services, print from Women in Texas Government Exhibit Collection, Archives for Research on Women and Gender, University of Texas at San Antonio. 254

Barbara Rusling. Courtesy Barbara Rusling. 256

Dianne White Delisi. Courtesy Dianne White Delisi. 261

Sherri Greenberg. Courtesy Sherri Greenberg. 261

Peggy Hamric. Courtesy Peggy Hamric. 261

Christine Hernández. Courtesy Texas House of Representatives Media Services, print from Women in Texas Government Exhibit Collection, Archives for Research on Women and Gender, University of Texas at San Antonio. 261

Leticia San Miguel Van de Putte. Courtesy Leticia Van de Putte, photo by Zavell's, Inc., San Antonio. 262

Patricia Gray. Courtesy Patricia Gray. 262

Diana Dávila. Courtesy Diana Dávila. 262

Yvonne Davis. Courtesy Yvonne Davis. 262

Mary Diane Carver Denny. Courtesy Mary Denny. 263

Helen Giddings. Courtesy Helen Giddings, photo by Gittings, Dallas. 263

Vilma Luna. Courtesy Vilma Luna. 263

Nancy J. Jones Moffat. Courtesy Office of Nancy Moffat. 263

Jane Gray Nelson. Courtesy Texas Senate Media Services. 264

Elvira Reyna. Courtesy Elvira Reyna. 264

Florence Muriel Donald Shapiro. Courtesy Florence Shapiro. 264

Dawnna Dukes. Courtesy Dawnna Dukes. 264

Harryette Ehrhardt. Courtesy Harryette Ehrhardt. 265
Jessica Cristina Farrar. Courtesy Jessica Farrar, print from Women in Texas Government Exhibit Collection, Archives for Research on Women and Gender, University of Texas at San Antonio. 265
Judy Hawley. Courtesy Judy Hawley. 265
Arlene Wohlgemuth. Courtesy Arlene Wohlgemuth. 265
Beverly Woolley. Courtesy Beverly Woolley, photo by Lieber Photography, Houston. 266
Norma Chavez. Courtesy Norma Chavez. 266
Carolyn Galloway. Courtesy Carolyn Galloway. 266
Terri Hodge. Courtesy Terri Hodge. 266
Suzanna Gratia Hupp. Courtesy Suzanna Hupp. 267
Ruth Jones McClendon. Courtesy Ruth Jones McClendon. 267
Dora Olivo. Courtesy Dora Olivo. 267
Sue Palmer. Courtesy Sue Palmer. 267

INDEX

Boldfaced page numbers refer to the main discussions in Biographies and Snapshots.

47–48, 169–170; right-to-work amendment, 167–168, 221; and safety, 195, 199; Title VII of Civil Rights Act, 47–48; of welfare mothers, 205, 216; of women during World War II, 41. *See also* Labor unions; Salaries; State employees

Environmental issues, 153, 154, 157, 168, 177, 201, 207, 212, 213, 218, 224, 226, 227–228, 232, 234, 237, 241–242, 245, 249, 252–253. *See also* Conservation

Equal Credit Act, 7, 18, 54, 163

Equal Employment Opportunity Commission (EEOC), 48

Equal Legal Rights Amendment (ELRA), 6, 18, 46–47, 49–50, 53, 67n.49, 105, 111, 133–134, 139–140, 146, 153, 154, 195

Equal Pay Act of 1963, 47

Equal pay legislation, 42, 47, 99, 118, 204

Equal Rights Amendment (ERA), 35, 36, 38, 39–40, 42–43, 46, 47, 50–51, 55–56, 64n.20, 65n.26, 67n.47, 146, 148–149, 163, 164, 167, 170–171, 211, 231

ERA. *See* Equal Rights Amendment (ERA)

ERAmerica, 55

Ethics Advisory Committee (EAC), 180–181

Ethics reform, 180–181, 238, 247, 249

Ethnicity of women legislators, 22, 53–54, 145–146, 169, 170, 176, 182, 227, 233, 241, 254, 275, 285–286

Evans, Mrs. L. W., 30

Fain, Anna Kilpatrick, 64n.15, 80n.2, 81n.5

Fair housing commission, 18

Family law, 177, 218

Family planning. *See* Birth control

Family responsibilities of legislators, 15, 88, 120, 124, 156, 171, 183–184, 200, 227, 240, 242, 245, 247

Family violence, 19, 50, 55, 171, 205, 207–208, 212, 213, 224, 229, 231, 234

Family Violence Shelter Fund (FVSF), 207–208, 212

Farenthold, Frances Tarlton (Sissy), xii–xiii, 6, 12, 13, 22, 49, 52, 53, 100n.12, 146, **152–157**, 170, 177, 194, 199

Farm workers, 177, 204, 216, 221, 224, 228. *See also* Agriculture

Farnham, Marynia, 41

Farrar, Jessica Cristina, 251, **265**

Federal agencies. *See* specific agencies; and headings beginning with U.S.

Feminism: antifeminism, 41, 55–56; in 1970s, 50–55; "postfeminist" era, 56; radical feminists of 1960s, 48–49, 50; women legislators' acceptance of "feminist" label, 166, 208, 212, 213; women legislators' avoidance/rejection of label of "feminist," 7, 11, 15–17, 87–88, 105–106, 109, 119, 123–124, 126, 131, 148, 153, 159, 179, 200, 213, 237; women's liberation as human liberation, 195. *See also* Women's issues

Fenley, Florence, 44, **116–117**, 118

Ferguson, James, 31–32, 35, 78, 90

Ferguson, Miriam A. (Ma), xi, 18, 32–33, 35, 37, 39, 64n.14, 65n.21, 65n.24, 78–79, 83, 90

"Fergusonism," 35

Fifteenth Amendment, 29

Files (Still), Rae Mandette, 18, 44, 97, 109, **112–115**, 118, 119, 120, 121, 125

Flores, Yolanda Navarro, **250–251**

Ford, Gerald R., 52, 160, 231

Foster care: for children, 224, 246; for elderly, 207

Foundation for Women's Resources, 4

Fourteenth Amendment, 29

Freedom of information, 148, 155

Friedan, Betty, 48

Fund-raising and campaign finances, 7–8, 22, 59, 60, 79, 96, 125, 139, 159, 202, 204, 212, 226, 231

FVSF. *See* Family Violence Shelter Fund (FVSF)

Galloway, Carolyn, **266**

Gambling, 140, 141, 177, 188, 199, 215, 221

Garner, John Nance, 83, 117

198, 231, 235–236, 244–245, 252–253, 256–257; women on Republican National Committee, 159, 160, 174; and women's opposition to Miriam "Ma" Ferguson, 32; women's shifts from Democratic Party to, 198

Retirement and retirement benefits, 121, 161, 190, 213, 227, 236, 238

Reyna, Elvira, **264**

Richards, Ann, xiii, 4, 7–8, 18–19, 56–57, 150, 157, 163, 183, 186n.3, 224, 227, 229

Right-to-work amendment, 167–168, 221

Ripley, Kate, 40

Roads and highways, 93, 94, 109, 110, 111, 121, 131, 190, 205

Robinson, Phyllis, **219–220**

Roe vs. Wade, 7, 55, 99, 162, 163, 165

Rogers, Mary Beth, 4

Romo, Sylvia, xii, **254–255**

Roosevelt, Eleanor, 38, 43, 139

Roosevelt, Franklin D., 38, 44, 83, 141

Rosson, Margaret Ann (Peggy) Mulry, **248–250**

Rountree, Frances Mitchell, 39, **92–94**, 94n.1, 95

Ruckelshaus, Jill, 51

Rural schools, 36, 78, 83, 90, 95, 179–180, 207

Rusling, Barbara, 202, 203, **256–257**

Rutgers University Center for the American Woman and Politics, 157

Ryan, Mary, 62n.6

Safety, 192, 195, 199, 215

Salaries: equal pay for women, 42, 47, 99, 118, 204; of legislators, 72, 79, 83, 110, 121, 128, 194, 195, 224; "living wage" for women workers, 91; minimum wage law, 147, 199, 228; of state employees, 175, 177, 190; of teachers, 114, 134, 180, 201, 221

Sales tax, 90, 91, 97, 104, 140, 144, 167, 174, 190, 207, 244

Sanger, Margaret, 40

Santa Adiva, 27

Satterfield, Mrs. C. W., 88n.2, 91n.1

Schechter, Sue Ann Smith, **246–247**

Schlafly, Phyllis, 55, 56

Schools. *See* Education; Higher education

Segregation, 46, 127–128, 139

Senate, U.S. *See* U.S. Congress

Seventeenth Amendment, 142

Sexism: barriers to women as political candidates, 33, 58, 60, 64n.17, 142, 145, 153, 170; of Citadel Club in Driskill Hotel, 199–200; difficulties for women legislators in working within system, 239; double standard for women, 10; dress code for women in Texas Senate, 231; in education, 47–48, 96; in employment, 40, 41, 47–48; in fund-raising, 159; hostility toward women political candidates, 96–97, 112, 122–123, 126, 139, 142, 153; interruptions of women legislators by men, 20; Jordan on, 149; in legal profession, 105, 159, 218; male legislator's attempt to date woman legislator, 242; "no-win conundrum" and behavioral bargain, 10, 11–12; and "old boys' network," 9–10, 140, 154, 163, 164, 171, 183–184, 199, 237, 243, 249; paternalism toward women legislators, 4, 6, 10, 11–12, 14, 15, 19–20, 46, 78, 88, 103–104, 110, 121, 124, 126, 134, 140, 143n.14, 154, 163, 174, 177, 234, 239, 255; and physical appearance of women, 10, 12, 78, 103, 110, 123, 126, 178, 234; social and legal restrictions on women generally, 162; in state government employment, 9–10, 153–154, 170; against Tobolowsky, 134; against women judges, 97; and women legislators' avoidance/rejection of label of "feminist," 7, 11, 15–17, 87–88, 105–106, 109, 119, 123–124, 126, 131, 148, 153, 159, 200; women legislators not aware of, 124, 237; women legislators not represented in leadership positions, 224, 242–243; women legislators' responses to, 12–15, 147, 177, 178, 192, 228; women not

recognized as legislators, 200, 231; women's need to be better than male candidates and legislators, 109, 119, 229, 239; and women's place in home, 97, 123, 139, 140, 179, 234; women's restroom for legislators only, 255
Sexual abuse of children, 199, 234, 246
Sexual assault. *See* Rape
Sexual preference/orientation, 48, 50, 55, 56, 151n.15, 213
Shapiro, Florence Muriel Donald, 19–20, **264**
Sharp, Frank, 53, 155
Sharpstown bank fraud scandal, 13, 53, 99, 100n.12, 155–156, 159, 163, 170, 173
Shaw, Anna Howard, 38
Shea, Gwyn Clarkston, **221–222**
Sheppard-Towner Act, 36, 78
Shivers, Allan, 46, 84, 127, 131–132
Sierra Club, 218, 245, 252
Smith, Al, 79–80, 86, 90
Smith, Margaret Chase, 43, 66n.34
Smith, Preston, 53, 154, 155, 156
Smith vs. Allwright, 42
Spanish women settlers, 27
Spector, Rose, 57
Spousal abuse. *See* Family violence
Spousal support. *See* Alimony
Stalking, 19, 161, 205, 234, 253
State agencies: human services delivery by, 207; regulations of, 201; tort claims against, 253. *See also* specific agencies; and headings beginning with Texas
State contracts with minority- and women-owned businesses, 171, 242
State employees: benefits for, 164, 190, 227, 236; child care for employees of Capitol complex, 228; cost-cutting ideas of, 253; grievance procedure for, 184; salaries of, 175, 177, 190; sexism against, 9–10, 153–154, 170; social security for, 236
State hospitals for mentally ill. *See* Psychiatric hospitals
State legislatures: goal of 50 percent women in, 60; statistics on women in

state legislatures by state, 21, 22, 25n.38, 35, 56, 57. *See also* Texas Legislature; and names of specific legislators
Stevenson, Coke, 44, 97, 104
Stewart (Mills Reich), Marian Isabel (Maribelle), 44, **119–120**
Still, Rae Files. *See* Files (Still), Rae Mandette
Stop ERA, 55
Strikes, 40
Strong, Cora Gray, 39, 93, **95**
Suffrage movement. *See* Woman's suffrage
Suiter, Mary Elizabeth, 44, 109, **118–119**
Supreme Court of Texas. *See* Texas Supreme Court
Supreme Court, U.S. *See* U.S. Supreme Court
Sutton, Lou Nelle Callahan, **187–188**, 203n.3, 241
Sweatt vs. Painter, 43

Tailhook sexual harassment scandal, 161
Taxes: cigarette tax, 121, 201; corporate franchise tax, 177; corporate profits tax, 155, 167, 177; county tax collection, 95; "crime tax" district, 244; equalization of, 79, 195; gasoline tax, 155, 247; income tax, 91, 97, 140, 167, 195; for interstate carriers, 207; liquor tax, 91; opposition to increases in, 215, 244; poll tax, 49, 135, 146; property tax, 190, 227; for public schools, 113; reduction of, 180; sales tax, 90, 91, 97, 104, 140, 144, 167, 174, 190, 207, 244; tax credits for low-income workers, 148; "truth in taxation," 227
TCM. *See* Texas Congress of Mothers (TCM)
Teachers: certification for, 82, 134; competency examinations for, 207; education of, 82, 134, 207; job protection for pregnant teachers, 18, 163, 170; loyalty oath for, 113; married women as, 96; retirement benefits for,